D1384717

— The Public Archives of Canada

Michael B. Katz

The People of Hamilton, Canada West

Family and Class
in a Mid-Nineteenth-Century City

Harvard University Press
Cambridge, Massachusetts, and London, England   1975

Library of Congress Cataloging in Publication Data

Katz, Michael B
        The People of Hamilton, Canada West.
        (Harvard studies in urban history)
        Includes bibliographical references and index.
        1. Hamilton, Ont.—Social conditions.   2. Social
classes—Hamilton, Ont.   3. Family—Hamilton, Ont.
I. Title.   II. Series.
HN110.05K37   309.1'713'52   75–12642
        ISBN 0–674–66125–7

To the memory of Wilson Benson, Daniel Dewey, and other obscure and forgotten Canadians

Acknowledgments

THE RESEARCH ON which this book rests was supported by the Ontario Institute for Studies in Education from 1967 to 1973. Although I no longer have any official connection with the Canadian Social History Project there, I am exceedingly grateful for that support. I wrote most of this book at the Institute for Advanced Study in Princeton, New Jersey, during the academic year 1973–74, and I appreciate immensely the opportunity for quiet reflective work, the idyllic surroundings, excellent secretarial assistance, and good company that the Institute afforded me. My work there was partially supported by a National Science Foundation Grant (G53170X2). In particular I should like to extend thanks to the Director of the Institute, Carl Kaysen, for his hospitality and encouragement, and, collectively, to colleagues there who listened to some of the ideas in this book and, especially at two seminars, offered enormously useful criticism. Chapter One appeared in a slightly different form in the *Canadian Historical Review*, LIII, 4 (December 1972), 402–426, copyright 1972 by Michael B. Katz. Chapter Four was published in a somewhat different form in the *Journal of Social History* (Winter 1975), 1–29, copyright 1975 by Peter Stearns.

For several years I had the benefit of the help, comments, and criticism of a somewhat amorphous yet cohesive "project group" at the Ontario Institute for Studies in Education. The members of that group—students, colleagues and assistants—know how much I owe them. Particular thanks go to my assistant of several years, John Tiller, as well as to Haley Bamman, Maryse Choquette, Ian Davey, Michael Doucet, Mai-Liis Gering, Harvey Graff, Susan Houston, Eric Ricker and Ian Winchester.

Over the course of the last several years more colleagues than I can remember have offered helpful comments, ideas, and suggestions which are somehow reflected in this book. I trust they will understand that I cannot recall or report all of them. My thanks go especially to Stephan Thernstrom for his continued encouragement, his critical reading of drafts, and his careful examination of the finished manuscript. Paul Rutherford also gave the completed manuscript a discriminating and helpful reading, and Ann Orlov went beyond the call of her professional duties to assist the publication of this book. Throughout the last several years I have been at times sustained, inspired, and always stimulated by the exciting work of my good friend Theodore Hershberg and his Philadelphia Social History Project. Some other colleagues whose help deserves special mention are Stuart Blumin, Barbara Brenzel, David Gagan, Lawrence Glasco, Clyde Griffen, Peter Knights, R. S. Neal, Alison Prentice, Peter Ross, and Edward Shorter. Peter Laslett has kindly sent me a very thoughtful and helpful critique of some of the ideas in Chapter Five, which I shall have to consider carefully in future work.

One day a friend and one-time student, Gordon McLennan, arrived with a bit of graffiti which instantly became the project motto. It read: "When you are up to your ass in alligators, it is difficult to remind yourself that your initial objective was to drain the swamp." My wife and children have endured my frustrations with both the alligators and the swamp, which makes this book partly theirs.

MICHAEL B. KATZ

Toronto
March 1975

Contents

TABLES

FIGURES

THE PEOPLE OF HAMILTON, CANADA WEST

Hamilton is a beautiful town. It lies at the head of Burlington Bay, the extreme westerly point of Lake Ontario, in a charming basin, made by the abrupt falling off of the table land to the vast upper country beyond . . . This valley lies warm and sheltered, and with its gradual slope to the lake, to give it drainage, and its soil composed partially of the debris of the disintegrated mountain limestone above, is of wondrous fertility and fruitfulness. The town is scarcely twenty years old . . . and is the chief entrepo and commercial mart of the extensive upper country to the west. The position of the town cannot be excelled—indeed, rarely equalled. Its upper quarter overlooks the lake and bay; the broad valley of Dundas, some miles above; the neighboring heights and beautifully picturesque lands stretching out for miles opposite. Just behind the town, and hundreds of feet above it, is the mountain, which looks down upon the town itself, even away beyond Toronto and into the mighty misty blue of its far eastern boundary. (*New York Times,* quoted in the Hamilton *Daily Spectator and Journal of Commerce,* September 27, 1860)

Introduction

A high proportion of sociological research is in fact research on
myths which sociologists have invented . . . The academic and intellectual dissociation of history and sociology seems . . . to have had the
effect of deterring both disciplines from attending seriously to the
most important issues involved in the understanding of social transition. Many current accounts of the historian's past, requiring as
they do a wholesale rejection of any form of structural analysis, strike
me as no better suited than the normal version of the sociologist's
past to deal with these issues. (Philip Abrams, "The Sense of the
Past and the Origins of Sociology")

WHEN THE EDITOR of a Toronto newspaper wanted to insult
the aggressive commercial policy of the men who ruled and developed Hamilton in the late 1840s, he patronizingly called their
town the "ambitious little city." Rather than take offense, the
people of Hamilton, Canada West, led by Robert Smiley, pugna-
cious and successful young editor of the Tory *Spectator,* adopted
that designation as their city's unofficial emblem. It was, after all,
not that different from the official civic motto: "I Advance."[1] Both
were apt, for the municipal policy and development of Hamilton
reflected as through a magnifying glass the individual behavior of
its leading citizens. The aggressive, entrepreneurial activity of men
openly and proudly ambitious brought some of them wealth, most
of them anxiety, and many of them instability and periodic failure. The same could be said of the commercial city which they
controlled. As they pushed aggressively and optimistically to catch
and surpass their rival, Toronto, Hamilton's city fathers often
made unwise decisions, and the history of the city, a roaring success story for several years, suddenly became one of disaster, turmoil, and eventual slow recovery.

In the end Toronto won. By the 1870s Hamilton's prospects as

1

a commercial city had become dim, and its future, all could see, lay not in trade but in industry. In the 1890s when the transformation was complete and a group of local businessmen wished to publish a celebration of their city's virtues, they no longer referred to the "ambitious little city." Hamilton, instead, had become for them the "Birmingham of Canada."[2]

Everyone who wrote about Hamilton commented admiringly on its magnificent setting. At the head of Lake Ontario, about forty miles west of Toronto, Hamilton sloped upward from the water to a steep hill, a part of the Niagara escarpment known still as the Mountain. From the top the view extended out over the city, its surrounding farms and fields, and across the lake, "even," one commentator wrote, "away beyond Toronto and into the mighty misty blue . . ." What today has become largely the view of an industrial city, its shoreline disfigured by steel mills, its atmosphere by smoke, in the nineteenth century was a commanding prospect of a harbor brightened by the sails of many ships carrying dry goods, groceries, hardware, and other manufactured articles from across the Atlantic; of a city linked to great waterways by the Burlington Bay Canal (whose completion had assured Hamilton's dominance over its first rival, Dundas, about five miles away), and the center of a rich agricultural region whose grain and lumber the railroad would carry to its wharves. The expectations of the merchants who wagered on the future of Hamilton against Toronto (such as the Buchanans who moved their business there) were not irrational. The future of the city, from the point of view of a mid-nineteenth-century entrepreneur, did appear unlimited.[3]

It is no exaggeration to call Hamilton an instant city. In the few years between the time it officially became a city in 1846, when it housed only a few thousand people, and the end of that decade, its population increased 150 percent. The newcomers had been born, for the most part, in England, Scotland, Ireland, and, to a lesser extent, in the United States and elsewhere. They came for various reasons: poverty-stricken Irish people fleeing the potato famine and a depressed, exploited society; young Scottish merchants seeking their fortune; English artisans in search of opportunity and independence; fugitive slaves seeking freedom. As they sorted themselves out in their new setting, they created a complex and stratified society. With an instant population and class structure came, as well, the antagonisms and animosities of the Old World, evident especially when Irish Catholics and Ulstermen battled each other on the city's streets, or in the creation of a small Irish quarter and the avoidance of the Irish by the Scottish, who settled in other parts of the city.[4]

Still, despite their animosities, the people of Hamilton, perhaps because they were nearly all immigrants, moderated their racial prejudice. There was little of the virulent Know-Nothingism that disfigured American urban politics in the same period, for instance. In fact, people in the city could show at times a surprising sensitivity to cultural difference, as in the admiring and detailed portrait of a local Jewish wedding offered by the editor of the *Spectator* in 1861. Nowhere, perhaps, was the contrast between American and Canadian approaches to cultural or racial difference more evident than in the case of Blacks. True enough, Hamiltonians shared the racial prejudice of their time, but the comparison is a matter of degree. The editor of the *Spectator*, for example, pointed with good reason to the prosperity and solidity of the Black community in Hamilton. Although an abolitionist Black speaker encountered jeers at one meeting, when the Black Abolitionist Society protested its alleged exclusion from the procession preceding the laying of the cornerstone for the Crystal Palace, the organizers of the next festivities placed them not only in the procession but near its head, before any of the other ethnic societies, in fact, where they marched resplendent in white hats.[5]

The procession was the most important civic ritual in nineteenth-century Hamilton. On every pretext work stopped and dignitaries, civic officials, representatives of societies, fire companies, even, on one memorable occasion, the mechanics of the Great Western Railroad, all carrying their banners, marched through the thronged city streets to a public place where eminent men made speeches to rousing cheers. Often after the procession came a mass dinner and carousing at one of the local hotels, followed sometimes by a ball. These festive days were very different from the humorous, pathetic, or grotesque parades that mark holidays today. They were not peripheral entertainments but key events in which, if contemporary accounts can be believed, a large portion of the community participated as marchers or observers.

In a relatively small city like Hamilton all the prominent citizens still could crowd into one banquet hall to toast one another, eat together, and voice the optimism in the future of the city on which each very directly depended. Processions signified urban civic festivals, the only real sources of release, refreshment, and integration in the stratified, transient, and anxious world of the nineteenth-century city.[6]

Festivals, like the marching artisans, the deference at the heart of political culture, and the strong Tory tradition that dominated local provincial elections, evoked an older civic order that still flickered in commercial Hamilton. Marketing, for instance, took place as it must have in cities for centuries. Grocery stores and butcher shops did not dot the neighborhoods of this walking city. Rather, they clustered into two markets near the central district to which everyone had to come to buy food. The concentration of shopping in markets did not happen accidentally; it was promoted deliberately by the members of the City Council, who considered it a policy too self-evidently wise to require elaboration. Whatever the unstated reasons were, the centralization of shops acted as a magnet drawing the population to the center of the small city, countervailing to some extent the centrifugal forces of residential development and population transiency. The markets helped make Hamilton a place, keeping its streets full of people, carriages, and carts, noisy and dirty but alive and vibrant. At Christmastime when grocers and butchers decorated their stalls and their wares and the city illuminated the market place, farmers from the countryside arrived in wagons with their families to sell produce, buy trinkets and gifts, and join in the holiday spirit, making the center of the city a scarcely passable jumble of horses and carts.[7]

As befitted an older civic order, artisans still retained some sense of craft identity. When someone proposed a new method of measurement, the master tailors met, deliberated, and pronounced it acceptable. In the procession preceding the laying of the cornerstone for the Crystal Palace, pride of place went, appropriately, to the mechanics of the Great Western Railroad and to the Masons, not simply in their capacity as a fraternal order but as craftsmen entrusted with the construction of a public edifice which was to serve as a permanent exhibit of Hamilton's productive capacity and a monument to civic pride.[8]

It is hard to evaluate the grounds for civic pride. Some observers, writing letters to newspapers in England or the United States, commented on the cleanliness of Hamilton. But local people on occasion took a different view, complaining of dirt and mud on unpaved streets, of pigs running loose, of the existence of one place selling alcoholic beverages for every sixty-seven inhabitants. Surely, it would have been difficult to take pride in the miserable shanty in which was found a dead storekeeper, near his impoverished wife and crying infant, or in the misery and destitution starkly evident in the lives of the poor who crowded into the soup kitchen set up one especially hard winter by the Ladies Benevolent Society, or in the poor and dying people in the City Hospital, or in the emigrant sheds by the water.[9]

But pride was felt in the public buildings made of abundant local stone and in the magnificent mansions, such as Dundurn Castle built by Allan MacNab or Richard Juson's home on the Mountain, the temporary residence of the Prince of Wales and his retinue. Pride, too, in the early 1850s came from prosperity and growth. The population continued its upward trajectory and business was golden—until 1857.[10]

Then the depression struck. Population fell precipitously, most people leaving, it was said, for the United States; land values, which had soared, suddenly dropped; men were unable to pay their mortgages or rent; and the city was unable to collect taxes and hence to meet its large debts. In these circumstances Hamilton went bankrupt, and, legend has it, the city treasurer fled across the lake to Rochester, books in hand, to avoid the creditors. Whatever the truth of that story, the city quite suddenly entered on desperately difficult times. By late in 1860, however, the glimmer of prosperity again could be seen. The statistics of trade, for instance, improved in 1860 and 1861 as both imports and exports increased markedly, and population once again began to climb. It was to inspire hope and express confidence in its own future that the bankrupt city in 1860 encouraged the building of the Crystal Palace.[11]

The 1850s had been not only a decade of boom and bust but a decade of modernization. And the two were intimately related. Fittingly, the introduction of gas lamps on the streets ushered in the decade in 1851, illuminating, as it were, the bright future,

attesting to the stature of the city and the traffic on its thoroughfares. In the 1850s educational promoters successfully urged a
thorough reorganization and modernization of the school system
along lines that were, for the times, extremely progressive. The
city not only lighted its streets and reformed its schools but com-
missioned an elaborate, modern waterworks, whose financial problems contributed in no small measure to the city's bankruptcy.
But, of course, the great engine of modernization and prosperity
was the railroad. Its promoters successfully persuaded the city government to invest heavily in the Great Western Railroad, which
began to run through Hamilton, its headquarters, in the mid-
1850s. Unfortunately, the Great Western, like the waterworks,
encountered serious financial trouble during the depression, and
its inability to meet its debts also helped plunge the city into
insolvency.[12]

Though Hamilton had its fine residential areas, its railroad and
waterworks, and its new Central School, cultural life remained
thin. The circus, the appearance of General Tom Thumb, and
other road shows provided some variety. The Mechanics Institute,
the Mercantile Library Association, the Horticultural Society, the
Choirs all offered some entertainment. But Hamilton nonetheless
remained inescapably provincial, not a bad place, perhaps, for an
aspiring entrepreneur, but not a place with much to offer anyone
with an interest in the arts.

The hustling, ambitious city appeared on the verge of a comeback in 1861, still determined to pass Toronto as the leading city
in the region. Hamilton's entrepreneurs had not counted, however, on the Grand Trunk Railway which Toronto's promoters
strung out from their city straight through Hamilton's hinterland,
taking all the trade north of the railway away from the "ambitious
little city." Nonetheless, by 1861 some men could see that the future
lay not only in trade but even more in manufacturing. By that
time advocates of industry had begun a campaign to persuade the
entrepreneurs of the city that the future lay in the factory as
much, or more than, in the countinghouse. At first their successes
remained modest. In 1861 the Wanzers moved their sewing-machine
factory to Hamilton from Buffalo; someone partially manufactured shoes which were finished by hand; there were a prosperous
factory that made pianos, one that manufactured hats, and, of

course, the yards of the Great Western Railway and the construction of locomotives. Overall, in 1861 Hamilton remained a commercial city, though the future already was clear to anyone who read the signs. The ambitious little city would become the Birmingham of Canada.[13]

At one level this book is about Hamilton in its years as the "ambitious little city" in the mid-nineteenth century. Specifically, the chapters that follow describe social and family structure during a key decade in Hamilton's history. They explore the relationships among occupation, wealth, transiency, social mobility, ethnicity, property ownership, residential patterns, family composition, and the life cycle. The first objective of the book, thus, is to lay out in concrete and precise terms the primary social and family patterns in one nineteenth-century city and, where possible, to compare them to those in other cities. Unfortunately, the absence of comparable works on Canadian cities makes it necessary to draw comparisons almost exclusively between Hamilton and American or British cities, an obvious but currently insurmountable problem.

But the book has broader objectives as well. Ultimately, my interest extends beyond the history of Hamilton to the way in which the complex set of structures and organizations that make up the modern world emerged from the quite different features of traditional society. One key to understanding the process, I assume, lies in the identification and explanation of the effects of the transformation usually called industrialization. Industrialization, however, might be better considered as part of a process of modernization in which not only the technology and organization of production but institutional structures and the attitudes and behavior of ordinary human beings changed in fundamental ways.[14]

In a sense sociology always has tried to chart this transition. As Philip Abrams has said, the initial and most powerful thrust within sociology as a field of study has been "a diverse but sustained and remarkably coherent effort, first to identify industrialism as a type of society in contra-distinction to a pre-industrial type or types, and second to tell industrial man where industrialization is going. Every so often this main commitment of sociology appears to go underground . . . But on each occasion what was taken to be a grave turns out to have been only a tunnel . . ." In its attempts to draw contrasts between past and present, however, social theory, as Abrams also points out, makes assumptions about the nature of earlier societies which are often vague or incorrect. Despite the massive amount of empirical and theoretical work by social scientists, the precise nature of social patterns and social change prior to industrialization remains to an amazing degree unknown. The past, in contrast to what much social theory appears to assume, simply is not self-evident.[15]

The predominance of ungrounded assumption over hard knowledge about past societies reflects partly the traditional concerns of historians, who have been more interested in politics, great men, governmental policy, and ideas than in the patterns made by the everyday lives of people. Although part of the problem has been interest, part has been the difficulty of the subject matter as well. Discovering the composition of ordinary families in the past and learning about the typical experiences of nineteenth-century laborers over ten or twenty years are not straightforward tasks or ones which most historians have been trained to undertake. The sources always have been there, and some energetic historians have explored them on a fairly limited scale by hand. But the advent of electronic data-processing equipment in the last several years has made the sources accessible as never before. For the task of counting and tracing thousands of individuals, of sorting out masses of information about very large populations, is beyond the capacity and patience of even the most dedicated historian working by hand.[16]

The sources on which people have based their observations about the past also have contributed to the distortions in both popular thought and social theory. For the most part those sources have been literary, descriptions by more or less knowledgeable people—politicians, social reformers, novelists, journalists—of the times and conditions in which they lived. Unfortunately, perception is a very selective procedure, and these contemporary descriptions of social reality as often as not have proved generally unreliable, or at least only partially true.

Thus, for a variety of reasons we are left either with incorrect notions or with ignorance about much of the past. That ignorance is especially harmful because it has led scholars on occasion to ask the wrong questions as they have formulated social theory or undertaken historical research. A "high proportion of sociological research," as Philip Abrams has written, "is in fact research on myths which sociologists have invented." Two examples will make this point clear. Theoretical work on the impact of industrialization on the family has tried to explain the significance of a transition from the extended to the nuclear family. Historians have shown in recent years, however, that most people, at least in North America and western Europe, always have lived in nuclear families. The predominance of the extended family in traditional society is very simply a myth. Therefore, in this instance, the very question which social theory has set out to explore is meaningless. Similarly, historians, using twentieth-century notions about occupation, have defined social mobility in the mid-nineteenth century as movement between blue and white collar work. However, as this book will show, the distinction between blue and white collar or between manual and nonmanual work did not exist then with anything like the sharpness it has since assumed. In fact the structure of the world of work and the very definition of social mobility differed subtly and significantly from what they have become in modern (industrial) times. Asking the wrong questions, in this case, has weakened some of the work which itself set out to remedy deficiencies in our knowledge about social processes.[17]

From these examples it should be clear that at this point the right questions remain more important than the right answers. One object of social history should be to formulate questions that will guide research in ways not only theoretically fruitful but historically appropriate. That is, perhaps, the most important goal of this book.

There are reasonable grounds for believing that in important ways Hamilton resembled commercial cities of its era in both Canada and the United States. The commercial city was the dominant urban form of an era. Too often historical writing and social theory contrast rural with industrial life, comparing the organization of peasant society with the industrial city. That contrast is misleading. Urban forms have existed for a long time. Industrialization in North America did not create cities as much as interact with well-established urban patterns. The story of its progress does not describe a massive external influence simply transforming a passive population but, rather, a complex interchange in which old forms and customs adapted themselves to, co-opted, and shaped a new technology perhaps as much as the new technology itself refashioned the older order. Thus, in order to explain the effects of industrialization it is essential to describe with precision the features of the earlier urban world, of, that is, the commercial city.

Of course, Hamilton may have differed more than I imagine from other places. Perhaps it represented only one kind of commercial city, or a particularly idiosyncratic case in some important respect. That, however, can only be known through precise, comparative study. If this book sets provocative questions and hypotheses that spark such study, its goal will be achieved, even if the specific speculations it offers prove wrong.

It should be clear by now that this book is a mixture of hard data and rash speculation. The data can be interpreted in different ways, but at rock bottom they do provide a solid and enduring contribution which other historians who may disagree violently with what I offer as explanation nonetheless can use. One immense value of the sort of historical inquiry on which this book rests is that it offers historians the opportunity to build upon one another's work in a systematic and cumulative fashion. History never can become a science like physics or chemistry, but historians can increase enormously the extent to which the results of their research are useful in comparative inquiry, reproducible by other scholars and cumulative in character.

As for the speculations in this book, I hope they will be taken in the spirit in which they are offered. They are not propositions offered dogmatically, or absolute truths, or even, sometimes, very firmly grounded generalizations. They are interpretations which seem plausible, consistent with the data, and, I hope, useful to social theorists and historians. It would be unfair, I believe, to fault this book for not proving beyond reasonable doubt its major hypotheses; it would be entirely fair to fault it for offering hypotheses inconsistent with its evidence, logically implausible, or just uninteresting.

This is the first book to come from the project which I have directed for the last few years. That project uses Hamilton, Ontario, and its region as a case study in the development of social and family organization in the nineteenth century. Its sources and methods will be explained throughout the book, especially in Chapter One. Here it is important to note two aspects of the project. First, the project is ongoing. This book does not represent its completion, or even a full utilization of the rich and complex data that already have been gathered. There are many questions that I have not attempted to answer. Very simply, after about four years of work it seemed time to bring my thoughts together in an initial, extended statement. Hence I arbitrarily stopped the analysis of data at a point in time, took what I had with me, and went away to write what I could. This book is the result. Just how long this project of mine will last and what shape it will eventually take depends on a number of circumstances. In the immediate future I will carry the study forward in time, testing the hypotheses about the impact of social change which are developed in the following chapters. The patterns described in this book should provide a base line against which to measure and assess the impact of social forces at work in the latter part of the nineteenth century. They provide, as well, a standard with which to delineate the particularly urban aspects of social and family structure. For one of the important questions which remains unresolved is the extent to which the book portrays patterns and processes that were general or ones that were peculiar to the city. For instance, the massive population turnover that urban historians have found might have been thought typical of the city and emblematic of its pathology. But, it is quite clear, similar rates of transiency existed in the countryside; massive population turnover was a general feature of North American life in earlier times. It is unclear what other phenomena were general as well, and this is one of the major questions which historians should explore in the next few years.

The project on which this book rests was collaborative. For a few years many people worked in one capacity or another on the collection and analysis of the data. Their contributions influenced my thoughts profoundly. In particular, we tried to establish a working model of research in which a group of people exploited a common data base, each pursuing his own individual interests yet drawing on the group as a whole for support, criticism, and knowledge. My original plan was to write a book including a number of essays by different project members, but the book became too long and I have included only one essay, the geographical appendix by Ian Davey and Michael Doucet. The other essays will probably form the nucleus of a volume discussing methodological issues in the historical study of class and family.

The collaborative nature of our work—the way in which we found it possible to reconcile the interests and desire for autonomy of individual scholars with the need for collective wisdom and energy in the analysis of the massive data base we were assembling—should be stressed. For historians traditionally are a lonely lot. The classic image of the historian is the scholar working alone with his books or manuscripts in a library, unable to carry on very much dialogue with anyone else. We, to the contrary, experienced the exhilaration of continually testing our ideas with a group which had an intimate knowledge of the same sources and techniques. Through periodic project meetings we sustained for a few years a collective and collegial intellectual life which enriched our own thinking and gave us a new perspective on the organization of scholarly activity. In one form or another all the material in this book at some time was presented to the project group. It was argued over, sometimes fiercely, and there remained differences of interpretation among us. We did share, nonetheless, a sense of excitement at the potential of our work and a pleasure in our joint endeavor. The project meetings were the best seminars that most of us had attended in a long time.

Lest this description appear unduly romantic, I should point out that collaborative work has its own strains and exacts its own price. My advice to anyone undertaking a joint project would be to define roles, obligations, and expectations clearly at the outset in a way that will account for possible changes in project membership and location.

One issue which the project group discussed time and again, in one form or another, is a fundamental intellectual problem that underlies contemporary studies in social history; namely, the connection among structures, behaviors, and attitudes. What connection, for example, can we assume between the structure of the family and the attitudes and emotions of the people within it? Can we assume that growing up within a nineteenth-century extended family produced in a child a set of attitudes or a personality different from those that would have developed within a nuclear family? What inference can we draw from stability in the distribution of wealth across time? Would it breed resignation, frustration, or anger? There exist very little evidence and very little theory to enable us to answer these questions with any authority. At times, though, we can associate structural variation with differences in behavior, and this brings us closer to attitudes and to the consequences of structural difference. For instance, there was a relationship between the class, religion, and size of a family and its propensity to send its children to school. That tells us something about the consequences of each of those family characteristics. And it implies the existence of particular attitudes. Similarly, there was a definite connection between the country in which a poor man had been born and the likelihood that he would buy a house. That, too, is an association between structural variation and behavior that moves us closer to the inner lives of people. However, even in these cases an inferential leap must be made in assessing the consequences and impact of any social pattern.

To make that leap we draw sometimes on social theory. But that often involves an assumption that the theory, even if based on reliable contemporary data, applies equally to human beings of another era. Sociological and psychological concepts, though, do not necessarily represent formulations appropriate for all times and places; they are not frozen distillations of absolute truth or governing laws. The most elementary implication of the sociology of knowledge should lead us to expect intimate connections between the generation of social or behavioral theories and the contexts in which they arise. Thus we must ask: is a concept such as the authoritarian personality, developed in the twentieth century, applicable to slaveholders in the American South before the Civil War?[18] Or, as many have inquired, to what extent do the ideas of Freud reflect primarily the anxieties and emotional processes of late-nineteenth-century European bourgeois society? Or, to take an example on which this book should shed some light, is adolescence a concept which describes a perennial biological state or a phase in the life cycle that emerged at a particular moment in history? These questions are important because they illustrate the difficulty and the danger of applying social theory uncritically while making the inferential leap from structures to their consequences.

These questions point out, too, that the relationship between history and the other social sciences must not be passive. The role of the historian should not be merely to receive, applying other scholars' concepts, testing their theories, adopting their methods. Data about the past must form an integral part of any valid social scientific theory, and in the attempt to discover how the world works the historian is at least the equal—in potential if not in practice—of any other social scientist. Unfortunately, history lost its early place at the cutting edge of social science. That largely was the fault of historians who, as Hayden White has described brilliantly, failed to shed their nineteenth-century notions of art and science and refused to join the contemporary intellectual world.[19] There are comforting signs that the trend is changing, and this book is offered as part of the effort to cross the disciplinary boundaries that have become outmoded barriers to creative scholarship.

Finally, a word about the level and organization of this book. First of all, it assumes no prior knowledge of statistical concepts or methodology. To comprehend what follows it is necessary to know nothing more than how to count, nothing more complex than the meaning of percentages. Any reader should be able to study the tables and reach his own conclusions. Nor should it be necessary to know anything special about social concepts or theories. I have tried to show why each topic this book treats is significant, how it is defined, and what are some of the major relevant issues in its study. I do not want to mystify readers or convince them of interpretations with techniques which they do not understand. On the contrary, my hope is to persuade the wary and the uncommitted that systematic social history is neither esoteric nor dull, but rather, an exciting and powerful approach to the past.

The opening chapter of the book provides a reasonably comprehensive portrait of a commercial city in the mid-nineteenth century; in a general way it touches all the major questions which later chapters consider in more detail, specifies the sources and some of the methods of the study, and outlines some of its principal themes. (An appendix by Ian Davey and Michael Doucet delineates with precise detail the manner in which the geographic distribution of the population and its activities partially reflected its social divisions and its ethnic and economic functions.) The rest of the book argues that an apparent paradox best characterizes the social history of Hamilton as a commercial city; namely, the coexistence of the rigidity of its social, economic, and demographic structures with the immense transiency of its population and the fluid experience of its individual people. Chapter Two shows the persistence of structures of inequality. Chapter Three analyzes transiency and defines and delineates patterns of social mobility. Chapter Four explores the manner in which the themes of the preceding chapters were woven through the experience of one social group, the entrepreneurial class. Chapter Five examines the boundaries of the family, the life cycle, and some possible connections between the family and social change; it argues that though in part the family reflected, on the one hand, social and ethnic distinctions, and, on the other, the theme of stability and transiency, it nonetheless had a dynamic and a character of its own.

The object of this book, in the last analysis, is to try to change the perspective and the lens through which historians look at the commercial city. What they see there may be different from what I have found. But if they are persuaded or provoked to look in a new way, that goal will have been reached.

CHAPTER ONE

The People of a Canadian City, 1851–52

The premises from which we begin are not arbitrary ones, not dogmas, but real premises from which abstraction can only be made in the imagination. They are the real individuals, their activity and the material conditions under which they live, both those which they find already existing and those produced by their activity. These premises can thus be verified in a purely empirical way. (Karl Marx and Friedrich Engels, *The German Ideology Parts I and III*)

ON AN AVERAGE day in 1851 about fourteen thousand people awoke in Hamilton, Canada West. Most of them were quite unremarkable and thoroughly ordinary. In fact, there is no reason why the historian reading books, pamphlets, newspapers, or even diaries and letters should ever encounter more than seven hundred of them. The rest, at least ninety-five out of every hundred, remain invisible. Insofar as most written history is concerned, they might just as well never have lived.

One consequence of their invisibility has been that history, as usually written, represents the record of the articulate and prominent. We assume too easily, for example, that the speeches of politicians reflected the feelings and conditions of ordinary people. As another consequence, we lack a foundation on which to construct historical interpretations. After all, the activities, interactions, and movements of these invisible men and women formed the very stuff of past societies. Without a knowledge of how they lived, worked, behaved, and arranged themselves in relation to one another our understanding of any place and point in time must be partial, to say the least. Finally, we apply contemporary assumptions to past societies. We turn our everyday experiences of modern social relationships into models which we apply to the past. Because we believe, for instance, that we are more sophisticated than our ancestors about sex, marriage, and the spacing of children, we imagine that they must have married younger and reproduced as fast as nature would allow. Neither of these assumptions, as it happens, is true.

The problem, of course, is evidence. How are we to write with meaning of the life of an ordinary laborer, shoemaker, or clerk in a nineteenth-century city? Or trace the most common patterns among important social features such as occupation, wealth, religion, ethnicity, family size, and school attendance? Those questions can be answered more directly and in a more straightforward manner than often imagined, as I hope to make clear in the rest of this chapter. My purpose is threefold: first, to show the range of questions about ordinary nineteenth-century people that may be asked and answered; second, to sketch in a preliminary fashion what I take to be the primary social and demographic patterns within a mid-nineteenth-century Canadian city; third, to set out the major themes and topics which the rest of this book will explore in more detail. The two great themes of nineteenth-century urban history, I shall argue, are transiency and inequality. This chapter will consider these two themes, as well as the nature of the family and household. For differences in family and household structure reflected, in part, the broad economic distinctions within urban society. The chapters that follow will contend that inequality represents the underlying structural rigidity of the society while transiency reflects the continual flow of people throughout the city's relatively fixed structures. The central intellectual task for the student of past societies, I believe, is to find a satisfactory way of interrelating structural rigidity and personal transiency.

At the beginning two caveats are necessary. First, the quantitative information presented here remains partial; it is drawn from a great many detailed tables.[1] Second, the figures given are approximate. Such must be the case with most historical data. However, and this is the important point, the magnitudes, the differences between groups, may be taken, I believe, as a fair representation of the situation as it existed.

The manuscript census contains the most valuable information about individuals and households within nineteenth-century cities.

For individuals the census from 1851 onward lists, among other
items, name, age, birthplace, religion, occupation, school attendance, and birth or death within the year. It provides a residential location for each household and a description of the kind of
house occupied; it permits the differentiation of relatives from
nonrelatives and the rough delineation of the relationships of
household members to one another. In some cases it provides information about the business of the household head by listing
other property, such as a store or shop owned, and the number of
people employed. Assessment rolls supplement the manuscript
census with detailed economic information, usually about each
adult member of the work force. The assessment lists income over
a certain level, real property, personal property, and some other
economic and personal characteristics, including the occupation
of each person assessed, the owner of the dwelling, and hence,
whether the individual was an owner or renter of property. (In
some instances a man who rents one house or store owns another;
in other cases individuals own property around the city. These
bits of information about individuals may be gathered together to
present a more complete economic profile.) Published city directories corroborate the information from other sources and provide,
additionally, the exact residential address of people and, in the
case of proprietors, the address of their business if outside the
home. Directories also include listings of people in various important political, financial, and voluntary positions within the city.
Many other sources which list information about ordinary people
supplement the census, assessment, and directory. Newspapers constitute the richest of these; mined systematically they yield an
enormous amount of information about the activities of people
within the city. There are also marriage records, church records,
records of voluntary societies and educational institutions, cemetery records, and listings of other sorts as well. Each of these
sources may be studied by itself and the patterns it presents may
be analyzed and compared with those found in other places. If
the same individuals appear in different records, it is possible to
build up rich and well-documented portraits of the lives of even
the most ordinary people.[2]

The project on which this book rests uses all the various records
described above. Its most general purpose has been to analyze the

impact of modernization on urban social and family structure, using Hamilton, Ontario, as a case study. It deals with the years 1851 through 1891, at the least; its basis is coded information about all, and not a sample, of the individuals listed in all the sources, studied at differing intervals.

The principal sources for this chapter, which discusses primarily the early 1850s, are the manuscript census of 1851, the assessment roll of 1852 (compiled three months after the census), the city directory of 1853 (the first published within the city), the marriage registers of 1842–1869, and two local newspapers, one for both 1851 and 1852 and one for 1852.[3] In some instances the analysis rests on one source alone, in others on two or more sources combined.

The sources for Hamilton as well as the studies of American cities make clear that transiency forms the first great theme of a nineteenth-century city. The most careful students of transiency to date, Stephan Thernstrom and Peter Knights, both conclude from their studies of Boston that far more people lived within the city in the course of a year than the census taker could find present at any one point in time. The census of 1880 listed the population of Boston as 363,000, that of 1890 as 448,000. However, during those ten years Thernstrom and Knights estimate that about one and a half million different people actually lived within the city. Elsewhere Knights has estimated that twice as many artisans in some crafts plied their trade within the city in the course of a year as might be found there at any given moment. Other historians have found similar high rates of transience: for instance, Howard Chudacoff for Omaha, Nebraska; Paul Worthman for Birmingham, Alabama; Anders Norberg and Sune Åkerman for rural Sweden; and David Gagan for rural Peel County, Ontario. Eric Hobsbawm's tramping artisans, quite obviously, were an international as well as a British phenomenon, in both city and countryside.[4]

Mass transiency also characterized the population of Hamilton, as the following evidence shows. The assessment roll of 1852 listed 2552 people. Through careful linkage by hand (later replicated by computer) we have been able to join only 1955 of them to people listed on the census, which had been taken three months earlier. (There is no reason to assume that the intervening three months were unusual in any way.) Even with a generous allowance for error, large numbers of people could not be found; they had moved into the city during the intervening three months. In the same way a comparable percentage of household heads listed on the census could not be found three months later on the assessment; most of them had left the city. Similarly, fewer than half the people on census or assessment could be found listed in the city directory compiled about a year and a half later, and there were a great many people listed in the directory and not on either census or assessment. Death records point to the same conclusion. Each household head was required to record on the census the name of any person within his household who had died during the preceding year. Hamilton cemetery and church records for both 1851 and 1861 reveal, however, that the number of people who actually died within the city far exceeded the number recorded on the census. Only a few can be linked to families resident within the city at the time the census was taken.[5] In most instances the families apparently had left the city. It is difficult to estimate the number of deaths that fall into this category; certainly it is not less than a number half again as large as the number of deaths recorded on the census. In all, only about 35 percent of the people present in 1851 could be located on the census taken a decade later.

The population, this evidence suggests, contained two major groupings. The first consisted of relatively permanent residents who persisted within the city for at least several years. This group comprised between one third and two fifths of the population. The remainder were transients, people passing through the city, remaining for periods lasting between a few months and a few years.

Many of the transients were heads of household, not primarily, as might be suspected, young men drifting around the countryside. The age distribution among the transient heads of household closely resembled that among the more permanent. If anything, the transients were on the average very slightly older. Nor, as one might expect, were the transients all people of little skill and low status. The percentage of laborers among the transients (15 percent) was only slightly higher than among the more permanent residents. Indeed, many people with skilled or entrepreneurial jobs moved from place to place: the transients included twenty-

four merchants, fifty-eight clerks, seven lawyers, fifty-one shoemakers, twenty-eight tailors, and so on.

Although the transients approximated the rest of the population
in age and occupation, they differed in two critical respects: wealth
and property. Homeowners were about three times more likely to
remain in the city than renters. Within every occupational category, the people who remained within the city were wealthier.[6]
Thus it was the *poorer* merchants, shoemakers, lawyers, and even
the poorer laborers who migrated most frequently. All of this
points to the coexistence of two social structures within nineteenth-
century society: one relatively fixed, consisting of people successful
at their work, even if that work was laboring; the other a floating
social structure composed of failures, people poorer and less successful at their work, even if that work was professional, drifting
from place to place in search of success.[7] This situation may have
prevailed only in prosperous times, however; as a later chapter will
show, the relations between transiency and wealth appear to have
been different during a depression.

The significance of transiency as a key feature of social structure
in both Boston, Massachusetts, and Hamilton, Ontario, becomes
especially evident in light of the fundamental differences between
the two cities. Late-nineteenth-century Boston had become an
industrial city; mid-century Hamilton remained a small, commercial one. Yet through both flowed, in Knights and Thernstrom's
phrase, "men in motion"; transiency formed an integral and
international feature of nineteenth-century society and one not
immediately altered by industrialization.

The relationship between work place and residence underscores
the nonindustrial nature of Hamilton. The separation of work
from residence has been one of the most profound consequences
of industrialization; conversely, the degree to which they remain
united provides a rough guide to the extent of industrial development within a society. Contemporary sociologists contrast the
organization of family and work place by pointing to their basic
structural differences in terms of authority relationships, criteria
for rewards, and so on. They argue that people must play radically
different roles in the two settings. It becomes the task of the
family and the school to teach the individual to make the transi-

tion between home and work and to learn to live with the sorts of internal switching required by a continual shifting from the personal and warm relations of the family to the impersonal, bureaucratic organization of work. This dichotomy in roles came about as a consequence of modern work organization, namely, the separation of residence and work place. Its implication for the psychology of the individual person and for the functions of family and school make the shift profoundly significant.[8]

It is almost impossible to state precisely the proportion of men who were self-employed and the proportion who worked at home in Hamilton in the 1850s. What follows is a rough estimate of the minimum numbers in each category.[9]

In 1851, 1142 male household heads were employees and 957 were employers. Adding 1310 male adult boarders, almost all of whom were employees, gives a total male work force of 3409, of which 2452 or 74 percent were not self-employed and 26 percent were. Given the approximate nature of the figures, it would be unwise to claim more than that between a quarter and a third of the men within the city worked for themselves. Certainly, this is evidence enough to point to a contrast with contemporary society.

Of the self-employed men about 137 (comprising roughly half of the proprietors of businesses and of the attorneys) worked away from their homes. Interestingly, if the proportion had been based on the number of businesses, not the number of proprietors, the proportion uniting work and residence would have been much higher. For many businesses were partnerships in which one member lived at the place of business and the other elsewhere. On the basis of this estimate approximately 14 percent of self-employed men worked away from their place of residence as did 72 percent of all employed males or 60 percent of household heads. Put another way, at least four out of ten households combined the function of place of work and place of residence for some of their members. That figure clearly demonstrates the nonindustrial character of economic life within the city. This is not to say, however, that large-scale manufacturing had not begun in this region of Canada. The nearby mill town of Dundas, for instance, was related to Hamilton, I suspect, somewhat as Lowell was to Boston.

Even though many people had to leave home each day to go to work, few spent their time in large, formal settings. Most people, regardless of where their job was done, worked in small groups. According to the census of 1851 (which is undoubtedly an under-enumeration in this respect), there were within the city 282 artisan shops, stores, offices, and manufactories. The proprietors of over half of these (52 percent) listed no employees. A further twenty-five listed one, and an additional sixty listed between two and five employees. Only thirty places had between six and ten employees and but a handful had more than ten. The city government complements this picture of smallness and informality, for the city employed approximately fifteen people full-time, a few others part-time, and spent annually only about £18,000 to 20,000.[10]

The preceding discussion has described features of a mid-nineteenth-century city that might be located almost anywhere in North America or Great Britain. However, one feature of Hamilton marked it as distinctively Canadian and, at the same time, emphasized the importance of transiency: the birthplaces of its residents. Only about 9 percent of Hamilton's work force had been born in Canada West. Immigrants made up the rest, about 29 percent from England and Wales, 18 percent from Scotland, 32 percent from Ireland, 8 percent from the United States, and the rest from various other places. Hamilton remained an immigrant city for at least a decade, as the figures for the birthplace of household heads in 1861 reveal. In a double sense the people of Hamilton were "men in motion." Thus in the origins of their people early Canadian cities differed fundamentally from cities in the United States and Great Britain. The consequences of this demographic difference might provide a fruitful perspective from which to begin the comparative study of national development and national character.

The immigrants to Hamilton did not gather themselves into ghettos, though there were significant clusters of people of similar origin living near one another. In Appendix One Ian Davey and Michael Doucet explore the social ecology of Hamilton in considerable detail. In general, despite some clustering and a modest tendency for the wealthy to live near the center of the city and the poor on the periphery, people of all degrees of wealth dwelled in close proximity to one another, the poor and the affluent intermingling on the same streets far more, probably, than they do in 1975.[11] Indeed, the extent to which the nineteenth-century city differed from today's urban environment is already clear. The transiency, the newness, and the intermingling of its population, the small scale of its enterprise, the high degree of self-employment, and the continued unity of work and residence: all define a situation which our own experience of urban life prepares us poorly to comprehend, but which, as historians, we must try to recapture.

In fact, it is easy to be nostalgic about small commercial cities. The absence of large-scale industry, the informality of government, and the lack of bureaucratic forms suggest an urban style both more cohesive and personal than that which we know today. We can imagine them without much difficulty: cities filled with more warmth and less tension than those today; stable, neighborly, easy places in which to live; the communities which our urban places have ceased to be. Unfortunately, the image that emerges from empirical study of nineteenth-century cities does not support the nostalgic vision. From one perspective it is partly contradicted by the facts of transiency. The continual circulation of population prevented the formation of stable and closely integrated communities within nineteenth-century cities. At the same time, sharp inequalities in wealth and power reinforced the pressures of population mobility against cohesion and integration, and the experience of entrepreneurs revealed contentiousness and continual struggle at the heart of the city's economic life. Together these features made the nineteenth-century city, even before industrialization, a place at least as harsh, as insecure, and as overwhelming as urban environments of the late twentieth century.

It is scarcely novel to assert that sharp inequalities existed within nineteenth-century cities or to posit a sharply graduated rank ordering of people. What should be stressed about that inequality is that, first, it may have been greater even than we have imagined; second, it underlay other social differences among people, such as household size and attitudes toward education; and third, it shaped political patterns and processes. In short, the division of people on most social measures corresponded to the economic differences among them. Social, political, and economic power overlapped and interlocked, creating a sharply divided society in which a small percentage of the people retained a near monopoly on all the resources necessary to the well-being of the rest.

There are various ways to measure the division of wealth within a community, and each one, each scale, yields a different result.[12] One division is property ownership: about one quarter of the population of Hamilton owned all the real property within the city. Roughly three quarters of the people rented their living accommodations and owned no other real property whatsoever. The most affluent 10 percent of the population held about 88 percent of the wealth represented by the possession of property. From a slightly different perspective, people in the top ten *income* percentiles (as reported on the assessment) earned nearly half the income within the city, and this figure, for a variety of reasons, is undoubtedly greatly understated. At the other extreme the poorest 40 percent earned a little over 1 percent of the income. Measured on a third scale, one designed to show economic ranking, the pattern of inequality is similar. Although here "wealth" represents a construct of different items and does not correspond exactly to either total income or assessed property, it is, nonetheless, the best available indicator of economic rank. On the basis of this measure, the wealthiest tenth of the people controlled about 60 percent of the wealth within the city and the poorest two fifths about 6 percent.

The scale of economic ranking also reveals differences in the wealth of the various sectors of the city's economy. The people engaged in building, about 14 percent of the work force (indicating the rapid expansion of the city), held only about 7 percent of the city's wealth; similarly, those engaged in some form of manufacturing (primarily artisans), about one quarter of the work force, had only 15 percent of the wealth. Likewise, as might be expected, the unskilled and semiskilled laborers, about 22 percent of the work force, had less than 5 percent of the wealth. At the other extreme those engaged in professions, about 4 percent of the work force, held over 7 percent of the wealth, and the men in commerce, about a quarter of the work force, controlled nearly 59 percent of the wealth, a figure which underscores the clear commercial basis of the city.

Religious and ethnic groups, like the various sectors of the economy, shared unequally in the city's wealth. Of the various immigrant and religious groups, the Irish and the Catholics fared worst. It is fair, I have argued elsewhere, to consider as poor the people in the lowest forty economic ranks. Using this criterion,

47 percent of the working population born in Ireland were poor,
as were 54 percent of those who were Catholic, and 56 percent of
the Irish Catholics. This, of course, is not a surprising finding.
On the other hand, it might be supposed that the English and
the Anglicans were disproportionately wealthy, but this was not
the case. Both of these groups formed a microcosm of the larger
social structure, distributed quite normally among different economic categories. The Free Church Presbyterians did rather better, but the most affluent group, considering both the number of
poor and of well-to-do, were the Wesleyan Methodists. In terms
of birthplace, the native Canadians and Americans fared best, a
prosperity no doubt reflecting the problems of trans-Atlantic migration rather than inherent ethnic capacity or style. Of the Canadians 32 percent were well-to-do, as were 31 percent of the
Americans.[13]

It is difficult to associate economic rank with standard of living
and to demarcate with precision the line separating the poor from
the comfortable. To say that the fortieth economic rank marks
the spot at which poverty ceased means that it was the point at
which people probably no longer had to struggle for and occasionally do without the necessities of life. Poverty in nineteenth-
century cities did not mean the absence of luxuries—simple Spartan
living with good home-grown food and sturdy home-sewn clothes.
Poverty meant absolute deprivation: hunger, cold, sickness, and
misery, with almost no place to turn for relief. The poor within
Hamilton, it is important to remember, remained quite at the
mercy of the well-to-do, who not only controlled employment
opportunity and housing but dispensed what little welfare there
was as a gift, not as a right. The Ladies Benevolent Society, a
voluntary and paternalistic body, formed in effect the city welfare
department. Financed by charitable donations and grants from the
City Council, it assigned teams of gracious ladies to roam the
streets, locate worthy poor women, and dispense loaves of bread,
sometimes coal and groceries, even occasionally rent. The City
Council coped with massive numbers of immigrants overcrowding
the combination hospital and poorhouse by transporting newly
arrived Irish people in wagonloads to country towns where they
were summarily left. Clearly, the Council believed such widespread
poverty to be only a temporary problem, which could be solved

by simple expedients that did not require the permanent and institutionalized extension of public responsibility for individual welfare.[14]

Aside from economic hardship, poverty in Hamilton meant powerlessness and invisibility. The lack of public provision for welfare reveals part of the powerlessness: the poor had no assistance on which they could draw as a right. Nor could they make their wants heard in any legal way, as the suffrage restrictions show. Less than half the adult males in Hamilton owned or rented enough property to vote in elections for the Legislative Assembly; 53 percent of all adult men, or 43 percent of household heads, could not meet the economic requirements for suffrage. Neither could 80 percent of the laborers, 56 percent of the artisans, or 59 percent of the business employees (primarily clerks). Many more, however, could vote in civic elections. The invisibility that accompanied powerlessness is harder to demonstrate; its existence has come to light by comparing the records of the Ladies Benevolent Society with the manuscript census. The Society's records contain a month-by-month listing of the recipients of welfare. An attempt to find these names on the census, even for the very month in which the census had been taken, located very few of them. Perhaps they were simply passed by, a blot on the city that it was well to ignore.

Even within a relatively simple society like Hamilton's, the affluent had tangible means of demonstrating their degree of success, most notably the employment of servants. It was at the eightieth economic rank that a family became more likely than not to employ domestic help, and the likelihood increased with each higher rank on the scale. Overall, about one quarter of the families in Hamilton had a servant living with them. If Hobsbawm's assertion that the possession of a servant defined middle-class status applies to Canada as well as England, then the percentage of households without servants indicates, again, the magnitude of the working class in Hamilton.[15] (The terminology of class is a delicate and complex issue. I shall argue later for a three-class structure—entrepreneurial, artisan, and laboring.) Most of the servants, 60 percent, had been born in Ireland and 47 percent were Catholic. By and large young girls, slightly more than half of them were under twenty years old, and three quarters were under twenty-five. Nearly nine out of ten servants were females, 93 percent unmarried, although some of these had children. Families that employed servants were likely to live in a brick or stone house of two or more stories, surrounded by a large plot of land. Like the employment of servants, houses of these types were more likely than not to be found at the eightieth economic rank; the size of the plot attached to the dwelling increased most often at the ninetieth rank.

Household size also increased quite directly with wealth. To take one example, 15 percent of the households in the 20–40th ranks were large (eight or more members), compared to 30 percent of those in the 60–80th and 61 percent of those in the top 1 percent. Little relationship, however, existed between wealth and number of children. The presence of servants, boarders, and relatives accounted for the larger household size of the wealthy. In fact, servants, boarders, and relatives all lived more frequently with affluent than with poor families. School attendance also varied directly with economic standing. Families with no servants sent only slightly more than a third of their school-age children to school; families with one servant sent just over half; families with more than one servant sent still larger proportions. Wealthier people also kept their children in school longer. Twenty-two percent of the fourteen-year-old children from families with no servants had attended school, compared to 42 percent of those from families with one servant and 82 percent of those from families with two servants. The employment of servants, the occupancy of a large brick or stone house, a spacious plot of land, a large household, the steady and prolonged attendance of one's children at school: these constituted the principal means through which the affluent demonstrated their success to their neighbors.

The affluent of the city solidified their economic control with political power. Not only did property qualifications exclude most of the poor from voting, but the wealthy monopolized local political offices. Despite the fact that nearly 30 percent of elected city officials called themselves by an artisan title, most were wealthy. They were by no means workingmen in the late-twentieth-century sense, that is, manual workers employed by a firm; rather, they were prosperous master craftsmen and employers. Of the elected officials, nearly 70 percent were in the top ten economic ranks;

83 percent were in the top twenty. In the two years 1851–52, 42 percent of the wealthiest 1 percent of the work force held political office.

To understand the exercise of power within the city it is necessary to grasp the extent of overlap of membership in elite positions. Measured grossly from listings in the newspaper, the overlap of membership in three elites—people elected to city political offices, business officials, and officers of voluntary societies—is striking and, beyond question, statistically significant.[16] Of the forty-eight elected city officials, for instance, fifteen were business officials, twenty-one were officers of voluntary societies, and eight were jurors. Of the 130 business officials, fifteen were elected city officials, forty-one officers of voluntary societies, thirty-six petitioners (asking the city for favors), and twelve jurors. Among 196 officers of voluntary societies (a very high figure, suggesting an extraordinarily important role for voluntary activity within this society), twenty-one were elected city officials, forty-one business officials, eight appointed city officials, six school trustees, and eighteen jurors. Of the seventy-four jurors who served during 1851 and 1852, eight were elected officials, twelve were business officials, and one was an appointed city official. Ten people were elected city officials, business officials, and officers of voluntary societies simultaneously.

Measures designed to test statistical significance—to see whether or not such results could have occurred by chance—tell the same story. The relationships were strong and real. The unmistakable overlap among elites underlines the interconnections among economic, political, and social power within this nineteenth-century city. More than that, the relation of people in elite positions to petitioners and jurors is revealing. A poor or unimportant man in Hamilton, it is quite clear, lacked the temerity to ask the city for favors; in fact, if he incurred its displeasure, he was not even tried by a jury of his peers.[17]

Just as poverty and powerlessness brought invisibility, so affluence and power made a man visible. On the basis of their mention in local newspapers the people of the city may be divided into three groups according to their "visibility": those "invisible" (not mentioned in the newspapers at all), about 94 percent of the population in 1851; those moderately "visible" (mentioned once or twice); and those highly "visible," mentioned five or more times, about 1 percent of the population. Who then were the highly visible people? They were, as might be expected, the members of the interlocking elites. Highly visible people comprised more than half of the following categories: elected and appointed city and county officials, business officials, officers of voluntary societies, school trustees, petitioners, jurors, advertisers, union members (only six were mentioned in the newspapers at all), political committee members, and people publicly honored. Interestingly, as with the case of overlap among various sorts of officeholders, jurors and petitioners interconnect with the most powerful men within the city.[18]

These interconnections among kinds of power within Hamilton pose important comparative questions. Did economic, social, and political power exist in a closer relationship at that time than they do at present? What impact did industrialization have upon their interrelationship? Is the curve of inequality steady over time, or did it widen in the initial stages of industrialization and then diminish in the twentieth century? Whatever the answers to these questions may be, the detailed examination of the distribution of income and power should help dispel any lingering nostalgia about the existence of equality and community in nineteenth-century cities.

Was Hamilton an especially unequal place? The little evidence that can be used for comparative purposes suggests not. Within nineteenth-century North America, industrialization, urban growth, and complexity may have increased the already unequal distribution of wealth. Certainly, Robert Gallman's analysis of the distribution of wealth supports that conclusion. Unfortunately, it is extraordinarily difficult to compare the distribution of wealth in any two past places with precision; differences in the way sources have been compiled, variations in patterns of property ownership, and the peculiarities of local economies make comparative analysis exceedingly hazardous. Nonetheless, it is instructive to compare the results of some other inquiries into nineteenth-century wealth-holding with the pattern that existed in Hamilton, if only to make a rough estimate about the representativeness of distribution there.

Robert Gallman, in his national study, estimated that in 1860 the richest 1 percent of the American population held 24 percent of the wealth, a figure identical to my estimation for Hamilton in 1861; and Gallman's other figures, especially his estimate that the wealthiest 5 percent held 53 to 55 percent of the wealth, are not too far from mine for Hamilton, where the wealthiest fifth had 50 percent of the assessed wealth. In his analysis, for 1860, of Milwaukee, Wisconsin, a city substantially more industrialized than Hamilton at that time, Lee Soltow found that the wealthiest 16 percent of the male population held about 80 percent of the wealth, compared to 77 percent held by the wealthiest 5 percent in Hamilton; the wealthiest 3.6 percent in Milwaukee had 58 percent compared to 50 percent held by the wealthiest 5 percent in Hamilton. Similarly, Edward Pessen's figures suggest a greater degree of inequality in two places that were larger, more complex, and more economically developed than Hamilton, namely, Brooklyn and Boston. In Brooklyn in 1841 people in the 90–99th economic percentiles held 41 percent of the wealth compared to 39 percent for people of comparable standing in Hamilton in 1852. However, the wealthiest 1 percent held twice as much as their counterparts in Hamilton, 42 compared to 21 percent. In Boston, in 1848, the wealthiest fifth of the population held 96 percent of the wealth, compared to 74 percent in Hamilton. It would be especially helpful if the degree of property ownership in each of these places could be compared, for it may be that proportionally fewer people owned real estate in very large cities, in which case real estate would have increased in value and been concentrated in the hands of a smaller number of people. Since the value of real property determines such a significant portion of individual wealth in all these studies, the spread of property ownership could account for what appears to be the rough relationship between increased urban size and complexity and economic inequality. The one study comparing home ownership in five nineteenth-century cities supports this line of reasoning. For in 1860 in the four small or medium-sized cities the proportion of home ownership did not vary to any great degree, hovering around 30 percent, while in the one large metropolis, Philadelphia, only 13 percent of the adult males owned the homes in which they lived.[19]

A number of common notions about families as well as communities in earlier times are dispelled by detailed examination of actual cases. It is often thought that the nuclear family emerged as a consequence of industrialization, that in early times people married at very young ages, and that the poor, especially, had very large families. None of these propositions is true. Clear relationships existed between transiency and inequality, the two great themes of the nineteenth-century city, and the domestic arrangements of its people. However, to some extent the family and household exhibited characteristics partially independent of wealth and related (sometimes inexplicably, it seems, at this stage of research) to other measures. Thus, it is important to consider family and household structure by themselves.

The formation of the family through marriage is the logical starting point. Statistics for this subject are based upon the marriage registers for Wentworth County covering the years 1842–1869.[20] Marriage patterns within Wentworth County were endogamous. Of 5327 brides, 4443 resided in Wentworth County as did 4026 of the same total number of grooms. It is to be expected that most brides would be from Wentworth County, since marriage customarily takes place at the bride's residence. More notable is the small proportion of local women who married men from outside the county. Nevertheless, the majority of marriages throughout the period involved people who had both been born outside Ontario and, indeed, outside Canada.

For the most part the figures for age of marriage contradict the stereotypes of early marriage among the people of earlier times. In fact, marriage age in Hamilton was comparable to that in more traditional European societies. The mean age of marriage for men was 27.7, the median 25.7; 61 percent of grooms were twenty-five years old or over; 25 percent were over thirty. Brides were considerably younger, about four years on the average, their mean marriage age being 23.2 and the median 21.8. Just over one quarter of the girls married before they were twenty, and 72 percent had married by the time they were twenty-five. Both religion and birthplace influenced marriage age, though of the two birthplace appeared stronger. Younger marriages were slightly more common among Baptists and "Protestants" and later marriages more common among Presbyterians. Similarly, Scottish people married notably later than other groups. People born in Canada West married the youngest by far. No unusual distributions of age existed among brides and grooms born in England, the United States, or, contrary to what might be expected, Ireland.[21]

Figures for births, like those for marriages, do not support common notions about Catholic families. From what I can tell at this point, the birthrate among Catholics or Irish-born people was no higher than among the population as a whole. To the contrary, the congruence between the percentage of total births in the city occurring among a particular group and that group's percentage of the total population, as reported in the census, stands out as especially striking. Thus, Catholics aged 20–29 formed 18 percent of the household heads of that age group within the city; to them occurred 18 percent of the births among that age group. The poor formed 26 percent of the household heads; they had 27 percent of the births. It would be tedious to continue to present these figures; with one exception they remain the same for ethnicity, religion, and wealth. That exception, and an interesting one, is the people born in French Canada, who formed a tiny 0.4 percent of the 20–29-year-olds but accounted for 2 percent of the births, a disproportion consistent with trends in French-Canadian demography.[22] Fertility rates (defined here for each ethnic group as children 0–15/women 16–45) show the same thing: for Irish Catholics the rate was 2.5; for Irish Protestants 2.6; Scottish Presbyterians, 2.9; English Protestants, 2.7; (English) Canadian-born Protestants, 2.3.

This initial survey of Hamilton's demography would be incomplete without some mention of death and death rates. At this juncture it is not possible to discuss with precision the relations among death rate, age at death, and other social variables, such as religion, ethnicity, and wealth. I do know that the infant mortality rate was staggeringly high. Of 210 people recorded on the census as having died, 106 or 51 percent were five years old or younger; all but twenty-one, or 10 percent, were under the age of fifty. Initial surveys show no relationships of significance between infant mortality or overall mortality and either wealth or ethnicity.

Figures for the number of children within a household are generally, though not completely, consistent with the statistics of marriage and birth. Among the heads of households as a whole, 55 percent had small families (0–2 children); 36 percent had medium-sized families (3–5 children), and 10 percent had large families (6

or more children). Of course, age distribution affects any discussion of family size. Thus, to have a fair basis of comparison
I shall discuss only heads of household aged 40–49, those whose
families were both complete and, to the largest extent, still living
together. Of the 40–49-year-old household heads, 37 percent had
small families, 44 percent had medium-sized ones, and 18 percent
had large numbers of children. The mean size of all households
was 5.8; where the head was in his forties it was 6.5; the mean
number of children for all age groups was 2.5, and for men in
their forties, 3.3.

First of all, as with births, family size among the 40–49-year-olds
shows little relation to wealth.[23] The poor did not breed more
quickly than the rest of the population. In fact, the only discernible relation between wealth and number of children works in the
other direction. Among the heads of household as a whole 0.3
percent of the very poorest people, those in the bottom twenty
economic percentiles, had a large number of children compared to
15 percent of those in the 95–99th percentiles. Among the 40-49-
year-old household heads the poorest men had no children about
twice as often as most other groups; similarly, they had the smallest percentage of medium-sized families of any group. Considering
all ages together, the mean number of children among the poorest
20 percent of household heads was 0.54, and among the wealthiest
1 percent, 3.32. Between these ranges, however, scores are quite
similar. One other difference, which relates to economic standing,
shows the same trend. Transients, who were poorer than the more
permanent residents, had a slightly lower mean number of children despite their similarity in age.

An examination of the mean number of children among 40–49-
year-old household heads highlights some ethnic and religious
distinctions generally unrelated to wealth. North Americans, natives of Canada West and the United States, had small families.
The lowest mean score, 2.40, was that of the Americans, followed
by the Canadians, the English, the Irish, and the Scottish in that
order. These figures reflect the late marriage age of Scottish
people. Among religious groups those with heavily Scottish membership ranked high in mean number of children among 40–49-
year-olds. At the other end of the scale the denomination with the
smallest mean family size, the Baptist, was heavily American in

origin. The mean size for the Catholics was quite average for the 40–49-year-olds, although their mean for the 20–29-year-olds was the highest in that cohort, which indicates that Catholics had more of their children when they were younger, not, as is often thought, a greater number in all than did other groups.[24]

It is difficult to draw many conclusions about the mean family size of different occupational groups, for research reveals systematic differences in 1851 but not in 1861. Nor is it possible to say much about birth control, except that in a time of depression men definitely postponed marriage. It is quite likely, given the evidence of scholars studying English society, that some form of birth control was in use, an hypothesis with which my demographic conclusions do not seem inconsistent. In Hamilton the aspiring business classes, at least, may have begun to practice some form of family limitation by the mid-nineteenth-century.[25]

Certainly distinctions in family size existed between men engaged in commerce and other nonmanual workers. Relatively small family size (merchants in 1851 averaged 1.78 children) remained more a hallmark of men with an entrepreneurial outlook than a badge separating white and blue collar workers in the modern sense. This becomes apparent from the mean family size of the other (nonentrepreneurial) nonmanual groups: the mean family size of teachers, for instance, 3.71, was the highest of any group; the mean for gentlemen was 2.89, the same as for laborers and tinsmiths; and the mean for lawyers fluctuated strangely with age. All of this suggests that in the mind of the aspiring entrepreneur the possibility of limiting the number of his offspring had become linked with increasing his wealth.

As already observed, the size of his household rather than the number of his children marked a wealthy man. Boarders, servants, relatives, and visitors, as well as his wife and children, composed his household. There were fewer extended families in this commercial city than might be expected; relatives other than husband, wife, and children lived in only 15 percent of the households. Like the families Peter Laslett and his associates have studied in England over a period of four hundred years, those in Hamilton remained overwhelmingly nuclear. As with servants, relatives lived most frequently in the households of the well-to-do; they were present in 4 percent of the poorest 20 percent of the households and in 24 percent of those in the 95–99th economic ranks.[26]

The same is true of boarders, who were found in 28 percent of the households. They lived, however, with 8 percent and 15 percent of the families in the 0–20th and 20–40th economic ranks, respectively, and with 46 percent of those in the 90–95th. There were boarders, in fact, in more than four out of ten households within each group above the eightieth economic rank, a somewhat surprising finding, for it might be expected that boarders would be most likely to live with poorer families who needed the extra income. This not being the case, the identity of boarders and their place within the household should be examined.

The presence of boarders in so many households reflects an important characteristic of social life: it was extremely unusual for people to live alone; everyone was expected to live within a family setting. Because only about 1 percent of the work force lived by themselves, large numbers of young unmarried people living alone clearly represent a modern development. The earlier pattern of residence, moreover, constituted an informal system of social control. For young men, close supervision with constant scrutiny of their behavior constituted the other side of the warmth of living in a family grouping. Boarding the young men of the town provided the affluent with a convenient means of keeping a close check on them.

Most of the boarders, 71 percent, were men; 14 percent of them were married, which accounts in large part for the women and children listed as boarders. Like servants, boarders were young, though not quite so young: 34 percent were under twenty and a further 52 percent between twenty and twenty-four years old; 84 percent were under thirty. They came more often from Ireland than from elsewhere, in 43 percent of the cases, but a sizable group, 19 percent, had been born in Canada West. A little over one third of the boarders were Catholic, the largest single figure for any denomination, and the rest were scattered among other religious groups. Boarders followed a staggering variety of occupations: many, about 54 percent, were craftsmen of one sort or another; of the remainder, about 13 percent were laborers and 8 percent clerks. Spinsters, widows, and women following domestic occupations like dressmaking frequently boarded, as did a few young professionals—nine lawyers and seven physicians, probably establishing themselves in practice.

These figures suggested at first that many boarders were young men living with their employers in households that combined work and residence. A close comparison of the occupations of boarders and their landlords demolished that hypothesis, however. It is extremely difficult to determine if a boarder and a household head might have worked together, for occupational terminology was vague and sometimes misleading. But in most cases it was clear that no reasonable connection could be made. Not only occupation but class seemed to make little difference. Laborers lived with judges, physicians, attorneys, and gentlemen, as well as with fellow laborers, molders, and widows. Widows, in fact, took in many boarders, obviously a way to make a little money. Other than that, there seems little pattern in the distribution of boarders by occupation, except that in a number of instances clerks and men employed in foundries lived at their place of work. Overall, slightly more than 9 percent of the boarders might have been living with their employers.

Other obvious principles on which boarders might have selected their residence are religion and ethnicity. Perhaps young men entering the city looked for families of similar ethnic and religious backgrounds with whom to live, whatever their occupation might be. In most cases this did not happen. There was some tendency for Irish and for Catholic boarders to choose landlords of the same background, and a very slight tendency for the English and the Anglicans to do the same. But in no instance did those dwelling with people of similar religion or ethnic background constitute a majority.

In short, it appears that other factors were more important in the choice of a lodging, such as convenience, price, and the presence of friends living there or nearby. The population of Hamilton was expanding rapidly, increasing between 1850 and 1852 from about ten to fourteen thousand. The practical result of this increase must have been a severe strain on housing facilities. Perhaps rooms were in such short supply that people took whatever they could find. Perhaps, too, there was great pressure on anyone with a spare bed to take in someone. That is probably why so many of the more affluent citizens with larger houses had boarders.

Although it is as important to discover the behavioral patterns associated with types of families and households as to determine their size and structure, there are fewer indexes of behavior than of structure on which to base systematic observations. One of the most readily available, and most interesting, is school attendance. The analysis of school attendance links parental attitudes to social, demographic, and economic measures, and to family size as well. It thus provides a way of joining the family and household to the larger social context in which they were embedded.[27]

Of all the children in the city aged 5–16 in 1851, 50 percent attended school at some time during the year. Rather more boys than girls attended at each age level. Very few children entered school before the age of six. At the age of six a third began to attend, but the ages from seven to thirteen were the period of heaviest school attendance, the proportion attending exceeding 40 percent only in each of those years. The peaks were reached between the ages of nine and eleven, the only time when more than half of the age group attended school.

Part of the variation in school attendance can be explained by family size. It is often thought that small families provide settings conducive to education. Indeed, twentieth-century studies have shown an inverse relation between school achievement and scores on intelligence tests, and family size. According to the data, this contemporary relationship did not hold in the nineteenth century. The percentage of school-age children attending school generally increased with the number of children in the family. This relationship held even for the youngest and eldest children attending school: 3 percent of children aged 3–5 from families with two children attended school, compared to 10 percent from families with five children; and 18 percent of 15–16-year-old children from families with two children attended school, compared to 23 percent from families with five children.

The birthplace of the head of household also affected school attendance. Irish fathers were least likely to send their children to school. The fraction of Irish children aged 5–16 attending school was under one third. For two groups, however, it was over one half; these were the Scottish and the native Canadians. The relations between religion and attendance reinforce these findings: fewer than 30 percent of Catholic children attended schools, compared to over 50 percent for the Church of Scotland and the Wesleyan Methodists and over 60 percent for Free Church Presbyterians. Scottish Presbyterianism should obviously be added to family size as an important factor promoting school attendance. Factors other than class accounted for part of the low attendance of Catholics, for their school attendance rose dramatically after the introduction of Catholic schools later in the decade.

If wealth is measured by the possession of servants, the relation between wealth and school attendance is striking. That relation supports the observations of school promoters who perceived their problem in terms of persuading poor families to school their children. Insofar as educational reform was impelled by a perception of idle children from poor homes wandering the streets, it was based on a very real situation.

The relations between occupation and school attendance spoil the neatness of the foregoing analysis, for they fail to adhere completely to the boundaries set by wealth, ethnicity, and religion. Lawyers, for instance, sent few of their children to school; it is entirely possible that they hired private tutors. Tinsmiths, on the other hand, were exceptionally conscious of schooling: 85 percent of their school-age children attended school during 1851, a figure exceeded only by the children of teachers, 92 percent of whom had attended. Laborers, as could be expected, were at the bottom; less than one quarter of their school-age children went to school in 1851, compared, for instance, to 46 percent of the children of merchants and 58 percent of the children of physicians. Differences among artisan groups parallel those among professionals; 38 percent of shoemakers' school-age children attended school, for instance, as did 54 percent of the children of cabinetmakers. There are at present no explanations for most of these differences.

Although school attendance often followed economic lines, it is clear that cultural and social factors intervened to complicate the final pattern. Two of these factors are noteworthy: North Americans kept their children in school somewhat longer than other groups; and the relationship between wealth, Catholicism, and Irish origin, on the one hand, and low school attendance, on the other, did not hold among the very youngest age groups. Perhaps schools served as baby-sitting agencies for large, poor families, relieving the parents of pressure at home and permitting the mother to work. At the same time, affluent parents of large families may have realized that they were unable to teach at home certain basic skills which it was traditional for children to learn before they started school at age seven. They may have used the school to accomplish what, given the size of their families, would otherwise have had to be done by private tutors.

But all conclusions must remain tentative at best. The most I can say is this: the people who most frequently sent children to school were well-to-do, had larger-than-average families, and had been born in Scotland or North America. Those sending the fewest were poor, Irish Catholic, and laborers. The same groups generally kept the most and the fewest children in school past the usual school-leaving age. But the figures for early school attendance revealed slightly different rankings, which indicates that early schooling served important economic functions for some poor families and important psychological functions for some large, wealthy families. The relations between occupation and schooling are unclear, aside from the figures for laborers. Why did lawyers send so few children? Why did tinsmiths send so many? These questions cannot be answered at present; like so many of the findings discussed in this chapter they remain beginnings rather than firm conclusions.

Clearly, the complex family and household patterns in Hamilton defy simple general descriptions. Equally clearly, they contradict many commonly held assumptions about preindustrial families. Men and women married relatively late, later probably than most people do today. In the vast majority of instances they formed nuclear families, the more wealthy adding a servant, a boarder, or, in comparatively few instances, a relative. Almost everybody, whether married or not, young or old, lived in a family. Within families there existed relatively little difference in the number of children born to parents of different economic conditions. Ethnicity and religion, in fact, remained more influential than wealth in determining age of marriage and number of children. The traditional image of the frugal, self-denying, and ambitious Scot emerges intact; the picture of the indulgent, overbreeding Irish Catholic is shattered. In fact, there were at least two types of households within the city. At one extreme was the Irish Catholic laborer living with his wife and two or three children in a one-and-a-half-story frame house. At the other extreme, but perhaps on the same street, lived the prosperous merchant with his wife, two or three children, a servant, and a boarder in a three-story stone house surrounded by a spacious plot of land. Most other families fell somewhere between. It will take a good deal more analysis to isolate other widespread family types, and a good deal of imaginative research into other sorts of sources to explain the results that emerge; to answer, that is, a question such as, "Why did American Baptists have small families?"

It is also important to ask whether the relations between family size and ethnicity that existed in Hamilton were present in other Canadian cities as well. That, in turn, is part of the larger issue of representativeness. How can one know that the findings from Hamilton have meaning for any other place? From one viewpoint the question is irrelevant. Every city's history is at the same time unique and representative of larger trends and forces. More than that, the relationships I wish to study can be investigated only on the local level. Even if Hamilton turns out to be less "representative" than one might wish, its study is important because it provides a datum with which to begin an analysis of what is special and what is general within nineteenth-century cities in Canada and elsewhere.

Hamilton was not representative of some things: it was not like villages and rural areas, for instance. On the other hand, it should have resembled in many ways the commercial cities of nineteenth-century Britain and the United States. Most of all, it was not too unlike other cities in Canada West. That is clear from studying published census figures for a number of Canadian cities. It is striking to observe the extent of similarity among Kingston, London, Toronto, and Hamilton with respect to the birthplace and religion of their residents; their age structures and sex ratios; their birth and death rates; and even their occupational structures. From these similarities it is obvious that Hamilton was structurally similar to other cities in Canada West. On that basis some general observations can be made about the nature of a commercial Canadian city.[28]

First, even in the mid-nineteenth century a relatively small commercial city was an enormously complex place. Simple general statements about its society, families, households, or spatial patterns are inadequate to convey the richness of its structural patterns. Economically, even before industrialization Canadian cities were highly differentiated. Socially, they were highly stratified.

Second, the family prior to industrialization was a more rational and "modern" organization than has often been suspected. Even at that early date people clearly related decisions about marriage and often about the size of their families to other, undoubtedly economic considerations. The difference between the earlier and the modern family does not rest in structure; both are nuclear. It lies, rather, in the number of children born to the average couple; in the composition of the household; and in the clear relation between household size and affluence.

Third, in no sense can we think of commercial cities as communities defined by stability, integration, and egalitarianism. The problem of inequality has already been touched on. The facts of transiency destroy any further illusions about community; the population simply changed too rapidly.

Fourth, the articulation of various structures with one another produced a powerful concentration of interlocking forms of power in the hands of a very small group of people. Household structure, political power, school attendance—the privileges that this society had to offer—all related to wealth. The distribution of men by economic rank corresponded to their division on most other social measures. Looked at another way, the business elite, the political elite, and the voluntary elite overlapped to a striking and significant extent. It is already evident that the political elite overlapped with the top rungs of the scale of economic rank. There is every reason to believe that the others did so as well.

The group that controlled economic, political, and social power within Hamilton contained at most 10 percent of the household heads. People within elite positions formed slightly more than 8 percent of men aged twenty and older. This figure is quite close to the 10 percent estimated elsewhere as wealthy. It is close, in fact, to the approximately 75 percent of elected officials who were within the top ten income percentiles. About 8 or 10 percent of the adult men, at the very maximum, controlled virtually all the resources necessary to the health, well-being, and prosperity of the rest.

In Hamilton the rulers, the owners, and the rich were by and large the same people. They clearly headed the stratification system. At the bottom the grouping was likewise clear: poor, propertyless, powerless men made up about 40 percent of the work force or between a fifth and a quarter of the household heads. The rest fall in between. About 40 percent were marginal; they owned no property and possessed no power, but they were prosperous enough to differentiate themselves from the poorest families. Their margin seems so slim and the consequences of falling so awful, however, that these people must have lived in constant tension and fear. Between them and the wealthy, comprising about a fifth of the families, was a qualitatively more affluent group. Most of them employed a servant and lived in a brick house which they owned. They were likely to vote in elections for the Legislative Assembly but were still not very likely to hold political office.

These four groups existed within Hamilton in the middle of the nineteenth century. Ranked according to wealth, power, and ownership, they form somewhat overlapping but nonetheless distinguishable clusters of people holding a similar position on each scale. Were they classes? That depends on the definition of class, which will be discussed in Chapter Four. No matter what the definition, however, it would be difficult to deny that class was a fundamental fact of life in mid-nineteenth-century urban Canada.[29]

CHAPTER TWO

The Structure of Inequality, 1851 and 1861

An unchanging, unchangeable social structure may well be essential to a swiftly changing population.   (Peter Laslett)

THE TWO GREAT themes of nineteenth-century urban history were transiency and inequality. It is easy enough for the historian to document each. It is much more difficult to explain their interrelations. This chapter will contend that there existed within the nineteenth-century city fixed, deep structures unaltered by the identity of the people who passed through them; and the next chapter will document the dimensions of transiency. The nineteenth-century city may be thought of as a society constructed in layers, each of which had room for a relatively fixed proportion of the population. Neither population growth nor depression nor transiency altered this structured inequality very much prior to the modernizing influence of technological change and industrial development. In fact it may be—as the quotation from Peter Laslett asserts—that structural rigidity counterbalanced transiency.[1] Persistent patterns of inequality preserved social stability and assured the continuity of social forms by staving off the chaos and anomie that otherwise might have accompanied a population moving with such astonishing rapidity.

There were four kinds of persistent structures within Hamilton between 1851 and 1861: (1) the occupational structure, or the proportion of the population engaged in various sorts of work; (2) the division of wealth, or the proportion of the wealth held by people in each economic rank; (3) the social and demographic identity of different economic ranks, or the characteristics of the

44

people with varying amounts of wealth; (4) the distance between the people of different social ranks, or the degree of social stratification. To the extent that notable change did occur, it increased the sharpness of social divisions by expanding the distance between rich and poor.

Two objections may be made to my argument that the existence of nearly identical social and economic structures at the start and close of a decade of rapid population turnover, depression, and political activity signifies structural stability or rigidity within the society. Critics may claim that: (1) identity at two points in time is an insufficient condition on which to base a conclusion, as the same result might have occurred by accident; (2) that one decade is too short a span of time on which to base any conclusions. Neither of these objections bears very much weight in this particular context.

The first criticism is weaker than the second because it is more ahistorical. Social structural patterns do not arise by accident. It is inconceivable that the social, economic, and demographic aspects of society resemble the pieces of colored glass in a child's kaleidoscope, which fall randomly into patterns with the turn of a tube. Social systems have an underlying logic that makes patterns at any point in time assume the shape they do. The social scientist must discover that logic. A similar structure in the same society at two points in time obviously means that the features which remained alike did not change. And the reason they did not change was that the pattern of interrelationships and dependency binding them together had not altered in any significant way. Should critics reply that, while this argument is appealing, confirming evidence from a decade later would be needed to make it conclusive, that claim, likewise, would be weak. For my hypothesis maintains that these structures did change in time, though exactly how and in what sequence I am not certain. They did alter, I suspect strongly, during the process of modernization, represented most concretely by industrial development. The decade in which industrial development initially increased most sharply in Hamilton was that of the 1860s.[2] Thus a change in structural patterns by 1871 would not discredit the argument that structural rigidity characterized the society prior to the onset of industrialization. Certainly, I would prefer to have data that

enabled comparisons of the sort offered in this chapter to be made
for an urban commercial society, or for any sort of society, across
a longer span of time, but I must work with what I have.

The second criticism questions basing conclusions upon the
experience of a decade. The question, which has no easy answer,
might be rephrased like this: how much can happen in a decade?
From the point of view of the demographic historian working
with series of data that span centuries, a decade represents a speck
of time, a possibly random acceleration or reversal in an otherwise
smooth curve. To the historian who examines societies more
closely, however, or to anyone living from day to day, a decade is a
long time. Significant social, economic, and cultural change can
occur in a period of ten years, as the student of depressions, race
relations, or the intellectual and institutional history of the 1960s
can testify. Thus there is little reason to dismiss an argument
which postulates either stability or change or, as is the case in
this book, some combination of the two, as characteristic of a
decade. Where a permanent change is postulated, as in Chapter
Five on the family, the evidence of what happened later will be
conclusive. But there is no reason to dismiss the fact that change
may have begun or been especially accelerated during a particular
span of time. The criticism might also be raised that the decade
of the 1850s was somehow abnormal because of the depression.
Very simply, I reject the idea of historical normalcy. It is impossible to sift out the process of economic fluctuation from other
historical developments. Given the fact that economic highs and
lows have followed each other with some regularity for a long
time, there is no reason to consider a period of prosperity any
more normal than one of depression. Indeed, the rhythm of
historical change in all institutions and behaviors must bear a
complex relationship to recurrent economic cycles. To explain
the origins or development of a particular social form, such as the
modern family or social stratification, in terms of both long-term
processes like modernization and short-term crises like depressions
is a distinctly historical procedure. It is one corrective historians
can inject into sociological theories that are singularly devoid of
contextual considerations and based on unexamined assumptions
of steady, evolutionary progress.

Twentieth-century images of social change have been conditioned unrealistically by evolutionary notions of progress.[3] Change is expected to be gradual, unidirectional, and incremental. Societies, it is tempting to say, do not change quickly; social change is, rather, a slow and piecemeal operation in which the outline of familiar forms gradually fades into hazy nostalgic background as new shapes emerge fuzzily, incoherently, and gradually crystallize into a new landscape. This image of societal change is not only overly simplistic but very possibly wrong. Any examination of the historical record will certainly muddy, block, and change the direction of streams of evolutionary progress. More than that, perhaps the correct image of social change is one of quick leaps from pattern to pattern rather than gradual development. If social systems have coherence, then perhaps their features change all together, not piecemeal, and speedily rather than gradually. The anthropologist Clifford Geertz, for instance, has argued: "Social system change is . . . multidimensional, a matter at once of redefining the framework of meaning in terms of which behavior takes place, the organizational forms through which it is effected, and the pattern of sentiments, conscious and not, in terms of which it is motivated." Writing of a Modjokuto village, Geertz shows how structures which persisted throughout the pre-1940 period crumbled relatively quickly as a result of the war.[4] My somewhat analogous hypothesis is that the commercial city formed a social system which persisted across time and with minor deviations across space, at least within the Atlantic commercial world. Its features—its social and family structure, its economic order, its power relations, even its cultural and intellectual life—were woven into patterns reproduced in varying though recognizable forms in both the Old World and the New. The modern industrial city, in this speculation, represents another pattern altogether, not merely an outgrowth or adaptation of the old, and one, moreover, that came about rather suddenly in terms of historical time. If this argument holds, then Hamilton in 1861 was more like Salem, Massachusetts, in 1800 than like the Hamilton it was to become in 1881 or 1891. This chapter, consequently, not merely delineates the patterns of one nineteenth-century city, but it attempts to formulate the structure of inequality in the urban form that dominated the life of the era.

To those critics who remain skeptical about the validity of

studying one city or one decade, I acknowledge that conclusions about nineteenth-century society cannot be made on the basis of the study of one city. This would be the case even if the data spanned a longer period of time and were richer than those presented here. Definitive answers to questions must be based on the comparative study of many places at varying points in time. The problem in making that comparison is that we simply have not formulated the most significant and important questions. Knowledge about the way in which past societies were put together and worked remains so primitive and the hypotheses arising from sociological theory so crude and ahistorical that we must grope for richer and more subtle, historical, and potentially rewarding analytical frameworks to guide research, comparative and otherwise. That I see as the primary value of this book. By abandoning caution a bit more than may be prudent in a book which must run the gauntlet of scholarly critics, I have set out a series of propositions that are not only testable in other settings but historically sensible, theoretically fruitful, and, just possibly, true. It is as a set of plausible and worthwhile historical hypotheses that I hope readers will approach the chapters in this book.

Before turning to the data which support my argument for structural stability, the historical and theoretical significance of that argument should be considered. Social structural distinctions which remain relatively fixed cannot be overlooked: they must of necessity be highly visible to almost everyone within a society. For social distinctions take a concrete form; in the case of Hamilton, for instance, a variety of tangible factors fused into a series of social identities by which people could be placed, by and large easily and precisely, on a hierarchy. The confluence of wealth, power, and life style at one point in time was described in the last chapter; this chapter will demonstrate its persistence across a decade; and Chapter Four will explore the interrelation of economic and political power through a study of individual cases. These examinations of networks of wealth, power, and life-style show that the objective characteristics of social stratification coalesced or, to use the phrase of sociologist Donald Treiman, crystallized. The importance of this crystallization lies in its possible consequences.[5]

Donald Treiman postulates that "the strength of the association between 'objective' status characteristics and subjective class identification depends upon the degree of crystallization of the objective characteristics in a society—the more crystallized statuses are, the more likely subjective identification will depend upon objective characteristics . . . And, as a corollary of this, the degree of status crystallization of a society should determine the degree of class cleavage of the society, a point which has been recognized from de Tocqueville on."[6] Treiman's speculation provides, first, a working hypothesis about the nature of social attitudes. If he is right, the hard crystallization of objective social features in Hamilton points to a clear and widespread consensus about the nature of social ranking on the part of the people within the city. Their awareness of differences in social rank should have been acute and, regardless of their position, largely the same. Indeed, if the degree of class *cleavage* as well as class *consciousness* follows from the crystallization of tangible components of stratification, then sharp and deep divisions of social class cut through nineteenth-century urban Ontario society.

All of this raises an intriguing methodological possibility, well worth further study. Measures that can be extracted from assessments, censuses, directories, and newspapers permit the historian to plot the extent to which the objective features of class have crystallized at various times. It should be entirely feasible to construct indexes that express the degree of crystallization in ways comparable, to some degree, across time and place. Given the assumptions in this line of argument, the historian can use these comparisons to contrast the degree of class consciousness and class division within a society. Quantitative historical studies might thus provide a relatively sensitive indicator of the way in which people in past times viewed themselves and their communities.

Accepting traditional assumptions about the nature of social development, one would expect the degree of social crystallization to decrease in a linear fashion throughout modern history. Certainly this conclusion may be drawn from a recent essay by Talcott Parsons.[7] The connection among property, political power, and ascribed status formed the basis of social differentiation within aristocratic societies; it remained strong, though in an altered form, during the early period of bourgeois ascendancy; and it eroded, especially through the growth of bureaucracy and scientific and technical elites, in contemporary times. The implication of this argument, given Treiman's hypothesis, is that the coalescence of objective class characteristics lessened, bringing a decreased awareness of class and a reduced degree of class cleavage throughout the last century or so. This is a simplification of a complex argument, but nonetheless it expresses conventional wisdom about the subject and is in itself a simplification of history. It is important both for its statement of a testable hypothesis about the history of social structure and for the assumption on which that hypothesis rests: namely, that the degree of association among objective class characteristics has decreased steadily, albeit imperfectly, throughout time. If that assumption should prove incorrect, a widely shared theory of stratification would crumble. Another aspect of the same theory of stratification postulates that the nuclear family developed as a concomitant of industrialization, thus reducing the influence of kinship on the maintenance of status. This assumption about the family has been proved wrong, and massively so. The family has been nuclear in most places throughout the largest part of its history.[8] A third dimension of the theory considers widespread geographic mobility to be a feature of modern social structure, which contrasts markedly to the localism of past times.[9] This, too, is a serious inaccuracy. In fact, the historical movement may have been in quite the opposite direction, a diminishing of transiency during industrialization.[10] Thus recent historical scholarship has knocked out two props from the theory of stratification. There is no reason to predict on the basis of the evidence that the aspect of the theory with which this chapter is concerned—the decline in the crystallization of class attributes—will prove unfounded as well. But the experience of historians studying the family and mobility does suggest that it can no longer be accepted simply as part of conventional wisdom. Thus the investigation of the interconnections between the various indicators of rank and the stability in their distribution—the subject matter of this chapter—connects with one of the major theories of stratification. It provides a baseline against which to measure the nature of social change wrought by modernization, to speculate about the change in social attitudes and class cleavage, and to assess the way in which contemporary social theory reflects or distorts historical data.

The documentation of structural stability begins with a consideration of occupational structure. Schemes for classifying occupational structure often confuse two purposes: the ranking of occupations in a vertical or hierarchical fashion according to criteria of wealth, status, power, or some combination of these attributes; and the arranging of occupations according to functional groups, that is, on the basis of the similarity of their role within the economy or of the sort of industry of which they are a part. In examining structural stability I shall adhere to the distinction between vertical and functional classification. Table 2.1 groups occupations functionally. The lack of change between 1851 and 1861 stands out starkly, for despite all the problems of occupational classification and the looseness with which people used occupational terms, despite the depression and mass transiency, the proportion of the population engaged in different sorts of work remained remarkably stable. The proportion in agriculture (1.3 percent) remained exactly the same; that in building stayed quite similar (15.1 and 13.9 percent); and, quite extraordinarily, the percentage in manufacturing remained about 26 percent. Similarly, the share of the work force in commerce shifted only from 26.8 to 24.5 percent; in the professions it remained 4.3 percent, and in semiskilled and unskilled labor it hardly moved, from 23.5 percent to 23.1 percent.

In fact, during the decade there were only two changes of significance; both occurred in tiny groups and were important merely as harbingers of the future. The proportion in transport rose, with the coming of the railroad, from 1 percent to 3.1 percent; and the percentage in public service increased from 1.7 percent to 3 percent, perhaps reflecting the fact that the size of public bureaucracy is not proportional to the size of population but rises at a geometric rate. Within the manufacturing sector of the occupational structure, only the clothing trades (predominantly shoemaking and tailoring) declined notably during the decade, from 11.2 percent to 7.8 percent, a consequence no doubt of technological innovation, especially the introduction of the sewing machine during the 1850s. The only trades to increase, again a

TABLE 2.1 Horizontal occupational structure, assessed males,
          1851 and 1861

Occupational group	1851		1861		Percent increase in number, 1851–1861
	Number	Percent of male work force	Number	Percent of male work force	
Agriculture	23	1.3	38	1.3	65.2
Building	277	15.1	406	13.9	46.6
Manufacturing	477	26.0	760	25.9	59.3
Food	70	3.8	93	3.2	32.9
Jewelry	6	0.3	13	0.4	116.7
Print and art	25	1.4	52	1.8	108.0
Metal	32	1.7	98	3.3	206.3
Transport trades	86	4.7	101	3.4	17.4
Clothing	206	11.2	228	7.8	10.7
Home furnishing	21	1.1	76	2.6	261.9
Mechanic	14	0.8	56	1.9	300.0
Building material	12	0.7	16	0.5	33.3
Other trades	5	0.3	27	0.9	440.0
Transport	19	1.0	91	3.1	378.9
Commerce	494	26.8	718	24.5	45.3
Professions	80	4.3	127	4.3	58.8
Nonprofessional services	6	0.3	24	0.8	300.0
Unskilled and semi-skilled labor	432	23.5	676	23.1	56.5
Public service	32	1.7	89	3.0	178.1
Total	1840		2929		59.2

tiny proportion but noteworthy in terms of the future, were the mechanical, which rose from .8 percent to 1.9 percent of the work force.

Thus, in each year about one quarter of the adult men worked in commercial occupations, another quarter in laboring jobs, a third quarter in skilled trades, about 15 percent in construction, just under 5 percent in the professions, and the rest in a variety of different capacities. To what degree, the question becomes, were these proportions typical of other nineteenth-century cities? It is too early in the history of comparative social research to answer definitively. Recently, however, five historians, including myself, studying five nineteenth-century cities, undertook a pilot study testing the similarities between places and the ways in which comparisons might be made. We concluded that the occupational structures of the five cities—Hamilton, Ontario; Poughkeepsie, Buffalo, and Kingston, New York; and Philadelphia, Pennsylvania —despite differences in geography, ethnic composition, and history showed striking similarities in the early 1860s.[11] And I have already pointed out that the occupational structure of Hamilton was remarkably like that of other Ontario cities in 1851. It is likely, then, that the occupational distribution just examined reveals a division of labor not merely idiosyncratic to Hamilton but, at the least, common to North American commercial cities in the nineteenth century.

Within Hamilton the division of wealth during the 1850s remained as remarkably stable as the occupational structure. The stability revealed between 1851 and 1861 appears especially significant in view of the problems of measurement encountered in determining an individual's wealth. The figure used here is the composite one that I call economic ranking, which consists of the sum of an individual's assessed worth based on all his property holdings throughout the city. The amount of rent paid by a tenant is credited to both the tenant and his landlord, and thus a considerable amount of money is used twice in the calculations. The justification for this is that we have considered the amount of rent paid by a man, combined with any reported income, personal property, or other assessed possessions, to be the best available *proxy* for his true worth. Extensive work with the scale of economic ranking produced through this procedure has justified its use and proved to our satisfaction that it gives the best indicator of the economic rank of an individual within the city and of his relative (not absolute) wealth in relation to the rest of the population.[12] The underreporting of wealth, which we assume was common in both 1851 and 1861 (though not significantly different in either year), adds to the general problem of creating a scale. Finally, in order to make comparisons even more difficult, between 1851 and 1861 the unit of currency on which the assessment was based changed from pounds to dollars. For all these reasons not too much precision should be expected in the comparisons of the division of wealth, and not too much weight should be placed on small differences. Despite all the problems and the researchers' caution, one conclusion has emerged with overwhelming clarity: the amount of wealth held by people in each economic rank remained almost identical in 1851 and 1861, as Table 2.2 shows. Assuming that the differences are accurate reflections of trends, the share of the wealthiest people, the upper 10 percent, increased from 60 to 63 percent; that of the middle-ranking groups, the people in the 40th–80th economic ranks, dipped very slightly from 20 to 18 percent; and that of the poorest 40 percent remained the most stable, dropping only from 6 to 5 percent. The stability in these distributions underlines the stark inequality already observed in Chapter One. At the same time it displays a deeply etched pattern of inequality. The identity of the people in the various economic ranks shifted, due to transiency and social mobility, but their share of the total wealth and the consequent distance between social groups remained the same, insofar as they can be measured by the data at hand.

Although the identity of the people in the various economic ranks altered, the social, demographic, and occupational charac-

TABLE 2.2 Distribution of total assessed
wealth by economic ranks,
1851 and 1861

Economic rank	Percentage of total wealth[a]	
	1851	1861
0–19 percentile	2	1
20–39 percentile	4	4
40–59 percentile	7	5
60–79 percentile	13	13
80–89 percentile	14	14
90–94 percentile	13	13
95–98 percentile	26	26
99–100 percentile	21	24
	100	100

a Percentages rounded.

teristics of those who occupied them remained remarkably similar. It is as though when a person left the city someone with similar features entered to take his place. As the word "his" in the last sentence shows, the discussion of inequality and its characteristics in most of this chapter refers to the male work force. But sex was as sharp and permanent a form of social and economic division as any other. Just as the structure of inequality among men changed very little during the decade, the place of women within the city altered hardly at all, unless it was to slide downwards on the unhappy road from difficult to desperate.

What has been called the "cult of true womanhood" reverberated in Hamilton as elsewhere throughout the Victorian world.[13] At once a sentimental idealization of feminine influence and a mawkish celebration of domesticity, the cult of true womanhood was also an ideology that kept women in their place, which is to say, in the home and out of the world of work. One Dr. Querner, for instance, put the whole case with perfection at the Burlington Temple on December 10, 1860: "Nothing," he said, "exerts a more ennobling influence on the character of man than association with a true and virtuous woman. Her naturally more soft and gentle form harbors also a milder mind. Modesty and a higher sense of morality are the gifts which the Creator has imparted to her in a richer measure than to men." The role of woman was, first, to improve her man, "to rein the wildness of the manly character, to smoothen his harshness, to soften his stubbornness, to spur his spirit of enterprise and emulation, to wipe out his delusions and bitter experiences, to mitigate his misfortunes." After her man, or more accurately, at the same time, came her influence over her children: "the blessed influence of mothers, who principally have to sow the seed for further flourishing in the hearts of their children." Thus woman reigned supremely important—"the most diligent architect in the temple of arts and science . . . the most noble educator of our character, the most earnest improver of our soul." Yet she had no existence of her own. Her role was to serve her husband, her children, and, through them, her society. Woman should know her "proper sphere." Predictably, the "labours of a woman are naturally divided betwixt the nursery, the kitchen, the sewing cushion, the garden." Some women, it is true, did somewhat more, but they made Dr. Querner a trifle uneasy: "Female artists and authors are pleasing and agreeable phenomena, but exceptions rather to the general rule ordained by the Creator of having 'the right thing in the right place.' "[14]

If women were more virtuous and noble than men, they were also potentially more base. Elevated upon an exalted pedestal, they had nowhere to go but off and down. And there was no halfway position: a woman who dropped from her pedestal fell into the mud. As Dr. Querner said, "how much lower than the lowest man does she become, how degraded does she appear, when, forgetful or regardless of all consequences, she neglects the duties proper to her position, stains her fair name, and falls into the vices common to the lowest grades of society." A woman such as that wrought only "mischief," breaking "that band . . . which binds the family together by the homely fireside," destroying with "wicked hands that which she should protect and cultivate with care."[15]

Man had all the freedom of action in nineteenth-century society. He could fail, sin, or simply lose his temper and a good woman would stand by ready to forgive, comfort, and send him forth once more. Not surprisingly, only the women who stepped outside the Victorian ideal of wife and mother could succeed as well as men. Ironically, women were probably the ones who upset the social system most in nineteenth-century Hamilton where wealth and status, reward and virtue were expected to accompany each other as visible manifestations of the rectitude and moral order of society. The two most independently successful women in mid-nineteenth-century Hamilton were Mrs. Matilda Tolman and Mrs. Annie Hibbard, and they were madams. One wintry night in 1851 a police magistrate broke up a brawl at a house of ill fame, rented from no less a person than the Honorable Samuel Mills. Ellen Gardiner, one of the unfortunate women charged with smashing "sundry panes of glass in a fit of passion," turned angry at her accusers, especially the madam of the house, Mrs. Matilda Tolman, who pressed charges against her. Ellen, in revenge, accused Mrs. Tolman of keeping a house of ill fame, something apparently well known, which she did not deny, though she did deny the second and apparently more serious of Ellen's charges, selling liquor without a license. But Ellen produced a witness, and Mrs. Tolman, shifting from accuser to accused, was fined. There are two remarkable aspects to this pathetically funny case. One is the description of Mrs. Tolman, "a tall, shewy looking *lady,* with a very jaunty and self-satisfied air—very handsomely attired in a purple velvet bonnet, a stylish silk polka and fur boa," who eventually left the court with *"characteristic dignity."* The other is the ease with which she paid her fine. She was fined, in all, seven pounds, fifteen shillings, a very large sum in those days, the amount an ordinary laborer might earn for two months' work. Yet, with anger but no difficulty, Mrs. Tolman paid her fine. Not having money with her, she produced on the spot a gold watch which she offered to leave as security while she returned home to collect her cash. The court refused, dispatching a constable with Mrs. Tolman to her house where, indeed, the money was duly paid. The same easy financial state appeared in the case of Mrs. Annie Hibbard. Once Ellen Gardiner had started pointing the finger, she appeared unwilling to stop and produced a list of local madams. Mrs. Hibbard, operating "in the most populous part of King Street" (like other prosperous local businesses) was one of them. Fined five pounds, two shillings, sixpence, Mrs. Hibbard, though enraged, promptly paid the full amount. So did Charlotte Chewett and Mrs. Delia Jane.[16] Obviously, these women had very significant sums of ready cash. They were, to repeat, the only independently successful women found in Hamilton. But in their case social respectability did not accompany wealth, as it did for even the shadiest of male entrepreneurs. These madams were the most glaring anomalies in a social system where wealth, status, and power coalesced into a neat and acknowledged gradation of social ranks.

For most women, however, opportunities remained extremely limited between 1851 and 1861; if anything, their situation worsened. In each year most of the employed women did menial work: 72 percent were servants in 1851 and 59 percent ten years later; in both years about 14 percent were dressmakers, seamstresses, or milliners, occupations suitable enough in terms of the ideology of female domesticity but offering irregular work at low wages. Few women (thirteen in 1851 and ten in 1861) could be positively identified as prostitutes, but undoubtedly there were very many

more. Some of the dressmakers especially, if they followed the
pattern common in London, must have resorted to part-time prostitution simply to earn enough money to stay alive.[17]

By 1861 the occupational situation had improved somewhat
from one point of view. The number of women aged fifteen and
over working as servants had dropped from 827 to 802 despite an
increase in population. In 1851 perhaps 4 percent of the women
might have been considered marginally middle-class (teachers, innkeepers, grocers, clerks, tax collectors); by 1861 that figure was
11 percent, including even one physician. At the same time, women
followed a somewhat greater variety of occupations, forty-one in
1851 and fifty-four in 1861.

Simultaneously, certain trends offset the apparent gains in occupation. First of all, the percentage of adult women employed
decreased slightly from 25 to 21 percent. Extremely large increases in the number of widows, 133 percent, and in the number of spinsters, 97 percent, took place at the same time, although
the number of households rose only 40 percent. Thus more women
than before needed employment, but relatively fewer jobs existed.
This unhappy situation resulted from demographic and economic
problems. Following the massive outmigration of young men during the depression, the sex ratios among people of the most marriageable ages became badly skewed. Among people born in
England the percentage of men to women among 16–20-year-olds
dropped from 97 to 68 percent during the decade, and the percentage among the 21–25-year-olds decreased from 96 to 80 percent.
Even among native Canadians the proportion dropped from 95
to 74 percent and from 90 to 72 percent. Among the Irish the
problem was most severe, the percentage among the 21–25-year-olds
plummeting from 74 to 46 percent. These figures make the increase in the percentage of spinsters easy to understand.

The decline in employment opportunities came about most
markedly through the drop in the number of families able to afford a servant. The proportion of families employing a servant
actually declined from 30 to 21 percent during the decade, most
likely a result of the depression. It is possible that male mortality
may have increased during the depression, thus increasing the
number of widows. Or a number of women may have been aban-

doned by their men, who left in search of better opportunities, and may simply have called themselves widows. At any rate, the absence of men may have left vacancies in some occupations which were considered relatively suitable for women, particularly inn-keeping and storekeeping. This availability of openings, coupled with a doubling in the number of women teachers (part of an international trend toward the feminization of teaching, which proceeded more slowly in Canada than in the United States), produced the small but notable increase in the number of women in less menial occupations.[18]

The situation of female household heads underlines the plight of women. There were, as might be expected, many more female household heads in 1861 than in 1851, an increase, in fact, of 115 percent, which was 75 percent greater than the increase in the total number of households. However, the percentage of female household heads actually listing themselves as widows declined from 92 to 86 percent, while the number calling themselves married (with their husbands by implication gone) increased from eleven to thirty-six, or from 5 to 7 percent, and the number showing themselves unmarried jumped from seven to thirty-four, or from three to seven percent, a relatively large increase. These trends point to a probable rise in the number of deserted women and to a possible increase in illegitimacy, which could have resulted from the desperation accompanying grossly unbalanced sex ratios.

Women who headed households were not young. In 1851 their average age was forty-five; in 1861 it was forty-six. They were thoroughly representative of all religions and birthplaces, although there were slightly more Irish among them than in the population as a whole. Nor did they have especially small families, their mean number of children dropping only from 2.4 to 2.2, a figure quite consistent with the city average. It is perhaps for this reason—the presence of children at home—along with the relatively restricted job opportunities, that most of the widows who headed households, 75 percent, did not list themselves as employed. With young children they could not very well become servants because most servants lived in. Without some small amount of capital they could not start a little business, such as a grocery store or an inn.

At best they might take in boarders and washing or do some sewing at home. In view of the inadequacy of welfare at this time, most of these women must have lived in stark poverty.[19]

Indeed, the absence of servants in the homes of all but a very few reveals that most of the households headed by women lacked resources. On the other hand, a relatively substantial proportion had boarders. Between 1851 and 1861, however, the number of boarders dropped among female household heads, as it did among the population as a whole. Among widows, for instance, the decrease was from 77 per hundred to 41. Thus even this supplementary source of income became increasingly scarce at the very time that other economic factors were worsening.

A number of factors intertwined by 1861 to make the prospects for a young woman in Hamilton exceedingly bleak: her chances of finding a husband had decreased; employment opportunities, with a few exceptions, had shrunk slightly; women who had married were increasingly left alone with their children either through death or desertion; and women who lacked men lived for the most part in poverty.

At both ends of the decade, sex formed an independent component of the system of stratification within nineteenth-century Hamilton. Women who worked could be considered by and large a homogeneous group with respect to wealth: they were poor, at the very bottom of the work force. Women who did not work fared according to the means which they had been left by men. A few managed to maintain a respectable position, but most formed an impoverished and dependent class, eking out an existence with the aid of charity and odd jobs. Like the occupational structure among men and the division of wealth, sexual stratification was one of the stable structural forms of inequality within this nineteenth-century city.

The pattern of ethnic stratification made up a second stable structural form of inequality. By ethnicity I mean not just birthplace, religion, or race but, usually though not exclusively, a combination that provides what might be thought of as a cultural identity. In this respect the definition of Stanley Lieberson is especially useful; he defines "ethnic" in a broad sense, "including groups that are differentiated on either cultural or physical criteria. This includes groups that are commonly called races, as well as populations that are distinguished on the basis of language, religion, foreign origin, history or other cultural characteristics." A society may be considered stratified along ethnic lines, continues Lieberson, "if the ethnic groups have differential access to either economic position or political power in a way that cannot be explained through the operation of other forms of stratification in the society."[20] This was precisely the case in Hamilton, where ethnic and economic stratifications superimposed themselves upon one another, creating a complex and sharply differentiated social system. The most relevant ethnic groupings are not precisely clear. Certainly one was Irish Catholic, a second Irish Protestant, a third Black. Beyond that I will postulate four other principal divisions relevant to the mid-nineteenth century: Scottish Presbyterians, English Protestants, Canadian Protestants, and Canadian Catholics. Perhaps the English group should be differentiated further along religious lines, but for the purpose of this analysis one group will suffice.

The significance of ethnic stratification is well argued, again, by Stanley Lieberson, who puts his case in terms especially relevant to Canada. Lieberson points out that ethnic stratification is a legitimate and autonomous area for study since only ethnic "strata hold the potential for forming their own separate nation-state." A society stratified along ethnic lines contains a potential for fission not present in any other form of stratification. At the same time complex relations exist between ethnic and other systems of stratification within the same society. As Lieberson contends, "the presence of ethnic stratification that cross-cuts economic groups will tend to reduce the cohesiveness of class."[21] If the distribution of rewards within ethnic groups closely parallels that within the society as a whole—if each ethnic group comprises relatively substantial proportions of people who are poor, well-to-do, and of middling circumstances—then class conflict should be muted. For in an economically stratified society ethnic solidarity, a sense of unity among members of the same ethnic groups in different economic ranks, will blunt hostility and frustration by creating bonds among people and, more importantly, offering a symbol of hope and aspiration which encourages dreams of individual social mobility rather than social revolution. Conversely, the overlaying of class and ethnic concentration—the clustering of ethnic groups within specific economic ranks—should heighten class consciousness. In this situation, issues of ethnic solidarity, feelings of discrimination and deprivation, superimpose themselves upon one another. Examples easily come to mind: in Canada, Quebec nationalism might be viewed in these terms, and in the United States, movements of black power and separatism. A sense of superiority and privilege, of course, can intertwine with a sense of ethnic identity in the same way, as evidenced by the solidarity sometimes felt by wealthy families of old, native stock. It becomes, thus, a matter of considerable importance to investigate the ethnic stratification system and discover the extent to which it blunted or superimposed itself upon other social divisions.

The relations between ethnicity and wealth in Hamilton are demonstrated by Table 2.3. In 1851, 56 percent of Irish Catholics were poor (0–39th economic percentiles), compared to 67 percent in 1861. At the same time their assessed population increase, 76 percent, nearly doubled that of the city as a whole.[22] The Irish Protestants, stagnating in terms of assessed population with a small 7 percent increase, remained about 40 percent poor and 20 percent well-to-do (80–100th economic percentile). Scottish Presbyterians were downwardly mobile as a group, the percentage of poor among them increasing from 29 to 37 percent while the proportion of well-to-do dropped from 24 to 19 percent. This was probably a function of the heavy immigration of relatively poor artisans, for the total number of assessed Scottish Presbyterians jumped a hefty 92 percent during the decade. English Protestants, on the other hand, showed very little change, 28 percent remaining poor and the well-to-do varying only from 21 to 23 percent; their assessed population increase, 32 percent, was quite average for the city as a whole. The Canadian Protestants increased in number surprisingly little, 25 percent—perhaps because of heavy outmigration from the city during the depression—but they improved their already strong position; the poor decreased from 26 to 18 percent and the well-to-do rose from 34 to 40 percent. Finally, Blacks, who increased their numbers about 64 percent during the decade, remained 61 percent poor, a proportion of poor people rather less than that among the Irish Catholics in 1861.

Looked at another way, in 1851 Irish Catholics made up 20

TABLE 2.3 Economic rank as related to ethnicity, 1851 and 1861[a]

Ethnic group	Year	Percent in economic ranks				Number	Percent of total population	Percent increase in group
		0–39	40–79	80–89	90–100			
Irish Catholic	1851	55.7	37.0	4.6	2.8	284	14.5	
	1861	67.2	26.4	3.4	3.0	500	18.2	76.1
Irish Protestant	1851	39.8	40.6	10.5	9.1	352	18.0	
	1861	40.0	39.6	8.5	11.9	377	13.7	7.1
Scottish Presbyterian	1851	28.6	47.1	11.7	12.4	248	12.7	
	1861	37.0	44.1	9.5	9.4	476	17.3	91.9
English Protestant	1851	27.6	51.4	11.6	9.5	545	27.9	
	1861	27.9	49.0	11.7	11.4	720	26.2	32.1
Canadian Protestant	1851	25.5	40.4	18.2	16.0	176	9.0	
	1861	18.2	41.8	15.5	24.5	220	8.0	25.0
Canadian Catholic	1851	61.1	27.8	5.6	5.6	18	0.9	
	1861	33.3	54.1	12.5	0.0	24	0.9	33.3
Black	1851	61.2	30.5	8.3	0.0	36	1.8	
	1861	61.0	35.5	1.7	1.7	59	2.1	63.9
Other	1851	27.2	44.7	10.5	17.6	295	15.1	
	1861	32.4	43.8	11.4	12.4	370	13.5	25.4
All	1851	34.6	44.2	10.7	10.4	1954	99.9	
	1861	38.9	41.2	9.4	10.1	2746	99.9	40.5

	Percent of poorest 20%		Percent of wealthiest 10%		Percent of total population	
	1851	1861	1851	1861	1851	1861
Irish Catholic	20.1	44.6	3.9	5.2	14.5	18.2
Irish Protestant	23.0	12.6	15.7	15.6	18.0	13.7
Scottish Presbyterian	10.5	8.8	15.2	15.6	12.7	17.3
English Protestant	20.1	14.3	25.5	28.5	27.9	26.2
Canadian Protestant	8.6	3.8	13.7	18.8	9.0	8.0
Canadian Catholic	1.3	0.8	0.5	0.0	0.9	0.9
Black	3.5	4.0	0.0	0.3	1.8	2.1
Other	12.8	11.0	25.5	16.0	15.1	13.5

[a] Entire population linked from census to assessment.

percent of the poor in the city, whereas in 1861 they constituted 45 percent, an increase by no means accounted for by their population growth. Taking into account the effects of population increase, this represented the only large shift in an ethnic group's share of poverty or wealth. It provides solid evidence that the position of Irish Catholics actually declined, an issue which will be explored later. At this point it is important to note that the relationships between ethnicity and wealth remained stable throughout the decade, although the extremities of the stratification system became somewhat accentuated. The distribution of ethnic groups throughout a variety of economic ranks should have served to lessen the abrasiveness of economic divisions. In one major and glaring exception, the case of the Irish Catholics, poverty and ethnicity coalesced in a way that heightened the potential for social conflict and animosity. The convergence of ethnic and economic stratification among Irish Catholics was reinforced by their experience of social mobility, for Irish Catholic men climbed out of poverty far less easily and less frequently than did men of other ethnic backgrounds.

For the most part, the relationships between ethnicity and occupation reinforce the economic distinctions. Ethnic occupational patterns, however, provide a more precise delineation of the role of each major group. During the decade the Scottish-born, between 15 and 20 percent of the population, became increasingly dominant in the building trades, especially among masons (increasing from 30 to 43 percent of the total), and in a few miscellaneous trades: increasing among gardeners from 30 to 41 percent, among bakers from 27 to 56 percent, and among mariners from 30 to 37 percent. They remained prominent, too, among confectioners, though declining from 43 to 33 percent. Throughout the decade the Scottish remained dominant in commercial occupations; they were the businessmen of Hamilton, their proportion rising from 33 to 39 percent of merchants and remaining about 40 percent of bookkeepers and 30 percent of clerks.

The English-born had a much less skewed occupational profile than the Scottish. Although scattered throughout most occupations, they did dominate a few trades: butchers (70 percent and 61 percent in 1851 and 1861); cabinetmakers in 1851 (about two thirds); tinsmiths (nearly half each year); engineers in 1861 (about half). In addition, they formed a preponderant share of the physicians, 41 percent in 1851 and 44 percent in 1861.

The Canadian-born Protestants, not surprisingly, had desirable jobs more often than any other ethnic group. They comprised a disproportionately large share of men in commerce, medicine, law, and even of "gentlemen." In each year Canadian-born people made up only about 9 percent of all household heads. By 1861, however, they formed 43 percent of the bankers, replacing the Scots who had dominated banking a decade earlier. Similarly, they increased their share of attorneys from 28 to 39 percent, this time at the expense of the English, whose proportion dropped by exactly the same amount. Simultaneously, the proportion of both Canadian physicians and "gentlemen" rose from 17 to 22 percent. Clearly, if Hamilton had an ethnic elite, it was the Protestant native-born. The advantages of being native did not extend, however, to being North American, especially if one were black. For the American-born, the group which included most Blacks, dominated only one traditionally black trade; in 1851 they composed 67 percent of the barbers, increasing their share to 75 percent a decade later.

The occupational profile of the Irish Catholics was distinctive if dismal, and they may even have been forced out of some trades in which they had had a foothold in 1851. For instance, in the building trades the Irish Catholic plasterers dropped from 20 to 13 percent, the painters from 11 to 3 percent, and the carpenters from 22 to 11 percent. Similarly, the proportion of Irish Catholic bakers dropped from 18 to 4 percent, of cabinetmakers from 22 percent to none, and, among blacksmiths, where they remained highest, from 33 to 26 percent. Irish Catholics retained their position among shoemakers, one of the least desirable trades, slipping only from 24 to 22 percent, but they dropped among mariners from 29 to 3.3 percent. Very simply, it appeared that when the English or Scottish moved into a trade, the Irish Catholics moved, or more likely *were* moved, out. The only positive change among Irish Catholics was that a small number managed to become grocers and tavern keepers. The number of Irish Catholic grocers and small storekeepers rose from thirteen to thirty-eight, and the number of innkeepers, tavernkeepers, and the like increased from six to twenty-five. In each year there were only a few Irish Catholics in any other white collar position. Thus it appears that the path of social mobility for Irish Catholics led through petty proprietorship. After all, this makes good sense: small taverns or neighborhood groceries required relatively little capital or prior skill and were the sorts of businesses in which ethnic identity probably was an advantage. Indeed, one fragmentary piece of evidence indicates that Catholics gave their business to other Catholics when they could. As a whole the Irish Catholics were concentrated in low-paying occupations, such as blacksmiths (noted already) and carters, of which they formed 50 percent in 1851 and 40 percent in 1861. And, of course, they were dominant among laborers. The number of Irish Catholic laborers rose during the decade from 258 to 342, a slight slip from 65 to 59 percent of the total.

It was the peculiar combination of being Irish and Catholic, rather than one and not the other, that was a problem, as appears from contrasting the Irish-born with the Canadian-born Catholics, who fared very much better. For instance, the proportion of Canadian-born Catholics who were poor, though comparable to that among the Irish at the start of the decade, dropped sharply to only 33 percent by 1861. The different proportion of Irish and Canadian Catholic girls employed as resident servants also points to the difference between the groups: in both 1851 and 1861 over half of the Irish Catholic girls aged 16–20 were servants. Since most girls probably did not remain servants for five years, this means that at some point in their late adolescence most Irish Catholic girls probably worked as servants. On the other hand, substantial but much smaller numbers of Canadian Catholic girls of the same age were servants, 27 percent in 1851 and 34 percent in 1861. There were striking occupational differences between Canadian and Irish Catholic heads of household as well. The Canadians were about three and a half times less likely than the Irish to be laborers, for instance. In 1851 about half the Canadian-born Catholics worked in some capacity in commerce, primarily as clerks, compared to only about 10 percent of the Irish-born. It is true that the difference in the sizes of the two ethnic groups makes comparisons dangerous; the Canadian-born Catholics were a tiny group. Nonetheless, the magnitude of these occupational discrep-

TABLE 2.4 Occupational structure, Irish and Canadian-born Catholic male household heads, 1851 and 1861

Occupational group	Irish Catholic				Canadian Catholic			
	1851		1861		1851		1861	
	Number	Percent	Number	Percent	Number	Percent	Number	Percent
Professional	3	0.6	2	0.3	0	0	1	4.0
Commercial	43	9.5	79	13.5	6	50.0	5	20.0
Skilled artisan	109	24.1	119	20.4	4	33.3	14	56.0
Semiskilled	29	6.4	26	4.5	0	0	1	4.0
Laborer	258	57.0	342	58.6	2	16.7	4	16.0
Other	11	2.4	16	2.7	0	0	0	0.0
Total	453	100.0	584	100.0	12	100.0	25	100.0

ancies cannot be doubted. *Irish* Catholicism, rather than Catholicism by itself, proved the major handicap.

Irish birth alone was not the main problem, for Irish Protestants fared much better economically than Irish Catholics. Interestingly, Irish Protestants dominated one occupation, that of constable. In both 1851 and 1861 half the constables in Hamilton were Irish Protestants. How this appeared to the large Irish Catholic population, which still occasionally rioted with their countrymen from Ulster, can only be imagined.[23] It may well have added an additional abrasive element to the Irish Catholics' frequent encounters with authority. (Of the 374 people arrested in 1847, 161 were Irish.)

It appears that the Irish Catholics fared even worse occupationally than the small Black community—about thirty-eight families in 1851 and eighty-one a decade later, though these figures are probably an underenumeration. Although about three fifths of them were poor, the proportion of unskilled and semiskilled workers among Blacks declined from 47 to 38 percent during the decade; the proportion in skilled trades rose correspondingly from 37 to 49 percent; and those in commerce and the professions increased from 8 to 14 percent. Blacks, in fact, were scattered among a wide variety of occupations, giving them, in all, a more favorable occupational distribution than the Irish Catholics. In 1851 about 20 percent and in 1861 about 24 percent of Blacks owned their own homes, very respectable proportions, and 50 percent of Black household heads present in 1851 remained in the city a decade later, a figure higher than that of any other ethnic group and a clear indication of Black stability and modest prosperity. Among Blacks, moreover, there were fewer female-headed households than among either the Irish Catholics or the population as a whole, again a sign that the Black community fared relatively well in urban Canada.[24]

Occupation, ethnicity, and wealth combined in nineteenth-century Hamilton to form distinctive clusters. It is not hard to identify the most prominent ones: prosperous Scottish businessmen; Scottish masons; wealthy Canadian merchants and professionals; and poor Irish Catholic laborers. The ability to identify these clusters should not be confused with the capacity to explain their existence, however. That undertaking is beyond the scope of this book, for it requires an understanding of the experiences of each group of people before they migrated to Canada.[25] Primarily important here is the constancy of these clusters in Hamilton throughout the decade. The only major changes were the increased flow of Scots into the building trades, the movement of Canadians into banking and law, and the apparent squeezing of Irish Catholics out of a few trades. Overall, the relations among ethnicity, occupation, and wealth support the theme of structural stability within this nineteenth-century city, and the pattern of ethnic distribution within occupations reinforces my earlier observation that ethnic stratification cut two ways: the distribution of some major ethnic groups throughout the occupational structure diminished the force of class antagonism, while the concentration of Irish Catholics among the laborers heightened the potential for class consciousness and social conflict. It is difficult to assess the balance of forces. On the whole, it is reasonable to imagine that the three-part equation of poverty, laboring, and Irish Catholicism yielded a result at once unmistakable and unforgettable, injecting a nasty undercurrent of racism and distrust into the power relations of a grossly unequal society.

Given the structural persistence in occupation, division of wealth, and sexual and ethnic patterns of inequality, it could be expected that the relationship between wealth and occupations would remain relatively stable as well. Here I will use the vertical mode of classifying occupations, putting them into a rank order designed to express their socioeconomic standing. Table 2.5 has five ranks based on the scale used in the five-cities project. The five historians undertaking that project developed a scale for classifying the 113 most common occupations in their five cities in 1861, classifications which accounted for about three quarters of the male work force.[26] I have added to those occupations all the rest in which at least ten or more assessed males were employed in 1861 and have divided them as appeared appropriate. Appendix Two lists the specific occupations by rank order.

The relations between the five occupational categories and economic rank remained sharp and clear throughout the decade. In 1851, 7 percent of the people in the highest category were poor and 41 percent wealthy; in 1861 the proportions were 6 percent and 40 percent. In 1851, 74 percent of the people in the bottom

TABLE 2.5 Occupational rank as related to economic rank, 1851 and 1861

Occupational rank group[a]	1851					1861				
	Percent in economic rank					Percent in economic rank				
	0–39	40–79	80–89	90–100	Number	0–39	40–79	80–89	90–100	Number
I	6.8	31.4	21.0	40.5	309	6.3	35.1	18.5	39.8	382
II	25.1	45.7	18.3	10.9	311	13.2	56.6	15.6	14.6	486
III	38.7	49.8	7.1	4.5	871	47.9	40.5	6.6	4.9	878
IV	46.8	46.8	5.2	1.3	77	55.8	39.5	3.5	1.2	86
V	73.9	23.6	1.9	0.6	322	83.6	15.3	0.8	0.3	652

Source: Assessment rolls.

[a] Based on scale used in five-cities project, but including all male occupations with ten or more assessed individuals in 1861.

rank were poor and 0.6 percent wealthy; in 1861 the proportions were 84 percent and 0.3 percent. An index of economic standing shows the relative position of each occupational rank across the decade. The index is derived by subtracting the number of poor (0–39th percentile) within a group from the number of wealthy (90–100th). In this case it shows that the position of the middle- and lower ranking groups worsened somewhat during the decade, though in each year the relation between the index and the occupational hierarchy was perfectly linear, that is, the scores for each group decreased with each step down the occupational ladder.

The preceding discussion of occupation remains crude in at least one respect: it lumps together in the same category occupations whose rewards differed. By contrast, Table 2.7 shows the detailed economic standing of a number of the most important individual occupations. Of most interest here is the variation in wealth within and between specific trades. In each skilled trade there were poor and wealthy craftsmen; it is impossible to predict the income of a man simply by knowing what trade he followed, although one can be sure of its average remuneration. Second, the rewards available in different trades varied substantially. Some men, such as tinsmiths, did as well as most small businessmen or as clerks; others lived much less comfortably. Quite obviously, one cannot with any justification consider men who identified themselves with a skilled artisan label as composing a homogeneous economic category. Differences between trades are as important

TABLE 2.6 Index of economic standing
of occupational groups,
1851 and 1861

Occupational group	Index	
	1851	1861
I	34	34
II	−14	1
III	−34	−43
IV	−46	−55
V	−73	−83

TABLE 2.7 Comparative economic standing, selected occupations, 1851 and 1861

Occupation	Percent poor[a]		Percent well-to-do[b]		Number	
	1851	1861	1851	1861	1851	1861
Professional and commercial						
Agent	35.3	22.0	35.4	29.2	17	41
Attorney	7.4	1.9	69.2	59.6	24	52
Clergy	10.5	7.4	31.7	33.3	19	27
Clerk	45.2	22.4	11.1	10.2	135	107
Gentleman	11.7	11.9	52.4	54.9	103	118
Grocer	4.0	6.4	40.0	43.9	25	95
Inn or tavern keeper	0	6.4	55.2	40.5	76	94
Merchant	2.5	1.0	69.4	78.1	121	96
Physician	5.0	0	75.0	51.7	20	31
Trades						
Baker	44.0	36.0	32.0	16.0	25	25
Blacksmith	45.8	43.3	4.2	5.7	48	53
Butcher	55.6	51.6	13.9	6.4	36	31
Cabinetmaker	59.2	39.4	4.6	10.5	76	38
Carpenter	28.7	42.5	7.7	12.0	181	233
Machinist	45.0	26.9	5.0	15.3	20	26
Mason	45.0	42.1	5.0	10.6	60	57
Molder	36.0	33.3	0	3.3	25	30
Painter	25.9	55.7	12.9	13.4	31	52
Plasterer	21.4	53.6	14.2	17.8	14	28
Printer	17.6	30.0	29.4	13.4	17	30
Shoemaker	40.0	46.6	8.7	13.6	115	103
Tailor	47.0	46.0	9.4	14.0	85	100
Tinsmith	14.3	19.2	25.1	23.1	28	26
Semiskilled and unskilled labor						
Laborer	75.5	84.9	2.4	0.7	342	626
Mariner	48.4	56.7	15.1	8.1	33	37
Teamster	45.2	57.2	0	0	31	19

[a] 0–39th economic percentile.
[b] 80–100th economic percentile.

discriminators in predicting the wealth of individuals as the familiar but crude manual-nonmanual distinction.[27]

The major trades can be divided into five groups on the basis of a comparison of their economic standing in 1851 and 1861. In the discussion that follows, "stable" means that the average rank of a trade varied little across the decade. The groups are as follows: stable prosperous trades (engineer, tinsmith, carriage maker); stable average trades (baker, carpenter, shoemaker, molder, tailor, mason, gardener, and butcher); stable poor trades (blacksmith); increasingly prosperous trades (saddler, confectioner, machinist, and cabinetmaker); and finally, trades whose rewards were declining (printer, plasterer, and painter). Twelve of the nineteen major trades remained quite stable in economic standing, which emphasizes once again the theme of structural persistence. What is more, those trades whose rewards were declining all shared one characteristic: the number of men within them expanded rapidly. The number of printers increased 75 percent, plasterers 100 percent, and painters 68 percent. No other major trade increased as much as any of these five. The cause of their declining rewards appears to have been an oversupply of labor which simply outstripped demand.

The age composition of trades did not contaminate the relation between supply and reward. It might be thought that it was not only an increased number of men but an influx of young men, in particular, that brought about the decline in the position of a trade. This supposition can be dismissed. In each of the three declining occupations the proportion of young men—those below the age of thirty—dropped notably: from 65 to 40 percent of printers; from 48 to 23 percent of plasterers, and from 42 to 26 percent of painters. Unlike the situation in 1851, described in my essay in *Nineteenth Century Cities,* there was no apparent relation in 1861 between the prosperity of a trade and its age structure.[28] There were some trades, besides those in obvious decline, which young men did not enter. The most striking example is the tailors, among whom the proportion of men under thirty was more than halved, from 40 to 19 percent. Young men could sense the way in which technological innovation, such as the sewing machine, had eroded the future of once stable crafts. The only occupations in which the proportion of young men remained stable in 1851 and 1861 were grocer and tavernkeeper, jobs which could be entered by men who had turned away from trades and were seek-

TABLE 2.8 Selected trades: growth and economic standing,
1851 and 1861[a]

Trade	Number 1851	Number 1861	Percent change	Index of economic standing[b] 1851	Index of economic standing[b] 1861
Stable trades[c]					
Renumerative					
1. Engineer	12	17	+ 42	+ 9	+ 6
2. Tinsmith	28	26	− 7	+11	+ 4
3. Carriage maker	21	23	+ 10	+ 5	0
Average					
4. Baker	25	25	0	−12	−20
5. Carpenter	181	233	+ 29	−22	−31
6. Shoemaker	115	103	− 10	−31	−31
7. Molder	25	30	+ 20	−36	−30
8. Tailor	85	100	+ 18	−37	−32
9. Mason	60	57	− 5	−46	−32
10. Gardener	19	19	0	−11	−31
11. Butcher	36	31	− 14	−47	−46
Poor					
12. Blacksmith	48	53	+ 10	−42	−35
Rising trades[d]					
13. Saddler	13	17	+ 31	−27	+24
14. Confectioner	11	10	− 9	− 9	+10
15. Machinist	20	26	+ 30	−40	−11
16. Cabinetmaker	76	38	− 50	−53	−29
Falling trades[e]					
17. Printer	17	30	+ 75	+13	−17
18. Plasterer	14	28	+100	− 7	−36
19. Painter	31	52	+ 68	−15	−42

[a] Based on household heads linked from census to assessment.

[b] Percent wealthy (90–100th percentile) minus percent poor (0–39th percentile).

[c] Economic position relatively unchanging.

[d] Economic position improving.

[e] Economic position deteriorating.

ing potentially profitable work that required little special skill or training, and laborer, to which a fixed proportion probably turned more from necessity than from choice.

Although relations between age and occupation shifted somewhat during the decade, the overall relations between age and wealth remained about the same. In each year more young heads of household, those aged 20–29, were poor, 29 percent in 1851 and 45 percent in 1861. At the same time, the general rise in the proportion of poor within each age category reflected the difficulties of the job market for young men during the depression.

Not only ethnicity, occupation, and age, but family and household structure as well retained the same overall relation to wealth in both 1851 and 1861.[29] Table 2.9 shows the association of number of children with economic rank. For the distribution to be random the percentage in each cell should be roughly the same. In fact, in each year the only marked deviation—the only notable relation between the number of children born to a couple and its wealth—was the association of a large number of children with high economic rank. In 1851, 15 percent of poor families had a large number of children, compared to 23 percent of those who were wealthy (90th rank and above); in 1861 the figures were strikingly similar, 14 percent and 23 percent, respectively. Likewise, the relations between total household size and economic rank remained stable and linear: the wealthiest families had the largest households, except that by 1861 there were fewer large households even among the wealthy. In 1851 the wealthy were about two and a half times as likely as the poor to have a large household (8 or more members); in 1861 they were four times as likely. In each year the poor were two and a half times more likely than the wealthy to have a small household (1–3 members), and the percentage of small households among the poor rose from 26 to 34 percent. Relations between economic rank and the presence of relatives in the household, though less dramatic, are nonetheless also clear. In 1851 the wealthy were about two and a half times more likely than the poor to have a relative as a member of their household. Over the decade the difference decreased as the proportion of relatives in wealthy households declined somewhat and the proportion living with the poor increased a little. As a result, at the end of the decade the wealthy were one and a half times more likely than

TABLE 2.9 Age and household structure as related to economic rank, 1851 and 1861

Age and household structure	1851					1861				
	Percent in economic rank					Percent in economic rank				
	0–39	40–79	80–89	90–100	Number	0–39	40–79	80–89	90–100	Number
Age										
Under 20	66.7	33.3	0	0	3	100.0	—	—	—	2
20–29	28.9	56.0	9.2	5.9	284	44.7	43.2	7.2	4.9	387
30–39	22.9	51.0	12.5	13.6	559	37.9	43.5	9.6	9.0	958
40–49	27.5	46.0	13.4	13.1	426	37.4	38.2	10.7	13.7	728
50–59	25.2	48.2	16.6	10.0	187	37.7	40.3	9.5	12.5	409
60 and over	31.8	44.5	9.1	14.5	110	39.1	40.7	8.1	12.1	258
Household structure										
Children at home										
None	20.4	19.1	23.7	20.1	316	20.8	22.2	19.3	17.1	525
1–2	35.8	30.9	39.9	34.2	558	39.0	36.4	29.1	32.4	997
3–4	28.5	25.0	24.2	22.8	401	26.4	26.9	29.5	27.2	758
5 and over	15.3	19.0	21.2	22.9	294	13.8	14.5	22.1	23.3	466
Household size										
1–3	25.8	19.6	11.3	10.9	304	33.5	21.8	15.9	12.9	691
4–7	54.0	44.5	47.9	41.2	853	56.3	59.0	50.8	48.1	1539
8 and over	20.2	35.9	40.8	47.9	412	10.2	19.2	33.3	39.0	516
Household members										
Relative	9.2	12.1	19.1	22.8	231	12.5	17.9	18.2	18.1	435
Boarder	20.0	28.2	47.4	50.5	487	12.4	26.8	31.8	27.5	566
Relative or boarder	27.5	39.0	58.8	59.4	638	22.6	37.6	43.8	40.1	894
Servant	13.4	32.2	58.8	64.1	538	6.5	12.8	47.3	68.3	637
Total proportion of linked household heads	26.1	49.7	12.4	11.7	1569	38.9	41.2	9.4	10.4	2746

the poor to house kin. The relations between economic rank and the presence of boarders in the household, though shifting slightly, also remained basically similar: in each year the wealthiest people were most likely to have a boarder living in their household, as the last chapter pointed out. During the decade, however, the proportion of boarders in the city dropped drastically, partially reflecting the outmigration of young men during the depression. In these circumstances only the middle-ranking households, perhaps because they were struck most seriously by the depression and needed extra income, retained the same proportion of boarders, while the percentage of both poor and wealthy households with boarders declined.

The employment of servants also reflected the squeeze in middle-ranking households during the depression. Although in each year the relation between economic rank and the employment of servants was perfectly linear, the distance between groups increased. In 1851, 13 percent of the poor and 64 percent of the wealthy employed at least one servant; in 1861 the proportions were 7 percent and 68 percent, respectively. At the same time the percentage of middle-ranking families employing a servant dropped sharply from 32 to 13 percent, a clear indication of their economic distress. Similarly, the proportion of home owners among poor and middle-ranking groups dropped notably, but, among the wealthy, home ownership actually increased. Thus, if household structure and the employment of servants can be taken as crude indicators, it appears that the wealthiest people survived the depression relatively unscathed while the middle-ranking groups suffered badly and the poor sank into an even more unhappy position.

Before leaving this comparative inquiry into the structure of inequality across the decade, the issue of home ownership should be considered. The pattern of home ownership did not entirely follow the rest of the socioeconomic structure, and, furthermore, property ownership was of extraordinary importance within nineteenth-century society. Only about 30 percent of the people in this medium-sized nineteenth-century city owned the house in which they lived, a proportion comparable to that in Buffalo, Kingston, and Poughkeepsie, New York, at the same time.[30] Unfortunately, simple characteristics did not distinguish owners from renters. To the contrary, patterns of home ownership reflected all the complexities of class, ethnic, and demographic structure in Hamilton. There are six particular reasons why it is important to unravel those patterns and determine the sorts of people most likely to own their own homes.

First, land operated as a medium of speculation in much the same way as the stock market does today. In the period before safe banking and institutionalized opportunities for routine investment developed, trading in land was a preeminent economic activity.

Second, the study of home ownership contributes to an understanding of the degree of equality, or inequality, within a society. Today a generally widespread desire for home ownership is assumed, a desire which is frustrated by the cost of land, credit, and inflation. Moreover, the quality of a society may be measured implicitly by the number of people within it who can own the houses in which they live. Whether or not this was the case a century and more ago, it is undeniable that the pattern of home ownership throws light on the distribution of goods and is one of the few relatively concrete measures which can be used comparatively across time and place.

Third, home ownership is important because it provides insight into cultural values. The determination to buy a house was not, and is not, entirely a matter of class. In contemporary Toronto, for example, the wealthy young professionals who choose to rent an apartment and preserve a goodly share of their income for entertainment and luxuries are as familiar a phenomenon as the extended household of immigrant kin living together, saving, and pooling their money in order to buy land. There is no reason to assume that cultural values, or differences in life style, did not interact with economic rank in the past as they do in the present, though unraveling the two is extraordinarily difficult. The study of who did and did not choose to buy a house is an approach to the problem that looks at one of the activities in which class and culture interact.

Fourth, home ownership related directly to another of the major dimensions of nineteenth-century society, namely, transiency. Those people who owned their own homes also chose to leave the city less frequently.

Fifth, home ownership bore at least an oblique relation to upward social mobility, as the next chapter will make clear. The acquisition of a house, in certain types of cases, may have been the first step in a climb upwards through the economic rank order.

Finally, property ownership in the nineteenth-century played a role subtly different from and even more critical than that in contemporary stratification. And home ownership provides the readiest indicator of the possession of property in a more general sense. As Parsons points out, occupation largely has superseded property as the primary source of household income among the well-to-do. At the same time, and most importantly, there has been "a relative dissociation of rights to property income from effective control of the means of production." In an earlier period, notes Parsons, the "Marxian synthesis" portrayed accurately "the *codetermination* of class status by economic *and* political factors—ownership of economic facilities giving *control,* in a political sense, of the firm as an organization." In nineteenth-century Hamilton, entrepreneurs effectively controlled their firms in a very direct sense, and ownership of property brought political power in the form of the right to vote and hold office. At the same time ownership of housing gave the capacity to rent, to evict, and to set prices, thus to control in a very intimate way the lives and well-being of people. At the upper end of the economic rank order the power that property brought could be enormous; at the lowest it was still substantial. For the acquisition of even the most modest of houses by an immigrant laborer meant shedding the uncontrolled, potentially arbitrary or whimsical power of a landlord and acquiring at least a slight hedge against the devastating, periodic unemployment endemic to the life of a manual worker prior to the introduction of insurance. In his book *Poverty* (1904) Robert Hunter bluntly made the same point about the importance of property:

> A propertyless person is one without any economic reserve power. He is in no position to ward off the sufferings which must frequently come to most persons depending wholly upon their ability to labor and upon the demand of the community for their services . . . The loss of profits or earnings from property is a serious loss to thousands of families more or less dependent upon incomes from that source; but the classes who possess no property, not even a home from which they may not be evicted,

must of necessity pursue that precarious livelihood which depends solely upon health and strength and upon economic conditions, which may, or may not, at any time, require the services of the worker. Security of livelihood in the present state of society comes only with the possession of property.

To discuss the ownership of property, therefore, is to explore the linchpin in the structure of inequality in a nineteenth-century city.[31]

The subject of transiency and persistence within the city, which will be treated at length in the next chapter, is closely related to home ownership. People who remained in the city between the taking of the census and assessment, a period of about three months in both 1851 and 1861, were between two and two and a half times more likely to own their own homes than people who left. Considering only the population linked between census and assessment at one point in time, about half of those who owned their own homes in 1851 remained in the city a decade later, compared to about a third of those who rented. At the end of the decade, 54 percent of all the people who had remained in the city owned their own homes compared to 43 percent of the same group at its beginning. And this happened at a time when the proportion of home owners in the population as a whole dropped from 34 to 28 percent, a figure not only smaller but moving in the opposite direction. In 1861, 43 percent of the home owners had been in the city ten years earlier, compared to 12 percent of the renters. Thus the conclusion is unmistakable: home owners were far more likely to remain in the city than people who rented. And those who remained were more likely to buy a house than those who entered the city during the decade. In order, therefore, to understand why some men were transient, it is necessary to explain why others bought homes.

The first social dimension through which to study home ownership is class, or, more precisely, the socioeconomic ranking of the people, which may be indicated by either wealth or occupation. Wealth is the more straightforward of the two indicators. In each year there was a completely linear relation between wealth and home ownership, with the proportion of owners at each level rising until roughly half of the wealthiest 10 percent owned their own homes. But tidy as this is, it explains only part of the problem. For although half of the wealthy owned their own homes, half did not. And conversely, in 1851 a substantial share, about a fifth of the people in the bottom forty economic ranks, managed to own their own homes. Thus although in a general way it can be said that the wealthier a man the more likely he was to own his own home, there still remains a great deal of variation to be explained.

Occupation, unlike wealth, does not explain very much. As Table 2.10 shows, within the same occupational rank there existed wide discrepancies among the proportions of home owners in various specific occupations: 37 percent of merchants owned their own homes in 1861 but only 13 percent of physicians, to take one example. Laborers more frequently owned homes than clerks, to take another. Only one occupation ranks consistently and understandably high: 57 percent and 53 percent of carpenters, in 1851 and 1861 respectively, owned their own homes, a figure no doubt reflecting the ability of carpenters to build the roofs over their own heads.

Within individual occupations, wealth remained an important factor in determining home ownership. For instance, 36.5 percent of all merchants owned their own houses in 1861, but only 19 percent of those merchants in the 40–79th economic ranks were owners, compared to 30 percent of those in the 80–89th and 44 percent of those in the 90–100th percentiles. Among carpenters and even among laborers the proportion of home owners was higher among the wealthier men within each occupation. Once more, wealth was more important than occupational title in determining individual rank within nineteenth-century society.

The relatively small differences in home ownership among ethnic groups—substantially smaller than the differences in wealth—are nevertheless striking. Although the relations between ethnicity and home ownership partially reflect wealth, the association is imperfect, especially in the case of the Irish Catholics. Particularly among people in relatively low-ranking occupations, cultural factors partially counteracted wealth and lessened the distinction between ethnic groups. Table 2.11 shows, for example, that among laborers the Irish Protestants ranked first among the major groups in each year, with home owners at 36 percent and 27 percent. In 1861, 17 percent of Irish Catholic laborers owned their homes

TABLE 2.10 Home ownership by occupation, ranked economically,
1851 and 1861

Occupation by economic rank	Percent home owners 1851	1861	Number in occupation 1851	1861	Occupation by economic rank	Percent home owners 1851	1861	Number in occupation 1851	1861
Lawyers					Clerks				
0–39	—	—	—	—	0–39	6.3	0.0	16	3
40–79	0.0	0.0	3	6	40–79	15.4	16.7	39	48
80–89	28.6	18.2	7	7	80–89	16.7	25.0	9	4
90–100	100.0	58.8	5	17	90–100	50.0	0.0	2	1
All	46.7	40.0	15	30	All	13.6	15.0	66	56
Physicians					Carpenters				
0–39	—	—	—	—	0–39	47.8	30.1	23	76
40–79	0.0	9.1	3	11	40–79	53.4	64.8	88	91
80–89	33.3	11.1	9	9	80–89	88.9	93.8	9	16
90–100	66.7	33.3	3	3	90–100	100.0	70.0	4	10
All	53.3	13.0	15	23	All	56.5	53.1	124	193
Clergy					Tailors				
0–39	0.0	0.0	2	2	0–39	12.5	24.3	24	37
40–79	42.9	0.0	7	11	40–79	25.8	35.5	31	31
80–89	50.0	33.3	4	3	80–89	0.0	50.0	2	4
90–100	100.0	66.7	2	3	90–100	100.0	33.3	4	3
All	53.3	16.8	15	19	All	24.6	33.3	61	75
Gentlemen					Shoemakers				
0–39	50.0	11.1	2	9	0–39	19.0	25.7	21	35
40–79	31.3	31.3	33	32	40–79	21.3	27.8	47	36
80–89	73.3	70.0	15	10	80–89	20.0	40.0	5	5
90–100	92.3	78.6	26	28	90–100	20.0	50.0	5	6
All	62.5	51.2	76	79	All	20.5	29.3	78	82
Merchants					Laborers				
0–39	—	0.0	—	1	0–39	18.5	11.9	168	353
40–79	20.7	19.0	29	21	40–79	44.0	38.0	50	71
80–89	15.4	30.0	13	20	80–89	60.0	0.0	5	2
90–100	46.9	44.4	49	54	90–100	100.0	0.0	1	1
All	33.7	36.5	91	96	All	25.5	16.2	224	427
Innkeepers									
0–39	—	25.0	—	4					
40–79	24.1	17.9	29	39					
80–89	13.6	26.1	22	23					
90–100	40.0	18.8	15	16					
All	24.6	20.7	66	82					

compared to 9 percent of Scottish Presbyterians, 13 percent of English Protestants, and no Canadian Protestants. The same pattern generally held among shoemakers: 33 percent and 40 percent of Irish Catholic shoemakers owned their own homes in 1851 and 1861 respectively, compared to 23 percent and 31 percent of Irish Protestants, 14 percent and 25 percent of Scottish Presbyterians, and 17 percent and 23 percent of English Protestants. The propensity of the Irish to own property showed only at the lower end of the occupational hierarchy. Among more prosperous callings no significant ethnic differences in home ownership existed. For some reason poor Irishmen more often bought homes than poor Englishmen, Scots, or Canadians.[32] The explanation undoubtedly rests in the place of land within Irish or perhaps peasant culture, a subject well worth exploring.

Besides class and ethnicity, home ownership should be considered in terms of the life cycle, for it increased with age, peaking at middle age and then declining slightly. In 1851 the drop apparently started after people had passed their forties; ten years later home ownership peaked among the 50–59-year-olds. In general, as people married in their late twenties, established households, and had children, they increasingly bought their own homes. As they aged, their economic position often worsened and they sold their homes, perhaps to obtain money with which to live in their old age. Although speculative, this interpretation is consistent with others that point to an onset of economic difficulty in old age.

The size of a man's family as well as his age influenced his decision to buy a house. Men with large numbers of children, as Table 2.12 shows, were more likely to own their own home. Among the 30–39-year-olds in 1851, 71 percent of those men with no children rented, compared to 60 percent of those with three or four children. Among 40–49-year-olds in 1861, to take another example, 71 percent of families without children rented, as did 63 percent of those with three or four children and 57 percent with five or more.

Even more striking is the relation among home ownership, wealth, and family size, also shown in Table 2.12. Among the poor in 1851, 90 percent of the families without children rented, compared to 80 percent of those with three or four children and 72

TABLE 2.11 Home ownership by occupation, divided ethnically, 1851 and 1861[a]

Occupation by ethnic group	Percent home owners		Number in occupation	
	1851–52	1861	1851–52	1861
Lawyers				
Irish Catholic	—	—	—	—
Irish Protestant	50.0	20.0	2	5
Scottish Presbyterian	33.3	25.0	3	4
English Protestant	50.0	50.0	6	8
Canadian Protestant	50.0	54.5	4	11
Canadian Catholic	—	—	—	—
Black	—	—	—	—
Other	—	0.0	—	2
All	46.7	40.0	15	30
Physicians				
Irish Catholic	100.0	—	1	—
Irish Protestant	50.0	100.0	2	2
Scottish Presbyterian	0.0	0.0	1	2
English Protestant	0.0	100.0	2	2
Canadian Protestant	25.0	11.1	4	9
Canadian Catholic	—	—	—	—
Black	0.0	—	1	—
Other	25.0	25.0	4	8
All	33.3	13.0	15	23
Clergy				
Irish Catholic	100.0	—	1	—
Irish Protestant	60.0	60.0	5	6
Scottish Presbyterian	0.0	50.0	1	2
English Protestant	66.7	100.0	3	2
Canadian Protestant	50.0	100.0	2	1
Canadian Catholic	—	—	—	—
Black	50.0	—	2	—
Other	0.0	100.0	1	9
All	53.3	16.8	15	20
Gentlemen				
Irish Catholic	50.0	50.0	2	2
Irish Protestant	73.3	60.6	15	17
Scottish Presbyterian	50.0	36.4	4	11
English Protestant	51.7	57.7	29	26
Canadian Protestant	66.7	22.2	12	9
Canadian Catholic	—	—	—	—

TABLE 2.11 (continued)

Occupation by ethnic group	Percent home owners		Number in occupation	
	1851–52	1861	1851–52	1861
Black	—	—	—	—
Other	64.3	41.7	14	12
All	60.5	51.2	76	77
Merchants[b]				
Irish Catholic	100.0	100.0	5	1
Irish Protestant	35.7	43.8	14	16
Scottish Presbyterian	50.0	29.4	18	17
English Protestant	21.1	55.0	19	20
Canadian Protestant	53.3	33.3	15	18
Canadian Catholic	0.0	—	1	—
Black	—	—	—	—
Other	25.3	19.0	19	21
All	33.7	36.5	91	93
Inn and hotel keepers				
Irish Catholic	25.0	15.6	8	13
Irish Protestant	33.3	30.8	18	13
Scottish Presbyterian	40.0	33.3	5	6
English Protestant	25.0	21.4	16	28
Canadian Protestant	0.0	11.1	5	9
Canadian Catholic	—	—	—	—
Black	0.0	0.0	1	3
Other	15.4	20.0	13	10
All	24.6	20.7	66	82
Clerks				
Irish Catholic	0.0	100.0	2	2
Irish Protestant	0.0	20.0	7	5
Scottish Presbyterian	15.4	5.6	13	17
English Protestant	30.0	20.8	20	24
Canadian Protestant	0.0	25.0	8	4
Canadian Catholic	—	—	—	—
Black	0.0	—	1	—
Other	9.1	25.0	11	4
All	13.6	15.0	62	56
Carpenters				
Irish Catholic	61.5	63.2	13	19
Irish Protestant	50.0	37.5	16	16
Scottish Presbyterian	50.0	56.9	28	58
English Protestant	62.8	56.9	43	58

TABLE 2.11 (continued)

Occupation by ethnic group	Percent home owners		Number in occupation	
	1851–52	1861	1851–52	1861
Canadian Protestant	66.3	56.3	12	16
Canadian Catholic	0.0	25.0	1	4
Black	—	33.3	—	3
Other	36.4	47.4	11	19
All	56.5	53.1	124	193
Tailors				
Irish Catholic	13.3	25.0	15	12
Irish Protestant	25.0	16.7	8	6
Scottish Presbyterian	16.7	44.5	6	18
English Protestant	26.3	29.2	19	24
Canadian Protestant	33.3	66.7	3	6
Canadian Catholic	0.0	—	1	—
Black	—	0.0	—	1
Other	44.4	25.0	9	8
All	24.6	33.3	61	75
Shoemakers				
Irish Catholic	33.3	40.0	15	15
Irish Protestant	22.8	30.8	22	13
Scottish Presbyterian	14.3	25.0	7	12
English Protestant	16.7	23.3	24	30
Canadian Protestant	100.0	—	1	—
Canadian Catholic	—	—	—	—
Black	—	0.0	—	1
Other	11.1	—	9	—
All	20.5	29.3	78	71
Laborers				
Irish Catholic	22.5	16.8	102	202
Irish Protestant	36.4	27.1	44	70
Scottish Presbyterian	30.0	8.9	10	45
English Protestant	16.7	13.2	30	53
Canadian Protestant	50.0	0.0	4	5
Canadian Catholic	0.0	33.3	2	3
Black	17.2	18.8	11	16
Other	30.0	3.0	20	33
All	25.5	16.2	223	427

[a] All persons linked from census to assessment.

[b] Includes all merchants: commission, hardware, etc.

percent of those with five or more. Among the middle-ranking the same thing held true in 1861: 76 percent without children rented compared to 63 percent with three or four children and 59 percent with five or more. The pattern held as well among people still higher on the economic scale. In short, at least as much as his ethnicity, a man's age and the size of his family acted independently of his occupation and wealth to affect his decision to rent or to buy the house in which he lived.

Many people, of course, owned more than one house, and rent formed a very important source of income within the city. Table 2.13 shows for selected occupations in 1861 the ratio between the number of properties owned and the number of men in each occupation, thus providing a rough index of the propensity of various sorts of people toward multiple property ownership. Even this very crude measure reveals with startling regularity that people in public office and public employees were multiple property holders. The four men who identified themselves as aldermen owned among them twenty-seven houses; the high bailiff owned six, the chamberlain four, the mayor four. Even the five bailiffs, in a not very prestigious occupation, owned eleven; the gaoler owned two, and the three policemen six. This unmistakably close association between the acquisition of land and the holding of public office raises the question whether public office served to enhance private wealth. Indeed, it does not speak well for the ability of the public officers of mid-nineteenth-century Hamilton to distinguish between their public duties and their personal gain.

The spatial distribution of home ownership throughout the city reflected the same dimensions—class, ethnicity, and life cycle.[33] As Figure 2.1 indicates, home ownership was usual in some of the wealthy areas, such as the district of expensive homes nestled at the foot of the Mountain, and in the newly developed, deliberately exclusive east end. In two poor districts, on the other hand, home ownership was exceptionally prominent, a reflection of ethnic influence. For these districts were the heart of Cork Town, the Irish section of the city, and the high incidence of ownership here reflected the propensity of the Irish to buy their own homes, however humble they might be. Finally, some of the districts where large families predominated also showed a high incidence of home ownership. Only one district that was high in families with chil-

TABLE 2.12 Home ownership and family size, by age and economic rank, 1851 and 1861

Age and economic rank	Households, 1851					Households, 1861				
	Children (%)				Number of households	Children (%)				Number of households
	None	1–2	3–4	5 or more		None	1–2	3–4	5 or more	
Age										
20–29										
Home owner	21.0	19.5	27.0	66.7	75	9.8	7.8	20.8	0.0	38
Renter	79.0	80.5	73.0	33.3	274	90.2	92.2	79.2	100.0	333
Number	(176)	(133)	(37)	(3)	349	(112)	(204)	(53)	(2)	371
30–39										
Home owner	29.1	34.5	40.4	38.7	206	16.2	23.1	30.2	36.5	234
Renter	70.9	65.5	59.6	61.3	376	83.8	76.9	69.8	63.5	669
Number	(141)	(200)	(166)	(75)	582	(160)	(324)	(315)	(104)	903
40–49										
Home owner	34.9	41.9	36.1	46.1	176	29.3	31.1	36.7	42.9	250
Renter	65.1	58.1	63.9	53.9	259	70.7	68.9	63.3	57.1	443
Number	(89)	(93)	(101)	(152)	435	(92)	(193)	(196)	(212)	693
50–59										
Home owner	48.1	40.0	36.2	36.2	73	47.5	37.9	40.0	42.9	158
Renter	51.9	60.0	63.8	63.8	113	52.5	62.1	60.0	57.1	230
Number	(27)	(65)	(47)	(47)	186	(58)	(132)	(100)	(98)	388

Age and economic rank	Households, 1851					Households, 1861				
	Children (%)				Number of households	Children (%)				Number of households
	None	1–2	3–4	5 or more		None	1–2	3–4	5 or more	
60 or more										
Home owner	40.0	68.3	44.4	60.0	60	43.3	39.6	32.2	30.3	92
Renter	60.0	31.7	55.6	40.0	53	56.7	60.4	67.8	69.7	151
Number	(35)	(41)	(27)	(10)	113	(60)	(101)	(59)	(23)	243
Economic rank										
0–39										
Home owner	9.8	24.6	20.2	27.6	93	14.7	15.8	17.6	19.9	166
Renter	90.2	75.4	79.8	72.4	334	85.3	84.2	82.4	80.1	830
Number	(126)	(133)	(107)	(61)	427	(184)	(392)	(284)	(136)	996
40–79										
Home owner	25.2	33.3	40.0	34.3	289	24.0	25.7	37.3	41.1	340
Renter	74.8	66.7	60.0	65.7	557	76.0	74.3	62.7	58.9	750
Number	(226)	(286)	(199)	(135)	846	(208)	(400)	(292)	(190)	1090
80–89										
Home owner	35.6	37.7	42.2	51.1	83	37.3	42.5	44.6	58.5	111
Renter	64.4	62.3	57.8	48.9	121	72.7	57.5	55.4	41.5	137
Number	(59)	(59)	(45)	(41)	204	(45)	(74)	(75)	(54)	248
90–100										
Home owner	61.4	65.6	64.3	61.9	128	53.3	50.0	60.8	69.4	156
Renter	38.6	34.4	35.7	38.1	74	46.7	50.0	39.2	30.6	113
Number	(57)	(61)	(42)	(42)	202	(45)	(88)	(74)	(62)	269

TABLE 2.13 Multiple property ownership in selected occupations,
1861: ratio of number of properties owned to number in
occupation

Occupation by ratio group	Number in occupation	Number of properties owned	Ratio
Group I (ratio 5 to 6.9)			
Alderman	4	27	6.8
High bailiff	1	6	6.0
M.P.	2	11	5.5
Trustee	1	5	5.0
Courier	1	5	5.0
Group II (ratio 4 to 4.9)			
Agent	41	181	4.4
Chamberlain	1	4	4.0
Mayor	1	4	4.0
Stage driver	1	4	4.0
Group III (ratio 3 to 3.9)			
Gentleman	118	402	3.4
Chandler	4	13	3.3
Builder	16	48	3.0
Ice dealer	2	6	3.0
Lathe maker	4	12	3.0
Weaver	1	3	3.0
Yeoman	4	12	3.0
Watchman	1	3	3.0
Group IV (ratio 2 to 2.9)			
Banker	15	43	2.9
Brick maker	5	11	2.2
Bailiff	5	11	2.2
Coroner	1	2	2.0
Gaoler	1	2	2.0
Miller	1	2	2.0
Miner	1	2	2.0
Policeman	3	6	2.0
Tallow chandler	2	4	2.0
Quarryman	1	2	2.0
Bank teller	1	2	2.0
Member, Superior Court	2	4	2.0
Appraiser	2	4	2.0

Source: Assessment only.

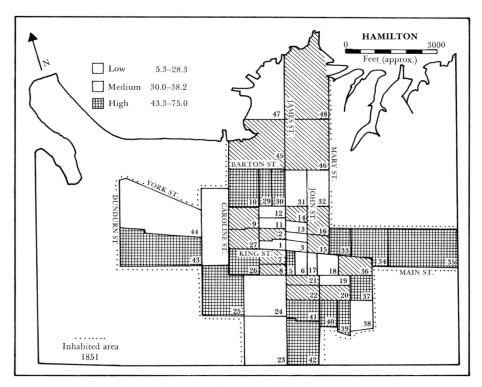

FIGURE 2.1 Percent of households owning at least one house

dren was low in home ownership, while six districts were high on both measures.[34]

To some extent the spatial distribution of home ownership reflected influences besides class, ethnicity, and life cycle. One of these was simply the pattern of landholding. The Stinsons, for instance, owned large segments of two central districts and rented out accommodation, keeping the proportion of home ownership there low. The east end ranked high in both home ownership and wealth because the man who owned large tracts of land deliberately decided to construct a district of broad, tree-lined boulevards with homes for the upper middle class.[35] Home ownership was marked, too, in especially desirable locations, such as those along major access routes.

To summarize, patterns of home ownership were extremely complex, reflecting both the independent and the overlapping influences of class, ethnicity, and life cycle. The spatial distribution of home ownership largely reflected these influences, and apparently the decision to buy a home often reflected or brought about a decision to remain within the city. Despite the complexity of its explanation, throughout the decade home ownership maintained, practically unchanged, its relationship with class and ethnicity. Like the occupational structure, the division of wealth, and the pattern of sexual and ethnic stratification, the structure of home ownership remained virtually the same.

This chapter has argued that there were four persistent structures in Hamilton between 1851 and 1861, and it has documented that assertation by showing that:

(1) the proportion of people in the various sectors of the work force remained almost identical;

(2) the share of the total wealth controlled by each economic rank stayed almost exactly the same;

(3) the characteristics of people in different economic ranks remained quite similar: occupations earned relatively similar rewards; household characteristics, with few exceptions, had almost identical relations with wealth; and the economic distribution of people of different sexes and different ethnic and religious backgrounds retained nearly the same shape;

(4) for the most part, the distance among economic, occupational, and ethnic ranks altered very little.

If anything, during the decade the poor became a little poorer, the middle rank experienced serious economic problems during the depression, and the rich became somewhat richer, thus slightly enlarging the degree of stratification at the extremes. But the data are too imprecise and the differences too small to make that conclusion other than speculative. Overall the most outstanding feature of the stratification system is its similarity at both ends of the decade.

The persistence of these structures is significant in three fundamental ways.

First, it provides a base line against which to measure the kind of social change that accompanied industrialization and against which to interpret shifts in other social features. For instance, the kinds of change in the life cycle that will be described in Chapter Five happened independently of changes in class structure, which points to some degree of independence between the family and the system of stratification, an intriguing hypothesis which must be tested.

Second, the basic structure of a nineteenth-century city prior to industrialization is now clear. By watching to see which of the four structures broke first, and by following their altered relations, it will be possible to identify the way in which economic, technological, and organizational change affected social structure. It will be possible to learn whether change happened gradually, one structure at a time dissolving slowly, and finally eroding another; or whether the whole pattern crumbled as a new order, a genuinely altered system of relations, emerged to replace the old. At the other extreme, by concentrating on the persistence of these structures it should be possible to frame questions about the mechanisms which preserve stability within a society. Here at last is a basis on which to conceptualize the relation of inequality to transiency. For it seems likely that Peter Laslett is right: that the rigidity of the social and economic order preserved the stability of a place whose population was in flux. The paths on which thousands of people passed through Hamilton in the 1850s were not arranged randomly. They were deeply etched, and, for the most part, straight. That is why the people moving along them rarely collided.[36] Perhaps the history of the relations between transiency and social structure has a moral for the revolutionary. To change social structure he must first slow down migration: human nature yearns for stability; lacking continuity in human relations, people seek it in social forms. If people are to accept a change in social structures, they must at least preserve the familiarity of the faces around them. This is a speculation and no more, but it bears study.

Finally, the persistence of structures leads to a more sophisticated understanding of class. The persisting crystallization of the objective features of social stratification, as I contended at the beginning of this chapter, accentuated the visibility and rigidity of class structure. One of the great problems for the historian is to understand the social divisions that were meaningful to people in a past society. Now for at least one city it is possible to perceive what those divisions were and to put the thousands of people with diverse characteristics into categories that they would understand and confirm if they could step out of the past and read this book.

CHAPTER THREE

Transiency and Social Mobility

Seven, eight, nine, and as high as thirteen weeks were not infrequently occupied by sailing vessels on the voyage; and the consequent suffering experienced on such occasions, the news of which, when transmitted by the sufferers to relatives at home, had spread an universal dread of a trip to America, and I must confess that I was not without my misgivings; but the incentive to brave the danger was caused by my desire to achieve a home and independence in the Western World which the force of circumstances had denied me in the land of my birth . . . I had been industriously engaged for five years climbing the ladder of fortune, and here I was at the lowermost rung. (Wilson Benson)

THOUGH FEW PEOPLE at the time would have thought so, one of the more remarkable men who wandered about Canada West during the mid-nineteenth-century was Wilson Benson. Wilson Benson was an Irish Protestant immigrant who lived on the edge of poverty, drifted from job to job and place to place, exercised no authority or power within any community, and lived, in short, the hard obscure life common to most people of his day. What makes him remarkable is that in his declining years Wilson Benson decided to leave a record of his life. His brief autobiography remains a poignant document embodying in fifty-six pages more authentic social history than most scholars have produced in volumes four or five times that size. With foresight for which the historian must be forever grateful Wilson Benson set out to provide the future with a primary source. The pages that follow will use what he has written, I hope in the manner which he intended. For "my humble aim," wrote Benson, "has been to preserve, from oblivion and the ashes of the past, a sketch which might serve future generations in the compilation of a future history of Western Canada (Ontario)."[1]

Wilson Benson's sketch has special value because he was a representative man. Without the background which statistical analysis has provided it would have been easy to dismiss him as a plucky unlucky fellow, interesting and quaint but hardly like the mass of immigrants who settled Canada West. But we know differently: the themes of Wilson Benson's life were woven through the lives of most people who lived and worked in mid-nineteenth-century Ontario. His life, therefore, merits considerably more than a passing look. And it is appropriate to study his life at this point because its main motifs—his transiency, his search for success, and their interrelation—are the subjects of this chapter.

Wilson Benson was born in Belfast in December 1821, his father the proprietor of a weaving shop employing several men. Within roughly a year his mother died, and soon afterward his father moved to the Townland of Drumnasue near Portadown, where he married a widow. The new wife had been in difficult circumstances and the rent of her small farm was seriously in arrears, but Wilson's father paid the back rent, built a new house, and made improvements to the property. Unfortunately, Wilson's father was not a shrewd man, for he neglected to have his wife's lease transferred to his own name. And one day, when Wilson was twelve years old, his stepmother's sons by her first marriage simply claimed possession of the property, ejecting Wilson, Mr. Benson, and presumably their mother with virtually no compensation. Losing his own mother in infancy had been Wilson's first piece of bad luck. This was the second; it set a pattern that would haunt him throughout his life.

"Suddenly," claimed Wilson, he was "reduced to penury."[2] The victim of instant downward social mobility for reasons beyond his control, Wilson at the age of twelve had to leave home to work, and he hired himself out to one William Cullen for three months at a wage of four shillings sixpence. Then he found a slightly better position as apprentice to a reedmaker, William Hyde, who paid him six shillings sixpence. Here too he stayed but a few months, returning to his father, who now lived in the Townland of Mullantine, to attend school for a few months, the only full-time formal education he ever received. Not long afterwards, probably in 1835, with twelve shillings sixpence in his pocket and "the usual accompaniment of a traveling Irishman—a sturdy blackthorn stick," Wilson left for Scotland with his married sister, who had been visiting their father.[3] At her home in Maybole they found her husband ill and, for some unspecified reason, all set off for Glasgow, sleeping along the way in haystacks. In Glasgow Wilson's brother-in-law found work as a weaver and Wilson as a piecer in a cotton mill. But Wilson apparently found life in the mill unsatisfactory and soon persuaded a wholesale merchant from Belfast, one John White, to give him eighteen pence' worth of goods on account. With this stock Wilson set off peddling, earning a substantial eight shillings in his first week. Not knowing what to do with his money, he deposited it with a weaver named Robert Young. After twenty-one weeks Wilson's brother-in-law decided to tramp to the Lothians and Wilson agreed to go with him, first seeking to collect his money from Robert Young, who told him to return some other time. Thus without his money Wilson went with his brother-in-law in the direction of Edinburgh. In Edinburgh once again he managed to obtain a stack of fancy articles and set off peddling. After a while he joined another boy and a girl making porridge for three hundred hands at harvest time.

Apparently anxious to strike out on his own at last, Wilson, now about sixteen years old, returned to Glasgow to claim his money, but after "three days of fruitless pleading," he knew that Robert Young would never return it,[4] and so he headed back to Belfast where he worked for his old employer William Hyde for six months and then for an unspecified reason went to work for James Ford in the Townland of Crueberg near Pointzpass in the County of Armagh. After six months there, perhaps weary of wandering, Wilson returned to his father for two months before apprenticing himself to William Courtney of the Townland of Bottle Hill in the Parish of Kilmore, where he learned linen weaving for three years and nine months, an extraordinarily long time for him to remain in one place or at one job. Although at the end of the time he had a trade, his wages had been so low that Wilson had to appeal to his father for money for clothes. While at Bottle Hill, Wilson had the first of his successive accidents, severely cutting his left hand when running from a field with his friends who had been frightened by a sound they took to be the police coming to arrest them for some minor caper. During the same period he attended night school and learned to write, and he sometimes went to Sabbath School where he learned a variety of things and, perhaps most importantly, met Jemima Hewitt. After his apprenticeship Wilson moved in with his father again and established himself as a weaver, taking in piecework under the putting-out system.

At the same time his friendship with Jemima Hewitt, who was a sixteen-year-old dressmaker (Wilson was eighteen) developed, and, despite their youthfulness, they decided to marry, in secret because they feared the objections of their parents on account of their age. However, their parents "heartily acquiesced in" their "little ruse," although it was extremely unusual for Irish couples to marry so young. Wilson Benson's early marriage was, insofar as I can tell, the most unrepresentative aspect of his life history.[5]

Frustrated by his prospects in Ireland, Wilson determined to take his bride to North America in the spring, and he began the "customary preparations," including "letters from friends in Ireland to friends in Canada." Despite an intercontinental network of friends and kin Wilson approached the trip with trepidation, not out of fear of a new country but from terror of the Atlantic crossing. His "incentive to brave the danger," he wrote, "was caused by my desire to achieve a home and independence in the Western World which the force of circumstances had denied me in the land of my birth."[6]

Wilson and Jemima sailed on the *Sarah Stewart* on 28 March 1841. The hazards of an ocean crossing clearly had not been exaggerated, for their ship nearly capsized in a storm, illness broke out on board, and in the fog off the Bank of Newfoundland the ship nearly collided with another vessel. After they arrived at Montreal, the Bensons set off for Kingston on a barge which stopped for an hour at Brockville, where Wilson and Jemima disembarked to look around the town, only to find on their return that the barge had left without them. Leaving Jemima in Brockville Wilson followed the barge to Kingston, where he found that their trunk had been opened and most of their valuables stolen. Once again the victim of his own ineptitude and some bad luck, Wilson returned to Brockville.

Pretending they were brother and sister, Wilson and Jemima set out to look for work. Jemima found a place as a resident domestic servant almost immediately; Wilson was much less fortunate. For a while he managed to work at weaving three miles from

Brockville. Then he hired himself to a farmer named Phillips, who wanted someone to plow his fields. Wilson had never farmed or plowed and had no idea how to proceed. For a few days he managed to find odd jobs that enabled him to delay the start of plowing, but when the inevitable moment came his performance was a disaster. He was sacked seven days after he had begun to work for the farmer, and his autobiography contains some uncharacteristically caustic remarks about Phillips and his wife. For a while afterward Wilson worked as a porter at a hotel in Brockville, apprenticing himself subsequently for six months to a Scottish baker named James Nicolson. Wilson at this time only wanted to learn a trade which he could practice in Ireland with more success than weaving. But "experience taught me that a journeyman baker was not that profession."[7]

Even less promising, however, was his next attempt to learn a new trade. Wilson apprenticed himself to a shoemaker but stayed only two days, "convinced . . . that 'lasts' and 'pegs' and 'wax ends' would not last me in pegging out an existence to the end of my days." After rejecting shoemaking Wilson went to work, presumably as a laborer, in an agricultural implements factory "employing a great number of hands." Persuading his employer to keep him on despite a general cut in staff, Wilson earned a comfortable fourteen dollars a month, which enabled him to rent a house and live with his wife, who worked as a dressmaker.[8] In the spring, presumably of 1843, his employer left Brockville for Toronto, taking Wilson with him. On board the steamer Wilson worked as a cook, finding at last a trade which he apparently enjoyed. Once more Wilson entrusted his money to someone, this time with happy results; his ex-employer not only returned the money but interest as well. Despite this, Wilson decided to stay on the steamer for the entire season and left some months later with a promise of employment again the next year.

When the season on the boat was over, Wilson moved his wife to Kingston where they opened a small, "tolerably successful" store selling groceries and miscellaneous articles. The next spring, with his wife presumably minding the store, Wilson shipped again on the same boat. In the course of his life as a mariner, Wilson met "many of the leading men of that day" and heard their discussions of the fiercely partisan politics of the time. The process had an interesting result: "These episodes in my steamboat life not only amused me, but furnished food for reflection, and awakened in me a new and lively interest in the country, and begat a feeling of identity in its welfare which supplanted the yearning desire I had hitherto entertained of returning to my native land."[9] Gradually and unconsciously, despite himself, Wilson Benson had become a Canadian.

After the shipping season of 1844, his captain gave Wilson a supply of oysters, which he spent the winter peddling throughout the Kingston district until he returned to the boat in the spring. The next season, however, was interrupted by a serious eye infection, cured only by an operation after fruitless visits to several physicians. After his operation, Wilson finished the season working on several different boats and then spent two months as a watchman before setting off to peddle once again.

During the peddling season his brother-in-law persuaded Wilson to join him in the Township of Richmond. There Wilson bought an acre of land, built a "snug house," and at the same time opened a general grocery store, staffed by his wife while he went off peddling his "miscellaneous stock of wares." Wilson's autobiography tells little about his experiences on the road, but it does refer to one occasion when, accompanied by a "female friend," he playfully evaded a toll collector.[10] (Why did Wilson include this incident? Was it male bravado? Or a way of indicating that men on the road found ways of compensating for the absence of their wives?) Wilson's contentment, alas, was not permanent. For with characteristic lack of forethought he made almost the same mistake his father had made more than twenty-five years before: he neglected to obtain title to the land on which he lived. Thus in the spring when the man from whom he had bought the land fell into debt, the sheriff seized Wilson's acre and his house. Despite all his improvements, Wilson received by way of compensation only one cow worth seventeen dollars. With justification he wrote, "This was a stunning blow to the future prospects I had pictured to myself."[11]

Nonetheless, Wilson, always ready to turn adversity to good uses, decided to buy a second cow, return to Kingston, and open a dairy. This he did, and once again all appeared well when accident struck: "Soon after a neighbour's cow broke into my stable,

and gored one of my cows, so that she died in three weeks afterwards." Thus ended the dairy business. In language that revealed
at once his ambition, despair, and image of society, Wilson wrote,
"I had been industriously engaged for five years climbing the
ladder of fortune, and here I was at the lowermost rung."[12]

Reduced again suddenly to the bottom of the ladder of fortune,
Wilson turned to what he knew and shipped on board a steamer
as cook. When the shipping season ended he moved his family
once more, this time to Toronto, where he opened a small store
on Victoria Street to sell miscellaneous goods. While his wife
tended the store, he went between Kingston and Toronto trading
vegetables, which he found sufficiently cheap in Toronto to make
the trip worthwhile. The next spring, though he cooked on board
a boat again, his luck improved. For some time Wilson had suffered from ague on board ship, and that spring in a dream he
discovered the ingredients for a cure, which worked not only for
him but for someone else on board as well. Thus encouraged he
set off in the winter of 1848 peddling his ague cure throughout
the Niagara district and the West (passing undoubtedly through
Hamilton) and "cured hundreds of cases," a success which left him
in "comfortable circumstances."[13]

On shipboard the following spring Wilson once more had a
memorable trip, for two reasons: at considerable risk to himself
he helped a fugitive slave escape from the United States, and the
trip that year was so rough and unpleasant that he decided to give
up his seasonal stints on the lakes and rivers, a decision to which
he adhered for the rest of his life. One day during the following
winter Wilson and his eldest son were returning to Toronto from
a peddling trip when Wilson saw smoke rising in the sky. With
an awful premonition he knew it to be his house and store, and
he was right. Once again his extraordinary bad luck undercut the
modest stability he had achieved. But opportunity, as always, appeared almost at once when his brother-in-law again presented a
plan, this time to move to Orangeville. Wilson dispatched his wife
to inspect and after her return decided to make the move, strength-
ened in his decision, interestingly, by learning of the death of his
father.[14] Perhaps this finally ended what lingering plans he might
have had for returning to Ireland and freed him to commit himself to the New World in a way he had not done before. In 1849

he moved with his family to Orangeville, then a village with only three houses. Always the opportunist, he took with him a cask of whiskey which he sold to the thirsty settlers at considerable profit. Although with his usual misfortune he cut his foot badly and was unable to walk for six weeks, Wilson managed surprisingly well as a farmer, considering his lack of experience and his unfortunate week at the Phillips' farm.

At the close of his second year as a farmer, Wilson and a friend carried their grain by sleigh to McLaughlin's mill, Mono Village, taking along a bottle of whiskey to treat the miller and some friends. When they arrived, Wilson left his sacks of grain by the door and went inside with his friends. Returning later he discovered that his grist—eight bushels of wheat—had disappeared. "One thing I was assured of," wrote Wilson with his curious naiveté, "neither Mr. Irwin nor Mr. Dodds took it; and the only supposititious [sic] idea I entertain on the subject is, that the relative fairies of the McLaughlins had followed them from Ireland—for I often there heard they were great meal thieves—and spirited away my flour, shorts, bran, bags and all."[15] Wilson may or may not have found solace for his loss in an Irish folktale, but it is significant that after a decade in the New World he should invoke it as an explanation. Whether or not the relative fairies of the McLaughlins had crossed the Atlantic, Irish culture certainly had.

After only two years of eking out a living in Orangeville, contending with the privations and hardships of pioneer life, Wilson heard about land farther away in Grey County, supposedly a veritable "Garden of Eden."[16] So once again, though this time as a committed farmer, Wilson trudged off in search of opportunity and bought land in Artemesia township. In order to retain title to the land Wilson had to make continual improvements, which called for twelve or thirteen arduous trips between Artemesia and Orangeville before he moved his family on 14 February 1851, a strange time to move in a cold and wild country. Life in Grey County was at first even more primitive and difficult than in Orangeville. Following his first harvest, for instance, Wilson had to transport his grain forty-four miles through the snow to find a mill, a journey reduced to eleven miles the next year but still, as he pointed out, one of enormous difficulty during the winter.

Throughout the next decade Wilson remained on the farm, scratching out a living. It was not until August 1860 that disaster once again struck, this time with the sudden death of his wife, followed shortly by that of their youngest daughter. Although depressed, Wilson somehow managed to carry on until, about a year later, he remarried.[17] Despite a near-fatal accident caused by a runaway horse in 1863, and broken ribs sustained after falling through a hayloft in 1870, nothing exceptionally unfortunate happened to Wilson until 1873 when he was almost killed by a threshing machine. The accident, which crushed his arm, leg, and head, left him immobile for weeks. Eventually he could stand and walk, but one arm and leg remained almost powerless. The doctors in Toronto felt that a man of his age (interestingly, only about fifty-two) and weakened condition could not withstand the "second shock" to his "nervous system" which breaking and resetting the bones would require. Thus Wilson accepted his fate, and made the last move he recorded. Unable to farm anymore he took his family to the village of Markdale, where he opened a small store and lived in "very moderate circumstances." Although he painfully felt his infirmities each day, Wilson remained basically irrepressible as he undertook the writing of his autobiography: "my natural buoyancy of spirits keeps me consoled, and activity of mind prevents me, in a great measure, experiencing the loss of my limbs."[18]

Wilson Benson was a representative nineteenth-century Canadian first and foremost because he was a transient. Like more than nine out of ten of the adult men in urban Ontario during his time, Wilson Benson was an emigrant. More than that, like the great majority of nineteenth-century men whom historians have attempted to trace, Wilson Benson moved often. Those without much knowledge of nineteenth-century people might assume that the ease with which Wilson moved himself and his family from place to place revealed an especially rootless and unstable character. But it was not so. The statistics to be presented later in this chapter offer convincing evidence that transiency was a way of life shared by the mass of the population. Little is known, however, about the rhythms, directions, and motivating forces of the mass movement that kept the populations of nineteenth-century places in a continual state of flux.

In dealing with the problem of interpreting transiency the experience of Wilson Benson is especially suggestive. Table 3.1 reviews his movements, which fall into clusters: first he moved within a relatively small area around Ireland; then came a jump of some distance to Scotland, followed by a succession of short moves. After the Scottish experience Benson returned to Ireland, moving around again within a relatively small area. The migration from Ireland to Canada, obviously, was the major move of his life. But within Canada he continued to change residence rapidly, again within relatively short distances, until he settled for two decades in Grey County. When he was in an area, Benson moved frequently but not far. There is every reason to suspect that this was not an uncommon pattern.[19]

Benson's movements were not rhythmical. The circumstances that caused him to move his family from place to place were related only marginally to the natural rhythms of the seasons, or even to the rhythms of his life. He moved often before and after

TABLE 3.1 Wilson Benson's major residential changes

Date	Place
1821	Belfast (Ire.)
ca. 1822	Drumnasue (Ire.)
1836	Glasgow (Scot.)
1837	Edinburgh (Scot.)
1837	Glasgow (Scot.)
1838	Armagh County (Ire.)
1838	Mullantine (Ire.)
1838	Bottle Hill (Ire.)
1841	Brockville (C.W.)[a]
1843	Kingston (C.W.)
1847	Township of Richmond (C.W.)
1847	Kingston (C.W.)
1847	Toronto (C.W.)
1849	Orangeville (C.W.)
1851	Artemesia (Grey County, C.W.)
1873 or 1874	Village of Markdale (Ont.)

[a] Canada West.

he was married, before and after he had children. However, although he could be called a transient, Wilson could not be called a drifter. For he was not an irresponsible loafer but, to the contrary, a hard-working man in search of success. At the grossest level one might say that his motivation remained economic; he kept looking for the main chance. At a more subtle level his wandering can be read as a search for independence, a striving not only for economic security but for a steady livelihood that would leave him beholden to no man, master of himself, free of employer and middleman. Yet, it is important not to impute to Wilson a planned rationality which he did not possess. With the exception of the deliberate move to Canada, most of the time he went from place to place more or less on the spur of the moment: his sister invited him back to Scotland; his brother-in-law wanted to change jobs; a brother-in-law asked him to come and live in Richmond; someone told him that Grey County was a second Garden of Eden. When he stopped moving it was because he more or less had settled, which sounds like a tautology but is not. His life finally fell into place: a decent farm which he owned, a reasonable rate of return, and an independence which he found satisfying. Why he found it in Grey County rather than in Orangeville is not possible to know. What is clear, though, is that a process of settling happened, and he just stayed put until he could farm no longer. It was not a conscious decision not to move again; things just worked out that way.

The role of circumstance and accident, I suspect, also united Wilson Benson's life to the lives of his contemporaries in Canada West. The search for tidy reasons to explain why some men moved and others did not will never succeed; the statistics of transiency will remain important and inscrutable artifacts of a past way of life because, very simply, many men moved for reasons as unsystematic as Wilson Benson's. Their cow was gored and their dairy ruined; their house burned down; they were caught in a threshing machine and no longer able to farm. The role of accident, in short, undoubtedly has been underestimated as a deus ex machina of social history. One of the foundations of modern life is its increased predictability, on which bureaucratic organizations, modern governments, and economic systems must rely. But modern medicine, fire and accident insurance, and the routine search of land titles by lawyers were at best rudimentary at the time Wilson Benson lived, and the lack of each opened his life to an uncertainty which at some point made it unpredictable and frustrated his efforts for happiness and success. It might at first seem that Wilson Benson was especially accident prone; he hurt himself working, he lost lands and business, and, in fact, spent only nine or ten years free of serious disaster. But aside from his naively trusting disposition (which, since it apparently was characteristic of his father as well, may even have been fairly common at that time), there was nothing in his experience that might not happen, and probably did happen, to many people. The incidence of fire, mortality, and failure in earlier times provides evidence enough that this was the case, and nineteenth-century newspapers are full of the hideous accidents that befell ordinary people in the course of their everyday lives.

In a similar way Wilson Benson's experience confounds the attempt to plot rational patterns in the occupational changes that occurred in men's lives. Statistics of occupational mobility, such as those given later in this chapter, show considerable movement into and out of specific callings. But Wilson Benson's experience indicates that occupational change among men who lacked a profession or who had not established themselves successfully in a craft was more or less random. By and large, job titles tell little about the relative success or failure of a man except that he was doing something different, which in itself may be the best sign that he had not been particularly successful. Wilson Benson's occupational history is summarized in Table 3.2, which shows quite clearly that the sort of work one man might do varied enormously —cotton-mill piecer, peddler, porridge maker, weaver, cook, grocer, farmer, to name some of Wilson's jobs. At the same time Wilson's occupational history underscores a theme of this book: the artificiality of the line often drawn between manual and nonmanual work in nineteenth-century society. For when he was a peddler or storekeeper Wilson would be ranked among white collar or nonmanual workers; when he was a weaver or cook he would be considered manual labor. Yet the differences in rewards were marginal and the distinction in social position very likely nil.

All of this raises an exceedingly difficult question: did Wilson Benson's life exemplify upward social mobility? That question

TABLE 3.2 Wilson Benson's occupational history

Date	Occupation
1833	Apprentice unspecified
1833–35	Apprentice reedmaker
1836	Piecer in cotton mill
1836	Peddler
1837	Porridge maker
1837	Apprentice reedmaker
1838–40	Apprentice linen weaver
1840–41	Weaver
1842	Farm hand
1842	Porter
1842	Apprentice baker
1842	Apprentice shoemaker
1842	Agricultural implements factory (laborer)
1843	Cook on boat (seasonal)
1843	Storekeeper (groceries and miscellaneous articles)
1844	Cook on boat (seasonal)
1844–45	Peddler (oysters, seasonal)
1845–46	Cook on boat (seasonal)
1847	Watchman
1847	Peddler (seasonal)
1847	Storekeeper (miscellaneous goods)
1847	Dairyman and storekeeper
1847	Cook on boat (seasonal)
1847	Storekeeper
1848	Cook on boat (seasonal)
1848	Peddler (winter only, ague cure)
1849	Cook on boat (seasonal)
1849	Peddler (whiskey)
1849–73 or 74	Farmer
1873 or 1874 and afterwards	Storekeeper

cannot be answered on the basis of his successive occupations alone. To take only one example, when he changed work for the last time, from farmer to storekeeper, Wilson did not move upward on a social scale; he merely shifted into a kind of work which he could carry on in his crippled state. Had it not been for his accident he would have remained a farmer. The only measures that have much validity refer to his economic position, his degree of comfort and security, which can only be inferred. Obviously, Wilson never regained the security and prospects he had at the age of twelve before his stepmother's sons hardheartedly reclaimed the family farm and reduced Wilson to instant destitution. But he had improved his position from the time when he and Jemima had arrived penniless at Brockville, after their valuables had been stolen. For Wilson had become a property owner, able to support his family, albeit modestly. He might have achieved as much had he stayed in Ireland; it is impossible to know. The gain was not very large, but it was enough to raise him from the destitute to the struggling. It would be wrong, however, to describe his experience only as moderately upwardly mobile, for in the course of his first decade in Canada his luck changed often and, to use his phrase, he repeatedly began to climb the ladder of fortune only to fall back time and again to its lowermost rung.

The movement of Wilson Benson through geographic and social space does not exhaust his interest for the social historian, for other, though less immediately obvious, themes in his life most likely resembled those of many other men. One of these is the role of his family. Wilson was reticent about intimate relationships and uninformative concerning the details of domestic life about which historians long to know. Nonetheless, throughout most of his life the important role played by his family is clear. Although he left his father's home at the age of twelve, Wilson returned there periodically as long as he lived in Scotland or Ireland. His father's house was a place to which he could always go for rest and, undoubtedly, comfort. At the same time he felt he had a continuing claim on his father, for, at the end of his apprenticeship as a weaver when he lacked money, it was his father to whom Wilson turned for clothes. And, after his years of independent adventures, Wilson still considered it necessary to marry secretly because his father might disapprove. Indeed, as long as his father lived Wilson felt a continuing tie. Only after his father's death could he move to Orangeville without reservation and take up farming, a move which apparently signified his decision to remain permanently in the New World. The liberation he experienced on learning of his father's death testifies to the strength of the bond that had endured despite the ocean between them.

Wilson's family also repeatedly influenced his movements. He left home to accompany his sister; he followed his brother-in-law around Scotland; the urging of another brother-in-law prompted two of his most important moves within Canada. Although Wilson and his wife lived alone with their children, functioning for all practical purposes as a modal independent nuclear family, there existed always the consciousness of a kin network that partially shaped behavior. That network encompassed more than actual kin; for friends appeared almost an extension of the family. When Wilson was about to migrate to Canada, letters were sent to friends there, an act which, it is important to remark, Wilson called "customary." When he wished to be given goods on credit to peddle in Scotland, he turned to a merchant from his home town of Belfast. When he sought a miller for his flour near Orangeville, he went to a man whose family obviously had some connection with the grain business in Ireland, and whose family reputation Wilson knew and, in this case, should have heeded.[20]

The most important member of his family was, of course, his wife. Their need to separate so that she could find work as a domestic servant is a poignant commentary on contemporary social customs. Their subsequent division of labor shows that one income was not sufficient to maintain life in nineteenth-century urban Canada. Not even a store brought in enough to make it unnecessary for Wilson to leave his wife and search for alternative employment in every season. Wilson's relation with his wife was not one-sided but was a partnership. For not only did she tend the family store but shared in making important decisions, going herself to evaluate the prospects for a family move to Orangeville.

That Wilson's employment was so often seasonal underscores the well-known rhythm of work in earlier times. Not only on the farm but elsewhere, as in shipping and probably construction, to name two substantial sectors of the economy, work ended with the advent of winter. Indeed, the irregularity with which Wilson worked at times probably formed the most representative aspect of his life history.

One aspect of Wilson's personality deserves further comment: his generosity and trust. He simply deposited his money with no security with Robert Young; although Young refused to return the money Wilson did the same thing once again, this time with happier results. Like his father he paid for land without obtaining a proper deed. He took a gift to his miller friends and accepted a supernatural explanation when his grain disappeared from their doorway. At great risk to himself he helped a fugitive slave escape. Was this openness toward other people idiosyncratic to Wilson, or was it an aspect of Irish culture, or again, was it an engaging characteristic found more often among men in earlier centuries?

Certainly, although he lived for a long time in Canada, Wilson did not shed his Irish identity completely. He came there, in fact, as an Irishman intending to return to his beloved home as soon as he had acquired the skill necessary to make an independent living. But through a gradual and unconscious process he became a Canadian. Traveling the canals and lakes he listened to the people of his new country arguing its problems, and his interests and identity quietly shifted. Late in his life, wishing to leave a source for future historians of Ontario, he wrote: "Looking upon the history of one's country as an heirloom, to be preserved at all hazards, has been the chief incentive to my taking up my pen, in my humble way."[21] Canada he called his country; and he regarded its history as an heirloom, an inheritance of sentimental value which should be treasured. His identification had become complete.

Wilson Benson's experience is noteworthy for the light, however dim, it sheds on one other problem: the relation of the motivation of particular immigrant groups to that of native North Americans. One argument that the new wave of interest in ethnic history might level with some plausibility against the historians of social mobility is that they impute similar motives to all groups by assuming that the definition of social mobility was the same to Irishmen, Italians, or Jews as it was to native Canadians or Americans, and that their aspirations for success were similar. This assumption, it would follow in this sort of argument, confounds the cultural idiosyncracy and specialness of individual groups. For a few groups, such as particular fundamentalist religious sects or those wishing to establish a special communal way of life, there can be no quarrel with this viewpoint. Indeed, the same argument applies to similar groups that arose within North America. But the argument probably casts an unduly warm, romantic glow around ethnic groups in past times. It takes the contemporary celebration of ethnicity as an alternative to a monotonous, materialistic life style and transposes it wishfully into the past, hoping that ethnic groups in earlier centuries were indeed bent on other things than participating in the North American scramble for economic success. Alas, I have seen no evidence whatsoever to support that argument.

Wilson Benson, for instance, a not atypical Irishman, came to Canada with the intention of climbing "the ladder of fortune," and he followed a clearly opportunistic path, moving from job to job and place to place as fortune proved more elusive than he had hoped. Although Irish immigrants usually did not move very high up the ladder of fortune or make their way into the more lucrative and honorific callings, they could and did scrimp and save, modestly defining their aspirations as the acquisition of a bit of property and moderate security. And they pursued these goals with middling success, if the evidence in this book and elsewhere can be believed.[22]

Nonetheless, there was something about Wilson Benson's attitudes and behavior that distinguished him from people today. Although it is tempting to attribute that peculiarity to his Irishness and thereby endow it with special charm, it is safer and probably more accurate to identify it as premodern. Wilson, though not a peasant, lacked the calculating discipline that subservience to time, large work settings, and technology have imposed on modern man. He followed opportunity, not a plan; he trusted; he found it difficult and unpleasant to remain at routine confining work in either factory or shop. He disliked most of all dependence. That is what drove him from Ireland, and in his own way he sought whenever possible to have no employer but himself. Wilson was neither a rural nor an urban man; in his case the distinction is almost meaningless. For he moved back and forth between town and country eradicating the boundaries between them with the pride and pluck that picked him up after each disaster and propelled him on to be always his own man.

Wilson sensed that the immense social changes he had witnessed called for an approach to life different from his own. When he went to Grey County it was a primitive place; when he left, there was "a market at our own door—the sound of railway and steam whistles, of mills and manufactories, where a few short years ago resounded the howl of the wolf. Innumerable villages, containing mills and manufactories, and general stores of merchandise now mark the spot which was overgrown by dense forest fifteen or twenty years ago." With this modernization of the land in mind, and the hope that his book would help others "clear the shoals of which I have ran [sic] aground," Wilson claimed, in direct contrast to his own life, that "the only true road to prosperity and social greatness" lay in a "well-matured, well-directed course of action laid down in youth for the guidance of our future lives, combined with unwavering purpose in execution." By the end of his life the transformation that experience had worked in his consciousness had made Wilson Benson not only a Canadian but a modern man.[23]

If Wilson Benson was a representative nineteenth-century man, then it is important to discover the cumulative impact of thousands of similar lives upon social development. What difference did it make that men in earlier times moved from place to place and job to job with such frequency? From one point of view an answer appears obvious: it made difficult the formation of communities and worked against the social integration of people into the places in which they lived. Transiency introduced an instability into society and made problematical even the definition of the population of any one place. Did the population of a place comprise the people living there for any specifiable period of time, or all those present at any one moment even though many would be gone within hours, days, or weeks? Although the implications of transiency for an understanding of community appear straightforward, its meaning for political life is ambiguous. There exist various ways in which the relationship among transiency, class, social mobility, and political consciousness can be construed, but one general question underlies virtually all formulations: what conditions promoted or retarded the growth of militant political beliefs and actions among the working class in earlier times?

A traditional answer, as Joan Scott points out in a superb essay, is that transients brought with them the virus of political discontent. Unstable, disoriented by moving from country to city, lacking the familiar restraints of community or religion, transients formed the "dangerous classes," the militant political rabble, of cities in earlier times. One historian, Scott argues, views "early working-class protest in Western Europe" as arising "from economic dislocations, and he sees the occupations most prone to radicalism as those that are least stable and most isolated from 'normal' social life." Her own study of the workers of Carmaux has led Scott to an opposite conclusion. There "incidences of militant working-class action" grew "as miners and glassworkers became increasingly attached to the city." In her view geographic stability accompanied an increased identification of the working class with the city as its source of livelihood and nurtured the will to take militant action to prevent the erosion of traditional rewards. Scott's argument is not unlike one put forward by Stephan Thernstrom and Peter Knights, who stress that "high rates of transiency for blue collar workers presumably left them alienated but invisible and politically impotent, and minimized the likelihood of effective organized efforts to reshape capitalist society." Thernstrom and Knights sought to explain the lack of working-class political militancy in America; Scott sought the reasons for the increased militancy of the working-class glassblowers and mineworkers of Carmaux. Both found answers in the process of population movement. The militant defense of their hard-earned position by the workers of Carmaux and the alienated apathy of American workers formed opposite sides of the same demographic coin. Unlike the settled men of Carmaux, American workers failed to identify their own economic success with any particular place. One might extend the argument and add that transiency worked against militancy by retarding the development of the common consciousness necessary to transform an economic group into a social class.[24]

Although the foregoing argument is persuasive, it is not without problems, as a fine essay by Clyde Griffen shows. Griffen speculates about the relations among transiency, mobility, and political consciousness for the workers of Poughkeepsie, New York, where he finds no growth of political or class militancy among the minority of workers who settled in the city for a decade or more. Unlike the settled glassblowers and miners of Carmaux the men of Poughkeepsie apparently accepted without question the political and social system within which they worked. "The high rate of persistence among the more successful in every occupation and nationality group," writes Griffen, "reduced the likelihood of protest against the status quo . . . the successful easily justified for most citizens their sense of Poughkeepsie's promise for their own advancement." Similarly, Thernstrom has argued elsewhere that the comparative ease with which poor immigrant workers managed to acquire property blunted the edge of their discontent and reinforced their image of America as a land of opportunity.[25] Geographic stability, from this perspective, follows from economic success; this success, even though extremely modest, reinforces the image of a land of opportunity. Where the promise of social mobility appears real it develops in men a commitment to the social system within which they and their children will try to rise.

These two views of the relationship of transiency to political militancy—that settled workers are most militant and that settled workers are not militant at all—are not contradictory. The crux of the matter is its context: the opportunities for economic success within a particular setting. In Carmaux upwardly mobile workers were not especially militant; it was, to the contrary, those who felt a sense of threat to their prospects, a blockage of expected and customary opportunity, who developed into a political class. In Poughkeepsie, according to Griffen, settled workers, sensing no threat to their future, remained nonmilitant. Geographical stability apparently promoted social stability and political inaction in settings where opportunities for economic advancement were not only available but perceived as attainable. Geographic stability promoted militancy, on the other hand, where advancement appeared blocked or customary rewards threatened.

The same might be said of transiency. In accordance with the older view, rootlessness and transiency probably did contribute to political militancy in some situations. When men moved alone or with their families, going like Wilson Benson from one relatively small work setting to another, rarely making a friend, continually encountering strangers, then the circumstances of their lives worked against the formation of any particularly sharp political attitudes or the taking of collective action. On the other hand, when circumstances threw crowds of rootless, wandering, exploited men together, a setting for the growth of militancy instantly appeared. When, to take one instance, the railroad brought together gangs of laborers to work under harsh conditions, it created the setting in which a collective sense of discontent could develop and take shape. In similar cases, the alienation and frustration devel-

oped by a life of wandering from one menial and unpleasant job
to another might have worked precisely in accordance with the
traditional argument, promoting the growth of an explosive, unruly lower class.

Clearly, much more historical evidence must be gathered before
any very definite conclusions can be reached about the complex
question of the political implications of transiency. There do seem
to be reasonable grounds, however, for supposing that the effects
of transiency or of its opposite, stability, were closely related to
the nature of opportunity within any particular place. And it
therefore makes good sense to study transiency and social mobility
together, seeking if not an answer at least a reasonable hypothesis
about their interrelation in nineteenth-century Ontario.

Nonetheless, transiency and social mobility were distinct processes, and special considerations govern the study of each. Transiency of course stands for a particular kind of migratory behavior,
and migration has already been studied intensively, if somewhat
inconclusively, as a glance at some general features of its literature
reveals. Most studies have found the life cycle to be a critical
variable in migration. Children usually accompany their parents;
people in their late teens and early twenties often strike out on
their own in search of jobs, in pursuit of education, or to accompany or join a spouse. People with families usually are more
settled; and old people simply do not move around very much if
they can help it. Thus it is usual to find migration decreasing
through about the age of fifteen and then increasing sharply until
the mid-twenties when it starts to decline, leveling off among
people over sixty.[26] The sexual distribution of migrants is less
clear than their age characteristics. One review of studies on migration reported little sex difference, but Sidney Goldstein's study
of Norristown found a substantial excess of men among migrants
to that city. The resolution of these different conclusions probably
lies in factors affecting individual migratory situations. One of
these might be cultural patterns: it has been customary in some
societies for men to migrate first, finding a job and establishing
a home before sending for their families. In other circumstances
industrial practices may determine migratory patterns if, for instance, particular industries attempt to attract young unmarried

men. In other circumstances, as in Ireland, women have migrated from country to city more than men, or, as in the New England mills, to take specific jobs.[27] Thus the sexual distribution of migrants probably related quite closely to specific situations. Wherever migration is studied, however, home ownership has a settling effect, a conclusion which applies to both past and present.[28]

The discussion of the class origins of migrants is not especially consistent. Usually class has been measured by occupation, which this book shows to be an imprecise indicator for times past, and most studies report rather small differences in the rates of migration for various occupational groups. In contemporary society it appears that white-collar workers move from place to place (as opposed to moving within the same city or town) more frequently than do manual workers. Although the contemporary working class seems more, or at least not less, rooted than the middle class, historical studies of nineteenth-century places prior to industrialization show an opposite pattern: there it was the semiskilled and unskilled manual workers who moved more frequently than men in more rewarding and prestigous callings.[29] Part of the explanation for this difference rests, undoubtedly, on the nature of job opportunities and the labor market, which today has become quite national for certain categories of workers, such as computer technicians, professors, and business executives. At present it may be that the ability to locate a satisfactory job prior to moving has become a critical factor and that it is easier for a professor or executive from one city to find a job in another than it is for a factory worker. In a similar fashion, and contrary to what historians find in nineteenth-century America, Gareth Stedman Jones explains how the imperatives of the labor market in late-nineteenth-century London trapped workers within particular sections of the city.[30]

Similarly to social class, little that is definitive can be said about the migratory experience of different ethnic groups in past times. Stephan Thernstrom has argued convincingly that the conventional historical image of ethnic groups huddled together in ghettoes and relatively immobile must be revised. Immigrants of various national origins and their children moved no less frequently than natives, and the amazing population mobility within nineteenth-century society was both a native and an immigrant phenomenon.[31] Nonetheless, the precise differences in the mobility rates and patterns of different ethnic groups remain unknown.

Contemporary studies show migrants on the whole to be better educated and more intelligent (as measured by tests) than the average person in the population from which they come. And there are some indications that in the past migrants were more literate as well. As one historian has observed, this is little more than a restatement of the old notion that the more ambitious and energetic young men went off to seek their fortunes. Still, its implications for the study of nineteenth-century North American society are important; for at that time commentators hostile to immigrants fostered the notion of illiterate peasant hordes, the dregs of the Old World, descending upon the North American continent. If it should be the case that the more able and energetic members of European societies migrated, then these critics were wrong, and Canada and the United States received continual infusions of select populations. Of course, once again a distinction must be made between types of migration. The more ambitious and able young men on European or rural North American farms may have left for the city in search of opportunity while the least able laborers may have drifted from city to city unable to hold any one job for very long. It would be odd indeed if the propensity of various sorts of people to migrate was unaffected by the distance and direction of the move, by the conditions in which they lived, and by their experience of success or failure. Thus no theory of migration which does not account for the context in which movement takes place can capture the complexity of the process as it actually exists. It may be possible, ultimately, to specify the kinds of conditions in which the more or less able members of a population are likely to migrate, but it is unlikely that any general statements about the ability of migrants will be valid for all circumstances.[32]

The motivation behind migration remains an elusive issue. Most contemporary students probably would agree on the inadequacy of economic explanations which assume a "rational man" acting to maximize his return. Certainly, personal and social factors—such as housing, the quality of schools, the nature of life style, and so on—play an enormous role in the decision to move, and probably always have. Some students of the subject, like Julian Wolpert, rejecting simplistic economic explanations, have tried to construct behavioral models, but their models operate at a fairly high level of abstraction. The historian will probably feel easier with the superb attempt to discover and describe the motives of migrants by Charlotte Erickson, in her book *Invisible Immigrants,* which in part argues that Scottish and English immigrants following different occupations came to the New World for subtly different reasons. The purest economic motives were to be found among farmers, who, seeking to overcome their "discontent arising out of economic ambition," bought farms in America. Industrial workers who sought farms, on the other hand, stressed independence more than any other factor (as did Wilson Benson): "gaining a livelihood without having to work for, or take orders from, anyone, be he employer or landlord." To some men independence meant as well the ownership of land; to all it meant "freedom from an authority or master." Artisans came not so much to escape from a job as to avoid changing their trade; they left not pushed by impoverishment but attracted by the opportunity for economic advancement and the prospect of their own house and garden. They were, interestingly, the most politically conscious of the immigrants that Erickson studied. Unlike other groups, clerical workers subordinated economic reasons to personal, family, and status concerns when they migrated, and, in contrast to all the others, they completely sundered family ties when they departed from England and Scotland.[33]

Whatever their motivation, one characteristic shared by many migrants has been their propensity to move frequently. For historical and contemporary studies both point to the prevalence of recurrent migration. Within many populations there have been, it would seem, two clusters of people: the relatively stable, and the transient. For example, Sidney Goldstein, summarizing some of the findings of his Norristown study, wrote:

> From the point of view of the significance of migration to cultural and social change, these data suggest that it might be desirable to distinguish in our population between the continuous residents and the repeated migrants: those who tend to remain stationary in locality and those who make repeated moves from one place of residence to another. The fact that the out-migrants from a com-

munity tend to be the in-migrants of an earlier year suggests that despite a high migration rate, continuous residents constitute a core population group which gives stability to what otherwise might be a highly unstable social organization.[34]

T. H. Hollingsworth, reviewing migration studies for the benefit of historians, makes the same point, and adds its implication for the determination of rates of population mobility: "Migrants go to a town but often do not stay there long. When they move again, quite often they go back to where they first came from. This means that measuring migration rates over ten years gives us much lower rates than if we measured them over five years. Taking just a single year would give a still higher annual migration rate."[35] Hollingsworth might have been writing about Wilson Benson, about the people of Boston, Massachusetts, or about those in Hamilton, Ontario, for that matter.

The difficulty of agreeing upon a standard measure for the rate of migration and of securing comparable data across a long period of time make especially hard the comparison of rates of mobility between either places or dates. Thus the historical rhythm of migration and its relation to major social changes such as industrialization remains obscure. Evidence compiled by Thernstrom from his own and other studies raises the possibility that the high rate of geographic mobility in the mid-nineteenth century tapered off gradually until, roughly, the period after the First World War, when it began to increase once again. Sidney Goldstein's work on Norristown, on the other hand, shows a decrease in geographic mobility from about 1910 to 1950.[36] The problem with assessing this evidence is twofold. First, it is not based on a comparison of representative places but on ones that just happened to be studied. Second, the studies of mobility have used different data sources and different methods of record linkage, that is, of determining whether a person present at one point in time was still there at some later date. Recent research shows quite decisively that both the nature of the sources and the techniques of record linkage dramatically affect the mobility rates that one discovers.[37] Thus it is difficult to know exactly how much weight can be placed upon the comparative analysis of various studies. If in fact additional research does support the pattern that these studies cumulatively show, it will present a powerful and important hypothesis about the relationship between geographic mobility and industrialization, namely, that migration decreased with industrialization until the integration of national labor markets and mass communications developed sufficiently to overcome the stabilizing force exerted by mechanization, the shift of work setting to the factory, and bureaucratic organization.

Although the historical rhythm of geographic mobility remains unclear, one fact has been established. The internal movement from place to place within past societies was astonishingly high, a conclusion which holds for a varied collection of places throughout a long span of time. For it was not an urban phenomenon, or one restricted to the nineteenth century, or one limited to Anglo-Saxon countries. In a recent paper Roger Schofield, for instance, points to the high mobility rates within preindustrial English villages. In one of these in which he studied the eighteenth century, 61 percent of the people present at one time could not be found a decade later; one third had died, the rest had left. Similarly, two Swedish scholars have reported: "Recent studies of Swedish agricultural communities in the 19th and early 20th centuries indicate a substantial internal migration, and it appears that at least some areas in the agricultural sector had astonishingly high mobility rates." David Gagan, likewise, in a study of rural society in nineteenth-century Ontario has been discovering rates of population mobility comparable to those claimed for urban areas. For the period under consideration here Thernstrom has compiled the figures from published American studies he considers reliable. Although there are no comparable Canadian studies, there is no reason to expect that in this area there would be much difference between the two societies in the mid-nineteenth century. For the years 1850–1860 the proportion of population persistence (the number of adult males apparently present in the same place at both ends of the decade) was 39 percent for Boston, 32 percent for Philadelphia, 40 percent for Waltham, and 53 percent for Northampton.[38] The rate for Hamilton, Canada West, was between 35 and 40 percent, depending upon the way deaths are considered. This similarity, of course, adds some weight to the claim made in this book that Hamilton was a reasonably representative mid-nineteenth-century city.

Within Hamilton not only the dimensions of transiency but the distinctions between transients and persisters reflected in a general way what other studies of migration have discovered. The analysis of transiency in this chapter uses four sources: the assessment of 1852, the census of 1851, the assessment of 1861, and the census of 1861. These four sources, in turn, provide four different populations:

(1) people linked from the assessment of 1852 to the census of 1851;

(2) people linked from the assessment of 1861 to the census of 1861;

(3) people linked from the census of 1851 to the census of 1861;

(4) people linked across all four sources.

In the pages that follow I shall refer to each of these populations at various points, calling the people linked between any two of them "persisters" and those unlinked "transients." The accuracy with which those labels can be applied depends not only on the completeness of the sources and the care with which they are coded for analysis but on the process of searching for the same people on two or more sources and the way in which their identity is determined. That process, known as historical record linkage, is emerging as a field of study of enormous theoretical and practical complexity.[39] There is little need to dwell on the process here except to emphasize the obvious point that the method of record linkage which is used directly affects the rates of persistence that are found. The rules by which two people listed on different sources are compared determine the identity of persisters and transients. And, as Ian Winchester has made clear, those rules are set in each case by the researcher, who must make choices among a variety of alternatives. Thus, it is vitally important for scholars publishing work based on record linkage to specify the rules they have followed. In this way others can replicate either their study or their procedures, something essential to comparative work. For if historians are to compare the degree to which people persisted in Hamilton and Boston, they must use rates which have been determined in the same way. The point may seem elementary, but it is not. As of this writing I know of no published study in the English language in which the techniques and rules used to link records have been specified in a way that permits another scholar to use the same ones in his work. This situation soon will be altered by the publication of work in progress. But it does mean that none of the studies published to date can be compared with one another in any but the most general way. The differences between rates of persistence compiled by Thernstrom, for instance, might all be accounted for by differences in techniques of record linkage, or, on the other hand, they might be real. There is no way of resolving that question at present.

Thus far in this study a variety of techniques of record linkage have been used. To join the census of 1851 and the assessment of 1852, the first record linkage task, an intelligent research assistant thoroughly familiar with the data simply began working by hand and employing his intuitive judgment. Ian Winchester then used this hand linkage as the basis for studying the problems encountered in the process, devising with that information an automated technique with which the linkage was replicated. The census of 1861 and assessment of 1861 were joined by a semi-automated technique, which is described in Appendix Three. The census of 1851 and 1861 and the four-way linkage were done with a fully automated technique. At that time, since we lacked the data with which to make proper estimates of probability, such as that described by Ian Winchester, we developed by trial and error an additive weighting system, which is listed in the same appendix. Our methods are not infallible, and they may not have achieved the best possible results, but any scholar can link his own data by using our rules and can achieve results which, at the least, may be compared to ours with some confidence.

Generally speaking, historians have considered the rate of persistence to be the percentage of a population that can be linked from one source to another compiled later in time. This is an inadequate measure, as only a little observation will show. It neglects to correct, first of all, for death rate; secondly, for errors in census taking or those ambiguities in the data that make linkage impossible; or, third, for human errors in coding the material. In the case of the census-to-census linkage reported in this chapter many women have been missed because of name changes after marriage. As of yet, no one has devised a systematic way of correcting persistence figures for these sources of error. It will be easiest to establish death rates, but we do not know, for instance, if transients and persisters had the same death rates, or if people who died within the city should be considered potential persisters. Nor is it even clear whether the sex ratios among transients and persisters were the same. Aside from Peter Knights, no one has tried to measure the underenumeration in nineteenth-century censuses, nor is there any way as yet of estimating the margin of error due to incorrect enumeration and ambiguity. The point of these remarks is not to undercut what follows but to emphasize that the persistence figures given here, even those derived from careful linkage procedures, should be considered estimates which probably overstate the amount of transiency. It would be surprising if that overstatement were much more than 10 percent, and in fact it may be a good deal less. None of the necessary corrections, therefore, will alter the fact that transiency was a major characteristic of nineteenth-century society. The rate of persistence, as Hollingsworth emphasized in the passage quoted earlier, is by no means the same thing as the rate of total population movement. Thernstrom and Knights have shown quite conclusively that the amount of movement into and out of a nineteenth-century city during the course of a year likely equaled the total population that could be found there at any one moment. Thus the amount of population movement during a decade was actually very much larger than the rate of transiency measured by studying only the two ends of a decade.[40]

Of all the males in Hamilton in 1851, 31.3 percent appeared on the census ten years later, compared to only 28 percent of the females, a figure artificially low because of name change upon marriage, as Table 3.3 indicates. If the sex ratios among transients and persisters were identical, the rate of persistence should be increased about 5 percent to 33 percent. Thus a minimum of about one third of the population remained alive and living in the city at the end of a decade. Household heads, as might be expected, persisted rather more than the population as a whole: 35.3 percent of those present in 1851 were found on the 1861 census. Taking the percentage of married women who had become widows as a surrogate for deaths among household heads, the percentage of persistent households becomes 44 percent; if all these household heads had lived and remained within the city, the percentage of persistence for household heads could have been raised a maximum of 7 or 8 percent. It is unlikely, however, that all would

TABLE 3.3 Dimensions of persistence, 1851–1861

	Number (N) in 1851	Number (N) persistent to 1861	Percent persistent
Males	6792	2124	31.3
Females	6838	1914[a]	28.0[a]
		2279[b]	33.3[b]
Household heads (HH)	2484	878	35.3
Surviving households[c]	2335	1027	44.0

[a] All linked.

[b] Corrected to make linked population have same sex ratio, assuming (a) understatement of females in linked population due to loss through marriage and (b) identical sex ratios for linked and unlinked populations:

$$\frac{\text{N Males 1861}}{\text{N Females 1861}} = \frac{\text{N Males linked}}{\text{N Females linked}}$$

$$\frac{9180}{9848} = \frac{2124}{X}; \quad X = 2279$$

[c] Surviving households $= \dfrac{\text{N Households 1851} - \text{N Widows of 1851 HH located in 1861}}{\text{N HH linked 1851 to 1861} + \text{N Widows of 1851 HH located in 1861}}$

have remained, and it is thus fairly safe to assume that the rate of persistence of living household heads would be about 40 percent. Although this is higher than the rate among males generally, it is not a great deal higher, a fact which points to the existence of mass transiency among all sorts of people. Everybody, in short, was on the move. The transiency found in our other short-term linkages was also high: only about 80 percent of the people on the assessment role appeared on the census, a figure approximately the same for each end of the decade, and a finding consistent with the high, rapid population turnover reported for Boston by Thernstrom and Knights.

Although transiency was widespread, it was not entirely fortuitous. Some kinds of people were very much more likely to move than others. First, as with migratory populations in general, the life cycle influenced the decision to move or stay. Young men, as Table 3.4 shows, were definitely the most likely group to leave the city. In 1861, 35.8 percent of the males who had been 6–10-year-olds a decade earlier could be found in the city, compared to 27.6 percent of the 11–15-year-olds, 22.8 percent of the 16–20-year-olds, and 23.9 percent of the 21–25-year-olds. After the age of twenty-five, persistence increased: 32.4 percent of the 26–30-year-olds of 1851 remained in the city in 1861, which is especially interesting since the mean age of marriage for men was twenty-seven. (These figures omit women because of the unreliability of the persistence rates for them, especially at these ages, when most marriages would have occurred.)

People who had established families—married household heads or wives—remained in the city more often than other groups of people. Table 3.5 shows that of the persisters, 40.5 percent, compared to 26.5 percent of the transients, were married in 1851. Among the persisters there were almost 50 percent more household heads and almost 100 percent more wives than among the transients. Conversely, as would be expected, a much lower percentage of boarders and servants persisted, a fact consistent with the rates for different age groups since most boarders and servants were in their late teens or early twenties. Among household heads themselves, those with more complex families were somewhat less likely to move; that is, persisters rather more often than transients had children, boarders, relatives, and servants. Though these differ-

TABLE 3.4 Male persistence by age, 1851–1861

Age groups, 1851	Number in 1851	Number persistent to 1861	Percent persistent
1–5	1109	380	34.3
6–10	825	295	35.8
11–15	720	199	27.6
16–20	754	172	22.8
21–25	725	173	23.9
26–30	726	235	32.4
31–40	1006	354	35.2
41–50	567	195	34.4
51–60	238	90	37.8
61 and over	133	31	23.3

TABLE 3.5 Percentages of persistence and transiency
by household and marital status, 1851–1861

Household and marital status, 1851	Percent persistent (linked)	Percent transient (unlinked)
Household status		
Head	21.7	14.6
Wife	19.8	11.0
Child	44.1	39.9
Relative	3.3	5.0
Boarder	8.7	18.9
Servant	2.3	9.8
Other	0.1	0.8
Number	(4038)	(9592)
Marital status		
Single	55.8	68.5
Married	40.5	26.5
Widowed	3.7	5.0
Sex of household head		
Male	94.6	88.4
Female	5.4	11.6
Characteristics of household		
Child	80.7	77.3
Boarder	31.7	27.3
Relative	16.2	14.2
Boarder or relative	42.0	37.3
Servant	35.6	27.0

ences are consistent, they are not, with the exception of servants, especially large: 31.7 percent of persisting household heads had boarders living with them compared to 27.3 percent of transients; 80.7 percent had at least one child compared to 77.3 percent of transients; 16.2 percent had one or more relatives compared to 14.2 percent of those who left; while 35.6 percent of the household heads who stayed had a resident servant compared to 27 percent of those who left.

Clearly, the life cycle, reflected in age and household status, exerted an independent influence on persistence. The same cannot be said for ethnicity, which, according to Table 3.6, exerted no independent influence whatsoever. Certainly, there were fewer

TABLE 3.6 Demographic characteristics of differently linked groups, 1851–1861

Demographic characteristics	Population, census 1851		Linked census to census		Four-way link		Household heads linked census to census[a]	
	Number	Percent	Number	Percent	Number	Percent	Number	Percent
Birthplace								
England	1551	16.1	733	18.2	201	30.1	328	26.5
Scotland	892	9.2	420	10.4	131	19.6	220	17.8
Ireland	3417	35.4	1177	29.1	214	32.1	468	37.8
French Canada	46	0.5	10	0.2	4	0.6	4	0.3
Canada West	2904	30.1	1438	35.6	57	8.5	122	9.9
U.S.A.	560	5.6	194	4.8	49	7.3	74	7.3
Religion								
Anglican	2166	22.5	1057	26.2	178	26.7	313	25.3
Ch. of Scotland	227	2.4	138	3.4	22	3.3	43	3.5
Catholic	3015	31.3	948	23.5	104	15.6	292	23.6
Free Ch. Presbyt.	264	2.7	186	4.6	32	4.8	59	4.8
Presbyterian	846	8.8	418	10.4	76	11.4	124	10.0
Wesleyan Methodist	416	4.3	201	5.0	34	5.1	56	4.7
Methodist	838	8.7	375	9.3	74	11.4	115	9.3
Baptist	280	2.9	140	3.5	30	4.5	47	3.8
"Protestant"	1007	10.4	381	9.4	81	12.1	124	10.8
Sex								
Male	4705	48.8	2124	52.6	636	95.4	1052	85.0
Female	4940	51.2	1914	47.4	31	4.6	185	15.0
Race								
White	9508	98.6	3993	98.9	657	98.5	1218	98.5
Black	137	1.4	45	1.1	10	1.5	19	1.5

[a] All people with status of household head in 1861.

Irish persisters (29.1 percent) than there were Irish among the population as a whole (35.4 percent), as well as fewer Catholics (23.5 percent compared to 31.3 percent). Similarly, there were a few more English (18.2 percent) and Anglicans (26.2 percent) than among the population as a whole (16.1 percent and 22.5 percent respectively), and more native Canadians, 35.6 percent, than in the entire population, where there were 30.1 percent. All ethnic groups, it is abundantly clear, were on the move to a roughly similar extent. Although ethnicity may have influenced persistence through the propensity of poor Irishmen to buy houses, the differences between ethnic groups paralleled their varied economic status; undoubtedly their wealth, rather than any independent cultural factor, most often accounted for the small ethnic differential in the tendency to remain within the city.

The relation between wealth and transiency, however, was not simple. Tables 3.7A and 3.7B compare the wealth of linked people (persisters) and unlinked people (transients) on the census and assessment of the 1850s with those on the census and assessment of the 1860s. In each year comparable proportions of people apparently left the city in the three months between the compiling of the census and of the assessment, and in each year the transients followed occupations of every rank. In 1851, however, as Chapter One has already shown, the wealth of transients within each occupation was lower than the wealth of persisters. In 1861 the situation differed: the mean total assessed wealth of short-term transients and persisters was quite close: $189.90 for persisters and $206.50 for transients. This difference, moreover, remained quite consistent through almost all occupations, which points to the possible mediation of the relation between transiency and wealth by economic conditions. In the boom-like prosperity of the early 1850s the more ambitious and successful people stayed more frequently in the same place, sensing that conditions favored making money by settling down. In the depression of the late 1850s, however, the more aggressive and energetic people may have felt that opportunities had become limited where they were and set out in search of new ones, while more timid individuals, frightened by economic instability, clung to what little they had. This, certainly, is sheer speculation, but it is a hypothesis worth pursuing.[41]

Across the decade as a whole wealthier people were more likely

TABLE 3.7A Wealth and home ownership, by occupation, of people linked and unlinked from census to assessment, 1851–52 and 1861

Occupation[a]	1851–52				1861			
	Linked		Unlinked		Linked		Unlinked	
	Mean assessed wealth (£)	Number	Mean assessed wealth (£)	Number	Mean assessed wealth ($)	Number	Mean assessed wealth ($)	Number
Group 1	155.7	231	118.4	21	739.50	221	792.00	80
2	43.6	283	13.1	34	274.40	341	198.20	119
3	24.4	702	13.2	45	116.70	826	113.20	171
4	21.3	83	43.7	3	66.40	126	46.90	19
5	10.0	263	8.4	42	32.40	473	36.20	153
Others	32.8	392	34.2	46	190.30	579	204.60	448
All	42.3	1954	29.2	191	189.90	2566	206.50	990
	Percent home owners				Percent home owners			
Group 1	45.9		28.5		38.1		22.6	
2	20.7		8.8		24.1		4.4	
3	32.3		13.4		36.1		18.5	
4	30.1		0.0		29.8		11.8	
5	23.2		4.8		14.9		8.6	
Others	29.6		13.0		28.3		11.3	
All	30.4		12.0		28.7		12.4	

	Percent poor	Percent well-to-do	Percent poor	Percent well-to-do	Percent poor	Percent well-to-do	Percent poor	Percent well-to-do
Group 1	2.9	62.3	33.3	52.4	5.0	61.6	6.3	55.1
2	25.1	29.7	73.5	8.8	8.8	36.7	27.7	24.4
3	31.8	13.3	62.2	4.4	37.4	14.2	49.2	12.9
4	42.2	14.4	33.3	33.3	63.2	7.2	63.2	0.0
5	74.9	2.3	93.8	2.4	82.3	0.8	86.3	1.4
Others	36.2	18.9	65.2	10.9	34.5	20.2	36.6	24.4
All	34.6	21.1	65.4	11.9	38.9	19.9	43.4	20.7

Percent in occupational group

Group 1	11.8	11.0	8.0	8.1
2	14.5	17.8	12.4	12.0
3	35.9	23.6	30.1	17.3
4	4.2	1.6	4.6	1.9
5	13.5	22.0	17.2	15.5
Others	20.1	24.1	27.6	45.3
All	100.0	100.1	99.9	100.1

a Categories used in five-cities project.

TABLE 3.7B Percentage of people linked and unlinked from
census to assessment, 1861 only, by religion,
birthplace, and household characteristics[a]

Personal and household characteristics	Linked	Unlinked
Religion		
Anglican	30.3%	28.4%
Church of Scotland	8.6	8.0
Catholic	21.8	32.9
Free Church Presbyterian	9.7	8.4
Presbyterian	6.7	4.5
Wesleyan Methodist	13.1	10.1
Birthplace		
England	26.9	19.4
Scotland	20.5	17.1
Ireland	31.9	40.8
Canada West	8.7	8.2
U.S.A.	6.6	6.4
Household characteristics		
Female-headed	10.6	26.4
Headed by widow or widower	13.4	25.0
One or more boarders	21.6	15.4
One or more boarders or relatives	32.6	30.9
Servants	23.2	12.0
Relatives	15.8	17.9
Children	3.1	2.1
Total number of people	(2746)	(764)
Percentage of all people	78.0	22.0

[a] The mean age of persisters (linked) was 41.5; that of transients
(unlinked) was 41.0.

to persist within the city. According to Table 3.8, the rate of
persistence increased in a linear fashion with each economic rank:
from 34.8 percent to 42.8 percent to 47.9 percent to 52.7 percent.
Nonetheless, although the affluent were more likely to remain, the
proportion of persisters among them differed by only 18 percent
from the proportion of persisters among the poor. Thus wealth,
although important, accounted for only part of the difference
between those who moved and those who stayed, less, probably,
than did property ownership.

TABLE 3.8 Persistence of household heads by wealth, 1851–1861

| Economic rank | All linked from census '51 to assessment '52 | | All linked four-ways | | Persistence |
	Number	Percent	Number	Percent	Percent
0–39 percentile	411	26.1	143	21.5	34.8
40–79 percentile	780	49.7	334	50.1	42.8
80–89 percentile	194	12.4	93	13.9	47.9
90–100 percentile	184	11.8	97	14.5	52.7

Home ownership exerted an enormous influence on persistence. This hardly should be surprising for it is consistent with contemporary patterns of migration. As the figures on the relation between home ownership and persistence given in the last chapter showed, the persisters in each three-month period between the taking of the census and of the assessment were about two and a half times more likely to own their own homes than were the transients. Table 3.9 points out (lines 10 and 11) that of all the

TABLE 3.9 Home ownership and persistence, 1851–1861

Categories of home ownership and persistence	Number	Percent
(1) Household heads linked from 1851 census to 1852 assessment	1569	80.3
(2) Home owners among (1)	537	34.2
(3) Persisters among (2)	270	50.3
(4) Renters among (1)	1032	65.8
(5) Persisters among (4)	355	34.4
(6) Home ownership in 1851 among persisters to 1861	117	43.2
(7) Home ownership in 1861 among persisters from 1851	145	53.8
(8) Home ownership among all household heads linked from 1861 census to 1861 assessment	773	28.2
(9) Home owners in 1851 among home owners of 1861	270	34.9
(10) Persistence since 1851 of 1861 home owners	335	43.3
(11) Persistence since 1851 of 1861 renters	232	11.8

home owners in the city in 1861, 43.3 percent had been there a decade earlier, compared to 11.8 percent of the people who rented. Clearly, home ownership exerted more influence on persistence than any other factor. In fact, it was in some senses equivalent, for undoubtedly the decision to buy a house very often represented a commitment to remain within the city.

Occupation is no help in estimating the probability with which any given person might remain in Hamilton. Like ethnicity it exerted almost no independent effect, and, as Table 3.10 shows, there was virtually no pattern in the differing rates of persistence among people in the common occupations. Plasterers persisted most frequently, followed by lawyers. Laborers were exactly average, coming thirteenth in a list of twenty-seven occupations. Physicians, on the other hand, were twentieth on the list, and clergymen tied with tinsmiths for twenty-second place. Quite obviously, other factors—life cycle, wealth, and home ownership—acted through occupation to determine the rate of persistence among people in any trade or profession.

Two kinds of conclusions emerge from the statistics of persistence. First, of the major structural dimensions along which the population could be divided, wealth and life cycle but not ethnicity acted independently upon persistence. Young unmarried people and people with no children and less complex households moved more frequently than others. Wealthier people were also less likely to move. To a considerable extent these factors exercised their influence through their impact upon the decision of people to buy property, which was the single most important way in which transients and persisters differed.

Second, despite the differences between transients and persisters, *every* type of person apparently moved. The transients within nineteenth-century society were not solely the poor and propertyless or the young. To a striking extent people of all ages and conditions were on the move. Thernstrom and Knights have called nineteenth-century people "men in motion," and they are correct, except that women should be added to their phrase. The question that remains is what impact transiency had upon the places through which people passed, or upon the pattern of their lives.

Little is known about the way in which the migratory experiences of nineteenth-century people intersected with their success

TABLE 3.10 Persistence by occupation, 1851–1861

Rank	Occupation[a]	Number in 1851	Percent persistent to 1861
1	Plasterer	28	71.4
2	Lawyer	37	59.5
3	Porter	33	42.4
4	Carpenter	147	41.7
5	Innkeeper	41	41.5
6	Merchant	93	39.8
7	Grocer	39	38.5
8	Mason	58	37.9
9	Painter	53	37.7
10	Gentleman	79	36.7
11	Molder	57	35.1
12	Tailor	146	34.9
13	Laborer	718	34.2
14	Baker	39	33.3
15	Shoemaker	209	32.1
16	Clerk	230	27.8
17–18	{ Carriage maker	47	27.7
	{ Cabinetmaker	65	27.7
19	Stone cutter	40	27.5
20	Physician	26	26.9
21	Teamster	83	22.9
22–23	{ Tinsmith	69	21.7
	{ Clergyman	23	21.7
24	Printer	53	20.8
25	Servant (male)	107	17.8
26	Blacksmith	121	15.7
27	Dressmaker or milliner	103	13.6

[a] Includes all occupations in which ten or more people were linked between 1851 and 1861, plus physician and clergyman.

or failure in either a temporal or a causal fashion. And yet this is critical for interpreting the statistics of social mobility for the people who remained within any one community over time, a problem which will be considered later. From another perspective, however, transiency affected the opportunity for social advancement within individual communities. The departure from cities of people in all occupational and economic ranks meant that spaces existed at all social levels. Although the proportion of the population engaged in various sorts of work, the proportion in various occupational ranks, and the distribution of wealth remained about the same—although the shape of the stratification system and the degree of inequality did not alter very much— transiency loosened the social structure and counterbalanced the tendency toward rigidity within the social system. By leaving the city in such substantial proportions people at all occupational and economic levels created vacancies: room at the top, middle, and bottom of the rank order. In fact, in Hamilton enough people entered various sorts of work to keep the proportions about the same across one decade. The question becomes, then, to what extent the people within the city seized the opportunities created by transiency.

If the rate of upward occupational mobility had been high, part of the reason undoubtedly would have been the existence of an exceptional number of opportunities. But the converse would not be true. Individuals would not have been hampered by a lack of desirable places but by other causes, such as social and ethnic origin, or lack of education, capital, or ability. Transiency, thus, created openings in what otherwise could have been a relatively closed system. Whether those openings were entered by people already within the city or by newcomers is a critical question. For it partially defines the extent to which social characteristics, especially class and ethnicity, operated as barriers to individual advancement relatively independently of the structure of opportunity.

The degree to which people improve their standing can be taken as one indicator of the "openness" of a social system. It provides insight into the extent to which talent, hard work, or other deserving qualities find reward, or, to put it conversely, the degree to which inherited social advantages determine individual experiences. The degree of openness is one dimension along which societies usually can be thought to differ. Whether, in fact, traditional images of the relative lack of openness in European as contrasted to North American societies are valid remains a very live question. Despite the differences in the political systems and cultures of industrialized countries, S. M. Lipset and Reinhard Bendix have argued in a very influential book that the rate of

social mobility within them is more or less the same, though more
recently Peter Blau and Otis Dudley Duncan in their major work,
The American Occupational Structure, have disagreed with that
position to some extent.[42] The data with which to make comparisons about the differential openness of contemporary societies are
hard to compile. But even more complex and problematic is the
effort to compare societies, including the same society, across any
substantial span of time. Nevertheless, a comparative question lies
at the core of many mobility studies: has society become more or
less open over time? In part, the question is of theoretical importance for understanding the effects of modernization. In part,
though, it is also a political question central to the evaluation of
qualitative changes in social experience and the policies which
have produced them.

Whatever the actual curve of social mobility has been over time,
it is doubtful if the real situation has mattered as much as what
people believed it to be at any moment. The existence of nearly
unlimited opportunities for upward social mobility, as many commentators have pointed out, has been part of the American dream.
And it is this expectation of mobility, in one line of argument,
that has kept the American working class committed to a capitalist
social system, retarding the development of socialism in America.[43]
Has it been, then, the existence of an *ideology* of mobility that
has kept American workers capitalist in contrast to their counterparts in much of the rest of the world? The question, obviously,
can only be answered through comparative analysis, difficult and
fraught with methodological danger though it is. If in fact it
should be the case that rates of social mobility appear to have
been lower in Canada and in European countries than in America,
how much of the difference in political history would that fact
explain? The question, obviously, cannot be answered here; nonetheless, it frames the attempt to discover patterns of mobility in
individual communities. The historical study of social mobility
becomes, thus, in part an attempt to discover the extent to which
one especially important social process has shaped political culture.

The impetus to work in the area of historical social mobility
has come, of course, from American scholars, who have shown
the greatest interest in the topic. In their work, it should be
pointed out, social mobility often has become synonymous with

individual mobility. Nowhere, perhaps, is there a more obvious fit
between national ideology and scholarly preoccupation, even
among scholars of the Left. Although the American concern with
"making it" has inspired some of the most exciting and creative
historical work in decades, it sometimes has obscured the equally
important—and in terms of social justice probably more important—question of stratum mobility, that is, of the relative position
of social groups (defined by ethnicity, class, or some other attribute) over time. Put another way, the work has concentrated
more on the fate of individuals than on the nature and degree of
inequality. In fact, much of the work on social mobility has lacked
a sufficiently developed concern with social structure, for scholars
began to measure mobility before they had acquired any precise
understanding of the social structure in which mobility occurred.
This problem, which Blau and Duncan also point to as a feature
of contemporary mobility research, came partly from the easy
assumption with which most of us working in the area began:
namely, that the shape of past and present societies and the terms
in which they could be comprehended were not all that dissimilar.
It has taken some time to shake that assumption out of the minds
of historians, to question, for instance, the validity of the distinction between manual and nonmanual work in societies prior to
industrialization.[44]

The system of social stratification in nineteenth-century cities is
far from self-evident, as this book shows. Consequently, the question of exactly what constitutes social mobility deserves far more
attention than it has received. Social mobility, however, forms only
one aspect of a social system, and its importance can be exaggerated. It would seem more appropriate, especially at this stage
of research, to include mobility as one aspect of a research design
exploring stratification, rather than as the primary focus for research. Otherwise, an overemphasis on individual mobility might
deflect attention from both other dimensions of social structure
and other varieties of life experience. Although Americans are
peculiarly preoccupied with individual success, the mobility experience of a population is only one aspect of the many dimensions
of life that may be studied historically. The point sounds almost
trivial, but it requires emphasis. It cannot be assumed that individual social mobility formed the central life experience and

preoccupation of nineteenth-century people. Their geographic mobility may have been equally central to their lives and equally important in the dynamics of their society. At the same time, the relative improvement or deterioration in the position and living standards of different social strata may have had greater impact on the history of society than the movements of the marginal individuals who changed rank. Finally, reconstituting the life histories of individual people allows one to plot not only their occupational and economic experience but other dimensions of their lives as well, most notably their life cycle and domestic relations. For the most part the work in social structural history has paid little attention to these aspects of experience, while the students of family have paid too little regard to social structure.[45] The obvious direction for future research, which this book attempts to follow, is to join the two, showing their interconnections and their implications for individuals and for social development.

The purpose of these remarks has not been to argue against the study of social mobility but to urge that it not be made an exclusive topic of study; that it be studied in the context of social structure broadly conceived; and that the study of nineteenth-century people and places attempt to recapture the varieties of experience which were typical of the times.

This chapter considers individual social mobility in terms of the city's social structure. Chapter Two, which outlined the persistent dimensions of inequality, discussed, in effect, the question of stratum mobility. In many ways the discussion of individual mobility is incomplete, for a number of additional analyses could be made from the data at hand. Here I have surveyed the data on mobility in a preliminary fashion. The obvious importance of this survey and its relevance to the themes of the book overcame my hesitations about its preliminary character, and I consequently decided to include it. But, even more than the other sections of the book, this discussion of social mobility should be regarded as a progress report rather than a finished analysis.

The analysis of the mobility data develops arguments of two types, methodological and substantive. Although the two are not completely distinct, they can be distinguished in a general way.

Methodologically, this chapter illustrates the four dimensions along which social mobility may be measured and shows that the movements along each of them are not parallel. The amount of mobility revealed by each measure differs, and the relation among the measures is imperfect. Of the four—occupation, economic rank, servants, and property ownership—economic rank appears the most discriminating and useful. But the ideal measure of mobility would be an index that incorporated all four.

Substantively, the chapter makes a number of assertions. First, the social structure of the city may be pictured as a continuum with three rather large bulges at which people were relatively stuck, with transitional areas between. Second, most social mobility was extremely short in distance. Third, the amounts of upward and downward social mobility were more or less equivalent. Fourth, the amount of social mobility, especially when measured by wealth, was quite large. Fifth, among the poorer part of the population, the acquisition of property often preceded upward social mobility. Sixth, mobility affected age and ethnicity: youth was least stable in terms of social and economic position, and old age was frequently a time of downward mobility. As for ethnicity, the Irish, both Catholic and Protestant, remained stuck at the bottom of the economic and occupational rank orders much more frequently than did other groups. Seventh, occupational inheritance from father to son remained strong, especially among artisans, although it decreased as sons began to shift into clerical work and out of declining crafts. The sons of low-ranking fathers who were not Irish frequently moved upwards, but the sons of Irish Catholics inherited their fathers' low positions.

The data to be presented on social mobility concern two differently linked groups: the men linked from census to census (the two-way link), and the men linked from assessment to census in 1851 joined to those linked from assessment to census in 1861 (the four-way link). The analysis of social mobility, unfortunately, must be restricted to men until complete marriage information can be added to the file. Furthermore, the study of social mobility proceeds with a biased sample of the total population, skewed slightly toward wealthier, property-owning men with relatively large families. There is no way to determine whether the social-mobility experience of poor, propertyless, Irish Catholic laborers with two children who remained in the city was identical to that of men with the same characteristics who left. This is the central limitation of these findings, and, indeed, of almost all historical social mobility studies. The only exception is the work of Peter Knights, who traced part of a small sample of native outmigrants from Boston and discovered that their rate of social mobility appeared higher than that of people of similar standing who remained behind; the rate of property acquisition of outmigrants, for instance, was twice that of people who persisted in Boston. Knights' conclusions are consistent with the contemporary findings of Blau and Duncan, who report that migrants of all sorts are more upwardly mobile than comparable men who remain behind, be it on the farm, in a town, or even in the city from which the migrants came.[46] The implication of this finding, if it should be true for the nineteenth century as well (and that of course is an open question), remains ambiguous. From one point of view it would be tempting to infer that the inclusion of the experience of outmigrants would substantially increase the rate of mobility. However, nearly the entire population of Hamilton consisted of migrants: over 90 percent of the adult men had been born outside Canada, and most of the natives within the city had migrated there from somewhere else in Ontario. It is thus possible that the population as a whole was an exceptionally mobile group, and that to correct for the disproportional success of outmigrants it would be necessary to correct as well for the disproportionate success already achieved by the population which remained throughout the decade. The inability to resolve this question remains a fundamental weakness in the historical study of social mobility.

Aside from the problem of people who leave the city, two important methodological and conceptual difficulties hamper the historical study of social mobility. The first is record-linkage, the process of actually tracing people from one document to another, which has been mentioned already. The other is establishing a scale to measure mobility.

Most scales use occupation, but occupational classification remains a difficult issue, and no fully satisfactory scheme exists. Aside from that, individual occupational titles frequently, in the crafts usually, included people with a wide variety of incomes, statuses, and authority positions. A poor journeyman carpenter might have become a wealthy self-employed carpenter with a shop and several employees, but he would still be called, most likely, a carpenter. Would historians then be happy with the conclusion that he was socially immobile? I think not, but this would be precisely my conclusion if I relied solely on occupational measures. Some scholars, it should be pointed out, have been able to differentiate between self-employed master craftsmen and journeymen, and this gives their work a great deal more precision. Eventually it may be possible, through the use of directories and the industrial census, to do the same with my data, which would add considerably to the refinement with which I can analyze occupational movement.[47]

After occupation, the next most obvious measure of mobility is economic rank or wealth, which also contains unresolved problems. Wealth, as Thernstrom showed in his initial work in this area, correlated only imperfectly with occupational change in the nineteenth century.[48] By accepting an increase in wealth as an indication of upward mobility, an automatic correlation between wealth and social position is assumed in the minds of people who lived at the time. While this may have been, and probably often was, the case, there is no reason to believe that a perfect association existed in all instances. There are other problems with establishing reliable and comparable measures of wealth or economic rank, though these seem to me rather more tractable than the problem of occupational classification. In this chapter wealth refers to economic rank, and fortunately the Ontario assessment roles provide a far better source for studying wealth than is available to the students of most American communities. I suspect, nonetheless, that there may be more economic records available in American towns and cities than scholars have yet unearthed, and it may be possible to use economic ranking in studies of social structure and mobility more widely than usually has been thought feasible.

A third possible indicator of mobility, and again one found important by Thernstrom, is the acquisition of property. For some relatively poor people the purchase of a home formed an intensely important goal. Property ownership was the most important determinant of persistence within the city, a conclusion supported by Clyde Griffen in his study of Poughkeepsie, New York, in the same period.[49] Thus the purchase or loss of property may have represented a shift in social and economic rank, especially among the poorer and middling ranks of the population.

Finally, one other potential indicator of mid-nineteenth-century social mobility is readily at hand: the employment of one or more resident domestic servants. Following the example of others, I have suggested that it may have been the employment of a resident domestic servant that separated the middle and working classes. Certainly, the employment of servants acts nicely as a surrogate for wealth in the absence of economic information, separating out about a quarter of the population—a proportion then divisible into people with one and more than one servant—which appears clearly different from the rest with respect to wealth, standard of living, and, in part, behavior.[50] Thus, if a man either gains or loses a servant, there exist grounds for at least suspecting that he has changed his rank within society. Only a minority of the households, however, employed a servant at any one time. Hence, although the employment of servants should discriminate within a certain section of the population, it lumps together a large and clearly variegated portion into one indefensibly undifferentiated rank.

The word "rank" as it is used here assumes, in the manner of social mobility studies, the existence within society of an entity that might be called a "socioeconomic ranking," a series of vertically ordered positions rather homogeneous with respect to economic circumstances, social status, and probably power as well. Whereas either occupation, wealth, property, or servants might be taken as an indication of that rank, although the use of each is fraught with dangers and difficulties, the greatest problem arises from the fact that a change of position on one measure of mobility by no means automatically meant a change of position on any of the other three. Thus the problem of which measure to choose as an index, or what combination of measures, remains unsolved. In fact, the existence of a unitary socioeconomic ranking system within this society is itself an open question.

The remainder of this chapter is divided into four sections. The first delineates *intra*-generational mobility on each of the four dimensions considered separately. The second section shows the relations of each measure to the others. The third discusses the

interaction among the measures of mobility and two other principal structural elements within society: the ethnic structure, and
the age structure or life cycle. The final section takes up the
question of the extent to which rank was passed from father to
son, the issue of *inter*generational mobility.

In dealing with the question of occupational mobility I have
used again the five-level classification of 113 occupations, which
represent the vast majority of the employed people in the city,
plus the other occupations in which at least ten males were employed in 1861.[51] I have also added a sixth, residual, unclassifiable
category to take care of pensioners, students, lunatics, handicaps,
people without specific titles, and a few others. At times the
discussion is based on percentages derived from using all the occupations; at other times it represents only those classifiable into
the five levels and not the sixth. Within this occupational classification the second and fourth levels often appear transitional: it
is difficult to establish that a given occupation belongs in one of
them and not immediately above or below. Because a movement
from one of these strata to one adjacent often cannot be called
confidently a change of rank, I have sometimes collapsed one or
two categories, making a scale with either three or four levels. On
the five-level scale the top category consists primarily of merchants
and professionals; the second of clerks, minor public officials, and
smaller proprietors; the third and largest level contains primarily
skilled artisans; the fourth is dominated by semiskilled service
occupations (teamster, carter, porter, and servant); and the fifth
consists of unskilled workers, largely laborers. In the collapsed
categories, four and five are joined to create a stratum of semiskilled and unskilled workers; the first two are also collapsed to
create a rank for professional, commercial, and clerical jobs.

It is true, and troubling, that this occupational classification is
gross and runs counter, in some ways, to the precision for which
I have argued elsewhere.[52] Nevertheless it is, first, as good a scheme
as any available at this time and should command broad general
agreement among historians. Second, it is explicitly a vertical and
not a functional scheme and was developed solely with criteria
of ranking, not similarity of work, in mind. Third, it is used here
with discrimination and skepticism. More importantly, it is compared with ranking on other measures and its limitations con-

sequently highlighted. I believe that the simplest scale, the three-level one, is at once the crudest and the best—best because it is the most conservative. It obscures what may be some real shifts of occupational level, but it does not report many that are not actual changes to an occupation which on this scale has a higher rank. Still, the figures for change are only approximations; they miss some changes and they show others that undoubtedly are artifacts of synonymy. For instance, a man owning a shop which makes and sells shoes and employs several people might in 1851 call himself a shoemaker and in 1861 a merchant or shoe dealer. In either case his rank, even on the three-level scale, would change, but his work and position would remain the same. There is no way, using the same set of rules for all cases, that this situation can be prevented. Because all the figures here are really approximations, all percentages have been rounded; the tables, however, contain figures rounded to one decimal place.

In Table 3.11A, the first table dealing with occupational mobility, the figures in the cells represent the percentage of the people in a given occupational rank in 1851 who were in each occupational rank in 1861. Thus, 70.9 percent of the people in rank 1 in 1851 were in rank 1 in 1861, whereas 14.0 percent of them were in rank 2, and 8.1 percent in rank 3. Table 3.11A indicates that the top group in the occupational hierarchy, rank 1, increased slightly during the decade; in 1861, 15 percent of the working population were at the top compared to 13 percent in 1851. Within ranks 1, 2, 3, and 5 the rate of persistence did not differ very much, varying from 63 percent for rank 2 to 77 percent for rank 3 (primarily artisans). Nearly as stable as the artisans, as might be expected, were the people in the highest category, 71 percent of whom were in the same rank at each end of the decade. The people in group 4, the semiskilled teamsters, carters, porters, and so forth, had a very low rate of stability, only 23 percent remaining in the same rank, with 27 percent moving one rank higher and 21 percent dropping to the bottom. In the entire group, by far the greatest number of mobile men moved to the next rank above or below: for rank 1, this short-distance movement accounted for 85 percent of all changes; for rank 2, 88 percent; for 3, 90 percent; for 4, 71 percent; and for 5, 74 percent. (These last figures are not included in the table.) Thus, whatever

TABLE 3.11 Occupational mobility of people linked four ways, 1851–1861

A. All occupations

Occupational rank, 1861

		1	2	3	4	5	Unclas.	All ranks N	%
	1	70.9%	14.0%	8.1%	2.3%	1.2%	3.5%	86	12.9
Occupa-	2	14.7	62.5	9.6	0.7	5.1	7.4	136	20.4
tional	3	5.2	10.1	77.3	3.1	2.1	2.1	286	42.9
rank,	4	6.3	18.8	27.1	22.9	20.8	4.2	48	7.2
1851	5	0	10.4	15.6	9.1	64.9	0	77	11.5
	Unclas.	5.9	2.9	8.8	5.9	2.9	73.5	34	5.1
All ranks:	N	101	144	269	32	75	46	667	
	%	15.1	21.6	40.3	4.8	11.2	6.9		100.0

B. Classifiable occupations only

Occupational rank, 1861

		1	2	3	4–5	All ranks N	%
Occupa-	1	73.5%	14.5%	8.4%	3.6%	83	13.6
tional	2	15.9	67.5	10.3	6.3	126	20.6
rank,	3	5.4	10.4	78.9	5.4	280	45.8
1851	4–5	2.4	13.8	20.3	63.4	123	20.1
All ranks:	N	99	143	266	104	612	
	%	16.2	23.4	43.5	17.0		100.1

occupational mobility did exist was short-distanced. This pattern of predominantly short-distance mobility appears ubiquitous: Clyde Griffen, for instance, found it in Poughkeepsie; Thernstrom found it in Newburyport; and Blau and Duncan report the same pattern in their recent contemporary study.[53]

The patterns are even more striking when movement into an unclassifiable occupation is eliminated, as in Table 3.11B. The percentage of movement into the next rank above or below rises for rank 1 to 89 percent, for rank 2 to 94 percent, and for 3 to 94 percent as well. In both tables the rank stability is lowest for people at the bottom, which indicates that occupational mobility was greatest for people at the lowest level, the semiskilled and unskilled workers, an instance in which Hamilton differed from Griffen's Poughkeepsie. The 9 percent of people in rank 5, almost all laborers, who became porters, teamsters, and so on, may or may not have experienced mobility, but the 26 percent who became artisans, clerks, or small proprietors almost certainly did. (This figure is exaggerated because only a select group of laborers could be linked four ways. Among those linked two ways the percentage of movement into nonmanual work was 18 percent for laborers.)

Interestingly, people in high ranks more often slipped downward in occupational position than people in middle ones: 11 percent of people at the top dropped two or more ranks, compared to 2 percent of the artisans. After ten years, 4 percent of the people who had been in rank 1, 6 percent of those from 2, and 5 percent of artisans ended up in ranks 4 and 5, proportions remarkably close to one another.

There was, thus, a substantial amount of upward movement of people at the very bottom of the occupational rank order. The experience of the transitional group between laborers and artisans was unstable. Artisans remained solidly within their own rank, by and large, and the people at the top of the rank order moved down to a small but noticeable extent, in fact more frequently than the artisans.

It is important to determine not only movement within ranks, vertical mobility, but movement between different sorts of work, horizontal or functional mobility. Table 3.12 shows this type of mobility. Among craftsmen the percentage of people probably doing the same sort of work remained especially high in the building trades (79 percent of carpenters and cabinetmakers; 73 percent of masons; 90 percent of plasterers). It was lower among trades which were declining due to technological innovation (66 percent of shoemakers, 65 percent of tailors), and quite low among trades that may have required less skill or paid less well (painters 60 percent, bakers 54 percent). (The low 36 percent among printers is accounted for by their expansion in numbers, explained in Chapter Two.) Much the lowest rate of persistence existed, naturally, among what might be called the transitional occupations: teamsters, 16 percent; porters, 21 percent; servants, 5 percent. Clerks, also members of a transitional occupational group, were

TABLE 3.12 Occupational persistence of people linked two ways, 1851–1861

Occupation	Percent probably in same job, 1851–1861	Number in job		Percent change in occupational rank of persisters[a]		
		1851	1861	Same	Up	Down
Baker	53.8	13	7	69.2	7.7	23.1
Lawyer	95.4	22	26	95.5	—	4.5
Blacksmith	63.2	19	21	82.4	11.8	5.9
Cabinetmaker	78.8	18	18	83.3	5.6	11.1
Carpenter	78.6	103	127	89.8	4.1	6.1
Carriage Maker	69.2	13	10	83.3	—	16.7
Clerk	65.6	64	68	75.9	—	24.1
Grocer	60.0	15	36	80.0	—	20.0
Innkeeper	64.7	17	8	82.4	—	17.6
Laborer	73.8	183	248	82.3	17.8	—
Mason	72.7	22	20	81.8	13.6	4.5
Merchant	78.4	37	52	91.4	—	8.6
Molder	75.0	20	24	94.7	—	5.3
Painter	60.0	20	27	93.8	6.2	—
Plasterer	90.0	20	16	90.0	—	10.0
Printer	36.4	11	20	63.6	18.2	18.2
Servant (male)	5.3	19	12	47.1	52.9	—
Tailor	64.7	51	45	77.6	8.2	14.3
Teamster	15.8	19	8	73.7	26.3	—
Tinsmith	73.3	15	17	85.7	—	14.3
Gentleman	n.c.	29	37	91.7	—	8.3
Shoemaker	65.7	67	52	75.8	10.6	13.6
Porter	21.4	14	11	64.3	35.7	0

[a] Occupational rank based on three-category scale using only people in classifiable occupations.

n.c. = not computable, due to extreme ambiguity of designation.

less fixed in their jobs—66 percent—than the occupational groups above and below them. Interestingly, the stability among laborers (74 percent) matched that among artisans and merchants. Among the major occupations, attorneys, not surprisingly, remained in the same rank most often, in 95 percent of cases.

There emerges, thus, an image of vertical occupational structure fairly fixed at the top, middle (in the stable, remunerative trades), and bottom, with 75 to 80 percent of the people remaining at the same sort of work from decade to decade. In the interstices between the major points—the transitional occupations—much more movement existed. In addition, there was movement out of trades whose fortunes appeared to be declining and which offered relatively low rewards. Similarly, Blau and Duncan found that "the occupations located just above one of the two class boundaries— the lowest white-collar and the lowest blue-collar groups—have high rates of both inflow, especially from lower strata, and outflow, especially to higher strata, thus serving as channels for upward mobility." Transitional occupations, through which people pass on their way up or down the social rank order, may be a general feature of social systems in which there is a relatively high degree of mobility and a relative absence of rigid class boundaries.[54]

Based on a three-interval scale, the amounts of horizontal and upward movement out of the transitional occupations were almost equal. Among teamsters, 38 percent moved horizontally and 26 percent up; among porters, 43 percent horizontally and 36 percent up; and for servants the figures were 44 percent and 53 percent, respectively. The movement from the specific trades was more mixed; in none of the poor trades, however, did upward mobility exceed downward. In fact, in the case of the tailors the excess of downward movement was quite pronounced: 13 percent of tailors moved horizontally, 8 percent upwards, and 14 percent down. The largest downward mobility in a major group, however, occurred among clerks, 24 percent of whom dropped, indicating once more their transitional and marginal position. Thus within each rank the fate of people in different occupations varied more widely at times than the experience of each whole rank compared to the others. Insofar as the varying rates of movement into and out of the different occupations can be explained, they must be accounted for by factors which were peculiar to each occupation, such as technological innovation, wages, or perhaps labor supply.

The second measure of mobility, economic change, is illustrated in Table 3.13. It uses the familiar scale for economic rank, considering the people in the bottom forty economic percentiles poor; the next forty percentiles middle-income; the top 20 percent well-to-do; and the top 10 percent wealthy.

The quantity of economic movement is strikingly larger than

TABLE 3.13 Economic mobility, 1851–1861

		Economic rank, 1861					
						All ranks	
		0–39	40–79	80–89	90–100	N	%
Economic	0–39	49.0%	41.3%	4.9%	4.9%	143	21.4
rank,	40–79	22.8	50.6	13.5	13.2	334	50.1
1851	80–89	6.5	26.9	28.0	38.7	93	13.9
	90–100	5.2	12.4	13.4	69.1	97	14.5
All ranks:	N	157	264	91	155	667	
	%	23.5	39.6	13.6	23.2		99.9

the amount of occupational movement, even comparing this four-level economic scale to the five-level occupational scale used in Table 3.14, which should reduce the differences. There was a much more pronounced shift upward in the group as a whole, with an increase of the wealthy from 15 to 23 percent. At the same time, however, the proportions of poor men increased slightly from 21 to 24 percent, while the proportion of middle-rank men dropped from 50 to 40 percent. In the group as a whole, that is, movement was toward the extremes, indicating both upward and downward mobility.

Not surprisingly, the wealthiest men retained their economic rank most often, 69 percent remaining in the top 10 percent across the decade. The least stable were the men just below the top, again apparently a transitional group, only 28 percent of whom remained at the same economic level. About half of the middle-ranking and the poor, 49 percent and 51 percent respectively, remained in their ranks during the decade. As a whole, downward mobility was surprisingly sharp, most notably among the transient group, the men in the 80–89th percentile, 27 percent of whom dropped to the middle rank and 7 percent to the bottom. Even at the top there was considerable movement down, 31 percent, which was almost equally divided between the next rank and the middle, with 5 percent ending up among the poor. Not only the top but also the middle rung was dangerously slippery during this decade, for 23 percent of its occupants ended the decade poor, compared to 14 percent one notch higher and 13 percent at the top. Among the poor, most movement was one step upward, and, for the time, this was a giant step: 41 percent ended up in the middle ranks, 5 percent in the next highest, and 5 percent among the wealthy, a figure identical to the percentage of wealthy who dropped into poverty.

Thus a poor man who remained in the city had a slightly better than even chance of improving his economic position during the decade, while the chances that someone at the top would lose his position were about 3 out of 10. In a decade that is a great deal of movement.

Clearly, there was more change of economic than of occupational rank. Table 3.14 compares the two, using a simple three-rank scale. The greatest amount of occupational stability occurred at the top and middle, the least at the bottom. Similarly, the greatest amount of economic mobility occurred at the bottom and the least at the top. But the proportions were very different: 76 percent of the 40 percent of people at the middle of the occupational ladder stayed there during the decade, compared to only 51 percent of the half of the people of middling economic rank. In both cases the others moved in about equal proportions upward and downward. This means that a person of middling economic rank had a substantial 1-in-4 chance of slipping into poverty during the decade, compared to the slightly less than 1-in-10 chance that an artisan had of becoming a laborer. This economic instability highlights the insecurity which must have gnawed continuously at the people of the time. It shows their chances to have been much worse than patterns of occupational change indicate by themselves, and it confirms that the pervasive nineteenth-century fear of downward mobility had a very real basis in experience.

Table 3.14C shows that only 57 percent of the people remained stable economically (in one of three ranks of an extremely conservative classification), compared to 77 percent who remained at the same occupational level. In the case of both wealth and occupation, quite similar amounts of people moved upward and downward. These facts convey the image of a fluid society, with substantial and roughly equal amounts of upward and downward mobility. In fact, if almost half the people changed economic rank in the course of a decade, it is not unlikely that the great majority experienced some form of mobility, some change of social rank

TABLE 3.14 Occupational and economic mobility of people linked four ways, 1851–1861

		A. Occupational rank, 1861[a]					
						All ranks	
		Low	Middle	High	Unclas.	N	%
Occupa-	Low	57.4%	20.5%	14.8%	7.4%	122	18.3
tional	Middle	10.8	76.1	8.6	4.5	268	40.2
rank,	High	3.8	15.4	75.4	5.4	240	36.0
1851	Unclas.	13.5	8.1	5.4	73.0	37	5.5
All ranks:	N	104	269	233	61	667	
	%	15.6	40.3	34.9	9.1		100.0

		B. Economic rank, 1861[b]				
					All ranks	
		Low	Middle	High	N	%
Economic	Low	49.0%	41.3%	9.8%	143	21.4
rank,	Middle	22.8	50.6	26.5	334	50.1
1851	High	5.8	18.9	75.3	190	28.5
All ranks:	N	157	264	246	667	
	%	23.5	39.6	36.8		100.0

C. Comparison of economic and occupational mobility, 1851–1861[c]

Direction	Economic	Occupational[d]
Stable	57.3%	76.9%
Up	24.3	11.5
Down	19.2	11.7
Total number	(667)	(592)

[a] Occupational Rank:

        High = 1–2 (nonmanual)
        Middle = 3   (artisan)
        Low = 4–5 (semiskilled and unskilled)

[b] Economic Rank

        High = 80–100th percentile
        Middle = 40–79th percentile
        Low = 0–39th percentile

[c] Based on three-category scale.

[d] Classifiable occupations only.

or standard of living, within their lifetime. Interestingly, both Thernstrom and Griffen in their studies of American cities have found that upward mobility exceeded downward during each of the decades they studied, irrespective of depressions.[55] If their findings and mine are even roughly comparable, there was more downward mobility in urban Canada than in urban America, which might reflect, in turn, a more rigid social structure. At the moment this is only a speculation, though a tantalizing one.

Finally, Table 3.15 shows property and servant mobility. Property holding among the group as a whole increased from 43 to 54 percent during the decade, and a substantial 36 percent of renters acquired property, while a substantial but lower proportion, 23 percent, lost their property during the same period. With respect to servants, over half the group, 51 percent, had no servant in either year, while 21 percent had one at each end of the decade. At the same time 17 percent of the people lost all their servants while 11 percent acquired one or more.

Mobility on each of the four dimensions may be compared in

TABLE 3.15 Property and servant mobility, 1851–1861

A. Property mobility of household heads, 1851–1861

		1861			
				All heads	
		% Owner	% Renter	N	%
1851	% Owner	77.4	22.6	257	43.0
	% Renter	35.9	64.1	340	57.0
All heads:	N	321	276	597	
	%	53.8	46.2		100.0

B. Employment of servants 1851–1861

	Had none in 1851 or 1861	Lost all by 1861	Gained at least one by 1861	Had at least one in both 1851 and 1861
N	310	106	69	126
%	50.7	17.3	11.3	20.6

summary fashion through the phi coefficient. The phi coefficient is the square root of chi square divided by the number of cases. In tables such as these, in which the numbers of rows and columns are equal, a perfect relation between two variables will give a phi coefficient of one. The coefficient may thus be interpreted like a correlation coefficient. Values below .30 or .35 should not be considered significant.[56] The relationship for occupational rank in 1851 and 1861, shown in Table 3.16, was highest, .88, indicating less change of occupational rank than of position on any of the other scales. Next, and much lower, was economic rank, .58, followed at some distance by property status and servant status, .41 and .37. Men changed their position with respect to the ownership of property and the employment of servants more frequently than they altered their economic standing and very much more often than they changed their occupational rank, which leaves unsettled the problem of determining the best indicator of an overall change in social rank. That problem can be approached, first, by examining the interrelations among the patterns of mobility on each of the four measures. To what extent did the same people change rank simultaneously on different scales? The answer is disheartening for the formulation of a tidy statement.

Table 3.17A indicates the association between occupational and economic mobility: 77 percent of the men who remained in the same occupational rank remained in the same economic one as

TABLE 3.16 Value of phi coefficient for economic rank, occupation, property status, and servant status, 1851 and 1861[a]

Variable	Phi coefficient
Economic rank, 1851 and 1861	.58
Occupational rank, 1851 and 1861	.88
Property status, 1851 and 1861	.41
Servant status, 1851 and 1861	.37

[a] Economic and occupational rank are considered on the basis of the three categories, high, medium and low, described in text. Property and servant status refer to an individual's stability with respect to owning or renting, or employing or not employing. Thus three categories are used for each variable.

well, but so did 73 percent of the men who moved upward occupationally and 73 percent of those who moved downward. The
only connection in this table between occupational and economic
movement is that slightly more of those who moved upward occupationally also moved upward rather than downward economically, 18 percent to 14 percent, though this difference is probably
trivial. At the same time, 13 percent of the people moving down
in occupation moved down in economic rank, compared to 9
percent of the same group that moved up economically, again a
very small difference. In fact, most interesting is the evident cross-
directional movement: people moving down on one scale and up
on another.

Looked at another way the figures show the same trends: 55 percent of men who remained in the same economic rank remained
in the same occupational one, a percentage identical to that of
people remaining the same occupationally but moving up economically. But a difference does exist between these groups and
the economically downward, of whom 40 percent remained stable
in occupation. At the same time 27 percent of people who moved
down economically also moved down occupationally, compared to
the 16 percent of those who remained stable and 13 percent of
those upwardly mobile economically. Roughly the same proportion of men moved up occupationally among those in all three
economic categories, the stable, the upward, and the downward
moving. Once again the relative independence of movement on
the two mobility scales is evident.

Table 3.17B displays the patterns a little more exactly. The
greatest stability existed among men at the bottom; that is, those
people whose economic rank was lowest in both 1851 and 1861
(in 92 percent of the cases) most often stayed at the same occupational rank. In the rest of the table about 70 to 77 percent of the
men, with one exception, remained occupationally stable *whatever*
the nature or distance of their economic mobility. Those who
made the jump from the middle to the top of the economic ladder formed the exception. Among them 64 percent remained
occupationally stable, 26 percent moved up, and 10 percent down.
In fact, with the exception of the people who made the somewhat
ambiguous move from the middle of the economic rank to the
rung just below the wealthy, all of the three other groups of

TABLE 3.17 Occupational mobility by economic mobility and
economic rank

A. Occupational mobility and economic mobility, 1851–1861

		Occupational mobility			
		Stable	Up	Down	Number
Economic mobility	Stable	76.6%	72.8%	72.8%	426
	Up	17.5	18.3	14.1	98
	Down	5.8	8.9	13.0	45
	Total				569

		Economic mobility			
		Stable	Up	Down	Number
Occupational mobility	Stable	55.4%	55.1%	40.0%	308
	Up	28.9	31.6	33.3	169
	Down	15.7	13.3	26.6	92
	Total				569

B. Economic rank[a]

Occupational rank	Percent stable				Percent up				Percent down		Totals	
	1–1	2–2	3–3	4–4	1–2	2–3	2–4	3–4	2–1	3–2	N	%
Stable	91.7	72.6	70.8	74.2	75.4	77.0	64.2	74.3	72.9	72.7	445	72.7
Up	8.2	17.9	25.1	22.7	18.9	7.7	26.2	20.1	12.9	18.1	109	17.8
Down	0.0	9.6	4.2	3.0	5.7	15.4	9.6	5.7	14.1	9.1	58	9.5

[a] Economic rank

   1 =   0–39th percentile.
   2 = 40–79th percentile.
   3 = 80–89th percentile.
   4 = 90–100th percentile.

economically upwardly mobile people had a percentage of upward
occupational mobility that exceeded downward mobility by two
and a half to three and a half times. Nonetheless, the weakness of
the influence that economic and occupational mobility exerted
upon each other remains truly remarkable.

Relations between economic mobility and the acquisition of
property, however, were quite marked, as Table 3.18 shows. Peo-

ple who moved up economically were much more likely (30 percent) to acquire property than those who remained stable (16
percent) or moved down (18 percent). This was not because those
who remained economically stable already owned property, for the
difference in initial ownership between the stable and the upwardly mobile was only 3 percent (37 percent as compared to 34
percent). The downwardly mobile, on the other hand, were by far
the least likely to own property in each year—23 percent—and
the most likely to lose it—16 percent—compared to 9 percent of
stable and 7 percent of upwardly mobile men.

The association between occupational mobility and property
was much less pronounced, with one exception: the downwardly
mobile rented more often in each year (45 percent compared to
36 percent and 32 percent among the stable and upward) and
owned property less in either year (17 percent compared to 37
percent and 34 percent). However, by a small and insignificant
margin, the downwardly mobile occupationally were also the most
likely to acquire property. No differences at all existed between
property acquisition or loss on the one hand and occupational
stability or upward mobility on the other. Thus there was little
connection between occupation and property. The strong relation
of property acquisition to economic mobility, on the other hand,

TABLE 3.18 Property mobility by economic and occupational
mobility, 1851–1861

Economic and occupational rank	Property status				
	Owner 1851 and 1861	Gained property	Lost property	Renter 1851 and 1861	N
Economic					
Stable	37.4%	16.4%	8.9%	37.4%	305
Up	33.7	29.6	6.5	30.2	169
Down	22.8	17.9	16.3	43.1	123
Occupational					
Stable	35.6	19.3	8.6	36.4	405
Up	34.1	23.4	10.6	31.9	97
Down	17.0	24.5	13.2	45.3	53
All	33.5	20.5	9.4	36.6	

provides additional support for the view that wealth is superior to occupation as a measure of mobility.

As Table 3.19 shows, property *itself* appears to have influenced economic mobility, especially at the lower ranks: only 36 percent of poor property owners in 1851 remained poor in 1861 and 18 percent jumped two or three ranks, compared to 52 percent of poor renters who remained poor and 8 percent who moved up two or three ranks. The difference is evident though less marked at the middle rank, where 27 percent of renters dropped into poverty compared to but 16 percent of owners, though comparable numbers move up. At the top of the scale it is noteworthy that

TABLE 3.19 Economic and occupational mobility by property mobility, 1851–1861

			Economic rank, 1861				
			0–39	40–79	80–89	90–100	Number
Economic rank and property ownership, 1851	0–39	Owner	35.7%	46.4%	10.7%	7.1%	28
		Renter	52.2	40.0	3.5	4.3	115
	40–79	Owner	16.1	56.2	16.1	11.7	137
		Renter	27.4	46.7	11.7	14.2	197
	80–89	Owner	9.8	26.9	26.8	36.5	41
		Renter	3.9	25.5	29.4	41.1	51
	90–100	Owner	4.7	9.4	9.4	76.6	64
		Renter	6.1	18.2	21.2	54.5	33

			Occupational rank, 1861[a]				
			4–5	3	2	1	Number
Occupational rank and property ownership, 1851	4–5	Owner	60.0%	23.3%	6.7%	10.0%	30
		Renter	62.6	21.7	13.3	2.4	83
	3	Owner	5.0	81.5	10.9	2.5	119
		Renter	12.4	78.1	8.9	0.7	137
	2	Owner	2.9	17.1	57.1	22.9	35
		Renter	5.0	20.0	58.8	16.3	80
	1	Owner	3.6	16.4	10.9	69.1	55
		Renter	3.6	10.7	21.4	64.3	56

[a] Classifiable occupations only; 5 = low, 1 = high.

of the wealthiest 10 percent, 77 percent of property owners retained their economic rank compared to only 55 percent of renters, among whom 24 percent slipped two or more ranks. It appears, thus, that the acquisition of property exerted an independent influence on the improvement of economic standing. Why this should be so is an intriguing question. The relation may well have been temporal rather than causal; that is, the purchase of a house could have been the first step in a process of upward social mobility. Perhaps the personal qualities that led a man to buy a house (a greater sense of family responsibility, an ability to save, a desire for success?) also led to economic success. But it is not clear how this could be investigated. The relations between property and occupation, it should be added, though they run in the same direction, are muted and certainly not conclusive.

Finally, the employment of servants was connected to upward and downward movement in occupation and wealth. According to Table 3.20 the occupationally upward moving were most likely to have a servant in each year (28 percent compared to 19 percent and 24 percent among the stable and downwardly mobile) and least likely to have none either year (40 percent compared to 52 percent and 47 percent). They were also most likely to gain a servant during the decade (17 percent compared to 11 percent and 7 percent). The downwardly mobile occupationally, as might be expected, were most likely to lose all servants (22 percent compared to 16 percent and 18 percent). One must remember when interpreting these figures that all groups lost servants during this period. Thus relations between servants and occupational movement existed, but they were not especially strong.

The same relations existed between servants and economic rank, this time in almost the identical strength as those between servants and occupational rank. In all, 20 percent of economically upward-moving men gained a servant; 27 percent of the downwardly mobile lost all, and fewer downwardly mobile, 3 percent, gained a servant than did the men moving downward in occupation. In a number of cases, however, the acquisition of servants, economic mobility, and occupational mobility accompanied one another. Among the upwardly mobile economically, the group that gained servants by far most frequently were the forty men

TABLE 3.20 Employment of servants by economic and occupational
mobility, 1851–1861

Occupational and economic rank and mobility	Servants employed, 1851–1861				Number of employees
	None either year	Lost all	Gained at least one	At least one each year	
Occupational status, 1851–1861					
Stable	51.8	17.9	11.1	19.3	415
Up	40.2	15.5	16.5	27.8	97
Down	47.3	21.8	7.3	23.6	55
Economic rank, 1851–1861					
Stable	52.5	15.9	10.8	20.7	314
Up	40.5	12.5	20.1	26.8	165
Down	58.3	26.5	3.0	12.1	132
Economic mobility					
From middle to top rank	15.0	12.5	37.5	35.0	40
From top to middle rank	41.7	58.3	0	0	12
Occupational mobility					
From artisan to commercial or professional	28.6	14.3	28.6	28.6	14
From professional or commercial to artisan	42.9	28.6	14.3	14.3	7
From clerical to artisan	33.3	50.0	8.3	8.3	12

who climbed from the middle to the top of the rank order. This
group, as Table 3.17B indicated, had a high rate of upward occupational mobility. Conversely, exceptionally large percentages
of men who dropped from the wealthy and well-to-do ranks to
the middle of the economic order lost all their servants, as did
men who slipped from the professional, commercial, and clerical
to the artisan ranks. Thus, the acquisition or loss of servants often

seemed to mark the experience of the minority of men who were the most mobile, moving upward or downward, often by two ranks, on both economic and occupational scales. If this was indeed the case, then the acquisition or loss of servants may turn out to be the best quick index of mobility in the mid-nineteenth century.

Once again the phi coefficient provides a useful way of summarizing the relationships that have been discussed. These relationships between the major dimensions along which mobility can be measured were in general extremely weak, as Table 3.21 shows. Only in certain instances—the propensity of upwardly mobile poor men to own houses, or the employment of servants by people moving upward or downward on both occupational and economic ranks—did strong connections exist between the dimensions of mobility. Overall, the phi coefficients indicate a different situation. The coefficient of the relation between economic and occupational mobility was .10, between occupational mobility and property mobility .07, and between occupational mobility and servant mobility .08. These are insignificant scores and certainly should give pause to anyone tempted to infer general social mobility from occupational title alone. The relations of

TABLE 3.21 Value of phi coefficient for interrelation of major mobility variables, 1851–1861[a]

Economic mobility by occupational mobility	.10
Economic mobility by property mobility	.18
Occupational mobility by property mobility	.07
Economic mobility by servant mobility	.20
Occupational mobility by servant mobility	.08

[a] Economic and occupational mobility are measured on a three-category scale: stable, upward, downward. The categories themselves are based on the division of the data into three ranks, as described in the text. Property mobility also is divided into three categories: owning or renting property in both 1851 and 1861; owning in 1851 and losing by 1861; renting in 1851 and owning in 1861. For employment of servants the categories are as follows: having none or one or more servants in both 1851 and 1861; employing a servant in 1851 but not in 1861; not employing a servant in 1861 but having one in 1861.

property and servant mobility with economic mobility were higher, .18 and .20, respectively, but hardly impressive. Thus, the relative independence of each of these measures, which one would expect to show strong and consistent relations with one another, stands out as striking.

One obvious conclusion from this comparison is that an adequate index of social mobility must encompass all four measures of mobility. It should be possible to give each a rough weight according to what seems to be its overall importance. Then each person could be scored and a series of rankings derived that could be called a social mobility scale, encompassing wealth, status, and power.

The data do not allow the full range of variables to be introduced in order to explain the causes of individual mobility, but the impact of both the life cycle (for which age will act as a surrogate) and ethnicity can be considered. In part the mobility of men must also have been a function of their personal characteristics, their intelligence, energy, and perseverance; in all likelihood it will never be possible to say very much about the influence of these factors historically for the mass of people. Mobility may also have been related to education, perhaps even to the kind of neighborhood in which people grew up; at this point nothing can be said about these either, although their exploration ultimately should prove possible. Finally, however, mobility resulted from the opportunities available to men of different ages and of different ethnic backgrounds, and about this, even now, something can be said.

Consider first the relation between occupation and age, shown in Table 3.22. The clearest association existed between occupational mobility and old age, a finding which again appears to reflect an ubiquitous nineteenth-century situation: only 60 percent of the men aged 60 or over in 1851 remained in the same occupational rank across the decade, compared to over 70 percent of each of the other age cohorts. And 23 percent of the elderly dropped in rank, a figure about twice that of the nearest cohort. For the other age groups the figures were strikingly similar: about 70 to 75 percent of each cohort remained occupationally stable, about 16 to 17 percent moved up, and 7 to 12 percent down.[57]

There was more variation, as should be expected, in the rela-

TABLE 3.22 Occupational and economic mobility by age, 1851–1861

	Occupational rank, 1851–1861[a]			
Age, 1851	Stable	Up	Down	Number
Under 30	70.6%	17.1%	12.4%	299
30–39	75.3	16.0	8.6	324
40–49	76.3	16.3	7.4	215
50–59	71.6	16.2	12.2	74
60 and over	60.0	16.7	23.3	30
All				942
	Economic rank, 1851–1861[b]			
Under 30	35.3%	43.3%	21.3%	150
30–39	47.1	34.0	18.9	244
40–49	59.9	18.1	22.0	177
50–59	65.7	17.9	16.4	67
60 and over	48.3	24.1	27.6	29
All				667

[a] Based on census-to-census linkage.
[b] Based on census-assessment to census-assessment linkage.

tions between economic rank and age. Here most of the movement occurred among the young, with stability of economic rank increasing with age in a linear fashion until it began to decline among the elderly; that is, only 35 percent of men under thirty remained in the same economic rank, compared to 47 percent of those aged 30–39, 60 percent of the 40–49-year-olds, and, when the drop began, 48 percent of those over sixty. The elderly, the men sixty and over, were, as in the case of occupation, the most downwardly mobile; 28 percent of men aged 60 and over moved downward in economic rank while the most upwardly mobile, 43 percent, were the young, the men under thirty. In fact, upward mobility decreased in a linear fashion with age through the 50–59-year-old cohort.

Thus, men in their twenties and early thirties, as might be expected, were relatively unsettled, still establishing themselves in their careers, and their experience in these early years of work apparently was critical. If a life cycle can be inferred from these data, men who did not succeed early by and large did not succeed at all, though old age was something of a leveler. Indeed, the experience of men over sixty reinforces the conclusions offered in earlier chapters about the hardships of the elderly. Many of them, quite obviously, could not retain their jobs, and the ones who had been unable to save or acquire independent means were forced into unskilled work and sometimes poverty.

The relationships between age and property, illustrated in Table 3.23, reinforce these conclusions. The men under thirty were the least likely by far (17 percent compared to 32 percent for the nearest group) to own property in each year and the most likely, 45 percent, to rent at each end of the decade. But, of course, they were also the most likely to acquire property. In fact, the rate of property acquisition declines in a linear fashion,

TABLE 3.23 Property mobility and the employment of servants by age, 1851–1861

| | Property status, 1851–1861 | | | | |
Age, 1851	Owner each year	Gainer	Loser	Renter each year	Number
Under 30	16.8%	27.7%	10.1%	45.4%	119
30–39	31.8	21.5	11.7	35.0	223
40–49	43.0	18.2	6.1	32.7	165
50–59	37.5	12.5	9.4	40.6	64
60 and over	50.0	11.5	15.4	23.1	26
All	33.3	20.4	9.7	36.5	597

| | Servant status, 1851–1861 | | | | |
Age, 1851	At least one each year	Gained at least one	Lost all	None either year	Number of employees
Under 30	15.1%	18.6%	22.1%	44.4%	113
30–39	25.9	11.6	19.0	43.5	232
40–49	17.4	8.7	13.4	60.5	172
50–59	21.2	4.5	15.2	59.1	66
60 and over	10.7	10.7	14.3	64.3	28
All	20.6	11.3	17.3	50.7	611

from 28 percent of the under-30-year-olds in 1851 at the highest to 12 percent of the men sixty and over. Partly this reflects the fact that a greater proportion of each cohort owned houses to begin with. At the same time, and also consistent with the patterns already described, the men sixty and over were most likely (15 percent) to lose property and, interestingly, by far least likely to rent in each year. Thus property ownership depended partially on life cycle and partially on wealth, which confirms the analysis in Chapter Two using purely cross-sectional data.

As for servants, the relations with age are not quite so clear, though the problems of old age do show up to some extent. The men aged 60 and over were least likely (11 percent) to have a servant in each year, followed, predictably, by the youngest co-hort (15 percent). But this youngest group, interestingly, also most often gained (19 percent) *and* most often lost (22 percent) a servant. In fact, the propensity to acquire a servant declined in linear fashion through the 50–59-year-old cohort, rising some-what among the most elderly, which reflects, perhaps, a need for assistance on the part of infirm and well-to-do old people. In all, the trends in property owning and the employment of servants reinforce the conclusion that the early working years, until some-time after the age of thirty, were turbulent and critical, followed by twenty or thirty years of relative stability, which, in turn, were often succeeded by a decline into difficult circumstances during old age.

If age affected a man's chances somewhat, ethnicity did even more. Ethnicity formed an integral component in the system of stratification within nineteenth-century cities, influencing not only the overall distribution of rewards but the opportunities of individual people. Insofar as ethnic stratification could be made to stand for social stratification more generally, there was little stratum mobility during the decade, as Chapter Two showed. The Irish Catholics were as far behind all other groups in 1861 as in 1851 and the native Canadians had retained their lead.

Against this background, consider the experience of individuals within the major ethnic groups shown in Table 3.24. The Irish were by far the most likely to remain poor: 67 percent of the Irish Catholics and 61 percent of the Irish Protestants who were poor in 1851 remained poor a decade later, compared to an extraor-

TABLE 3.24 Economic and occupational mobility by ethnicity,
                1851–1861

| | Selected economic mobility | | | |
| | Remaining poor | | Becoming well-to-do | |
Ethnic group	Percent	Number[a]	Percent	Number[a]
Irish Catholic	66.7	45	3.2	9
Irish Protestant	61.3	31	4.0	36
Scottish Presbyterian	22.2	18	14.9	25
English Protestant	31.3	32	11.5	56
Canadian Protestant	20.0	5	6.8	26

| | Selected occupational mobility | | | |
| | Remaining in lowest rank | | Becoming nonmanual | |
	Percent	Number[a]	Percent	Number[a]
Irish Catholic	70.3	37	5.0	10
Irish Protestant	83.3	18	4.0	41
Scottish Presbyterian	50.0	14	2.4	35
English Protestant	56.6	23	1.1	70
Canadian Protestant	20.0	5	8.0	32

| | Economic mobility, whole group | | | |
	Stable	Up	Down	Number[b]
Irish Catholic	58.1%	24.7%	17.2%	93
Irish Protestant	53.7	23.1	23.1	121
Scottish Presbyterian	35.1	40.4	24.5	94
English Protestant	52.5	31.5	16.0	200
Canadian Protestant	41.3	37.9	20.7	58

| | Occupational mobility, whole classifiable group | | | |
	Stable	Up	Down	Number[b]
Irish Catholic	70.4%	16.0%	13.6%	81
Irish Protestant	76.9	11.1	12.0	108
Scottish Presbyterian	64.3	17.9	17.9	84
English Protestant	73.4	15.2	11.4	184
Canadian Protestant	66.0	16.0	18.0	50

[a] Total in ethnic group in rank, 1851.
[b] Total traceable and classifiable in ethnic group from 1851 to 1861.

dinarily low 22 percent of the Scottish Presbyterians, 31 percent of the English Protestants, and 20 percent of the Canadian Protestants. At the same time, few Irish, 3 to 4 percent, became wealthy compared to 15 percent of Scottish Presbyterians, 12 percent of English Protestants, and 7 percent of Canadian Protestants. For the Irish, poverty was a way of life. For the others it was a temporary problem.

The occupational statistics show the same thing: 70 percent of Irish Catholic men and 83 percent of Irish Protestants who were at the bottom of the occupational rank order in 1851 remained there in 1861, compared to only 50 percent of the Scottish Presbyterians, 57 percent of the English Protestants, and 20 percent of the Canadian Protestants. Laboring as well as poverty formed a way of life for the Irish and a temporary state for the other groups. Within the whole group, the Irish had the lowest rates of upward economic mobility—25 percent and 23 percent for Catholic and Protestant respectively—compared to 40 percent, 32 percent, and 38 percent for the other major groups. (Since the Irish were already at the bottom their rate of downward mobility is not relevant.) Of the non-Irish the English Protestants had the lowest rate of downward mobility, the Scottish Presbyterians the highest. There is, however, no difference among groups in the direction of mobility when *occupation* is the measure, indicating, once again, its imprecision as an overall index. For *each* ethnic group, it is important to emphasize, the percentage climbing out of poverty exceeded the percentage remaining laborers, which points to a significant process; namely, that people improved their economic position while remaining within an occupation. That is another reason why occupation by itself is an inadequate measure of mobility.

It is possible to imagine a society in which men remained relatively fixed within their occupational positions while their sons most often moved into different kinds of work and different ranks. A society is conceivable, that is, in which *intra*-generational mobility was low and *inter*generational mobility high. Hamilton, it appears, was not that sort of place.

Although my measures and indicators of intergenerational mobility remain imprecise and inadequate, they are nonetheless suggestive. Table 3.25A and 3.25B compare the occupations of sons living at home with those of their fathers. These tables are not based on a linked population but, rather, on all households in both 1851 and 1861, which is their strength. Their weakness is that occupation is the only measure of mobility available. Since the sons were living at home, they were not assessed as householders, and consequently I could not estimate their earnings.

TABLE 3.25A Fathers' and sons' status, 1851–1861[a]

			Son's occupation, first job			
			Professional or commercial	Skilled	Semi-skilled or unskilled	All
Father's occupation, 1851[b]	Professional or commercial	N	42	15	1	58
		%	72.4	25.9	1.7	28.2
	Skilled	N	6	85	4	95
		%	6.3	89.5	4.3	46.1
	Semiskilled or unskilled	N	1	15	37	53
		%	1.9	28.3	69.8	25.7
	All	N	49	115	42	206
		%	23.8	55.8	20.4	
Father's occupation, 1861[c]	Professional or commercial	N	49	16	4	69
		%	71.0	23.2	5.8	27.6
	Skilled	N	16	91	9	116
		%	13.8	78.4	7.8	46.4
	Semiskilled or unskilled	N	10	16	39	65
		%	15.4	24.6	60.0	26.0
	All	N	75	123	52	250
		%	30.0	49.2	20.8	

[a] Table includes only fathers and sons with occupations in five-cities categories. Professional or commercial = groups 1–2; skilled trade = 3; semiskilled or unskilled = 4–5.

[b] $\chi^2 = 197.5$ (significance greater than .001).
   $\phi = .92$

[c] $\chi^2 = 144$ (significance greater than .001).
   $\phi = .76$

Indeed, given their youth, it would be unwise to make any estimates about intergenerational economic mobility.

Table 3.25A shows the clear inheritance of occupational status. In 1851, 72 percent of sons of professional and clerical workers remained in the same occupational rank; 26 percent did skilled manual work (not necessarily indicating downward mobility), and only 2 percent became unskilled or semiskilled workers. Inheritance, however, was strongest among artisans—90 percent—with 6 percent of the sons moving into professional or clerical work and 4 percent dropping to unskilled and semiskilled jobs. Inheritance was lowest among the semiskilled and unskilled workers' sons, 70 percent, though that is still high. Of the remainder, 28 percent had moved up one rank and 2 percent had moved into professional and clerical work, precisely the proportion of top-ranked men's sons that dropped to the bottom of the rank order. Thus the overall distribution of fathers and sons was quite similar: 28 percent of fathers and 24 percent of sons were in professional and commercial occupations; 46 percent of fathers and 56 percent of sons were skilled workers; and 26 percent of fathers and 20 percent of sons did semiskilled or unskilled work.

By 1861 the degree of occupational inheritance had decreased generally. The proportion of sons of professional and clerical workers assuming their fathers' rank dropped only 1 percent, from 72 to 71 percent, but the percentage becoming semiskilled and unskilled workers increased from 2 to 6 percent during the decade. Occupational inheritance among skilled workers dropped from 90 to 78 percent, while the percentage of skilled workers' sons dropping in rank doubled, from 4 to 8 percent, and the percentage moving upwards increased from 6 to 14 percent. Among the semiskilled and unskilled workers occupational inheritance dropped from 70 to 60 percent while, intriguingly, the percentage of sons entering professional and clerical occupations jumped seven times, from 2 to 15 percent. (Again, note that the flow from *both* top to bottom and bottom to top increased by proportionally large amounts.) These changes were accounted for, partly, by the beginning of a shift of manual workers' sons into lower-level clerical occupations, a trend which probably signified less change in status than might at first appear. Nonetheless, occupational inheritance

in Hamilton remained higher than in Poughkeepsie, where only
68 percent of the first jobs of sons of skilled fathers were in the
skilled trades. Perhaps this indicated that Canadian social structure was more rigid, or, alternatively, it may have reflected a
slower pattern of technological change in Hamilton. Despite the
difference in magnitude, however, the trend was the same in both
places; in Poughkeepsie, too, occupational inheritance decreased
with successive cohorts.[58]

Interestingly, the shifts balanced one another so that the overall
distribution of fathers and sons remained quite similar: 28 percent and 30 percent, respectively, in professional and clerical
occupations; 46 percent and 49 percent among skilled workers;
and 26 percent and 21 percent among the semiskilled and unskilled.

The trends stand out even more clearly on a scale with five
ranks instead of three, shown in Table 3.25B. There the degree
of occupational inheritance between 1851 and 1861 increases only
in the small, transitional rank 4. It drops especially sharply in rank
1, from 46 to 18 percent, and at other ranks about 11 or 12 percent: at the bottom, from 68 to 56 percent, and at ranks 2 and 3
from 70 to 59 percent and from 90 to 78 percent.

Sons not only inherited their fathers' rank less frequently; they
also followed the same occupations less often, as Table 3.26 reveals. Part A of the table shows that in 1851 41 percent of sons had
an occupational title identical to their fathers. While not overwhelming, it is clearly a figure much greater than chance would
produce and reveals a strong tradition of occupational inheritance

TABLE 3.25B Percentage of sons living at home
in same occupational group
as father

Occupational group	1851	1861
1	46.4	17.9
2	70.0	58.5
3	89.5	78.4
4	61.5	70.0
5	67.5	56.4

TABLE 3.26 Fathers' and sons' occupational inheritance: sons living at home

A. Direct inheritance

	1851	1861
(1) Number of fathers	272	349
(2) Number of sons with identical occupations	184	100
(3) Percent of sons with identical occupations	40.8	28.7

B. Inheritance by trade[a]

	Sons' occupation											
	Identical or equivalent		Artisan		Professional		Commercial		Laborer or unskilled		Number	
Fathers' occupation	1851	1861	1851	1861	1851	1861	1851	1861	1851	1861	1851	1861
Baker	50.0%	66.7%	50.0%	0	0	0	0	33.3%	0	0	2	3
Attorney	50.0	0	0	33.3%	0	0	0	66.7	50.0%	0	2	3
Blacksmith	60.0	50.0	40.0	50.0	0	0	0	0	0	0	5	6
Bricklayer	100.0	100.0	0	0	0	0	0	0	0	0	5	1
Butcher	50.0	100.0	25.0	0	0	0	0	0	25.0	0	4	1
Cabinetmaker	100.0	40.0	0	40.0	0	0	0	0	20.0	0	4	5
Carpenter	70.8	57.5	20.7	24.3	0	0	8.4%	15.1	0	3.0%	24	33
Clerk	57.1	14.3	14.3	57.1	0	0	14.3	14.3	14.3	14.3	7	7
Laborer	69.1	52.7	26.3	36.0	0	1.8%	4.7	7.3	0	0	42	55
Merchant	100.0	100.0	0	0	0	0	0	0	0	0	1	2
Physician	0	50.0	0	0	100.0%	0	0	0	50.0	0	3	2
Tailor	58.3	20.0	16.7	20.0	0	20.0	8.3	20.0	16.7	20.0	12	5
Tinsmith	80.0	50.0	0	50.0	0	0	20.0	0	0	0	5	2
Shoemaker	52.9	27.3	35.4	40.9	5.9	0	5.9	9.0	0	22.7	17	22
Gentleman	13.6	11.8	36.4	23.5	13.6	11.8	36.4	53.0	0	0	22	17

a Classifiable trades only.

still in operation. By 1861 the overall degree of occupational inheritance had dropped to 29 percent, a very sizable difference. This occurred, as Chapter Five will show, at precisely the time when greatly increased numbers of sons were remaining at home longer and starting work later. They were not staying home, it is clear, to follow their fathers' trades.

The very small numbers within individual trades make it difficult to draw firm conclusions. Part B of the table hints at some interesting patterns, however. Among the sons of carpenters, on the whole a solid group, the drop in occupational inheritance was smaller (71 to 58 percent) than among two major trades which were declining because of technological innovation: shoemaking (53 to 27 percent), and tailoring (58 to 20 percent). Most sons of laborers who did not follow their fathers' occupation became artisans, with only a few entering commercial occupations. On the other hand, there was a noticeable movement of craftsmen's sons into clerical occupations. Although most boys who did not follow their fathers' craft entered another trade, the number entering clerical occupations rose from 8 to 15 percent of carpenters' sons, from 6 to 9 percent of shoemakers' sons, and from 8 to 20 percent of tailors' sons. At the same time, the plight of shoemakers in this period is underscored by the increase from 0 to 23 percent of their sons who became laborers. At the other end of the hierarchy the high rank of gentlemen is emphasized by the occupations of their sons; in 1851, 14 percent called themselves gentlemen and 50 percent were in professional or commercial occupations; ten years later the figures were 12 percent and 65 percent, respectively. In neither year did any gentleman's son become a laborer. There are, finally, too few sons of attorneys and merchants to make any meaningful claims about them. That, in itself, is interesting. It would seem that very few attorneys' sons living at home were employed, probably the result of prolonged schooling.

Clearly, then, occupational inheritance remained strong at mid-century but declined during the 1850s. Although most sons assumed the same occupational rank as their fathers, remarkably fewer did so in 1861 than in 1851. The increased movement was by no means all upward. For the increased proportion of laborers' sons moving upward was balanced by initially higher-ranking sons moving down. The implication of this movement is that fathers were decreasingly able automatically to pass on to their sons their occupational status. If this was indeed the case, it provides a logical background for the increased attention to the development of educational facilities and the increased school attendance during the same decade. The patterns point, perhaps, to the onset of a period of readjustment in which education began to intervene, as it does in the contemporary social structure, in the transmission of status from father to son. The impact of technology influenced this trend, for sons of men in crafts such as shoemaking and tailoring, in which mid-nineteenth-century technological developments eroded skill requirements, began to avoid their fathers' occupations. Lacking capital with which to establish businesses, shoemakers and tailors, anxious about the future of their sons, had a serious problem; perhaps that is why the artisans of Hamilton in the 1850s turned so eagerly to the new Central School and the facilities for secondary education which it offered.[59]

There is, finally, one more measure of intergenerational mobility: the experience of sons traced from 1851 to 1861. The occupation of these men in 1861 can be compared with their fathers' occupation ten years earlier. Unfortunately, the number in this case, shown in Table 3.27, is pitifully small. Of the entire population of Hamilton, traced from one census to another, only 151 sons could be found who lived at home with their fathers in 1851 and who were themselves employed in 1861. The reason, of course, is the extraordinary outmigration of young men. The smallness of the number precludes any refined analysis because even an analysis with gross categories must be based on tiny numbers. Therefore the results of Table 3.27, more than of any other table in this chapter, must be taken as suggestive only.

Most sons in professional, clerical, and skilled manual work assumed their fathers' rank, 67 percent of those in professional or clerical work and 74 percent of sons of artisans. For semiskilled and unskilled workers, the degree of inheritance, 53 percent, was much lower. Most of the sons of high-ranking fathers not at the top of the scale themselves were artisans, and only 4 percent were in semiskilled and unskilled work. Rather more, but not many

TABLE 3.27 Intergenerational occupational mobility,
1851–1861

		A. Sons and fathers[a]				
		1–2	3	4–5	N	%
Fathers'	1–2	67.4%	28.3%	4.3%	46	30.4
occu-	3	17.4	73.9	8.7	69	45.7
pational	4–5	13.9	33.3	52.8	36	23.9
rank,	N	48	76	27	151	
1851	%	31.8	50.3	17.9		

B. Mobility and ethnicity, 1851–1861

Ethnicity	Laborers' sons who remained laborers	
	%	N
Irish Catholic	75.0	12
Irish Protestant	50.0	2
Scottish Presbyterian	0	0
English Protestant	62.5	8

	Artisans' sons who remained artisans or became laborers		
	Artisans	Laborers	
	%	%	N
Irish Catholic	66.7	22.2	9
Irish Protestant	71.0	7.1	14
Scottish Presbyterian	93.8	0	16
English Protestant	76.9	7.7	26

[a] $\chi^2 = 65.2$ (significance greater than .001).
$\phi = .66$

more, 9 percent, of sons of artisans dropped to the lowest end of
the scale, while 14 percent of sons of men at the bottom moved
into professional or clerical jobs.

The striking thing about the figures in Table 3.27 is that they
are nearly identical to those in Table 3.26 for fathers and sons
living at home in 1861. And the relations are of similar magnitude: the phi coefficient for the occupation of sons living at home
in 1861 compared to the occupation of their fathers is .76; for
sons in 1861 compared to fathers in 1851 it is .66. This points to
the happy conclusion, given the small number found, that the

experience of sons living at home can be taken as a surrogate for the early job history of all sons, who probably would be very largely under the age of thirty in 1861. On the basis of the knowledge already gained of patterns during adulthood, specifically the relations between mobility and age, a fair prediction can be made of the amount of subsequent career mobility among members of a cohort in relation to their fathers' positions.

Table 3.27, part B, hints at some of the relations between mobility and ethnicity, though the numbers are tiny. Note that of the three major ethnic groups the percentage of Irish Catholic laborers' sons remaining laborers is by far the highest, 75 percent, compared to 50 percent of the Irish Protestants and 63 percent of the English Protestants. There were no Scottish fathers with laboring sons among those traced. Similarly, 22 percent of sons of Irish Catholic artisans became laborers, compared to only 7 percent of Irish Protestants, none of Scottish Presbyterians, and 8 percent of English Protestants. Clearly, the sons of Irish Catholics inherited not only their fathers' poverty but their ethnic handicaps as well. The fact that 70 percent of all Irish Catholic men who were laborers in 1851 remained in the same rank a decade later, as Table 3.24 showed, also indicates little if any improvement among their sons. In most cases these sons cannot properly be considered first-generation Canadians because most of them had been born in Ireland. The mobility patterns among sons of immigrants probably corresponded closely to the patterns among their fathers. The few Scottish Presbyterians who became laborers were able, by and large, to improve their position and to keep their sons from dropping back; the Irish Catholics, on the other hand, passed on both their poverty and their limited opportunity to their sons.

This first foray into mobility, despite all its limitations, has proved remarkably useful. Perhaps of most value is a methodological warning: occupational and economic mobility appear to be relatively independent of each other, and a reliance on occupation alone obscures a large amount of movement, masking the instability that marked the life experience of most people within mid-nineteenth-century society. Once again the image is presented of a population churning, this time in social rather than geographical space, within a fixed set of structures. These tentative conclusions are full of implication for the quality of experience at the time: not only opportunity but also disaster beckoned, and both could be seen all around. It is little wonder that the Victorians were an anxious people.

How these patterns changed over time can only be the subject of speculation. If the patterns here can be compared, even roughly, to American studies, then Hamilton differed from American cities in the extent to which upward and downward mobility nearly equaled each other. Not only students of nineteenth-century but of contemporary American society as well have reached the same conclusion: the United States is a land in which upward mobility has exceeded downward mobility, where success has come more often than failure. Although it is tempting to attribute the pattern and rate of mobility to the underlying properties of a modern industrial society, as Lipset and Bendix do, the experiences of various countries apparently are not quite so comparable as they indicate, a case which Blau and Duncan have made for contemporary societies. Little comparative historical evidence exists, though one recent study of Germany found lower rates of upward mobility than those reported by students of late-nineteenth and early-twentieth-century American cities who used roughly similar procedures.[60] Thus two rather different hypotheses can be framed about the nature of Hamilton in successive decades. One is that the differences between Hamilton on the one hand and Poughkeepsie and Boston on the other reflected different stages of development among not only the cities but also the societies in which they were embedded. From this perspective, as industrialization occurred the patterns of mobility in Hamilton would be expected to become more like those in American cities. According to the second hypothesis, the difference in mobility patterns reflected a difference in social structure, and that social structure grew not only from the level of industrialization but from peculiar demographic conditions and distinctive traditions. If this was the case, then the pattern of social mobility in Canadian cities would remain different from that in American ones, despite increasingly similar levels of industrial and technological sophistication. It is not possible as yet to assess which line of interpretation is more likely to prove true, or how they might be combined. But they do frame a question that connects historical studies of social mobility with both a larger body of social theory and a series of national historical traditions.

It is appropriate to end this chapter where it began, with the life of Wilson Benson. In one sense the chapter has been a prolonged attempt to show why Wilson Benson was a representative nineteenth-century man. The wandering, fluctuating search for success that led Wilson through Ireland, Scotland, and Upper Canada as he tried his hand at a variety of tasks from weaving and peddling to porridge-making, storekeeping, and farming marked, if my speculations are correct, the lives of many men. Though their specific experiences took many forms, shaped by culture, origin, and especially by accident, the transiency and the uncertain attempt to climb what Wilson Benson called the ladder of fortune were central themes in the lives of nineteenth-century people.

CHAPTER FOUR

The Entrepreneurial Class

By the uneasy class, I mean those who, not being labourers, suffer from agricultural distress, manufacturing distress, commercial distress, distress of the shipping interest, and many more kinds of distress . . . In English politics, the word distress is used more frequently than any other comprehensive word, except pauperism . . . the uneasy class consists of three-fourths, or rather perhaps nine-tenths, of all who are engaged in trades and professions, as well as all who, not being very rich, intend that their children should follow some industrious pursuit . . . the desire or obligation to establish children in the world is the same as before, while the difficulty of accomplishing that object is much greater, since beginners in trade require a much larger capital than formerly to obtain the same income as formerly; unfavourable accidents happen as before, while bankruptcies, complete or partial, are more frequent than ever. All those, therefore, whose incomes are derived from the employment of capital, except great capitalists, who can easily save out of diminished incomes, have smaller means of meeting heavier calls. Their existence is a continued struggle with difficulties. How to make the two ends meet, which way to turn, how to provide for one claim without neglecting another, how to escape ruin, or at least what they consider degradation, how on earth to manage for their children; these are the thoughts which trouble and perplex them. The anxious, vexed, or harassed class, would be a better name for them than the milder terms which I have used. (Edward Gibbon Wakefield, *England and America*)

ON MONDAY, February 3, 1851, the laborers building the Great Western Railroad near Dundas, Canada West, struck for the second time, demanding a raise in their wages from three shillings and three halfpence to three shillings and ninepence per day. To enforce their demands the strikers, armed with bludgeons, threatened the workers who wanted to remain on the job, marched through the streets of Dundas, and effectively stopped work on the railroad. Two days later in nearby Hamilton, Robert Smiley, editor of the *Spectator,* called on his fellow citizens to petition the government to send troops to end the strike, and within a few days he published a petition in which twenty-five property owners requested the Mayor to call for a public meeting. The Mayor called the meeting for noon, on Wednesday, February 12, at the City Hall. There the local Member of Parliament, the eminent Allan MacNab, moved an address to the Governor General, which was "carried by acclamation."

The address voiced the fear felt by its sponsors. Over nine hundred laborers had been employed already on the railroad and thousands more would be coming. The men already had struck twice, showing a willingness to resort to violence to achieve their ends. The people of Dundas were frightened, as were the "yeomen" living along the line of railroad construction; other laborers who opposed the strike threatened violence in retaliation. Clearly, protection had become necessary, and the government should dispatch troops to "overawe the turbulent, afford protection to the peaceable and industrious, and in case of necessity, aid the Civil power in enforcing the laws."[1]

The address showed no sympathy whatsoever for the strikers or their cause. They were simply unruly and dangerous laborers in need of discipline. What the address represented was a speedy mobilization of forces by a group acting upon its shared interests. Those interests belonged to a special portion of the community. The address was, in short, an example of class action and class conflict. The men who organized the meeting and engineered the petition were the leaders of one class within a nineteenth-century commercial city. I call it the entrepreneurial class, although I might as well have used the term "uneasy class," which Edward Gibbon Wakefield defined with such precision and insight. I shall argue that the entrepreneurial class comprised an overlapping elite governing economic, political, and associational life within this mid-nineteenth-century city. Individual members of this class, however, did not remain secure in their exercise of power and privilege. Partly through the uncertainties of economic life and partly through their own acquisitiveness and weakness, they failed nearly as often as they succeeded. Downward mobility, accompanied by aggressive, anxious, and competitive behavior, consequently formed an important motif in the experience of the entrepreneurial class.

In the manuscript census, assessment rolls, city directory, and newspaper there is information about twenty-one of the twenty-five men who signed the petition.[2] For nine of them this information is supplemented by credit records.[3] It should be understood, however, that the description given here of their involvement in the life of the city is a gross understatement. We know only of those activities which took place in 1851 or 1852 and were reported in newspapers; we know, for the most part, only the roster of officers of some of the voluntary associations. The actual involvement of each man must have been much greater over the course of his residence within the city. When this is remembered, the impressive patterns which emerge from even incomplete sources become all the more significant.

But twenty-five men do not make a class in a city of fourteen thousand. Whatever the degree to which these leading men met the criteria of a class, it is clearly absurd to dignify them with such a label unless it can be shown that they were representative of a much larger group which shared the same essential features. Fortunately, this was precisely the case.

Beginning with the newspapers, I have selected all the men involved in the city government; all listed as connected with banks, railroads, gasworks, waterworks, the telegraph, and insurance; the members, mainly officers, of the leading voluntary, benevolent, and philanthropic societies; and the men who participated in the organization of public events. Where possible I have added material culled from census and assessment rolls and, in fifty-one cases, from credit records. The main characteristics of this group of 161 men, including the twenty-five who signed the petition, are summarized in Table 4.1. The list by no means includes all the activities of all the men, but only those listed in the newspaper for 1851 and 1852, perhaps merely the tip of the iceberg. For instance, on the basis of newspapers alone it appears that thirty-six, or 22 percent, of these men had invested in railroads; but the actual stock subscription lists for the Great Western Railway provide another twenty-nine names, making a total of sixty-five, or 40 percent of this sample of the entrepreneurial class.[4] If the stock subscription lists from the other railroads promoted at the time could be located, the proportion, undoubtedly, would be higher still.

Proceeding to gather a group in this manner—that is, using visibility as measured by mention in the newspaper in one of a specified number of categories, rather than membership in a group which expressed its collective consciousness through a political action—produces a collection of men with characteristics similar to those of the signers of the petition considered by themselves. In all, the activists turned up in my loose and ragged net represent between 30 and 33 percent of the men in Hamilton's entrepreneurial class.[5]

Ten important observations can be made about the men who signed the petition and the entrepreneurial class of which they formed a part.

First, the signers were the leaders of their class, that is, the most prominent men in a representative variety of trades and businesses. The twenty-one signers represented twenty different occupations. Except for one minister, one gentleman, and Allan MacNab, the Member of Parliament, all were, despite the artisan titles of nine of them, businessmen. And MacNab certainly, and Distin (the "gentleman") probably, had business interests in the city. The artisan titles are deceptive because all the artisans were among the wealthiest 10 percent of the city's people. Two of them, the tinsmiths Jackson and Moore, were among the very richest men in Hamilton. At least seven of the nine men about whom information is most complete were the leaders in their business or trade. R. W. Harris was a partner in Buchanan and Harris, the largest firm in Canada, and president of the Great Western Railroad; Robert Smiley was not only editor of the *Spectator* but proprietor of the largest printing business in the country; T. N. Best, at the time of signing the petition, was Hamilton's leading auctioneer; T. Bickle soon became the city's leading druggist; Jackson and Moore appear to have been the largest tinsmiths, and James Osborne the leading grocer. All in all, the signers made up a remarkably representative collection of leaders from the most important businesses and trades within the city: flour merchant, insurance agent, auctioneer, druggist, hardware merchant, grocer, dry goods merchant, jeweler, printer,

TABLE 4.1 Characteristics and activities of 161 members of the entrepreneurial class, 1851–52

Characteristics and activities	Percent	Number
Occupational group		
Professional	14.3	23
Merchant, proprietor, or manufacturer	46.0	74
Trades	18.0	29
Public service	10.6	17
Other	11.2	18
Total number		161
Wealth		
0–39 percentile	0.7	1
40–59 percentile	4.3	6
60–79 percentile	11.5	16
80–89 percentile	21.6	30
90–94 percentile	25.2	35
95–98 percentile	28.1	39
99–100 percentile	8.6	12
Total number		139
Birthplace		
England	33.6	48
Scotland	23.1	33
Ireland	14.0	20
Canada West	18.9	27
U.S.A.	8.4	12
Other	2.1	3
Total number		143
Religion		
Protestant	95.6	129
Catholic	4.4	6
Total number		135
Age		
20–29	17.6	24
30–39	43.4	59
40–49	30.1	41
50–59	8.1	11
Over 60	0.7	1
Total number		136
Activities		
City Council	19.2	31
Railroads	40.4	65

Education[a]	22.4	36
Urban development[b]	44.1	71
Benevolent societies and philanthropy	35.4	57
Public events	49.0	79
Specific voluntary organizations		
Hamilton Association	9.9	16
Union Hook and Ladder	0.5	8
Choral Society	7.5	12
Horticultural Society	11.8	19
British Connexion Society	24.2	39
Member of at least one	34.2	55
voluntary organization	59.6	96
Jury duty	13.7	22

[a] Includes school trustees, officers of the Mechanics Institute and the Mercantile Library Association, and a few miscellaneous positions.

[b] Indicates involvement with insurance, building societies, banks, the Board of Trade, the gasworks or waterworks, and the telegraph.

banker; carpenter, shoemaker, tailor, tinsmith, tallow chandler, and mason. Professional men, however, were notably absent, with the exception of the one minister, whose presence veiled the repressive intent of the petition in complete respectability, and MacNab, an attorney by background but present because he was the most famous man in Hamilton. Whether this represented a cleavage within the city, a divergence of interest, or an interesting calculation of who in the crunch really counted remains unclear.[6] The occupations of the larger group, the 161 members of the entrepreneurial class, reveal similar patterns. Nearly half, compared to about a fifth of all employed men, were merchants, proprietors, or manufacturers, and nearly 15 percent, compared to 5 percent of all men, were professionals. From a different point of view, about 40 percent of the men in Hamilton practiced a skilled trade compared to about 18 percent of the activists, a figure no doubt still much too large since most men with artisan titles were well-to-do master craftsmen or manufacturers.

Second, the signers of the petition were entirely and by definition a propertied group. This is especially important because, first, it at once differentiates them from the mass of the adult male population, two thirds of whom owned no property whatsoever, and, second, because of the importance of property within nine-

teenth-century society. More than any other factor, the ownership
of property determined whether or not a man remained for a
decade within the city. Forty-three percent of all homeowners in
Hamilton in 1861 had been in the city a decade earlier, compared
to 12 percent of renters. Overall, the rate of persistence among
household heads who owned their own homes was at least 50
percent higher than among those who rented.[7]

Third, these men must have known one another well. Hamilton
was still small enough to be intimate at the upper reaches of its
commercial life, and, more than that, all of the nine signers about
whom detailed information exists had lived in the city since
some time in the 1840s, when the city had begun its meteoric
transformation from an overgrown village into a commercial
center. They were, for Hamilton, founding fathers. Yet most of
them were surprisingly young: 62 percent of the 161 members of
the entrepreneurial class were under the age of forty, reflecting,
undoubtedly, the youthfulness of the city itself.

Fourth, as might be expected, these were wealthy men. Of the
twenty-one signers whose economic position can be estimated,
nineteen were among the wealthiest 10 percent of the population.
Only the city inspector and the clergyman, Reverend Webster,
were somewhat less affluent. Of the larger group of 161 men, 62
percent were among the wealthiest 10 percent of men in the city,
and 83 percent were among the richest 20 percent.

Fifth, the signers of the petition had a deep personal involvement in the economic development of the city. At least thirteen
had interests in railroads, and at least seven were concerned with
the introduction of public utilities (gas and water), building
societies, and the Board of Trade. Among the larger group of men,
at least 40 percent participated in the greatest developmental
activity of the century, the railroad, and at least 44 percent
sponsored the other activities which I have classed as urban
development.

Sixth, these were general entrepreneurs as much as specialized
businessmen or tradesmen. Besides running their own businesses
and promoting railroads and utilities, most speculated in real
estate around the city, several loaned money, and a number were
officers of insurance companies.

Seventh, the signers were the political as well as the commercial leaders of the city. Allan MacNab was the Member of Parliament; six others served on the City Council in 1851 or 1852. Of the larger group, 19 percent served on the City Council in 1851 or 1852 and 14 percent on juries.

Eighth, they promoted education as well as railroads. Four of the signers were on school boards, one was an officer of the Mechanics Institute, and one was an officer of the Mercantile Library Association. They supplied the leadership in the modernization of the schools which took place in the 1850s, symbolized most effectively, as Ian Davey has demonstrated, by the founding of the Central School. Among the larger group of 161 entrepreneurs, 22 percent volunteered their time to promote education.[8]

Ninth, the signers led the social as well as the commercial and political life of the city. Seven were members of the founding committee of the British Connexion Society; at least five were officers of fraternal organizations; six were members of the Committee to Aid the Montreal Fire Victims; and three were prize winners in the Hamilton Horticultural Society. This brief foray into the organizational life of Hamilton has turned up records of the participation of twelve of the signers in voluntary associations. Relatively fewer, interestingly, participated in philanthropic than in fraternal, honorific, and public activities: one was an officer of the St. George's Society, one an officer of the St. Andrew's Benevolent Society, and one a trustee of the Orphan Asylum. This did not represent an indifference to philanthropic activity but a division of labor. Charity in Hamilton remained mostly an activity for women, as Haley Bamman has shown. At least twelve of the wives of the signers, for instance, were Visitors for the Ladies Benevolent Society.[9] The same pattern existed among the larger sample of entrepreneurial class members: 35 percent participated in benevolent and philanthropic activity, mostly through one of the benevolent societies or through raising funds to help victims of disasters. Few spent time in the actual operation of philanthropic societies or institutions, leaving this work for the most part, undoubtedly, to their wives. Finally, at least 60 percent were members, generally speaking, officers, of one of the city's leading voluntary societies, a percentage which grossly understates their participation.

Tenth, and finally, none of the signers was a Catholic. Although

about a quarter of Hamilton's population was Catholic, including
two thirds of its laborers, all the wealthy entrepreneurs who called
for troops to quell the striking laborers were Protestant. Within
the group of 161 entrepreneurial class members there were far
fewer Irish and far more Scottish and Canadian-born men than in
the population as a whole, and almost all of them, 155 out of 161,
were Protestant.

The entrepreneurial class formed an overlapping elite, governing all the major activities within the city, whose economic prosperity they had made, through their investments, identical with
their own. They invested the city's money in railroads and utilities, in which they were stockholders. They bought land which
the coming of the railroad would make more valuable. These
leading citizens made the public interests of Hamilton and their
private economic prospects the same. Nowhere was this more
evident than in the public debates which preceded the purchase
of a large block of railway stock by the city, an act which required
the city, already hard pressed, to go even more deeply into debt.
At a meeting in August 1849, called through a petition to the
Mayor, the assembled citizens of Hamilton voted overwhelmingly
to urge their City Council, which required legitimation rather
than encouragement, to purchase fifty thousand pounds' worth of
stock in the railroad. Arguing the case for the purchase, S. B.
Freeman predicted, "The property in the City would be greatly
enhanced in value, and in this manner we would be paid; and
again, if profits resulted from the road, we would possess them."
The "we," of course, was partly the city in its corporate capacity;
it was also its entrepreneurial class, who owned most of its land.
Pushing the case from another direction, again blending public
and private interest in a fortunate harmony, Freeman continued,
"Every person acquainted with the position of Hamilton, must be
aware, that without this road it would remain an inland town,
with little commerce and manufactures; but if this railroad were
once constructed, Hamilton would be the great mart for the
business of the West, as well as for a large portion of the United
States." Freeman conveniently forgot that the Burlington Bay
Canal had assured that Hamilton would no longer be an inland
town. And he was gloriously overoptimistic about the impact of
the railroad on the city's immediate future. Nonetheless, most

of his fellow citizens must have shared his hope. Eager for the success that the railroad would bring to their speculations, they saw nothing amiss in using the credit of the city to promote the value of their own investment. If they had been asked, they could not have distinguished between their own well-being and the good of the city.[10]

The men who governed the city did not always agree with one another. Indeed, as Eric Ricker has shown, squabbling and dissent marked City Council meetings, and some local elections were fiercely fought. Although Reformers and Tories often nominated candidates for City Council elections and waged highly partisan campaigns, there is no evidence whatsoever that the members of the two parties differed from each other socially or economically, or that they had divergent views of the future of the city; virtually all came from the entrepreneurial class. The only relationship discovered between behavior in City Council and some other characteristic was the association between behavior and the ward which a councillor represented. There were, apparently, extremely localized issues which divided councillors coming from different parts of the city. But this did not detract from what Eric Ricker, in his detailed analysis of city politics, has called "the mutuality of interests, of shared concerns and values, of the city's leadership cadre, and of Reformer and Tory alike."[11]

Hamilton was certainly governed by an elite. A relatively small group of men controlled employment, credit, housing, land, welfare, and political decisions. Recently Walter Glazer, discussing power in nineteenth-century cities, has pointed to Robert Presthus' argument that "the 'scope of a leader's activity' is the best indication of his relative power, and that the proportion of leaders with multiple, or 'overlapping,' areas of activity is the best comparable index of elitism." Hamilton, in this regard, must rank high. A minimum of thirteen, or 62 percent, of the men who signed the petition provided leadership in at least two areas of activity not directly related to their business. If my information were complete, the percentage very likely would be a good deal higher.[12]

The elite that dominated Hamilton met every requirement of a social class. First of all, its members had similar objective characteristics: wealth, power, and Protestantism. A conscious attempt to find the wealthiest and most active men within the city would have arrived, pretty closely, at the same group. Second, their status within the community was similar and high; leaders in their work, they were elected to various political and associational offices. Finally, they shared common interests, which they recognized as such and supported: the fortune of all as promoters followed closely the development of the city, especially the increasing value of its land, in which they speculated heavily. They knew this well, and their promotion of railroads, utilities, and schools undoubtedly reflected their perception of the contribution these modern innovations would make to the general prosperity of their city and their own fortunes. These men were bound not only by their common investment in the future of the city but in some instances by their investment in one another. They had lived within the city when it was much smaller; they were neighbors; they were one another's creditors and debtors; they participated in the same clubs, committees, and associations. Their ties were many and their interests were common. They were capable of defending those interests when they perceived them threatened—capable, in fact, of fast, vigorous, and effective action as in the case of the railroad strike of 1851. Their actions on that occasion justly can be called an instance of class consciousness.[13]

In the same way the actions of the City Council can be considered expressions of class consciousness, for the council consistently supported and, indeed, overinvested city funds in projects which reflected the financial interests of its members. The awareness of class within the city, finally, is hinted at by marriage practices. Although at this juncture the records of marriages remain incomplete, certain patterns appear quite vividly in even the fragmentary data at hand. In the eighteen marriages of children of the entrepreneurial class in which it has been possible to estimate the social standing of both partners, the bride and groom came from the same social class. At the other end of the scale, in thirty-four of the thirty-six Catholic marriages for which evidence about social rank can be found, both bride and groom came from the lowest ranks in Hamilton's society.[14] Clearly, consciousness of class pervaded this nineteenth-century city.

Though at once an elite and a social class, the entrepreneurs did not make up a traditional upper class. Few if any of them came from gentry families in Britain, and, as a new city, Hamilton lacked a social hierarchy governed by birth rather than achievement. Anyone with enough money and sufficient pretensions could style himself a gentleman. Many men who retired from active business to live on the proceeds of their real estate or other investments did this, even when, like Edward Jackson the gentleman-tinsmith, they had started their career as artisans. Similarly, it would not be more accurate to call the entrepreneurs a capitalist class, for this would carry with it the implication that Hamilton had a two-class society rather than three quite distinct classes: entrepreneurs, artisans, and laborers.[15]

Through its leadership of commercial, civic, and social affairs the entrepreneurial class extended its influence widely, diffusing its conception of the city's interests throughout much of the population. Undoubtedly, the members could mobilize a large segment of the city's work force to support their actions, even many people not of their class. Just how far the boundaries of the class extended is unclear. They cannot be drawn by occupational lines alone, because some of the wealthiest men had artisan titles, though, certainly, no one in a commercial or clerical occupation should be excluded. The class included the wealthiest people in business and trades, definitely the most prosperous 10 percent of the population. With minor figures included, the lower boundary might extend to roughly the wealthiest fifth or quarter, the group which I have argued elsewhere can be considered well-to-do, whose members were likely to display that badge of membership in the Victorian middle class, a resident domestic servant.[16]

Thus the entrepreneurial class exerted enormous influence over the commercial, political, and associational life of this nineteenth-century city. Young, aggressive, Protestant entrepreneurs worked to propel Hamilton into the mainstream of nineteenth-century social and economic development. Unfortunately, their zeal, their confusion of public and private interests, exemplified by their overcommitment of city resources to railroads in which they were investors, and their lack of restraint plunged the city into economic disaster during the depression of the late 1850s. Nor, as a group, were these men much more successful with their own than with the city's affairs. For the calm, solid facade of power conveyed by a static group portrait

masks the turmoil, striving, anxiety, and disaster that frequently
characterized the experience of the individual members of the
entrepreneurial class.

I have traced fifty-one of these men to the credit ledgers of
R. G. Dun and Company, the precursor of Dun and Bradstreet.
These remarkable sources, treasure troves of information about
careers, morals, business practices, and social values, were systematically compiled in New York from the reports of agents in the
field, men intimately familiar with the business life of the communities in which they lived. These ledgers, of course, do not
represent anything like a complete credit history of each firm.
Firms in Hamilton obtained credit both from Great Britain
(especially Glasgow and later Liverpool) and from local banks. In
fact, the Scottish and local Canadian banks probably represented
more important sources of credit in this period than American
ones. And local banks apparently used rather less rigorous criteria
in their decisions about credit than did the Americans who ad-
vised R. G. Dun and Company. For local sources usually continued to grant credit to men well after the Dun Company rater
had recommended otherwise to New York. Obviously, local
reputation, friendship, and a sense of interdependence in the local
business community outweighed to some extent purely rational
economic decisions.[17]

Especially striking, to one perusing the pages of case histories,
is the high incidence of business failure and its concomitant—
personal disaster. The number of men who remained solidly
wealthy and the number who failed during the period of their
lives captured in the credit records were roughly comparable:
twenty-two were well-to-do or wealthy whenever the local credit
rater made his report to New York; nineteen, or nearly 40 percent, failed. There were a few, but very few, cases of dramatic
upward mobility. Neither continuing wealthy nor failing, most men
struggled from year to year, their economic state marginal and fluctuating. The incidence of failure is especially high because, first, the
credit records cover only a portion of a man's career: for fifteen
men they span 1–5 years; for eleven others 6–10 years; for ten
men 11–15 years; for twelve men 16–20 years; and for three the
ledgers record more than twenty years. The rate of failure appears
high, too, because these men were at one time wealthy and

prominent, not petty proprietors of marginal concerns. These were aspiring entrepreneurs seeking credit in New York, and their frequent failure exemplifies one of the primary social processes within this nineteenth-century city: downward social mobility. As the preceding chapter estimated, about three tenths of the men who were wealthy in 1851 and remained in the city until 1861 slipped in economic rank.[18]

Curiously, most discussions of social mobility concern themselves more with upward than with downward movement, optimistically assuming that in a growing, modernizing society opportunities expand. What count are the rate and identity of those who move up, the degree to which the gates of opportunity swing relatively more open or shut, and the equity with which the chance to pass through them is distributed throughout the social structure. It is mainly the students of older societies, concerned especially with the downward mobility of younger sons in places where primogeniture is common, who have commented historically on downward mobility. The fault, according to Anselm Strauss, is not that of historians alone: modern sociological literature is replete with studies of upward but not of downward movement. Perhaps the students of social mobility, primarily American, have discounted the possibility that failure has formed a significant aspect of the national experience. Whatever the ideology of success has proclaimed to the contrary, nineteenth-century men would have been unlikely to make the same mistake. The fear of failure—if not for oneself, then for one's children—permeates nineteenth-century writing, expressing itself most concretely in the reforming of schools, which assumed increasing importance as agencies of middle-class social advancement, and in the diffusion of contraceptive practices, noticeable among the middle, or more precisely, the entrepreneurial (or "uneasy") class as early as 1870. Clearly the process and mechanisms of downward mobility deserve more attention than they have received.[19] For that reason especially I shall turn shortly to the cases of a number of men who failed.

Despite their confusion of the public and the private in their actions as civic officials, most entrepreneurs appeared relatively honest; credit raters reported questionable moral character in only seven instances and shady business practices in only seven, and not all of these were duplicates. Honest or not, there is some indication that mortality among entrepreneurs was relatively high. Eight of them or nearly 16 percent died during the period for which records exist and they were by no means elderly: three were in their thirties, two in their forties, and three in their fifties. Perhaps the anxiety and distress that Edward Gibbon Wakefield saw in England took its toll in Canada as well.

Certainly, the credit records convey an image of men scrambling anxiously for success. Twelve or almost a quarter of them changed partners at least once during the period of record, some several times. Indeed, only one or two partnerships not based on kinship survived during the years for which credit ledgers exist. There were, of course, many reasons for changing partners. One might be simply incompatibility, which would suggest very little about business life. But in many instances it is clear that partnership changes represented attempts to reorganize businesses in a way that would ease the burdens of credit, present a new face to those from whom credit was sought, or take advantage of new opportunities. The frequent changes of partnership in the Buchanan firms, described by Douglas McCalla, reveal all these reasons, assuming often a frantic quality. Changing the form of partnership, it appears, was often a form of artful dodge.[20]

Kinship, as the experience of partnerships indicates, was a fact of extraordinary importance in business life. Some form of kin ties was present in twenty-one or about 40 percent of the businesses run by Hamilton entrepreneurs. For the overwhelming part kin ties operated through the male line. In seventeen firms the partners were brothers, sometimes working together in Hamilton or running branches of the family firm in various places, with the Hamilton branch not infrequently dependent upon the capital and good name supplied by the headquarters of the family operation in Scotland or Montreal. In three cases the kinship tie was between father and son. In only two instances was it between a man and his son-in-law and in only one was a brother-in-law involved. (These figures total more than twenty-one because in one firm two brothers were assisted by their father and father-in-law and in another two brothers worked with their brother-in-law.) Bernard Farber, studying kinship connections in Salem, Massachusetts, businesses around the start of the nineteenth century, found much the same thing: the frequent existence of a kin connection, overwhelmingly that of brothers. It is possible that this remained a pattern of the Atlantic commercial world, intertwining the fates of firms, families, and even cities in a complex net of kin and commerce. It might be expected that kinship connections served as a buffer against the insecurity of commercial life, providing men with a hedge against the failure that happened all around them. If this had been the case, then kin-based businesses would have failed less frequently than others. Whatever people might have felt about this question at the time, kinship connection apparently had little impact on business success; eight of the twenty-one firms operated or supported by kin failed, a percentage quite comparable to that of the group as a whole. In fact, in some cases kinship ties may have promoted business failure. For instance, as Douglas McCalla has shown, Peter Buchanan continually protected his brother Isaac despite the latter's irresponsible behavior. Had Isaac not been a brother, Peter undoubtedly would have broken with him, thereby saving himself much anguish and preserving the stability of the firm.[21]

One other factor besides their common interest in urban development, membership in the same associations, wealth, and commercial orientation united these entrepreneurs; namely, their speculation in real estate. No matter what the nature of a man's business, he was expected to play the land market. Sometimes speculation spurred success; in other instances it was the cause of failure. Clearly, gambling in land, done with a touch of restraint and good sense, was no vice in the eyes of men who gave credit. Quite the contrary; it meant a man was enterprising, promising, and worthy. Among the men whom speculation ruined were J. and J. Moore, brothers, "stirring men of good business habits," who confined their activities primarily to lumber and land speculation, shifting wholly to land as its profitability increased, until in 1855 they "speculated beyond their means," ending "very hard up." Similarly, by 1861, E. H. McKinistry, once wealthy and even a mayor of Hamilton, was "utterly ruined by land speculations." Nonetheless, it was essential for a businessman to try: when in 1850 the credit rater reported on James Cumming, crockery merchant, he noted that despite his excellent character Cumming had no real estate and little capital. By 1858, however, when the now successful Cumming owned "a good deal of unencumbered property," his potential as a creditor was "very good." Nowhere, perhaps, is the equation of speculation with virtue clearer than in the paean to Isaac Buchanan that passed for a credit rating. The writer of the report stated, apparently unaware of the shaky foundation of Buchanan's fortune: "Has establishment in New York and other places. Has partners. Speculates. Active business man. President of the Great Western Railroad . . . as good as the Bank." What more could be said? The men of the time, however, did not need the prodding of the Dun company reporter to push them into speculating; everyone did it, whatever his occupation. Nehemiah Ford, a wealthy painter and once Mayor, owned "real estate worth at least twenty thousand dollars" in 1856; in 1844 Daniel McNab, a wholesale hardware merchant in business for ten years, had a "capital of ten thousand dollars in real estate, made it all himself"; Colin and John Ferrie, merchants, owned real estate worth one hundred thousand dollars, which enabled their credit rating to withstand the setback to their business caused by the unpaid accounts of the country merchants whom they supplied. Alexander Carpenter, one of the partners in the firm of Gurney and Carpenter, tinsmiths and iron founders, owned "a great deal of valuable land unencumbered."[22]

Nonetheless, speculation posed some real problems for the society in which it took place. One of these, as an article in the local newspaper pointed out, was the shortage of cash and the fragility of an economy based on the credit of overextended people. "The old farmer cannot buy a cleared farm every year and pay up his store debts . . . The newer settler cannot pay up his land instalments, clear fresh land every year, and support his family . . . The country merchant, after trusting out all his capital amongst long-winded customers, finds he cannot pay his debts . . . The merchant with too many irons in the fire, finds himself unable to meet his liabilities." In these instances the lack of money did not cause problems, as the hard-pressed claimed, but their own greed. "Their difficulties arise from their imprudence in attempting too much. They have gone beyond their means." Extending himself beyond his means was what one Irish emigrant, surveying the disasters that befell his contemporaries, determined to avoid: "I believe few will dispute my assertion," wrote Wilson Benson, "when I state that nine-tenths of the financial ills that have beset the first settlers throughout Canada may be traced to the facility with which they could become involved in debts, which hung like a millstone around their necks for a number of years, until, finally, either their energies became wasted so that they were no longer able to stem the current of compound interest, or their creditors sent in the sheriff to close the scene."[23]

Given the limited investment opportunities of the time, land occupied the place that the stock market someday would assume. As one historian has written recently, "The buying and selling of land for possible profit, whether on a very small or a very large scale, was almost a universal preoccupation, almost, it might be said, the Upper Canadian national game." As the primary source of investment and speculation in a commercial society, the importance of land hardly can be overestimated. Yet, strange to say, knowledge about the structure and mechanism of the nineteenth-century land market remains, to put it charitably, primitive.[24]

One other characteristic of business life needs to be pointed out: the interdependence of the entrepreneurial class. Wholesalers in Hamilton depended upon the fortune of the family business in Montreal or abroad, or upon capital and credit from New York, London, or Glasgow. Wholesalers and importers in turn supplied local retailers with both goods and credit. City merchants extended supplies on credit to their counterparts in the country. Thus when a firm in the country failed, it could shake a commercial house in the city. "Most customers," writes Douglas McCalla of the Buchanan firms, "depended for business survival on credit, and this gave the firm much power over them. But the Buchanans depended also on their customers. Credit created a more complex relationship between creditor and debtor than the sometimes simplified models of non-business historians would suggest." The entire commercial structure resembled a house of cards, fragile and insecure, based upon the credit of overextended people. If a powerful wholesaler wished, he could sustain a retailer for years. If for some reason, perhaps personal, the wholesaler disliked a man, he could close down his business practically overnight. This tissue of connectives made of credit created elaborate patterns of dependence throughout the city, its regions, and indeed, as McCalla has shown, throughout the Atlantic commercial world.[25]

Within the entrepreneurial class two or three strata can be isolated without undue difficulty. At the top were the very few men of at least temporarily unquestioned riches, as good, it was said, as the bank. These few men exerted enormous control through commanding the sources of credit which could make or break less wealthy men. Although direct evidence for this is lacking, it is not unlikely that they exerted enormous political as well as economic power through the deference of the rest of the entrepreneurial class, which in one way or another depended upon them. Below these men were the rest of the merchants, larger master artisans, and manufacturers, who composed a stratum united by aspiration and anxiety. For these, the great majority of the entrepreneurial class, the future remained always uncertain despite the prosperity of the moment. Although their wealth varied, they formed one stratum as the result of their common experience—their use of a specific business to acquire the capital with which to branch out into real-estate speculation, their fundamental insecurity, and their dependence upon credit. Below these men lay another stratum whose members can be identified only statistically from assessment and census records, for they were neither wealthy, important, nor controversial enough to find their way often into newspaper and credit records. These, of course, were the commercial employees, primarily clerks. It is not unlikely that young men viewed clerical occupations as an entrance into the entrepreneurial class through whose ranks they hoped to climb. Because they shared the aspirations, prejudices, and deference of their employers, they should be placed within the entrepreneurial class rather than in the class below it. (Later in the century the growth of bureaucratic forms of organization in both business and government broke this identification of the clerk with his employer and created a new social grouping which might be called the bureaucratic class.)[26]

These, then, were the primary patterns: business failure, kinship-based firms, frequent change of partners, ubiquitous real-estate speculation, and the interdependence of the entrepreneurial class through networks of credit. All of them were intertwined through the lives of Hamilton's entrepreneurs, as a consideration of several case histories will make clear.

Although business failure was a common occurrence, some entrepreneurs were fortunate enough to enjoy continued success. One man who on the surface fitted this category right up to his death in 1861 was R. W. Harris, import merchant and partner of Isaac Buchanan in a firm which in 1846 had at least thirty stores across Canada and which one credit-rater overoptimistically called "as good as the bank." Harris himself remained one of the richest men in Hamilton, but when he withdrew from the firm because of ill health, his assets had already begun to shrink as a result of the firm's grave and eventually fatal problems. Had he lived, Harris would almost certainly have been considered a failure. For in the 1870s Buchanan's business, which had gone too heavily into debt, finally collapsed, leaving Buchanan himself dependent upon the charity of his friends.[27]

A more unambiguous success story is that of Edward Jackson, in business in Hamilton since 1833, and D. Moore, partners and tinsmiths. Moore, the younger partner, had started in business at about the age of thirty, largely supported by Jackson, then retired. By 1848 Moore, "rich and young," owned real estate worth between ten and fifteen thousand dollars. In the same year Jackson, then director of the Gore Bank and "one of the wealthiest men in the city," came out of retirement to rejoin Moore in the firm, which at that point owned nine good stores, unencumbered, in the city. Although Jackson retired once more in 1857, within a decade his son had succeeded him. Moore, meanwhile, continued to prosper, forming and reforming a variety of complicated partnerships.

The final success story has, like Harris's, an unhappy ending. Robert Smiley, editor of the *Spectator*, who also dabbled in real estate, by 1852 conducted "about the best printing business in Canada." In 1854, Smiley, only thirty-five years old, married, of "good character and habits, honest and industrious," with a new store and dwelling house, seemed on the threshold of an illustrious career. But within a year his health failed, and in May 1855 he died, leaving his business to his brother, who continued its success.[28]

Another kind of entrepreneurial experience, even less common than success, was upward mobility. One variant consisted of turning a modest business into a lucrative one, as the story of T. Bickle, a Wesleyan Methodist druggist born in England, illustrates. Although little was known about Bickle when he began business in 1843, his firm was considered "good for a small amount," for Bickle, a cautious, hard-working man, had a "good moral character" and was "very penurious and tight." By 1849, though doing a good business, the firm was still "not that first rate," and business languished. During 1851, however, fortune finally came to T. Bickle and Sons, and the next year the credit report concluded that the firm, "doing well," was "good for all they want." Now secure, Bickle built himself "a fine residence;" four years later he was speculating, "building good houses" and buying land. In the early 1870s, with the firm reputed to have the finest retail trade in its line, T. Bickle retired, leaving the business to one of his sons, who shifted into wholesaling as well as retailing. Bickle's story presents a classic case in which business acumen, thrift, and hard work paid off: proof that the world worked in the way which nineteenth-century social thought had predicted.[29]

A second, even rarer type of social mobility was a climb into the entrepreneurial class from quite humble origins. Such was the experience of James Williams, contractor for the Buffalo, Brantford, and Goderich Railroad, who, "through persevering, industry and sobriety" had "from being a Journeyman Blacksmith, become an independent man. Has good property and extensive buildings on the main and other streets in Hamilton." Once again, morality and success appear intimately connected. In actuality, real estate had preserved Williams' position. For when his business encountered serious trouble, his extensive land holdings shielded him from ruin until he recovered, triumphing in a contract dispute against the Great Western Railroad. Wealthy enough, perhaps savoring his success, in 1856 Williams sold his foundry to Daniel G., whose experience was less fortunate.[30]

One of the most interesting patterns among the entrepreneurial class was that of skating on thin ice—prosperous to the world, but teetering always on the edge of disaster. Such was the case of James O., Grocer and General Merchant. O., a Free Church

Presbyterian, had been born in Scotland about 1811 and was extremely prominent in the city: a member of the City Council, a director of insurance companies, the gas and light company, and a savings fund; an officer in the Masons and the Mercantile Library Association; active in his church and among those who aided the Montreal Fire Victims and founded the British Connexion Society. O. lived with his wife, four children, three servants, a relative, and a boarder in a two-story brick house at 31 James Street; his property report put him among the wealthiest 5 percent of men within the city. Although O. was the very image of the rich, community-minded entrepreneur, all was not solid beneath the surface. First of all, he bought all his commercial stock from Buchanan and Harris (themselves deeply in debt and headed for disaster), to whom he was heavily and continually indebted from the 1840s onward. In 1849, said the credit investigator, he owned "some real estate but it is encumbered . . . much respected, careful, attentive and industrious. Considered solvent at home but if he asks credit in N.Y. should give an endorsement." The note of ambivalence continued: O., though safe himself, was supported by Buchanan and Harris, "who would take care of themselves should anything go wrong of which however there need be little fear." By 1853, O. had given up dry goods completely and was supporting himself as the leading grocer, worth about forty thousand dollars. He had not given up other forms of business activity, however, for he speculated a good deal, especially in railroad stock. For a time in the mid-1850s reports became much more positive, but in 1859 a note of caution once again crept in. O.'s property was in his wife's name, and he continued largely indebted to Buchanan and Harris. The next year the sharp-nosed E. W. discovered that the property, no longer in Mrs. O.'s name, had been mortgaged for about half its value and that O., despite his "pretty profitable" family trade, had heavy expenses and was "not doing much more than holding his own." Within a year, though prosperous to the world, O. was "hard up," fortunate indeed that Buchanan and Harris were "indulgent creditors." The next year, still "by no means strong," O. remained on the edge of failure, a situation which continued for at least the next decade and a half. Not a very desirable credit risk, he at least continued to hold his own through 1875, unlike his creditor, Buchanan, but in case of a reverse he had "not much to fall back on."[31]

Another firm, the R. brothers' dry goods business, illustrated by its repeated approach to failure the delicate problem of progressing without introducing innovations that would exceed the capacity of the community. The R.'s, Robert of Hamilton (aged 46 in 1851), and James of Montreal, began their business in Hamilton in the 1840s; a decade later its reputation within the city was high, "A No. 1." Although the partnership between the brothers formally dissolved in 1861, their connections remained close. Robert, worth about thirty thousand dollars, continued in Hamilton (as E. W. put it) "a perfect slave" to his "quiet snug business," conducted at "light expense" with "adequate capital . . . in every way worthy." But complacency proved an enemy almost as deadly as drink, which ruined more than one entrepreneur in Hamilton. By the late 1860s the firm was "not progressing. Rather sleepy and rusty"—dependent on the energy of Robert's young son of about twenty-one. As the R.'s began to encounter problems, they dropped in the estimation of credit raters: "Respectable people but weak capacity and capability." Robert, it was rumored, owed a great deal of money to his brother in Montreal. Searching for a way to modernize their business, the R.'s attempted to sweep out all the mustiness in one stroke by specializing in carpets and home furnishings. But these were kept by most general dry goods firms in Hamilton, and the city was not yet ready to sustain such a specialty business. Failing as a specialty house, the R.'s encountered increasing difficulty, falling behind in their debts and earning poor credit ratings in New York. Only when the firm shifted back into the general dry goods business in 1870 did it appear to make a comeback, "evidently more alive now than previous reports indicate."[32]

Through their connections, character, some skill, and some luck, the R.'s and James O. had held on. T. N. Best was not so lucky; his story represents another pattern, rise and fall. Best was an auctioneer, like Osborne a member of the City Council, and active as well in the Union Hook and Ladder Company, treasurer of the St. George's Society, and a member of the British Connexion Society. A "first-rate auctioneer," he had come to Hamilton in 1843 and opened a small auction shop with little means but excellent character, and his business increased until by 1851 he was "the best and the principal auctioneer in the town." Through 1856 Best continued successfully with no hint of difficulty. Then in May he suddenly failed, his company bankrupt and his goods sold, ironically—it must have been—at auction. Afterwards he continued as an auctioneer on a very small scale. In 1862 E. W. reported him as "honest and respectable but poor. Responsibility slight, but he will account for business placed in his hands."[33]

Daniel G., a former freight superintendent for the Great Western Railroad, who had bought James Williams' foundry, also experienced a precipitous rise and fall. G. had paid Williams thirty-six thousand dollars for the business, four thousand in cash and the rest in a mortgage, and had taken into partnership two young Englishmen, one of whom brought fifteen thousand dollars' capital, especially necessary in a business whose tools alone cost forty thousand dollars. A "good active businessman very much liked," G. was expected to "most likely do well." Through the 1850s he produced railway cars and locomotives for the Great Western, building up "a very large establishment doing a first-rate business." A man of exceptional "character and habits," G. was in "prime credit and not sued, owns a good deal of real estate." Nonetheless, when the depression struck, railroads encountered difficulties, and the contractors who depended upon their business suffered as credit became increasingly hard to obtain. By May 1858, his works "almost at a standstill," G. was heavily in debt, mainly to R. Juson (another one of the 161 entrepreneurs), and "pressed for want of money." A widower, then forty-five years old, G. went from bad to worse, and by 1859 his business had failed. As one credit report phrased it cruelly, "All to pieces. Worth nothing." Two years later, in answer to a telegram asking if a claim of three hundred dollars could be obtained against him, E. W. said of the once well-liked, prosperous, and upright G.: "Out. Not trustworthy." A man, it seems, was judged by what he had.[34]

Somewhat as in the case of G., problems of credit apparently ruined the Hilton brothers' hardware business. Supported also by Juson and Company, in which the younger brother, Edward, had been a partner, the Hiltons started business in the late 1850s with little capital but good credit, backed by their father in Montreal and a father-in-law in New Glasgow. They were young, "first-class business men, of good character and habits, steady and attentive," who survived the depression, reporting an excellent business in the difficult year of 1861. Nevertheless, the Hilton brothers encountered trouble in 1862 when, left with too much old stock, they were sued successfully by the City Bank. Fortunately, they were able to pay the judgment against them and regroup their resources, selling their retail stock to one of their clerks and shifting their activities into the wholesale business. Their future still appeared promising, not least because they were popular young men whom other wholesale houses would assist. Once more, however, the Hiltons encountered trouble, this time from customers who did not pay them very regularly or very well. Once more, too, they escaped failure through the assistance of relatives who endorsed their notes. Soon, however, with no longer even a bank account, they were "hardly able to get along at all." Although they always had been considered upright men, their financial difficulty colored their character in the eyes of the credit rater, who, sniffing failure, made a familiar reversal of judgment. "We think they are quite honest and straightforward, and will do nothing they think wrong. Still in large matters, people see things with different eyes." Then, almost miraculously, the Hilton brothers once more bounced back, trading on their popularity to make an arrangement with all large creditors for two years' extension without interest and to arrange for a line of credit with the Bank of Montreal. Although it appeared for a year that the Hiltons were doing nicely, in spite of dealing with a slightly shady class of customers, they could not quite succeed; in 1865, at last, they went under. Summing up their complex history, E. W. put the matter tersely, as usual: "worthy fellows who have had an insufficiency of capital to do business." Mid-nineteenth-century merchants had to withstand the inability of hard-pressed customers to pay, an absolutely fundamental problem, as Douglas McCalla has shown, as well as the general fluctuations of the business cycle. Both of these conditions required capital sufficient to tide a man over the doldrums, the depressions, and the ruin of his customers. They militated against the success of the small businessman and against the prospect of permanent upward mobility into the ranks of the entrepreneurs.[35]

The depression or a lack of sufficient capital brought ruin to some men. In other cases, like that of T. N. Best the auctioneer, failure appeared suddenly and inexplicably. Such was also the fate of C. J. Tracy and the brothers A. and A. A. Wyllie. The story of Tracy is especially interesting because he was one of the few Catholic entrepreneurs in the city. In the middle 1840s Tracy, then in his late twenties, began to deal in boots and shoes, building a modest business and a reputation as "honest and industrious." With six thousand dollars' worth of real estate, he was portrayed in the credit reports as solid, practical, and knowledgeable about his trade. A prominent man in the Roman Catholic Church, he always "had a good trade among the Catholics." Nonetheless, E. W. remained mildly contemptuous of Tracy, summing him up unkindly as a "plodding, hard-working man, small means and small business." When C. J. Tracy failed without warning five years later, it must have come as something of a surprise. It also came as a disaster, for his relatively small debt outshadowed his modest assets. One wonders if the religious prejudice of Protestant entrepreneurs closed to Tracy the flow of credit that went so freely to many other men of respectable character, good judgment, and solid ability. For Tracy failed for a trifle: his debt was only thirty-five hundred dollars.[36]

The final inexplicable failure shows the enormous and arbitrary control wielded by the richest firms in the city. In the early 1850s two young unmarried brothers, A. and A. A. Wyllie, entered the dry goods business without much capital. Nonetheless, they were "cautious; not likely to contract debts without seeing their way clear." The Wyllies, "Scotchmen . . . steady and hardworking," were prospering as late as June 1854. Then, only four months later, came the report that they had "been closed by Buchanan and Harris and Co., who supported them." In response to a query made several months later the local credit rater replied: "failed last fall and will pay 25 cents on the dollar; are not again in business, and will not be." What had the Wyllies done to anger their often indulgent supporters, Buchanan and Harris? Whatever it was, their failure reveals the power of those in control of credit and points to the potential for deference in politics and social life that arose out of the commercial structure of a nineteenth-century city. For what ambitious young man would oppose the large merchants and bankers who literally controlled his future?[37]

One reason for failure did appear to be independent of the structure of credit and the business cycle. It was, very simply, moral weakness. The entrepreneurial class in Hamilton had its share of shady and dissolute characters, who, if the stories in the credit ledgers can be believed, always received their just reward. It is true, of course, that reports on a man's character usually followed the curve of his success. Credit reports left the honor of few men unblemished after they had failed. And, for the most part, successful men appeared in their pages as paragons of virtue. Nonetheless, it is possible to isolate some cases in which reports of moral weakness preceded economic decline. One such case, interestingly, was that of Robert O., brother of the slightly suspect grocer James O. Robert O. was a successful jeweler, a "prudential Scotchman," highly respected in the late 1840s and early 1850s. The only jeweler of substance in the city for some time, Robert O. was a "keen intelligent man of business," who was "self made . . . never sued . . . and A No. 1." Once again, it was E. W. who blew the whistle in 1860, sounding the cautionary note that O.'s business was slow and that he was drinking "as much as usual." Throughout the next year O.'s drinking continued, though not yet to the injury of his business. It took another year for the denouement: "not improving. Still imbibes and we should hesitate to recommend. Lives from hand to mouth." Clearly, whatever the problems brought about by the depression, Robert O. brought his troubles partly upon himself. It is of special interest that until his financial decline started, credit raters found it unnecessary to comment on his longstanding and well-known fondness for the bottle.[38]

Rather similar and equally precipitous was the decline of the grocer William Gibson K. In July 1844, Samuel K., a 35-year-old Scottish grocer, took his brother William into the family firm, already capitalized at ten thousand dollars. Only four years later Samuel left the business himself, having made a "fortune." William, "a very careful, prudent Scotchman," though somewhat overextended, was "close, honest and attentive," qualities that augured well. But by 1851 reports about K. became openly ambivalent. Although he had made "a great deal of money," his business was "chiefly with the country and lower class in town," and he had "been drinking too much for a while past." Drink, it was now brought out, had killed his older brother Samuel. Nonetheless, despite his lower-class customers and bent elbow, William thrived. One year, indeed, the people of Hamilton elected him their mayor. William's habits and his success created a problem for the credit reporters. Men who drank too much and dealt among the lower class (perhaps the source of William's political support) should not succeed. The contradiction had to be resolved, and it was. The reports lost their tone of ambiguity, and K. once again found unqualified favor as, during the next five years, he prospered and bought valuable unencumbered land upon which he erected buildings with money secured by mortgage to McLaren and Taylor. Then suddenly in 1859 his old habits reasserted themselves: "Within two months has become dissipated and is neglecting his business . . . if he continues thus he will go down with a run," said E. W. A year later William Gibson K. went out of business and was ruined.[39]

Robert O. and William K. had one achievement in common: whatever their moral character, they managed for a time to convince the local business community that they were respectable, earnest, and promising. J. G. could not claim even that much. A Scottish Anglican shoemaker, G.'s property in 1851 put him among the wealthiest 5 percent of men within the city. He lived with his wife, three children, and a servant in a two-story frame house at 19 Catherine Street and had a shop on King Street. His involvement with civic affairs, as reported in the sources, was limited to winning a prize at the Hamilton Horticultural Society and signing the petition calling for troops to end the strike on the railroad. Beginning in the mid-1840s credit investigators warned about G.: "doubtful character, unsafe, not worthy of credit." Despite his poor character, G. continued to do a good business though raters considered him "doubtful even for a small amount." G. borrowed money which he refused to pay back and put his property in his family's name (a common ploy) to avoid its seizure in one of his many legal battles. "One says of him *nulla bona,* another says he is a humbug." His principal debt, which it appears he did not pay, was to none other than James Osborne, who of course was sustained through the indulgent credit of Buchanan and Harris, who were themselves sustained through indulgent bankers in Hamilton and creditors in Glasgow. In fact, G. did "his best to cheat his creditors." Strangely, though, he managed to prosper for over a decade even though by 1851 he was known generally in Hamilton as "Old Humbug." As time passed, the condemnations of Old Humbug became more direct: "cannot be trusted"; "a grand rascal"; "a confounded old scoundrel." By 1853 his property was all in the name of his 16-year-old daughter, and his condition was shakier than usual. At last immorality and failure conjoined, as they were supposed to do, and justice triumphed; in March 1855 G. was reported "worse off and a bigger rogue." By September he had failed: "out of business, no one would trust him."[40]

The final case study in failure is more ambiguous, and more poignant. It is hard to know whether its subject, Daniel D., was a victim of his luck, his bad judgment, or his good intentions. Clearly, here too some shady dealings precipitated business problems, but Daniel's exact role remains unclear. For some years Daniel, an American by birth, kept a successful saloon on King Street West, from which he made quite a lot of money. He lived, meanwhile, with his wife, five children, and three boarders in a two-story brick house on MacNab Street. He, too, was a prize winner in the Hamilton Horticultural Society and a signer of the petition. During the 1850s, Daniel sold his saloon and began supplying ice to houses throughout the city. Considered a safe man with good habits, the owner of a prosperous business as well as assorted real estate, his troubles began when his daughter married a jeweler, one C.H.V.N., sometime during the 1850s. V. N. was successful until the depression of the late 1850s, when his trade, like that of all the other jewelers in the city, began to fail. Daniel sustained his son-in-law through loans, eventually even purchasing the business, a move E. W. suspected as "a dodge to postpone the payment of pressing obligations." For a couple of years the business limped along in bad trouble, until in March 1864 a fortunate fire saved Daniel and V. N. from embarrassment. Daniel received eighty-five hundred dollars from the insurance company, "which fully and indeed more than covered the loss. The concern has no doubt been benefitted by fire and it gives them some cash capital which they always lacked." Nonetheless, unable to make a comeback, they went into insolvency in December, with a meeting of creditors scheduled for January 9, 1865. V. N., however, did not wait to face disgrace. Late in December he "absconded taking it is said monies with him—proceeds of forgeries." And so Daniel D., encumbered with a deserted daughter and five grandchildren who moved in with him, was left to face his creditors by himself. In 1871, at the age of seventy-three, still housing his daughter and her children, old Daniel, now a widower, was back in the ice business.[41]

These vignettes have carried the story of the entrepreneurial class a long way from the railroad strike of 1851. Their significance extends beyond the human interest they evoke, for they highlight the major themes and complex texture of commercial life within even a small city. Clearly, no simple general statements about the amount, direction, or rate of mobility could define the processes at work. What is needed is a subtle classification of the varieties of experience common in the nineteenth century, and the microcosm examined by this essay has captured some of them. The continuing prosperity of Edward Jackson, the climb into prominence of T. Bickle, the rise and fall of T. N. Best, and the failure of Old Humbug—all must have been repeated often among the people of Hamilton.

In a general sense insecurity dominated the life of the entrepreneurial class. Even among the prominent, the incidence of failure was staggeringly high, and the consequences of failing were dreadful. Insecurity bred suspicion, aggressiveness, and conflict that probably counterbalanced the cohesion which might otherwise have resulted from the close association of the same men in all the affairs of the city. Despite the leniency sometimes shown by local banks and creditors, commercial Hamilton was something of a jungle. The everyday business failures brought lawsuits in their wake. Indeed, the amount of litigation occasioned by commercial disputes, nonpayment of debts, and the winding up of failed businesses must have been enormous. The men who met at the Horticultural Society at night might meet, just as easily, in court the next day as antagonists. Hamilton, of course, was a small city; the people assiduously suing one another knew one another well. They hardly could avoid meeting on the street; very likely they were often neighbors. Through its fundamental insecurity and the amount of serious conflict it engendered, commercial life must have invaded personal relationships, isolating men from one another, creating small unstable factions, driving men inward to their families in search of warmth, outward to frantically hard work, and often away to another city where they might start anew. The unpleasantly shifting fate of the individual members of the entrepreneurial class forms the backdrop to the extraordinary frequency with which its members left the city: only 40 percent of the merchants and 28 percent of the clerks present in the city in 1851 could be found there ten years later.

And yet, these men were members of the same social class, with the same civic interests and goals, driven by similar ambitions and similar calculations on how the public good could promote their private prosperity. Competitors and sometimes antagonists, they could still unite when threatened by unruly laborers. But the smooth flow of power rippling out through the commercial, political, and associational life of the city could not veil the other face of the entrepreneurial class: the competition and squabbling among anxious, "uneasy" men scrambling for success amidst the constant threat and the frequent reality of failure. Hamilton was ruled by an elite whose powers extended simultaneously to all activities within the city. Some men managed, it is true, to maintain their position in that elite for decades. But others came and went, leaving the nature of the elite unaltered while the identity of its members swirled with the vicissitudes of commerce, the whims of creditors, the logic of character, and the vagaries of chance.

How does the experience of the entrepreneurial class relate to the general theme of structural stability and individual transiency explored in the preceding chapters? And what light does the identification of an entrepreneurial class shed upon the existence of other social classes within the city? The first question is easy to answer: the theme of stability and transiency which marked the life of the city as a whole characterized the experience of its entrepreneurial class. To answer the second question and define the other social classes is much more difficult, for only one group coherently organized itself in pursuit of its interests. Yet, as I have argued elsewhere, the potential for consciousness within a group should legitimately be included within a definition of class. If any group other than the entrepreneurs had a legitimate basis for potential consciousness and collective action, a similar set of objective characteristics, and a similar status, it was the laborers of Hamilton. Their acquiescence and docility may have reflected more their isolation from one another in small work settings than a lack of consciousness about the inequalities they faced. The first enterprise to bring them together in large numbers was the railroad; then they needed only a short time to organize sufficiently to express their class interests, striking against their employers and parading through the streets with bludgeons in hand. One might argue that in Hamilton the entrepreneurial class created for itself a proletariat.[42]

It is tempting to leave the class structure in two parts, arguing that other groups formed only transitional strata that were not properly classes. For the entrepreneurial and laboring classes divide nicely along the axes of ownership of property and ownership of the means of production. Unfortunately, the historical reality was more complex. Once again a conflict provides the needed clue: in 1852 a group of mechanics protested the "truck" system of payment by orders redeemable at certain stores rather than by cash. In their arguments the mechanics identified themselves and their own interests as set apart from the merchants and master tradesmen who employed them, and who, they believed, were consciously exploiting them. This incident suggests that a conscious middling interest existed within the city, buffeted between top and bottom, sometimes identifying with the entrepreneurial class, sometimes with the laboring class, and sometimes standing by itself. Certainly, artisans could be distinguished from laborers on a variety of objective dimensions: their wealth, their propensity to own property, the frequency with which they sent their children to school, perhaps even the age at which they died. There may have been distinct differences as well in the way in which merchants, artisans, and laborers organized their families, as Bernard Farber found for commercial Salem, Massachusetts, in the late eighteenth century. And finally, there is the evidence of patterns of social mobility, described in Chapter Three: movement took place within three relatively large and stable, hierarchically ordered groups, separated by unstable, transitional strata.[43]

Thus the class structure of this mid-nineteenth-century commercial city seems to have had three components: the entrepreneurial class, the artisan class, and the laboring class. But the fundamental division within Hamilton was ethnic as well as economic; the city was divided not between native and immigrant but between Irish Catholics and all the rest. That Irish Catholics were largely laborers and that the poor increasingly were Irish Catholic superimposed these two criteria of social division upon each other, giving to the class structure within the city a sharp edge of animosity and setting up a peculiarly strong latent source of conflict. What was especially frightening about the striking laborers on the Great Western was not only the threat they posed to the linchpin in the scheme of modernization but the simple unstated fact that they were Irish Catholics.

CHAPTER FIVE

Growing Up in the Nineteenth Century: Family, Household, and Youth

Whatever the previous ideal family structure was, during the transition toward relative modernization, the ideals always change toward what anthropologists and sociologists call a *multilineal conjugal family* unless they already took that form. (Marion J. Levy, Jr., *Modernization and the Structure of Societies*)

JOHN MOTTASHED, John Cawly, John Shea, Anthony Copp, and S. D. Sawyer were the heads of five quite ordinary families who lived in Hamilton in the middle of the nineteenth-century.

John Mottashed, a 52-year-old Protestant shoemaker, born in Ireland, lived on Hughson Street in a two-story stone house which he rented from T. Stinson. With him in 1851 lived his 40-year-old second wife, Mary Ann; his married, 24-year-old son Jonathan, a miller, and his 20-year-old daughter-in-law, Mary Anne; his other sons, John, twenty-two, George, seventeen, Robert, fourteen, Joseph, six, and Charles, one; his daughters, Mary, twelve, and Anne, eight; and his stepchildren, John Calvert, an 18-year-old shoemaker, and Sarah Calvert, fifteen years old. Throughout the 1850s John Mottashed ranked close to the middle of the population in wealth. Although he continued to live in the same house and to work in the same shop, which he owned, by 1861 the composition of his household had changed markedly. His married son and daughter-in-law no longer lived with him, and the three older boys—John, George, and Robert—had taken up his trade, while the youngest, Charles, and the girls, Mary and Anne, attended school. Joseph and the two step-children no longer lived at home. John Mottashed's family, however, had not stopped growing, for, perhaps surprisingly in light of her age, in 1853 his wife gave birth to another daughter, Ester, who, like her half-sister, was attending school in 1861.

John Cawly, another shoemaker, had an economic standing comparable to John Mottashed's. In 1851, Cawly, a 36-year-old Catholic born in Ireland, lived in a one-story frame house on Catherine Street with his wife Mary and their two daughters, aged 8 and 6, who attended school. His experiences during the next decade are not clear, but by 1861 John Cawly and his family had left the city, their destination unrecorded.

John Shea, an illiterate 40-year-old Irish Catholic laborer, lived near John Cawly in a one-story frame house on Tyburn Street with his 40-year-old wife Johana and their three sons, Patrick, nine, John, six, and Dennis, four. The two older boys attended school. A poor man, Shea probably earned less than about two thirds of the men in Hamilton, and his already precarious situation worsened during the decade. His wife died, leaving him to care for the boys, the oldest and youngest of whom remained at home while the middle son, John, went away to school. Overwhelmed by the problem of maintaining a family by himself, John Shea declined into deeper poverty: by 1861 he had become one of the poorest men in the city.

The story of Anthony Copp is happier. Copp, a 26-year-old Baptist tinsmith born in England, lived in 1851 with his recent Canadian bride, 22-year-old Milvina, in a two-story stone house on Hughson Street. With them lived Copp's unmarried 24-year-old brother, William, also a tinsmith, a young woman boarder who worked as a milliner, and two female servants, Mary Chandy, an Irish Catholic woman of thirty, and Susan Arab, a Canadian Baptist girl of fourteen. A prosperous man, Copp was wealthier than about 85 percent of the other men in Hamilton, and he owned six horses, a cow, and a tin shop employing thirteen hands. With this strong foundation, Copp prospered during the decade; by 1861, styling himself a manufacturer, he ranked among the wealthiest 5 percent of the population. In the meantime his family had expanded. Although his brother, the boarder, and the two servants no longer lived with him, there were now three children—Nelly, eight, Samuel, four, and a baby girl, two—as well as a new servant, 19-year-old Louise Johnson, a Methodist born in England.

Another successful man was S. D. Sawyer, an unmarried

American-born stove dealer, who in 1851 lived with the family of his younger brother, a machinist. A prosperous man, S. D. owned a horse and carriage for pleasure. By 1861 he and his brother had transformed and expanded their businesses into a substantial iron foundry. In 1853 S. D. married, and within the next eight years he had four children, three daughters and a son, all living on Victoria Avenue in his own household, which also included a 16-year-old English servant girl.

Are these five case histories of real families representative of common patterns, or was past family structure a bundle of fleeting and varied relationships, complex and incoherent? If, indeed, there was order to family structure, which case was typical, the extended family of John Mottashed in 1861, or the nuclear family of John Cawly at the same time? Did most households change their composition as rapidly as that of John Mottashed, Anthony Copp, or S. D. Sawyer's brother, or was stability over time more usual? Were any of the variations that existed related to the particular ethnic background or economic rank of the household head? Was it common for girls the ages of Susan Arab and Louise Johnson to work as servants, and for how long did they usually remain employed as domestics—until the age of thirty, like Mary Chandy, or was she an anomaly? Did young couples, like the children of John Mottashed, usually go to live with their parents after marriage, and did boys the age of his unmarried sons frequently remain at home, or did they more often go to live as boarders in the household of a friend, sibling, or stranger? Was John Mottashed's wife unusual in giving birth in her forties? How often did men like John Shea lose their wives through death?

It is not clear that any meaningful patterns can be constructed out of the answers to these questions, which may be mostly of antiquarian interest—intriguing, gossipy facts without much historical or theoretical significance. Peter Laslett has asked "whether the form of the family has in fact played as important a role in human development as the social sciences have assigned to it. It is possible to wonder whether our ancestors did always care about the form of the families in which they lived, whether they were large or small, simple or complicated, and even whether they contained kin or servants or strangers."[1] On the other hand, it may be possible to relate these domestic details to questions of social organization and social change, connecting the facts of household composition with the life cycle of people in times past, the complexities of social structure, and even the dynamics of modernization.

This chapter cannot do more than take a tentative step toward these vastly complex issues. Its approach is to arrange specific questions about the family into three large problems and to consider the extent to which the implications of the situation in Hamilton support, modify, or challenge what scholars recently have said about each. These three problems concern the boundaries of the family, the relation between the family and the life cycle, and the relation between the family and social change. From one perspective, the conclusions that the chapter reaches support the general argument of this book: within the city as a whole, household structure remained remarkably stable across the decade, but the composition of individual households frequently changed. The household, it will be argued, was basically simple or nuclear in structure with flexible boundaries expanding or contracting as circumstances required. These expansions and contractions related frequently to the presence within the household of a young person living a state of semi-autonomy, a phase of the life cycle common in times past but since virtually lost. Its loss during modernization reflects the prolongation of dependence of young people upon their families. The contraction of the stage of semi-autonomy reflected the assumption of a more specialized role by the family, whose boundaries became more sharply defined and rigid over time. The process, however, involved strains; for the curtailment of semi-autonomy began prior to the introduction of an institutional framework to contain and manage young people, who now passed the long period between puberty and marriage in new ways. The result was a very real crisis of youth in the nineteenth-century city.

The problem of the boundaries of the family provides a way of placing the question, perhaps a bit tired by now, of whether the family was nuclear or extended into a larger context. What kinds of people lived together under what circumstances is a question which involves the formation of the family through marriage, its size, and the addition of people other than husbands, wives, and children to any domestic group. At the same time, the issue of boundaries concerns the interconnections between families or between families and institutions: the extent to which boundaries should be stretched to encompass kin not residing with each other and the degree to which families shared a broad variety of tasks with each other and with other agencies in the community.

The relation of the family and life cycle raises, at one extreme, a question which cannot be answered here: how parents loved, punished, or taught children of different ages.[2] From another point of view, it asks to what extent people at various points in their life cycle found sustenance, support, or aggravation in their families. At what age and for what reasons, to take one important example, did children customarily leave their parents' household, and did that age relate to other major events, such as attending school, starting to work, or marrying? A similar question is important at the other end of the life cycle: did the elderly turn to their children customarily, or only in particular circumstances such as widowhood, poverty, or illness?

The connection between the family and social change concerns, first of all, the extent to which the boundaries of the family and the life cycle can be set in time and place. Were there systematic connections between particular patterns and social contexts? When, in what way, and why did these configurations alter? Lurking behind these questions is the contentious issue of the relationship of the family to modernization. Folk wisdom and even academic writing often teach that industrialization eroded the stability and importance of the family. But that may well turn out to be a simplistic view, for it is possible that the family did not weaken as much as change. If this should be the case, then the modern family is no less important than its counterpart, the happy scene of work and residence admired by preindustrial romantics. It is simply different.

The Boundaries of the Family

More than any other historian, Peter Laslett has confronted the question of the historical boundaries of the family. First raised in *The World We Have Lost*,[3] his hypothesis that throughout history most people have lived most of their lives in nuclear families challenged both conventional wisdom and sociological theory. It is the most radical and influential contemporary statement about the family in history and for that reason deserves close examination. Partially in order to test his contention, Laslett with the Cambridge Group for the History of Population and Social Structure has been systematically collecting all the available listings of inhabitants for preindustrial England. As a way of testing the representativeness of the English experience, moreover, the Cambridge Group sponsored a conference at which scholars investigating similar questions in other places compared their results. In his new book, *Household and Family in Past Time,* Laslett has brought together revisions of some of the conference papers and related material, including a long analytic introduction and his essay on the size of the household in England across four centuries. His introduction and essay present the most recent exposition of his basic argument and a summary of the available related data from various places in the world. Together they constitute the most complete discussion in English of the boundaries of the family.[4]

At the most general level, Laslett again argues his case that most European families have been nuclear at least since the start of recorded experience. Put in a negative fashion, his argument is that the extended or stem family was not the predominant form of family organization anywhere in the world for which data from any point in time have been found. The nuclear family, therefore, cannot have been, as social theorists have argued, a precondition of industrialization. Not only has the family remained nuclear in England for four hundred years, but until the twentieth century it stayed about the same size. This stability in average household size persisted throughout the onset of the industrial revolution and the demographic transition, the decline in marital fertility. Just why family size remained constant while fertility declined is a puzzle that still lacks an adequate solution.

Laslett not only advances an argument but puts forward a series of definitions, a taxonomy for classifying households, and the beginnings of an ideographic system to represent family and household structure. His belief that systematic comparative work requires the adoption of uniform categories certainly is right and his advocacy timely. Nonetheless, the classificatory scheme he adopts has a serious flaw.

Laslett points out, quite rightly, that people in times past used the words family and household loosely and interchangeably, too imprecisely, in fact, to make discrimination between the two possible. But the delineation of a sharp boundary between family and household is, in a sense, the very essence of the conceptual scheme which underlies his taxonomy. Thus Laslett proposes as a basic term *co-resident domestic group,* which refers to all the people living together within one dwelling. Within the co-resident domestic group he distinguishes among the conjugal family, the husband, wife and their children; the *household,* a less intimately related group consisting of the conjugal family plus co-residing kin and servants; and the *houseful,* people he terms "inmates," who have a less permanent and intimate relation with other members of the household, with whom, nonetheless, they reside. Within this last group Laslett places boarders, lodgers, and visitors, and it is this distinction that is the most questionable element in his scheme. Laslett also distinguishes between *dwelling* and *premises.* The dwelling is the actual building inhabited by the household; a household always lives in a dwelling. But members of the same household may live in separate buildings on the same plot of land, or in self-contained apartments in the same building. The space thus inhabited by the entire co-resident group Laslett calls the *premises.* The premises and the dwelling may or may not be identical.[5]

Despite his placement of servants within the household, Laslett includes only the conjugal family and kin when he classifies co-resident domestic groups into various types, a procedure which seems inconsistent with the logic underlying his scheme, though sensible enough on more intuitive grounds. He subsequently divides the variety of groups he finds into households with and without servants, though in practice he makes very little use of that distinction. The most serious weakness in the scheme, however, is the complete exclusion of boarders and lodgers from the household.

I dwell on Laslett's detailed scheme for classifying co-resident domestic groups because I shall use it shortly to describe the household in Hamilton and to compare it with the household in other places. For that reason it is worth describing in even more detail the terminology which Laslett employs. The first group he distinguishes consists of those people living alone without spouse, children, or other kin, though they might have boarders or servants dwelling with them; these people he calls *solitary family households.* Another category consists of unmarried people, whether related or not, living together, such as a group of friends or siblings; these he calls *no-family households.* Next, he separates out the co-resident domestic groups in which no kin live with the conjugal family. These are the *simple family households,* either a married couple with or without children or a widowed person with children. Families that contain kin he divides into two groups: those which contain unmarried kin and those which contain two or more married couples, such as two parents with their married son, daughter-in-law, and any children they might have. The first category, those with unmarried kin such as a widowed parent or a maiden sister, he calls *extended family households,* and those with two or more couples *multiple family households.* Laslett divides both the extended and multiple family households into subcategories according to the relation of the kin to the household head. Where the head of the household is the elder person, such as a parent, and the kin a younger one, such as the child, the relationship is considered *downward*; where the head of the household is the younger and the kin the elder, as in the case of a widowed parent living in her married daughter's house, the relation is considered *upward*. When the kin are of the same generation as the household head, the relation, as in the case of a married couple living with the husband's brother, is *lateral;* and if two or more of these conditions prevail, the household is put into a category called simply *combined*.[6]

Laslett used this classificatory scheme to compare the structure of co-resident domestic groups both between places in England and between England and other countries. In England and most of western Europe the overwhelming proportion of households, generally about three quarters, have been simple for as long as records exist. They consisted, that is, of a conjugal family and no other resident kin. Very few households at any time were multiple. Thus the classic extended or stem family consisting of married children living together with their spouses and parents in one household appears to have been exceedingly rare in western European history. This pattern, moreover, bore almost no relation to industrialization nor, in any given area, to the age gap between spouses, to household size, marriage age, the incidence of two-parent households, or the average number of children. Laslett did find different distributions of household types in Serbia and Japan, two of the areas with which he made comparisons. But even there, multiple family households, though much more common, did not form a majority of all co-resident domestic groups. Laslett is conscious of the objection that his classification may undervalue the existence of intimate relations between kin who lived near to each other though not in the same premises. This contention he dismisses rather abruptly, and not quite convincingly, with the assertion that had their relations been truly close kin would have dwelled together more often.[7]

Laslett also leaves unresolved two other problems neglected by his classification. One is the possibility of social class variation in household structure and size. Laslett touches class as a source of potential variation only briefly and rather inconclusively in his introductory essay, implying that the simple family household formed the modal experience of all social groups. In his essay on household size, however, he presents some fairly scanty evidence which nonetheless shows very consistent relations between household size and social rank as measured by occupation: the higher the rank, he found, the larger the household (defined, according to his scheme, as including kin and servants but excluding lodgers).[8] Laslett does not elaborate on the significance of this systematic variation or relate its implications to his conclusions about the structure, as distinct from the size, of the household. Nevertheless, other historians, Lutz Berkner, Michael Anderson, and Bernard Farber, to name three, have found class or wealth an extremely important determinant of household size and structure. The regularity with which class variation in household size and composition appears makes it seem, in fact, an ubiquitous and important feature of past societies, pointing to a link between social and family structure.[9]

The other problem with Laslett's scheme concerns the life cycle, or as he calls it, developmental cycle. In an important essay critical of Laslett, Lutz Berkner uses an Austrian village to show that household structure varied systematically with the life cycle: young, newly married couples frequently lived for a time with one set of parents, and elderly people often dwelled with their children. Although at any moment in time a majority of all households were simple, at one or more quite predictable times in their lives most people resided within a multiple-family household. Similarly, in an industrial English city, Preston, in 1851, Michael Anderson found that 43 percent of all childless men with wives of child-bering age did not head their own household, a proportion that dropped radically as their age and the number of their children increased. However, unlike the situation described by Berkner, very few elderly couples lived with kin.[10] It would be a telling blow to Laslett's argument if it should prove to be the case that in preindustrial England young married couples usually lived with their parents and elderly couples with their married children, an outcome which Laslett considers unlikely. For he contends that the area studied by Berkner deviated from the pattern dominant in both England and western Europe. As Laslett points out, the issue is a difficult one to resolve, because very few listings of inhabitants in English villages contain ages. On the basis of those that do list the ages of the people, it appears that both young and elderly couples usually dwelled alone. There are, additionally, ratios which specify the approximate proportion of households that would have been extended or multiple had most elderly people gone to live with one of their married children. The proportion of English households with kin has consistently been well below this level, Laslett states. Finally, the transiency of the population, a factor which he does not discuss, probably supports Laslett's argument that the simple family household predominated throughout the life cycle. Roger Schofield, for instance, has discovered rates of transiency in preindustrial English villages that match those reported here, in the previous chapter, for nineteenth-century cities. Thus distance separated the members of many conjugal families and made co-residence unlikely.[11] Perhaps the rate of transiency intervened between the life cycle and household structure by lessening the proportion of multiple or extended family households in areas where people moved often. It could be that the rate of transiency distinguishes the Austrian village described by Berkner from the English villages studied by Laslett.

Laslett has found little discussion of household structure in literary sources. From this he concludes that people generally did not think or care about the question very much; household structure, he maintains, was neither an ideological nor a cultural issue. Later on I shall present some evidence that calls into question Laslett's conclusion on this point, which, I can only surmise, must be based on an unduly narrow consideration of written sources, if Canadian and American material can be taken as any indication of what was written about similar subjects in Britain. Nonetheless, Laslett surely is right that a number of concrete factors shaped family structure. He points, for example, to Marion Levy's argument about the demographic limits of any population; there are only a limited number of grandparents available at any one time, a number especially low in earlier societies in which death came sooner than it does now.[12] Similarly, Laslett points to inheritance practices, economic circumstances, and other generally objective factors which, he contends, made the maintenance of simple family households more or less inevitable.

This conclusion leaves Laslett with a difficult problem: why has a belief in the prevalence of the extended family in earlier times persisted with such remarkable tenacity? If he could show that it was once the dominant household structure among the elite or was specially prized by them, Laslett argues, it might be possible to account for the hold of the extended family on the historical imagination, but, rather too abruptly, he dismisses this as unlikely. As a result he is left, he readily admits, with no very good answer, other than the unconvincing implication that the myth of the extended family has been the creation of contemporary intellectuals seeking the warm, close, and vital family life that they romantically imagine existed once upon a time.[13]

Laslett's interpretation of the boundaries of the family, or more precisely the co-resident domestic group, poses three questions of special importance here: (1) To what extent was Hamilton like other places? (2) Does Laslett's delineation of the boundaries of the family, notably his distinction among conjugal unit, household, and houseful, appear valid and useful? (3) Does the Hamilton experience offer clues to the puzzling persistence of the myth of the extended family? There are, of course, other important questions about the boundaries of the family. One is the extent to which ethnicity and class defined barriers to the formation of the family through marriage. Another is the permeability of the

boundaries between the family and community. In this part of
the chapter I shall touch only briefly on the question of marriage,
reserving speculation about the relation of family and community
for the last topic on social change.

The distribution of household types in Hamilton matched the
common pattern discovered in most parts of western Europe and
North America beginning, at least, in the sixteenth century. Table
5.1 shows that in Hamilton about four fifths of co-resident domestic groups consisted of simple family households; that is, they
contained no kin except married couples (or widowed persons)
and their children. In Preston, an industrial city in Lancashire, in
1851, 72 percent of all households were simple in structure; in the
English village of Ealing in 1599, the percentage was 78; in a
French village in 1788, it was 76; in England and Wales, as a
whole, in 1966, it was 73; in Buffalo, New York, in 1855 (not included in the table), it was 73 for natives and 84 for Irish-born
household heads.

The same conclusion emerges from comparing the proportion
of households with at least one resident relative: in Hamilton the
proportion varied between 15 and 16 percent between 1851 and
1861, compared to 22 percent in York, England, in 1851, and 23
percent in Preston at the same time, 13 percent in Ealing in 1599,
20 percent in Longuenesse in 1788, and 10 percent in the 100
English communities between 1564 and 1821 studied by Laslett
and his associates. Only in Serbia and Japan, among the areas
studied, did Laslett discover significant differences. Even there,
however, the simple family household existed as a far more important and widespread form, comprising 67 percent of households
in Belgrade in 1733 and 43 percent in Nishikomiya, Hama-issai-
chō, in 1713, more than usually is thought to have been the case.[14]

At one level, of course, these comparisons appear absurd. Eighteenth-century France, seventeenth-century England, eighteenth-
century Japan, and nineteenth-century Ontario were exceedingly
different societies. But that, of course, makes the similarity in the
structures of their co-resident domestic groups all the more striking. To be more precise, most people dwelled within simple
family households, and those who did not lived, more often than
any other way, with one or more unmarried relatives in extended
family households, as Table 5.2 indicates. In only a very few

TABLE 5.1 Comparative household composition and structure, 17th–20th centuries

Household (HH) composition and structure	Mid-19th century					17th–18th centuries					Laslett study	20th century
	Hamilton 1851	1861	York, 1851	Preston, 1851	Rural sample, 1851	England,[a] 1599	France,[b] 1788	Serbia,[c] 1733	Japan,[d] 1713	Rhode Island,[e] 1689	100 communities, England and Wales, 1564–1821	England and Wales, 1966
Mean HH size	5.8	5.3	4.8	5.4	5.5	4.8	5.1	7.1	5.0	5.9	4.8	3.0
HH with												
8 or more members	23%	17%	13%	23%	24%	13%	20%	27%	53%	27%	10%	1%
Children	78%	79%	66+%	81+%	74+%	72%	77%	77%	82%	87%	75%	n.a.
Relatives	15%	16%	22%	23%	27%	13%	20%	27%	53%	3%	10%	10%
Lodgers or boarders	29%	20%	21%[f]	23%	10%	n.a.	n.a.	n.a.	n.a.	n.a.	n.a.	n.a.
Servants	30%	21%	20%	10%[g]	28%[g]	34%	20%	30%	14%	30%	29%	0
Mean no. of children	2.4	2.4	1.8+	2.7	2.6	1.6	2.4	1.6	2.0	3.1	2.0	n.a.
HH structure[h]												
Solitary	5%	4%	n.a.	} 14%	17%	12%	1%	2%	7%	7%	n.a.	} 17%
No family	2%	2%	n.a.			2%	6%	2%	2%	0	n.a.	
Simple family HH	80%	79%	n.a.	72%	62%	78%	76%	67%	43%	90%	n.a.	73%
Extended family HH	11%	12%	n.a.	} 14%	21%	6%	14%	15%	27%	3%	n.a.	} 9%
Multiple family HH	2%	3%	n.a.			2%	3%	14%	21%	0	n.a.	
Indeterminate	0	1%	n.a.	0	0	0	0	0	0	0	n.a.	1%

Source: Peter Laslett, ed., *Household and Family in Past Time* (Cambridge, Eng., 1972), 77, 82, 83, 85; Michael Anderson, "Household Structure and the Industrial Revolution: Mid-nineteenth Century Preston in Comparative Perspective," in Laslett, *Household and Family,* 219, 220, 222.

n.a. = not available.

a Ealing, Middlesex: population 427.

b Longuenesse, Pas-de-Calais: population 333.

c Belgrade: population 1,357.

d Nishikomiya, Hama-issai-chō: population 653.

e Bristol: population 421.

f Definition in York study varies slightly.

g Includes apprentices.

h Terms defined in text.

instances in Hamilton, which was not at all unusual in this respect, did two or more married couples dwell together in a multiple family household: 2 percent in 1851 and 3 percent a decade later. The classic extended or stem family, parents dwelling with their married children, existed infrequently in nineteenth-century Hamilton, as it did in a sixteenth-century English village, an eighteenth-century French village, or a seventeenth-century New England town.

The purpose of these comparisons is not to explore the variation in household structure within Europe or among western European, North American, and other societies. Laslett's recent book pursues that task at length and with considerable success. My purpose here is a more modest one, namely, to suggest that the distribution of household structures in Hamilton fell well within the limits of what could be expected in most towns and cities in western Europe and North America. Hamilton's representativeness in this respect gives additional force to the more detailed discussion which follows, for it at least makes plausible the supposition that the other aspects of family life in Hamilton existed, with no more than a reasonable degree of variation, in a great many other places as well.

In the past, co-resident domestic groups often contained members other than married couples, their children, and assorted kin. These additional members were, primarily, boarders or lodgers and servants. "The substantial proportion of persons who turn out to be living in households other than those into which they were born," asserts Laslett, "looks to us like a sociological discovery."[15] In Hamilton, as Table 5.1 shows, boarders dwelled in 29 percent of households in 1851 compared to 20 percent a decade later. Similarly, there were boarders in about 23 percent of the households in Preston in 1851; in 21 percent of those in York at the same time; in 22 percent of native and 15 percent of Irish households in Buffalo, New York, in 1855; and in 16 percent in Detroit, Michigan, in 1850 (not shown in the table). In fact, Modell and Hareven recently estimated that boarders could be found in about 15 or 20 percent of the households in most nineteenth-century cities. Resident domestic servants remained common, too: they lived in 30 percent of the households in Hamilton in 1851 and

TABLE 5.2 Comparative household structure, 1851–1861

Household type	1851	1861	No other person in household 1851	1861	At least one boarder 1851	1861	At least one servant 1851	1861
Solitary								
Widowed	1.7%	1.8%	45.0%	61.9%	50.0%	23.8%	27.5%	20.6%
Single	3.1	2.4	34.7	54.8	56.9	40.7	18.0	15.5
Total	4.8	4.2						
No family								
Co-res. rel. or sib.	2.1	2.1	50.0	68.2	37.5	27.6	20.8	18.8
Simple								
Couple alone	11.0	10.8	49.0	70.3	34.1	20.4	30.6	15.2
Couple with child	58.3	56.0	52.4	65.3	28.3	19.6	31.8	22.3
Widower with child	5.4	5.8	60.5	69.8	26.7	20.5	19.4	12.7
Widow with child	5.1	6.0	58.8	72.0	24.3	19.9	21.8	12.8
Total	79.8	78.6						
Extended								
Upward	2.6	3.1	41.0	62.0	33.5	20.3	47.6	29.6
Downward[a]	—	0.2	—	66.7	—	33.3	—	0
Lateral	4.8	4.1	47.3	55.9	34.6	26.6	37.3	31.5
Down-lateral	1.1	1.4	40.0	62.5	40.0	22.9	44.0	22.9
G&G[b]	0.5	0.3	58.3	91.7	16.7	0	25.0	8.3
Combined	2.3	2.5	64.2	52.9	26.4	28.7	22.6	29.9
Total	11.3	11.6						
Multiple								
Up	0.3	0.3	14.3	50.0	57.2	40.0	57.2	10.0
Down	0.7	1.6	82.4	69.6	5.9	19.7	11.8	14.3
One level	0.7	0.6	50.0	59.1	43.8	31.8	12.6	31.8
Total	1.7	2.5						
Indeterminate	0.3	0.7	16.7	56.5	66.7	21.7	33.4	26.0

[a] Grandparents with grandchildren.
[b] Couple with their unmarried children and their grandchildren.

21 percent a decade later. Servants, similarly, dwelled in 20 percent of the households in the commercial city of York in 1851; in
10 percent of the households in Preston (a low percentage that
may reflect its large industrial work force); in 29 percent of the
households in the 100 communities that Laslett studied between
1564 and 1821; and in 12 percent of the households in Detroit in
1850. Finally, the proportion of all households with children appears to have been quite similar across time and among a wide
variety of places. In Hamilton, 78 percent of households in 1851
and 79 percent in 1861 contained children, compared to rather
more than 66 percent in York and 81 percent in Preston in 1851,
72 percent in Ealing in 1599, 77 percent in Longuenesse in 1788,
and 75 percent in Laslett's 100 communities between 1564 and
1821.[16]

In the 100 communities that Laslett studied for nearly three
centuries the average size of the household was about 4.8, a figure
which varied surprisingly little. Nonetheless, the mean household
size in Hamilton, which decreased from 5.8 to 5.3 during the
1850s, did not differ so much from its English counterpart as the
Laslett average might lead one to expect, for the average in Preston was 5.4 although in York it was 4.8. The smaller household
size in York reflected a lower mean number of children per household, a bit more than 1.8, compared to 2.4 in Hamilton in both
1851 and 1861, and 2.7 in Preston. In Michigan, for instance,
mean household size and average number of children varied together among three types of places in 1850: in the rural areas
where household size was largest, 5.4, there were 3.1 children per
household; in the city of Detroit, the average household size was
5.2 and the number of children 2.5; and, finally, in villages and
towns there were on the average 5.0 people and 2.4 children
per household. The variation in number of children among Preston, York, Hamilton, and Michigan probably stemmed from a
difference in age structure, with which, of course, number of children varies quite directly. Unfortunately, the comparative figures
necessary to make an estimate of family and household size that
controls for age have not been assembled.[17]

Household structure in Hamilton was not only representative
but stable, an observation which returns to the main theme of
this section. The distribution of household types remained remark-

ably constant across the decade: to reiterate, the proportion of simple family households varied only between 79 and 80 percent, and the percentages of extended households increased only from 11 to 12 and of multiple households from 2 to 3. Among extended family households the most common subtype remained the lateral, those in which kin members were of the same generation as the household head, usually a brother or sister of the husband or his wife. In only about 8 percent of households in 1851 and 10 percent in 1861 did adults of two or more generations, a married or widowed child with one or more parents, dwell together. Similarly, the average number of children per household (and the average age of household heads) did not alter at all. The decrease in the proportion of households with boarders and servants, and the consequent decline in average household size, constituted the only alteration in household composition during the decade. The cause of the decline in the proportion of households with boarders was the outmigration of young men, a phenomenon referred to in earlier chapters. The reduction in the proportion of households employing a resident domestic servant may have come about because of the economic hardships posed by the depression. Middle-income people, among whom the decline was sharpest, had been hit hard by the economic dislocations of the 1850s.[18] This interpretation is more likely to be valid than one which rests on labor supply, for the number of young women rose while the proportion employed declined.

The demography of Hamilton's population probably explains the remarkable stability in household structure. Two populations with similar birth, death, and marriage rates should have about the same proportion of married, widowed, and single adults. Given similar social rules governing the formation of households, the proportion of different sorts of household types should remain constant across time. Slightly surprising, nonetheless, is the relatively fixed proportion of kin available for distribution to various households in a city whose largely immigrant population entered and left with such rapidity.

Nonetheless, the overall stability of household structure should not be extended to the experience of individual households, as Table 5.3 shows. For the composition of individual households varied greatly over time even though the distribution of types remained virtually identical. Simply put, most households which had a boarder or a relative at the start of the decade no longer had one at the end: 72 percent of households had lost all their boarders and 71 percent had lost all their relatives between 1851 and 1861. A much lower proportion of households with either relative or boarder lost them, 34 percent; and a somewhat lower proportion, 30 percent, lost all their servants (which points to the fact that fluctuation in household type did not usually mean fluc-

TABLE 5.3 Changes in household structure and size of linked households, 1851 and 1861

	A. Household members					
	All households linked 1851 to 1861		All households linked 1851 to 1861			Unlinked households,
Members	Lost all	Acquired one or more	1851	1861	1851 or 1861	1851 At least one
Child	6.7%	57.6%	80.8%	85.1%	91.8%	77.3%
Boarder	71.8	16.1	31.7	20.0	42.7	27.2
Relative	71.2	11.8	16.2	14.6	26.1	14.1
Boarder or relative	34.4	24.9	42.0	31.2	56.4	37.3
Servant	29.6	16.3	35.6	28.8	46.1	27.0

	B. Household size		
Size	1851	1861	Unlinked, 1851
1	1.5%	0.7%	3.4%
2–4	18.1	19.2	38.6
5–7	43.2	39.5	37.4
8 or more	37.2	40.6	21.6

	C. Marital status of household head		
Status	1851	1861	Unlinked, 1851
Single	5.3%	1.3%	5.7%
Married	86.3	86.9	79.2
Widow	8.4	11.8	15.0

tuation in social status). Looked at another way, fewer households acquired one or more boarders or relatives during the decade: about 16 percent acquired a boarder and roughly the same proportion a servant; 12 percent gained a relative, and a substantial one quarter of all households traced across the decade gained either a relative or a boarder.

Thus, much larger proportions of households had a boarder or relative at one end of the decade or the other than at one point alone. These figures refer only to linked households, which accounts for the difference between them and the statistics in the table that refer to all households. Of all households, 32 percent in 1851 and 20 percent in 1861 contained at least one boarder; but 43 percent had a boarder dwelling within them in *either* 1851 *or* 1861. Similarly, relatives lived in 16 percent of households in 1851 and 15 percent in 1861, but in *either* 1851 *or* 1861, 26 percent of households contained kin. In 1851, 42 percent of households had either a relative or a boarder; in 1861, 31 percent of households had either a relative or a boarder. At *either* end of the decade, however, the proportion was much greater, 56 percent. Primarily, boarders and relatives were either young unmarried people or elderly widowed ones, probably moving into and out of households at fairly short intervals. As a consequence, if 56 percent of households had a boarder or relative living with them in one of two years a decade apart, undoubtedly many more had one dwelling with them at some other point during their existence. If, as I shall argue, boarders and relatives can be legitimately equated in terms of place within the household and a new category of extended households which includes both can be formulated, then the proportion of extended households rises dramatically (as Table 5.4 shows). Thus, observing the same households at more than one point in time reveals that a majority were extended, a radically different conclusion from the one reached before on the basis of Laslett's classification.

The transiency of household status mirrored the transiency of the population at large. At some point nearly every household probably contained either a boarder or relative. This does not mean, however, that the dominance of the simple family household should be abandoned. Rather, the static model of the household should be transformed into a dynamic model: the simple family

TABLE 5.4 Households classified two ways, 1851 and 1861

Household structure	Household Type A: relative and boarder not equivalent		Household Type B: relative and boarder equivalent	
	1851	1861	1851	1861
Solitary	4.8%	4.2%	2.2%	2.8%
No family	2.1	2.1	1.3	2.0
Simple	79.8	78.6	56.9	63.1
Extended	11.3	11.8	37.8	29.1
Multiple	1.7	2.5	1.7	2.5
Indeterminate	0.3	0.7	0	0.5
Total number	2313	3513	2313	3513

household remained the dominant household structure, but it was continually expanding and contracting. At some juncture in their lives the great majority of people most likely dwelled for a time with someone other than their parents, children, or spouse. They lived for a while in another household as kin, boarder, or servant, and probably a relative or a boarder lived for a while within their household. This transiency of household structure means that as children grew up they dwelled, at one time or another, in various types of households; or, to put it more accurately, almost all lived in a household to which, from time to time, someone else—a maiden aunt, a widowed grandparent, a young man in temporary need of a home, or a servant girl—became temporarily attached. In the light of this evidence, it does not make sense to ask, as one scholar did, whether growing up within an extended as opposed to a nuclear family altered the pattern of social mobility among middle-class youths in a nineteenth-century city. Now the question of the impact of different kinds of household structure on the life histories of individual young people, which once appeared to be an interesting and significant problem, has become virtually meaningless.[19]

These conclusions raise two major questions. First, is there any systematic way of accounting for the variation in household structure? Two major possibilities come to mind at once, class and life cycle; either of them might have influenced the kind of households in which people lived. The other question concerns the characteristics of relatives and boarders. How similar were these people and on what grounds can they be considered equivalent in their relation to the household in which they dwelled? The second question will be considered first, for it leads directly into one of the problems raised at the outset of this section: the adequacy with which Laslett defined the three areas of the co-resident domestic group—the conjugal unit, the household, and the houseful. Laslett's position can be challenged on three counts: the use of the terms family and household in earlier times; the reflection of this usage in the instructions given to census takers; and the similarity of relatives and boarders in age, marital status, and place within the household.

Laslett himself points to the ambiguity with which people in times past used the terms family and household, but his main purpose has been to sort out the distinctions that people made in practice rather than in language. Nonetheless, as in the case of occupational classification, we just as plausibly might draw initial guidance from the way in which words were actually used at the time. Occupational terminology, for example, blurred the distinction between master and journeyman, and this points to the absence of a rigid line between manual and nonmanual work in our contemporary sense. In a similar way the manner in which people blurred the distinction between kin and boarders offers a clue as to how they regarded their place within the household. Richard Wall quotes the following definition of a family from the introduction to the Enumeration Returns of the State Census of 1851:

> The first, most intimate, and perhaps most important community, is the family, not considered as the children of one parent, but as persons under one head; who is the occupier of the house, the householder, master, husband, or father; while the other members of the family are, the wife, children, servants, relatives, visitors, and persons constantly or accidentally in the house.[20]

Clearly, the compilers of the British census defined family more as scholars would depict household today, and they drew no firm distinction between relatives and boarders. Their remarks provide

no justification for Laslett's discrimination between household
and houseful.

Nor does Laslett's distinction find any support from a demographic comparison of relatives and boarders in Hamilton, who
were quite like each other in most of the essential ways. Table 5.5
compares boarders and relatives in 1861 only, but the demographic characteristics of both groups did not alter at all during
the decade. Their ages, first of all, were similar: the mean age

TABLE 5.5 Relatives and boarders compared, 1861

Demographic	Percent		Number	
characteristics	Relatives	Boarders	Relatives	Boarders
Age[a]				
Groups, 1–30				
1–5	13.4	6.8	146	108
6–10	8.0	3.4	88	55
11–15	11.5	6.3	125	100
16–20	12.7	17.3	138	276
21–25	12.5	23.6	137	377
26–30	8.4	15.4	91	245
Total under 31	66.5	72.8	725	1161
Sex and marital status				
Male	40.9	66.3	447	1065
Female	59.1	33.7	647	541
Single	68.5	79.0	749	1268
Married	12.5	12.8	137	205
Widowed	19.0	8.2	208	133
Birthplace				
England	11.6	18.9	127	304
Scotland	13.5	15.2	148	245
Ireland	23.6	23.8	258	381
Canada West	39.0	28.9	427	464
U.S.A.	6.7	7.5	73	120
Other	5.6	5.7	61	92
Total	100.0	100.0	1094	1606

[a] The mean age for relatives was 27.3, for boarders 26.2; the standard deviation for relatives was 21.3, for boarders 13.9; the median age for relatives was
22.3, for boarders 24.0.

of relatives was 27.3, and of boarders 26.2. Nearly two thirds of relatives compared to 73 percent of boarders were less than thirty-one years old. And about 13 percent of each group had married. Only in sex and widowhood did boarders and relatives differ. For 41 percent of relatives and 66 percent of boarders were male, while 19 percent of relatives compared to 8 percent of boarders had been widowed. There were also more very young relatives: 21 percent of them, compared to 10 percent of boarders, were under the age of eleven (very likely orphans). Thus, relatives consisted primarily of young, unmarried women, with a solid minority of widows and orphans; boarders were most often young, unmarried men. Both lived in intimate contact with other members of the household, sharing meals, I imagine, as well as occupying a room. In only a very few instances, moreover, could boarders have been employees of the household head. Rather, they were young men at a particular stage in their life cycle dwelling within another household whose responsibilities toward them included not only the provision of board and room but some sort of moral oversight as well.

Boarding, in short, formed part of the process of socialization. "In its urban, nineteenth-century manifestation," write Modell and Hareven, "boarding was an adaptation of a traditional middle-class practice to a situation in which large numbers of new urbanites, both foreign and native-born, usually young and with shallow resources, were thrown into a chaotic housing market. Confusion, economic considerations, and the need for socialization into the ways of the city all made a quasi-familial setting a very attractive proposition." Boarding, they conclude, provided young people with a "family surrogate." Neither boarders nor relatives were likely to work for the household head, and they did not substitute for servants. The only relation of consequence between household structure and servants was that households with resident kin were somewhat more likely than others to employ servants. The only possible distinction between boarders and relatives was economic: boarders paid the head of the household for their room and meals. But there is no evidence that relatives did not do so as well. Until there is some reason to believe otherwise, it is more plausible to suppose that relatives also paid as they were able; indeed, children often did contribute

from their earnings to the upkeep of the household.[21] Orvar
Löfgren has stated the lack of distinction between kin and non-kin
members of households especially clearly:

> There exists a tendency to use our present urban family system
> as a starting point for the reconstruction of earlier household
> forms. Instead of asking how the form and function of the *family*
> has changed during the last centuries, we ought to phrase the
> questions in a more neutral way:
> "What types of primary groups fulfilled the basic functions
> of production, consumption, socialization, etc., in peasant society,
> and to what extent do these groups coincide with the unit we call
> the family today?"
> As the Swedish ethnologist, Börje Hansen has stressed, our
> familial orientation may trap us into over-emphasizing the role
> of the family in peasant organization. He finds it highly probable
> that peasants viewed each other more often in terms of the house-
> hold or "farm people" to which they belonged than the kin group
> into which they were born . . . In the tasks of production, con-
> sumption and socialization no firm dividing line was drawn be-
> tween kin and non-kin members of the household.[22]

Thus the evidence is overwhelming: no very clear distinction
between relatives and boarders on the basis of language, demographic characteristics, or place within the household existed in
earlier societies or in nineteenth-century Hamilton. The distinction between boarders and relatives should therefore be minimized, boarders should be recognized as an integral part of the
household, and Laslett's distinction between household and houseful should be discarded.

The boundaries of individual households varied somewhat with
the social class of their heads. Chapters One and Two have explored some of the relations between wealth and the number of
children in a family. For the most part there was very little connection between the two. The very wealthy did have rather large
numbers of children and the poor somewhat fewer children than
usual; among 40–49-year-old men, for instance, the poorest had
no children about twice as often as other groups. But between the
extremes of wealth and poverty—in the great majority of instances
—there was little variation. Chapter One also pointed out the
congruence between the occupational groups' share and the ethnic
groups' share of both total population and total births. Fertility
rates, as Table 5.6 shows, support the conclusion offered there

on the relative lack of ethnic and class difference in birth rate. By fertility rate I mean the number of people in a group aged 0–15 divided by the number of women in the group aged 16–45. The groups considered here are ethnic, though the Irish Catholics may be taken as a surrogate for low social standing. Fertility rates among the largest ethnic groups remained stable across the decade: for the Irish Catholics 2.5 and 2.6; for the Scottish Presbyterians 2.9 and 2.7; for English Protestants 2.7 and 2.9; and for Canadian Protestants 2.3 and 2.2. These fertility rates show, first, that Irish Catholics, and by inference the poor, did not have exceptionally large numbers of children and, second, that the number of children born stayed about the same across the decade, a conclusion consistent with the stability in the mean number of children per family. They also point to the lower fertility of natives, a phenomenon discovered by Laurence Glasco for Buffalo in 1855 but still unexplained.[23]

Thus, for the most part, any class variation in household size could not have been the result of differential fertility. It was due, in fact, to the number of boarders and relatives. In each year a direct and linear relation existed between the wealth of a household head and boarders, relatives, and total household size. As Chapter Two, Table 2.9, indicated, 20 percent of the poor in

TABLE 5.6 Fertility by ethnic group, 1851 and 1861

| | Fertility rate[a] | |
Ethnic group	1851	1861
Irish Catholic	2.5	2.6
Irish Protestant	2.6	3.0
Scottish Presbyterian	2.9	2.7
English Protestant	2.7	2.9
Canadian Protestant	2.3	2.2
Canadian Catholic	1.9	2.8
Black	2.3	1.6
Other	2.4	2.3

[a] Measured by $\dfrac{\text{children aged 0–15}}{\text{women aged 16–45}}$.

1851 and 48 percent of the wealthy had large households, that is, ones with eight or more members; in 1861, the proportions were 10 and 39 percent. Conversely, in 1851, 26 percent of poor households had from one to three members compared to 11 percent of the wealthy; in 1861, similarly, the proportions were 34 and 13 percent. In 1861, 13 percent of poor and 18 percent of wealthy households contained a relative; 12 percent of poor and 28 percent of the wealthy had a boarder; and 7 percent of the poor and 68 percent of the wealthy employed a servant. The differences in 1851 were even more striking. One explanation for this, as Table 5.7 shows, is simply the size of the house in which the wealthy lived. For there was a direct connection between the size of houses (measured by the number of stories) and the presence of boarders. Whether the wealthy needed the income that boarders provided is difficult to determine; it may have been, as in New England in an earlier period, that social norms required young, single people to live within a household under the supervision of a surrogate parent. In these circumstances, it would have been the civic obligation of respectable families with extra space to take in homeless young men. Very likely, class differences affected the motivations of people who took boarders into their households. The many widows with boarders undoubtedly were supplementing meager incomes; and poor families, as Modell and Hareven have shown, often needed the income from boarders to replace the money lost when a working child moved out.[24]

TABLE 5.7 Number of boarders by house size and type, 1851 and 1861

Number of boarders	Percent of families with a house of two or more stories		Percent of families with a brick or stone house	
	1851	1861	1851	1861
None	35	39	23	22
One	47	51	34	68
Two or more	58	62	31	86

If those households which included either a relative or a boarder are classified as extended households, the variations between social classes appear dramatic. Again according to Table 2.9, 28 percent of poor households were extended in 1851 compared to 59 percent of wealthy households. As for the households with servants, a classification which gives an excellent indication of social standing, in 1851 a majority of the people employing two or more servants lived in extended households. Close to one half of the people with one resident servant, the group I have called middle-class, also had extended households, compared to less than a third of those without servants.

Hamilton was not unique in the extent to which household size and complexity increased with wealth and social standing. Although it is not yet possible to compare class differences in household size and structure precisely, all studies I have seen report the same general tendency: a linear increase with wealth. For instance, within Laslett's 100 communities the means of means for household size decreased nicely down the social scale from 7.54 for gentlemen to 5.60 for clergy to, at the other extreme, 4.34 for laborers and 3.74 for paupers. Similarly, measured on a social-class scale with three intervals, the mean proportion of households with kin declined from 5.31 to 4.66 to 4.48. Michael Anderson found that in mid-nineteenth-century Preston the proportion of households with kin dropped from 16 among people in trade to 7 and 8 among lower factory workers and laborers respectively. In Salem, Massachusetts, in 1790, Bernard Farber reports that the number of persons per family varied from 9.8 for merchants to 6.6 for shoemakers to 5.4 for laborers. And Lutz Berkner found that in the Austrian village of Waldviertel the percentage of extended families rose from 15 percent among the poorest peasants to 42 percent among the wealthiest.[25]

There is nothing surprising about this conclusion, which confirms the impressionistic evidence that comes from many sources. A large household composed of relatives, boarders, friends, visitors, and servants, as well as one's own children, was the setting in which most wealthy people lived in earlier times. This is revealed, to name one place, in Peter Laslett's discussions of gentry families in *The World We Have Lost*. It is the image of the family on the eve of modernity evoked with splendid, decadent richness in the movie *The Go-Between,* or, in a Canadian setting, in the books and television series *The White Oaks of Jalna.* As Alison Prentice has shown, it was also the ideal of the family that was expressed by prominent Upper Canadians early in the nineteenth century.[26]

This conclusion must be stressed, for it conflicts with the argument advanced by Laslett. Laslett omitted lodgers and boarders from his first recording of household members because he expected them to be a trivial and marginal category. Despite his belated recognition of their prevalence, he has not incorporated them fully into his concept of the household. Nor has he explored the implications of the class variations in household structure and size that appear in his data. Although those variations could be used to support an opposing argument, Laslett concludes that "it would seem impossible to specify the mechanism whereby such a tradition [the belief in the predominance of the extended family in earlier times] could survive over time . . . The wish to believe in the large and extended household as the ordinary institution of an earlier England and an earlier Europe, or as a standard feature of an earlier non-industrial world, is indeed a matter of ideology."[27]

But there is another explanation consistent with the data. It begins with Marion Levy's forceful argument on both theoretical and empirical grounds that the actual range of variation in family structure has been remarkably narrow. The majority of people, he contends, must always have lived within nuclear families. With this assumption he confronts the contradiction between the actual history of the family and its formulation in both popular and academic thought, which he thinks has failed to distinguish properly between ideal and actual family structures. Levy maintains that within every society two family structures coexist. One, which he calls the ideal structure, represents the official or institutionalized version of the family; it is what the family is supposed, and sometimes believed, to be like. Ideal family structures vary widely from place to place. The actual family structure, on the other hand, is exactly what its name implies, the way in which people do in fact live. This, Levy contends, varies much less than the ideal. Although the two structures may be related, at no point have they ever been identical; the disjunction between them has been a permanent feature of history.[28]

It is about the ideal family that historians most frequently write. It, after all, is found in the sentimental fiction, the sermons, and the tracts which form the evidence for traditional family history. Through this concentration on the ideal family scholars have come to believe in the dominance of the extended family in earlier times. It may be, despite what Laslett says, that an extended family structure formed the ideal of earlier societies in the same way that the ideal of the nuclear family dominates in modern times. (In fact, the nuclear family has become idealized to the point that social-work textbooks advise students that the reliance of their married clients upon parents, even a close relationship between married people and their parents, is unhealthy.)[29] Despite what may have been a dramatic shift in ideal family structure, the actual family has probably changed very little.

What evidence can be found to support the view that the large extended household was once the ideal family structure? Though Laslett claims that none exists, Alison Prentice has found some for Upper Canada, and I suspect that a good deal more could be discovered. Whatever the case may be with respect to literary sources, there certainly is a clue embedded in the quantitative material I have inspected. Acceptance of that clue, however, rests on two plausible but by no means proved assumptions. The first is that the ideal family at any point in time reflects the practices of the most visible, the elite, members of a society. The people with the highest status set the norms and standards by which others evaluate their own existence and life style. Thus, ideal family structures usually have had a firm foundation in the real families of the rich; as their practices have changed, social ideals, generally speaking, have followed. This statement, in turn, rests on an assumption that Michael Young and Peter Willmott recently have called the "principle of stratified diffusion," a reformulation of a principle at least as old as de Tocqueville, namely, emulation of the rich by the rest of society and the gradual diffusion throughout the social order of ideals and practices that were once the preserve of the wealthy.[30]

In virtually all places they have studied, historians have found that the size and complexity of households has increased with wealth or social standing. Perhaps most of the wealthy upper class or gentry in preindustrial England and early North America lived in a household which included members other than a married couple and their children. If the extended household was indeed predominant among the rich, then it was this minority of households which became at once the social ideal and the practice from which the household structure of all people has been generalized incorrectly. This speculation in no way contradicts the demographic findings of Laslett or the general conclusion that the co-resident domestic group of most people has been the simple family household. Although a majority of wealthy households may have been extended, their number remained too small to boost substantially the proportion of extended households within a society.

The discussion of Hamilton earlier in this chapter began with three questions about the boundaries of the family and household. First, to what extent was Hamilton like other places? The answer has been given that it was well within the range of normal household structures in western Europe and probably in North America. Second, how adequate are Laslett's distinctions among conjugal unit, household, and houseful? They do not appear to reflect historical circumstances with very much precision. The distinction between the household and houseful, which rests on a sharp analytic distinction between the place of kin and boarders, is probably untenable for the nineteenth century. Third, can we find a clue in the Hamilton experience that accounts for the tenaciousness of the myth of the extended family? Here the answer is a probable though somewhat hypothetical yes. The clue, the prevalence of extended households among the wealthy, raises the possibility that most wealthy households once were extended, thus creating and sustaining an ideal family structure which became diffused throughout the social order and was generalized incorrectly as the typical form of historical experience.

Other questions might be asked about the boundaries of the family. One especially pressing problem concerns the relationship between kin who did not dwell together. To what extent should the boundaries of the family be extended to nonresident kin? Should Laslett's definition be accepted, a definition which extends household membership to people living in the same apartment building or on the same land in separate dwellings, which he groups into the concept of common premises? This would take into account the case described by Philip Greven in colonial Andover, Massachusetts, where married children still effectively under the control of their fathers lived in separate houses on the family land that they were waiting to inherit. Such a group would be called a houseful and its various dwellings subsumed under the notion of premises. But what of the married children who simply lived near their parents and maintained a close, mutually supportive relationship? At this point we do not know how usual that situation was, though some initial work by Michael Anderson and Michael Doucet suggests that it might have been relatively common in the nineteenth century. Even if it was common, we have not yet developed a conceptual framework and classificatory scheme which enables us to encompass nonresident kin within the structure of co-resident domestic groups or to compare one society with another in this respect with any degree of precision. It is difficult to estimate what the results of such a study would show. However, the existence of mass transiency certainly must have militated against the retention of close contact among kin or friends who did not reside together. With such a large proportion of the population on the move, kin ties must have been difficult to retain with any degree of intensity. More recently, the possible slowing of working-class migration with the coming of industrialization, the invention of the telephone and the automobile, and the spread of relatively rapid and inexpensive public transportation may have promoted contact between kin, such as the close relations between married daughters and mothers that Young and Willmott found in East London or that exists in contemporary Toronto, according to a recent study.[31] These contemporary relations may be a modern phenomenon, however, rather than the survival of more ancient family patterns. But all this remains highly speculative; answers await research which must be even more intricate and subtle than the work on family and household structure that already has begun to recover the domestic experiences of ordinary people in times past.

Another unanswered question about the boundaries of the family concerns social class. Did social class divisions demarcate rigid boundaries within which but not between which families were formed? The answer must come from the records of marriages. If class distinctions created barriers, then marriage between members of different classes would be rare; the frequency of intermarriage provides a very sensitive indicator of the openness of a social system.[32] Unfortunately, evidence on interclass marriage is difficult to find in this period, for marriage registers list at the most only the name, age, religion, and address of bride, groom, parents, and witnesses, with no indication of occupation or wealth, which can only be determined by linking marriage records back to the census and assessment. The marriages now on file for Hamilton do not represent all marriages in this period, and so far only a sample of them have been linked back to the census and assessment. Nonetheless, the results are already instructive.

The first marriages traced were those of the children of the elite sample of 161 men discussed in the previous chapter. We were able to estimate the social class of both bride and groom in eighteen marriages of these children of the "entrepreneurial class." In no case did any children marry outside of their families' class. We also attempted to link those Catholic marriages which occurred between 1860 and 1862 (the years surrounding the census) in order to inspect patterns within a very different social group. In this case, we discovered thirty-six marriages. Thirty-four of them occurred within the same class; one of the other two might have been an example of upward mobility and one an example of downward mobility. But again, the overwhelming trend is clear. Although the numbers here are small, there is no reason to suspect that the marriages were unrepresentative. The reason why so few marriage records could be linked to census and assessment is that in only a minority of cases did the parents of both bride and groom live in Hamilton. In most marriages one or both partners were inmigrants to the city. In cases where the groom was employed and the bride's father lived in the city, some conclusion could be drawn about relative social rank. Otherwise, the presence of both fathers was necessary. In a number of instances the only parent was a widow whose economic rank could not be estimated. Thus it is unlikely that systematic differences in the relation between class and marriage existed for those couples whose social standing we could determine and those we could not determine.

Although much work on the social basis of marriage remains to be undertaken, the fragmentary marriage patterns described here might reflect relatively stong barriers between classes. The implications of this conclusion reverberate backward and forward through the other chapters of this book. For it strengthens the argument presented elsewhere on the rigidity, depth, and recognition of class lines, and it means that marriage probably did not serve as a means of social mobility to any significant extent.

Although the boundaries of the family were sharp when they confronted the class structure, the boundaries of the co-resident domestic group, which basically included parents and children, fluctuated easily and frequently as relatives, servants, and kin arrived and departed. The frequency with which the usual boundaries extended to embrace members other than parents and children varied somewhat according to class. Nonetheless, households of all sorts had someone other than an immediate family member dwelling within them at one time or another.

It is an open question whether the rest of the variation in household structure can be explained by the life cycle. Certainly household structure is one important issue in the analysis of the relation between the family and life cycle.

The Family and the Life Cycle

Insofar as a person's stage of life determined the kind of family in which he lived, it was the life cycle that created the boundaries of the family and household. The question of life cycle is important enough to merit independent inquiry from two perspectives. The first concerns the relation between the life-cycle stage of the household head and the household's size and structure. The other concerns the extent to which the relationship of the individual to the household in which he lived varied at different points in his life. The first leads us to ask, for instance: Were extended family households more common among young, recently married people than among the middle-aged? The second prompts us to inquire, to take one possibility: At what ages did individuals leave home? When they did leave, did they set up their own households or go to live in another house under some special arrangement?

Ideally the study of the life cycle should employ categories that are broader than age alone. Twenty-year-old married people should be differentiated, for instance, from 20-year-olds who are single. Michael Anderson has developed a sensitive and discriminating scheme which takes into account the age of the wife and the presence of children.[33] To some extent I shall be able to use broader categories here, but as yet I have no scheme that puts all the population into particular life-cycle categories. I shall have to move between types of categories, sometimes using age as a surrogate for a life-cycle phase, sometimes employing categories based on marital status, such as widow, or on household status, such as boarder.

One other problem deserves special mention. This is the difficulty of drawing inferences about the life cycle from a cross-sectional analysis, a dilemma faced by everyone who works with manuscript census materials. The census provides a static picture, a cross section of the population at a particular moment in time. To translate that into a dynamic portrait requires making some very large assumptions. For instance, if a quarter of the 21-year-old men and half of the 27-year-olds are married at a given point in time, I will assume that when the 27-year-olds were six years younger only a quarter of them had been married. A cross-sectional analysis provides no way to either prove or disprove this assumption. Although it is possible to imagine that for some reason the experience of 21-year-olds would change in six years, without evidence that such a change occurred it is equally plausible to entertain the other hypothesis, that experiences were comparable. Much of the analysis here rests on such assumptions. Sometimes it makes little difference, because the relation between age or life-cycle stage and a particular variable, such as the number of children in a family, is so congruent with common sense that it is difficult to imagine how circumstances could have changed enough to modify the patterns that emerge. In other instances the stability of age-related patterns across the decade helps confirm conclusions that might be more tenuous if they were based on one cross-sectional analysis at a single point in time. Fortunately, in some cases the linked population acts as a control. And whenever possible the changing experience of individual families and comparable age cohorts is traced over time. Comfortingly, those changes over time support some of the more controversial inferences in the cross-sectional data. But it is not possible in every case to confirm the inferences about life cycle that emerge from the analysis of individual censuses.

What, then, is the relation between household size and structure and the life cycle? Lutz Berkner has argued persuasively that at some point in their lives most people in a population might have lived within a multiple family household, though at any single point in time a majority of all households were simple or nuclear. "There may be," he says, "a normal series of stages that appear only rarely in a population because they last for only a short period of the family's cycle or in some cases do not appear at all. From this point of view, the extended family is merely a phase through which most families go. Since there is a good chance that the parents will still be alive, when a young couple marries, they begin marriage in an extended family. In time, the parents die, and the now middle-aged couple spend their years in a nuclear family. When one of their sons marries and brings his wife into the household the family is extended again." Although only 25 percent of all families in the Austrian village Berkner studied were extended, he found that 60 percent of those headed by a man aged 18–27 contained kin, compared to 45 percent of those where the head was aged 28–37, tapering off to 9 percent among men aged 48–57 but climbing among the eldest to 15 percent on account of the entry of married children. The kin who lived with younger heads of households were either parents or unmarried siblings; those who lived with the older ones were primarily married children.[34]

Michael Anderson also found that the life cycle influenced household composition. Although in Preston in 1851 "87 percent of all married couples headed their own households," about 40 percent either lived in lodgings or with kin immediately after marriage, "though most only for a few years." Similarly, later in life "some couples again gave up living in a household of their own and went and lived with others." The simple family household was the "normal pattern" for the population of Preston taken as a whole. Nonetheless, "a very large proportion of people in certain family statuses occupied some non-familial residential status. For the young married couple and for widowed persons (particularly the older widowed persons), kin-based residence was important."[35]

The pattern that Berkner and Anderson have found for an eighteenth-century Austrian village and for an English industrial town in the middle of the nineteenth century differs from the picture Laslett offers. For he maintains that the simple family household not only was the usual place of residence for the majority of the population but was, as well, the most common domestic arrangement among both young married couples and elderly people.[36] The situation in Hamilton supports Laslett rather more than Berkner or Anderson. Thus it is possible that Laslett is right, that the pattern Berkner found was not typical for English villages, at least. At the same time, Anderson's findings may be more representative of industrial cities like Preston than of English villages or commercial cities like Hamilton. Within cities, in fact, the critical factor may have been housing supply: when adequate housing was available, newly married couples lived by themselves; when it was not, they moved in with parents or into another household.

Within Hamilton the size of households and the number of children within them varied quite directly with the age of the household head; household structure varied considerably less; and the presence of boarders and relatives in any given household appears to have been largely accidental. In order to overcome the limitations of cross-sectional analysis I shall restrict the discussion here to those families remaining in the city for at least a decade. The size of these individual households, like their internal composition, changed markedly during the decade, as Table 5.8 shows. Except for those which were large (8 or more members) in 1851, a majority of households shifted from one size category to another during the decade. For instance, the percentage of households remaining "average" (5–7 members) was 47, and the percentage retaining 2–4 members was only 40.

Age brought about most of the change in household size. Households of young men, for instance, increased most notably: in 1851 only about 6 percent of household heads under the age of 30

TABLE 5.8 Household size for all people who were household heads in both 1851 and 1861

		Household size, 1861					
						All sizes	
		1	2–4	5–7	8 or more	N	%
Household size, 1851	1	16.7%	8.3%	41.6%	33.3%	12	1.5
	2–4	1.4	39.9	44.6	14.1	148	18.1
	5–7	0.3	18.7	46.7	34.3	353	43.2
	8 or more	0.3	10.2	28.3	61.2	304	37.2
All sizes:	N	6	157	322	332	817	
	%	0.7	19.2	39.5	40.6		100.0

presided over large households, compared to about 37 percent of the same men a decade later. As men passed the 40–49 period, their household size began to diminish: in 1851, about 39 percent of men that age headed a large household, compared to 33 percent a decade later. And among older men the drop was steepest, for the percentage of large households among men aged 50–59 dropped from 33 to 18 percent.

Household size also increased among men born a decade apart. Consider Table 5.9 on 30–39-year-old men: those born between 1811 and 1820 had large households less often than those born after 1820 (in 29 percent compared to 37 percent of instances). This increase in household size reflected another distinction between men born a decade apart, the number of children alive and at home. When men born between 1811 and 1820 were 30–39

TABLE 5.9 Household size and number of children of household heads aged 30–39: cohorts compared, 1851 and 1861

Birth date	Percent with large households (8 or more members)	Percent with 3–4 children at home	Percent with 5 or more children at home
1811–1820	29	31	14
1821 and after	37	43	22

years old, 31 percent had three or four children living at home
and 14 percent had five or more; when men born a decade later
reached the age 30–39 years these proportions increased to 43
and 22 percent, a very marked gain. Very likely, this increase did
not reflect any difference in the birth rate, which was generally
stable, but rather reflected a rise in the proportion of children
who remained at home well into their twenties, a phenomenon to
which I shall turn later.

In general, as might be expected, the relation between household size and age reflected the relation between age and number
of children. For instance, as Table 5.10 shows, those men under
the age of thirty in 1851 increased their family size during the
decade, for the most part; by 1861, 43 percent had three or four
children and 22 percent had five or more. Family size reached its
peak among men in their forties, when, as with household size, a
decline began. As an example, 37 percent of the men aged 40–49
with three or four children at home in 1851 had only one or two
there a decade later. The same decrease showed, of course, among
men over the age of fifty; 39 percent of those who had had three
or four children at home in 1851 had one or two in 1851 and 15
percent had none.

Aside from confirming what I would have predicted, these
relationships among household size, number of children, and age
are important for two reasons. First of all, they support the conclusion I drew earlier that most men had the greatest number of
children at home during their forties. More interestingly, and
forming a corollary to that argument, most couples had their last
child considerably later in life than they do today. Today most
women bear their last child around the age of twenty-six; in
earlier times it was at least a decade later.[37] In Hamilton in 1851,
according to Table 5.11, 60 percent of the 40–45-year-old married
women had a child aged 1–5, and 81 percent of married women
that age had a child aged 10 or younger, a proportion which
decreased to 77 percent a decade later. As Robert Wells has
pointed out in a fine essay, this decrease in the age at which
women cease to have children has had a profound impact on the
family, on relations between husbands and wives, and on women.[38]
For now a stage quite new in history has been added to the

TABLE 5.10 Number of children of all household heads, compared by age, linked 1851 and 1861

		Number of children, 1861				All children	
		0	1–2	3–4	5 or more	N	%
		Household head under 30, 1851					
Number of children, 1851	0	21.0%	33.8%	40.3%	4.9%	62	40.0
	1–2	4.4	14.7	44.1	36.8	68	43.9
	3–4	4.3	30.4	43.5	21.7	23	14.8
	5 or more	0.0	0.0	50.0	50.0	2	1.3
All children: N		17	38	66	34	155	
%		11.0	24.5	42.5	22.0		100.0
		Household head 30–39, 1851					
Number of children, 1851	0	46.2%	26.9%	19.2%	7.7%	52	17.3
	1–2	7.0	29.6	38.3	25.2	115	38.2
	3–4	1.1	16.3	31.5	51.1	92	30.6
	5 or more	7.1	7.1	16.7	69.1	42	14.0
All children: N		36	66	90	109	301	
%		12.0	21.9	29.9	36.2		100.0
		Household head 40–49, 1851					
Number of children, 1851	0	62.1%	27.6%	3.4%	3.4%	29	12.3
	1–2	26.4	49.1	17.0	7.5	53	22.5
	3–4	5.3	37.3	30.7	26.7	75	31.8
	5 or more	1.3	11.4	40.5	46.8	79	33.5
All children: N		37	71	65	63	236	
%		15.7	30.1	27.5	26.7		100.0
		Household head 50 or more, 1851					
Number of children, 1851	0	80.0%	6.7%	13.4%	0 %	15	12.0
	1–2	29.8	53.2	12.7	4.3	47	37.6
	3–4	15.2	39.4	39.4	6.1	33	26.4
	5 or more	3.3	33.3	43.3	20.0	30	24.0
All children: N		32	49	34	10	125	
%		25.6	39.2	27.2	8.0		100.0

family life-cycle: a prolonged period between the time at which the youngest child leaves home, on the one hand, and the onset of old age and the death of either husband or wife on the other. Before the late nineteenth or the early twentieth century, very few husbands and wives in Hamilton or elsewhere had more than a few, if any, years to live together after their children had left home. In fact, many of the younger children in families could expect to lose at least their father through death before they reached maturity.

Unlike the size of households or the number of children within them, the turnover in the number of boarders and relatives living with individual families cannot be explained by the age of the household head. Consider, for instance, only those household heads who had a boarder living with them in 1851: 74 percent of 20–29-year-olds had lost all their boarders by the end of the decade, compared to 66 percent of the 30–39-year-olds, 74 percent of the 40–49-year-olds, and 79 percent of the men aged 50 and over. The proportions for the loss of relatives by age were quite similar.

TABLE 5.11 Age of youngest child of all married women aged 40–45 living with their husbands, 1851 and 1861

Age of youngest child	Number of children		Percent of children	
	1851	1861	1851	1861
Age groups				
1–5	138	200	60.2	51.8
6–10	48	97	21.0	25.1
11 and over	43	89	18.8	23.1
Age year by year				
1	38	47	16.6	12.2
2	34	58	14.8	15.0
3	27	36	11.8	9.3
4	17	34	7.4	8.8
5	22	25	9.6	6.5
6	14	24	6.1	2.2

Somewhat more variation existed between the structure of individual households (defined in Laslett's terms) and the age of their heads, although once again the variation was small. In Table 5.12 the figures relate to all households, not just those traced across the decade. The most striking point is the stability in the distribution of household type by age across the decade: in each year about two thirds of men under the age of thirty headed simple family households compared to about four fifths of men in their thirties and 34 or 84 percent of men in their forties. Although households with no conjugal families ("no-family households") remained a quite small category, there were more of them among the young, about 6 percent among households headed by people under thirty, dropping to 2 percent among those in their thirties and between 0.5 and 1.0 percent among those in their forties. Similarly, younger people more often headed extended family households, though here too the differences are small, much less, for instance, than those reported by Berkner: 16 percent of households headed by someone under thirty were extended in 1861 compared to 12 percent of those in which the head was aged 30–39, a proportion which dropped to 8 or 9 percent among those aged 50 and over. The greatest proportion of extended family households contained a relative of the same generation as the household head; they were extended laterally, that is, more often than upward or downward. Most relatives were siblings of the household head or his wife.

Not surprisingly, the highest proportion of solitary and multiple households (those in which a person lived alone except for boarders and servants, and those in which two or more families lived together) existed among both the young and the old, those people most likely to be alone on account of widowhood or youth and those most likely to have either married children or living parents. Again it should be emphasized that even among the young and elderly these categories accounted for but a small proportion of the total: 10 percent of the youngest household heads lived as solitaries compared to 3 percent of the 40–49-year-olds and 7 percent of the most elderly. Multiple family households, on the other hand, accounted for about 2 percent of the young households, about 1 percent of those with a head aged

TABLE 5.12 Household structure by age, 1851 and 1861

Structural categories		Under 30		30–39		40–49		50–59		60 and over		All	
		1851	1861	1851	1861	1851	1861	1851	1861	1851	1861	1851	1861
Solitary	N	46	41	39	38	19	33	7	16	11	19	112	152
	%	10.0	7.3	4.9	3.3	3.0	3.6	2.5	3.0	7.0	5.6	4.8	4.3
No family	N	27	37	16	28	3	9	2	5	0	6	48	85
	%	5.9	6.6	2.0	2.4	0.5	1.0	0.7	0.9	0	1.8	2.1	2.4
Simple	N	306	373	636	946	513	760	245	436	126	251	1846	2766
	%	66.7	66.5	79.2	81.0	83.4	83.7	88.1	81.6	79.7	73.4	79.8	78.7
Extended	N	71	90	98	143	69	93	21	47	12	31	261	404
	%	15.5	16.0	12.2	12.3	11.2	10.3	7.6	8.8	7.6	9.1	11.3	11.5
Multiple	N	8	9	11	7	9	9	3	28	9	35	40	83
	%	1.7	1.6	1.4	0.6	1.5	0.9	1.1	5.3	5.7	10.2	1.7	2.4
Indeterminate	N	1	11	3	6	2	4	0	2	0	0	6	23
	%	0.2	2.0	0.4	0.5	0.3	0.4	0	0.4	0	0	0.3	0.7
All	N	459	561	803	1168	615	908	278	534	158	342	2313	3513
	%	100.0	100.0	100.0	100.0	100	25.8	100.0	100.0	6.8	9.7	100.0	100.0

30–39, and, in 1861, 10 percent of those headed by someone aged 60 or over.

These statistics mean, first, that most people of all ages headed simple family households. The exceptions consisted primarily of the young, who sometimes lived alone or with other young people, often relatives of their own generation, and the elderly, who were more likely to be widowed or alone or to have taken in their married children. It should be remembered, however, that 50 percent of the widows and 57 percent of the young people listed as solitaries actually had another person (excluded from the household by Laslett's definition) dwelling with them. Thus the number of people living entirely by themselves was negligible. Among the majority of household heads, those aged 30–60, the simple household remained the dominant type in over 80 percent of the cases.

The dominance of the simple family household becomes even clearer when examining the cases in which it has been thought that the life cycle most often influenced household structure: the young married couples and the elderly people, especially widows. In Hamilton, unlike Preston or the village Berkner describes, very few married couples lived with a parent. Instead, the vast majority established their own household immediately after marriage. Evidence to support this contention is shown in Table 5.13, which compares the number of men married at each age with the number who were household heads, giving an index generally of about 1.1. In other words, at every age there were ten married men who headed their own households for every one who did not but dwelled instead with parents or as a boarder. For men who married unusually early the figure was only a trifle higher. The index for women was 1.2, though in about one out of three instances very young married women, those under the age of twenty, dwelled in a household which their husbands did not head. Clearly, couples almost always established their own households upon marriage. Why, one might ask, did this pattern exist in Hamilton and not in Preston, where, according to Michael Anderson, quite a different practice prevailed? It could be that cultural norms differed in the two places, though the prevalence of Irish immigrants in both cities and the overwhelmingly British origins of Hamilton's population make this unlikely. Or it could be that industrialization had altered the traditional practices of

TABLE 5.13 Marriage by age and sex, all persons aged 18–30, 1851 and 1861

		Males								Females							
		Married or widower		Head of household		Index 1/2		All males		Married or widow		Head of household or wife		Index 1/2		All females	
Age		1851	1861	1851	1861	1851	1861	1851	1861	1851	1861	1851	1861	1851	1861	1851	1861
18	N	3	1	2	2	1.5	0.5	147	170	18	10	12	8	1.5	1.3	211	248
	%	2.0	0.6							8.5	4.0						
19	N	1	1	1	3	1.0	0.3	148	159	25	19	18	13	1.4	1.5	205	280
	%	0.7	0.6							12.2	6.8						
20	N	8	6	6	4	1.3	1.5	167	160	54	50	40	43	1.4	1.2	223	292
	%	4.8	3.8							24.2	17.1						
21	N	13	11	11	12	1.2	0.9	141	146	39	57	30	48	1.3	1.2	141	208
	%	9.2	7.5							27.7	27.4						
22	N	18	13	18	16	1.0	0.8	159	164	68	77	57	63	1.2	1.2	170	216
	%	11.3	7.9							40.0	35.6						
23	N	30	31	32	28	0.9	1.1	121	131	80	79	69	64	1.2	1.2	164	196
	%	24.8	23.7							48.8	40.3						
24	N	39	38	35	34	1.1	1.1	149	155	78	120	67	100	1.2	1.2	271	220
	%	26.2	24.5							28.8	54.5						
25	N	69	53	57	49	1.2	1.1	155	161	111	151	95	129	1.2	1.2	186	259
	%	44.5	32.9							59.7	58.3						
26	N	63	81	60	75	1.1	1.1	137	156	113	145	97	130	1.2	1.1	160	213
	%	46.0	51.9							70.6	72.3						
27	N	61	93	48	87	1.3	1.1	111	155	81	112	69	98	1.2	1.1	106	141
	%	55.0	60.0							76.4	79.4						
28	N	96	99	90	96	1.1	1.0	151	169	111	154	95	142	1.2	1.1	140	194
	%	63.6	64.3							79.3	79.4						
29	N	70	98	67	98	1.0	1.0	112	148	74	96	68	79	1.1	1.2	92	125
	%	62.5	66.2							80.4	76.8						
30	N	128	180	116	168	1.1	1.1	215	258	182	246	153	215	1.2	1.1	220	309
	%	59.5	69.8							82.7	79.6						

the people in Preston, in which case a change in Hamilton might be expected in succeeding decades, though there was none by 1871, by which time the city had become significantly more industrial. Or it might be that the residence patterns of young couples reflected a rate of transiency greater in Hamilton than in Preston. Perhaps far fewer couples in Hamilton had parents nearby with whom they could live. But without a knowledge of the rate of transiency in Preston it is not possible to do more than speculate on this intriguing issue. Most simply, housing may have been more available in Hamilton.

Widows apparently strove as much as young married couples to maintain their independence by retaining their own home as long as possible. As Table 5.14 shows, in 1851, 53 percent and in 1861, 69 percent of all widows in their forties headed their own households. This proportion did not drop notably until after the age of sixty, though even then, in 1861, 38 percent of widows, a not insignificant minority, headed their own households. Conversely, only 9 or 10 percent of widows in their forties lived with relatives, a proportion which rose with age to about a quarter of those in their fifties and about 45 percent of those aged 60 and over. As long as they had children at home whom they could support, widows chose to remain independent heads of their own house-

TABLE 5.14 Widows by household status and age, 1851 and 1861

| Age | Status in household | | | | | | | All widows | |
	Head	Child	Relative	Visitor	Boarder	Servant	Other	N	%
40–49									
1851	53.2%	—	10.3%	—	25.4%	11.1%	—	126	27.1
1861	69.2	2.7%	8.5	0.5%	11.2	6.9	1.6%	188	26.4
50–59									
1851	45.0	—	24.3	0.9	17.1	12.6	—	111	23.9
1861	57.9	0.5	21.6	0.5	9.2	9.2	1.0	199	25.6
60 and over									
1851	33.7	—	46.7	—	16.3	3.3	—	92	19.8
1861	38.2	—	44.3	0.9	12.3	1.9	2.4	212	24.4

holds. When their children left, the widows were alone and often destitute; they could take in boarders, as many did, or else go to live with someone else, perhaps preferably with a child, if that was possible, but if not, with some other relative, or failing that, in another household as a boarder.

The problem of widowhood in a nineteenth-century city must not be underestimated. It was, first of all, a frequent experience and, for some reason, an increasing one in the 1851–1861 decade. The percentage of widows among all adult women in Hamilton rose during the decade from 8 to 13 percent. When widowhood is considered by age, the magnitude of the problem and its increase become even clearer. Here we compare women living in the city in both 1851 and 1861 in order to eliminate the possibly distorting effects of transiency upon the results. The proportion of widows among women aged 50–59 increased from 26 to 39 percent. More women, as usually has been the case, were widowed than men: in 1861, 21 percent of all men in their sixties compared to 49 percent of women had been widowed. (This information has not been presented in tabular form.) Between 1851 and 1861, as Table 5.15A shows, 15 percent of married men and 34 percent of married women in their fifties became widowed. Among people ten years older, 32 percent of the married men lost their wives and 59 percent of the married women lost their husbands during the decade. Thus, most married women could expect widowhood. If their husbands had not left them well off, the threat of poverty could never have been far away. In fact, the destitution of elderly widows provided the stimulus to the most vigorously and systematically undertaken charity of the time, the Ladies Benevolent Society. Widowhood, as Table 5.15B indicates, reflected the fact that death came earlier to the poor. For in 1861 the proportion of widows among Irish Catholic women aged 40 or over was about eight times higher than that among Canadian-born Protestant women, the most well-to-do.

The case of widows highlights the insecurity and harshness of life in a nineteenth-century city; it also strengthens the argument for the predominance of the simple family household at all phases of the life cycle. For it shows that only when a person's situation had become desperate, only when old age and loneliness were combined, would a parent move in with her children. It is clear,

TABLE 5.15 Widows and widowers, 1851 and 1861

A. Married persons widowed between 1851 and 1861[a]

Age in 1851	Women	Men
25–29	9.4%	0.8%
30–39	14.8	3.8
40–49	23.7	10.7
50–59	33.8	14.6
60–69	58.8	32.4

B. Total widows among women aged 40 and over, by ethnicity[b]

Ethnic group	Percent		Number	
	1851	1861	1851	1861
English	51.0	44.6	22	74
Scottish	42.4	50.6	33	79
Irish Catholic	26.8	56.9	86	102
Irish Protestant	38.8	46.0	49	76
Canadian Catholic	—	11.0	17	45
Canadian Protestant	15.3	6.9	72	203
U.S.-born	26.8	34.1	26	44
Other	—	34.8	3	23

[a] Linked persons only.
[b] All women.

then, that household structure varied only partly with age. Whereas the variation in household size and the number of children in a family can be explained largely by age, household composition was influenced primarily by only two aspects of the life cycle, the greater volatility of domestic arrangements among the young and the problems of the elderly. The variations among age cohorts were not nearly large enough to account for the tremendous fluctuation in the composition of individual households across a decade. Nor was the influence of wealth a sufficient explanation. Whether or not a particular household contained a boarder or relative at any moment remained partly a function of wealth, slightly a consequence of age, but largely a result of chance.

Whether or not any individual person became a boarder,

relative, or servant, however, depended much less upon chance. For when the perspective shifts from the household to the individual, relationships with the life cycle become more systematic, especially the clear interactions among a number of key events in the lives of young people: leaving school, departing from home, starting to work, and marrying. These events intersected with one another in a way that gave to the experience of people whom today we would call adolescents a distinctly different pattern from that which it has since assumed. As much as anything, the prolongation of dependence upon parents during an extensive period of formal schooling, we imagine, marks the adolescent years in modern times as different from the experience of growing up in the past. And that belief, generally speaking, is correct. But less accurate is a popular belief that in earlier times a complete autonomy succeeded a relatively brief period of dependence as children left home to work and live on their own at an early age.

Joseph Kett summarizes the prevailing idea, of which he is critical, in this way: "The period of dependency, it is asserted, was very short in the early nineteenth century. Boys left home and became men at 15, if not earlier, and thus scarcely experienced a period of youth." To the contrary, argues Kett, a stage of "semi-dependence" intervened. In their semi-dependent years boys moved back and forth between school, where they were treated as children, and work, where they were adults. Often living with their parents while employed, boys escaped complete parental control during the time they earned money and acquired a partial autonomy on the job. This rotation among school, home, and work did not form a neat and identifiable pattern, Kett contends. "The experience of growing up differed, often profoundly, from one youth to the next," he writes, describing "the pattern of random experience" that marked the lives of young men and their families.[39] Experience may have been random in rural areas where the rhythm of existence differed from the city. But in Hamilton, experience assumed a more uniform pattern, though the element of chance or circumstance often muddied the tidier picture. In Hamilton, also, an important and largely lost stage of the life cycle which I call semi-autonomy can be identified. My definition of semi-autonomy differs somewhat from Kett's definition of semi-dependence. For semi-autonomy was anchored not solely in employment but also in place of residence. It consisted of the span of years between leaving home and marrying during which young men and women frequently worked and lived as members of a household other than that of their parents. If I am right, almost all young men and the majority of young women passed through a stage of semi-autonomy, which provided not only a convenient living arrangement for young people away from home but also a supervised environment in which to take the first step toward the independence that would arrive with marriage. At the same time, placing young people within a household gave the social system a means of containing the potentially disruptive behavior of youths on their own and of managing the lengthy and potentially turbulent period between puberty and marriage.

In places other than Hamilton, and very different from it, youths customarily left home to dwell in another household or several other households for some years prior to marriage. Writing of apprentices in seventeenth-century London, Steven R. Smith claims they "were no longer children; they had reached the stage of puberty and were sent out of their homes to live in the homes of others, almost as the children of other parents, but not quite."[40] Alan Macfarlane has described in great detail the family life of a seventeenth-century English clergyman, Ralph Josselin, who sent his children away from home between the ages of ten and fifteen, some to be educated, some to be servants and apprentices. At the same time, he took into his own home other, unrelated young people of the same age who acted as servants. Diaries, Macfarlane claims, show that it was common for men of Josselin's status or above it to follow the same custom; and when Macfarlane inspected parish records, he found that the practice seemed to be equally customary among more ordinary people. "In the years between puberty and marriage," writes Macfarlane, "approximately 2/3 of the males and 3/4 of the female children seem to have been living away from their parents." Among the wealthy, those missing children "were replaced by other people's children acting as servants." The poor, on the other hand, apparently lost their investment in their children and the labor that they might have provided. "The institution of servanthood might, therefore," Macfarlane speculates, "be regarded as a disguised means whereby wealth and labour flowed from the

poorer to the richer." Undoubtedly, the implications of the practice of sending children away from home do not stop here.
Though Macfarlane ends his discussion with a confession of
historical ignorance about details and a plea for research, he
offers some tantalizing speculations about the purpose of sending
children to live in another household. The custom might have
been "a mechanism for separating the generations at a time when
there might otherwise have been considerable difficulty" on
account of the protracted period between puberty and marriage.
Those difficulties could have involved incest, or they could have
centered around questions of authority within the family. Macfarlane also presents an argument (reminiscent of Edmund Morgan's report on the same practice in colonial New England) that
strangers might discipline children more easily "in the absence of
intimate and already fixed emotional ties," and that they might
provide a broader, richer variety of experience than children
found at home. The high rate of mortality could have influenced
the custom too, Macfarlane concludes, for "children would be
dispersed and would not be entirely dependent on parents who
were always likely to die before the children grew up."[41]

The custom of sending children away from home that prevailed
in seventeenth-century England lasted at least into the late
eighteenth century. Roger Schofield, examining the best listing
for the later period, has found fundamentally the same pattern in
Cardington, a Bedfordshire parish. "It is known from listings of
inhabitants," reports Schofield, "that children were frequently sent
out into service from about the age of 15 until marriage." Usually,
they not only left home but moved to a different parish as well.
As a consequence, two thirds "of the children of the previous
generation had left the parish to found families elsewhere, their
places being taken by the children of other parishes." The chances
that boys aged 10–14 would leave home were one in four; for
boys aged 15–19 the chances rose to four to one. During this time
a boy would live within another household, remaining unmarried
at least until the age of twenty. "The pattern is therefore one of a
general expectation for a boy to leave the parental home after
the age of 15, first as an unmarried servant, and then married, as
the head of his own family." Girls in this parish more often remained at home, participating in either lace making or textile

spinning. Young women aged 20–24 were equally likely to be at home or away. If a young woman had left home, she was 1.5 times more likely to be a servant than to be married. This age-specific information on mobility, Schofield rightly concludes, underlines "the paramount importance of the custom of sending children into service in determining the migratory experience of children for the ten years from the age of 15 until the mid-twenties," when they married.[42]

In the nineteenth century, Michael Anderson found, children frequently left home after the age of fifteen in rural areas of Lancashire, though in the industrial city of Preston they usually remained much longer with their parents, frequently until, and even after, they had married. In fact, Anderson speculates, the reason household size remained constant while fertility declined late in the nineteenth century could be "the rise in parent–married child co-residence, possibly to a level above its modern figure."[43]

These three studies, which stretch from the seventeenth through the mid-nineteenth century, point to the possibility that in pre-industrial England children gradually began to live at home longer, a trend which industrialization rapidly accelerated. Although Macfarlane and Schofield report that children left home frequently, Macfarlane, like Edmund Morgan for seventeenth-century New England, found that the exodus started after the age of ten; Schofield reports that it began primarily after the age of fifteen, a situation which seemed to prevail in rural Lancashire in the mid-nineteenth century. However, in the industrial city of Preston, children stayed at home much longer, which presumably meant a sudden break from custom for immigrants from the countryside, where traditional practices prevailed. If this sequence does signify a trend, then urban places on the verge of industrialization, like mid-nineteenth-century Hamilton, should show characteristics of both tradition and modernity. Comparisons, of course, can only be suggestive and limited at best, not just because so few studies have been made but even more because no one has examined in detail the experience of urban rather than village or rural youth in early England or North America.

In a general way Table 5.16 compares the experience of Hamilton with three other places: Cardington, the Bedfordshire parish

studied by Schofield; Preston in Lancashire; and the rural sample
of Lancashire examined by Anderson. The notable increase in the
proportion of young men and women of different ages remaining
at home with their parents constitutes the most striking and important trend. Whatever the nature of the connection might be,
it is apparent that in Hamilton industrialization and the prolongation of dependency accompanied each other. During the twenty
years of economic modernization between 1851 and 1871, the
proportion of male 15–19-year-olds remaining at home with their
parents, for instance, rose from 49 to 71 to 76 percent. Comparisons between the experience of Hamilton and elsewhere are
more striking in the case of young men than of young women.
The persistence of domestic service that was common among
young women until at least late in the nineteenth century probably gave their life cycle a continuity across time which was
lacking among young men, who were affected more immediately by
changes in apprenticeship and technology. In 1851, young men in
Hamilton and in rural Lancashire remained at home until roughly
the same age, which was longer than men had stayed at home in
late-eighteenth-century England but much shorter than in industrial Preston in the mid-nineteenth century. Throughout the
next two decades, a period when Hamilton began to acquire the
features of an industrial city, young men increasingly remained
at home longer, almost though not quite as long as they had stayed
at home in Preston. Similarly, young men left home somewhat
later in mid-nineteenth-century Buffalo, New York, which was
more developed industrially than Hamilton.[44] Tantalizing though
these comparisons are, they cannot be considered to substantiate
a trend of major historical and theoretical significance. Nonetheless, they do form a reasonable basis for a hypothesis about the
relationship between industrialization and the experience of
young people over time.

The age at which young people left home is only one event in
their lives about which information exists. The others are the age
at leaving school, starting work, and marrying. Plotting the interconnections among these major events makes it possible not only
to examine their sequence but also to use their systematic interaction as evidence that the pattern of massive early departure from

TABLE 5.16 Young people living with parents: comparative statistics

A. 15–19-year-olds in four places, various years

Place	Date	Males	Females
Cardington	1782	22%	71%
Rural Lancashire	1851	56	62
Hamilton	1851	49	46
Hamilton	1861	71	54
Hamilton	1871	76[a]	64[a]
Preston	1851	79	67

B. Native- and Irish-born young people in Hamilton and Buffalo, various years and age groups

	Native-born[b]			Irish-born[c]		
	Hamilton		Buffalo	Hamilton		Buffalo
Age groups	1851	1861	1855	1851	1861	1855
			Males			
15–17	69%	80%	83%	37%	70%	78%
18–19	43	66	71	24	34	62
20–22	35	49	39	18	44	32
23–25	21	37	24	16	23	14
			Females			
14–16	70	73	82	37	58	41
17–19	52	60	60	20	28	17
20–22	27	39	34	11	20	12
23–25	12	27	18	5	5	14

Sources: R. S. Schofield: "Age-Specific Mobility in an Eighteenth Century Rural English Parish," *Annals de Démographie Historique 1970* (Paris and The Hague, 1971), 261–274; Michael Anderson, "Household Structure and the Industrial Revolution: Mid-nineteenth Century Preston in Comparative Perspective," in Laslett, *Household and Family,* 234; Laurence Admiral Glasco, "Ethnicity and Social Structure: Irish, Germans and Native Born of Buffalo, New York, 1850–1860," unpub. diss., SUNY, Buffalo, 1973, 181–201.

[a] 1871: sample of approximately half the population.

[b] Native-born in Hamilton means Canadian Protestants; in Buffalo it means all U.S.-born whites.

[c] Irish in Hamilton means Irish Catholics; in Buffalo it means all Irish.

home was neither accidental nor ephemeral but part of a reasonably well-defined process of growing up in a nineteenth-century city. Figures 5.1–5.6 summarize these interactions in graphic form.

Consider first the case of young men in 1851, illustrated in Figure 5.1. Most lived at home through the age of sixteen, though there was a noticeable decrease after the age of ten: 88 percent of the 6–10-year-olds and 78 percent of the 11–15-year-olds lived with their parents. This proportion decreased steadily until at the age of twenty only one quarter and at twenty-five only 14 percent still lived in their parents' home. Those young men who did not live at home by and large were boarders in another household. Over a third of the 16-year-olds and half of the 19-year-olds, in fact at least 40 percent of all young men at each age between seventeen and twenty-five, lived as boarders. After the age of twenty-six the proportion began to drop as a majority of men married. Moreover, very few young men lived with kin—only between 3 and 5 percent at most ages between one and thirty.

The last age at which a majority of young men lived at home in 1851, the age of sixteen, was also the first year in which a majority, 51 percent, were employed. Young men, it would appear, left their parents' home when they first found work. After the age of sixteen, a sharp rise in employment took place, from 18 percent of the 11–15-year-olds to 70 percent of the 16–20-year-olds, 86 percent of the 21–25-year-olds, and 93 percent of the 26–30-year-olds. There was, of course, a corresponding decrease in the proportion of young men remaining at home.

School attendance decreased as the proportion of young men employed rose: 36 percent of the 11–15-year-olds attended school in 1851 compared to only 6 percent of the 16–20-year-olds. However, the proportion employed and the proportion attending school do not account for all the young men in any age cohort. Large numbers of young men neither worked nor went to school: nearly half (46 percent) of the 11–15-year-olds and about a quarter of the 16–20-year-olds remained in what must have been a state of partial idleness. Many adolescents must have roamed around the city with little or nothing to do, a situation which provides an objective underpinning for the desire felt by adults in this period to devise institutions that would take adolescents off the streets.

Most men married relatively late in their twenties: the first age

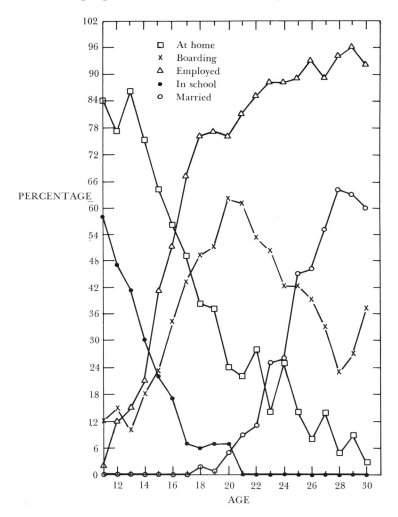

FIGURE 5.1 Young males at home, boarding, employed, in school, and
married, 1851

at which a majority were married was twenty-seven, although
many men married around the age of twenty-five. Few, moreover,
married before the age of twenty-three (only 11 percent of the
22-year-olds, for instance) and almost none before the age of
twenty-one (5 percent). Especially noteworthy is the remarkably

large number of men, 40 percent, who remained unmarried at the age of thirty, a phenomenon that cannot be accounted for by a lack of women of marriageable age. Rather, it points to a deliberate postponement of marriage, very likely for economic reasons. Clearly, men expected to establish themselves before they assumed the responsibilities of a family. And most must have worked several years before they took a wife; for instance, 86 percent of the 21–25-year-old men worked, but only 23 percent had married; 93 percent of the 26–30-year-olds were employed but only 58 percent were married. Most of the unmarried men who worked lived as boarders, probably trying to save enough money for marriage. Residential practices, in fact, reinforced the postponement of marriage, for young married couples almost always established their own households. Very few moved in with their parents, and thus young men could not count on their fathers to provide board and room during the early years of marriage while they sought to establish financial independence. The ability to support a family therefore had to precede marriage. Given the length of time between the onset of maturity and marriage and the social conventions prohibiting premarital sexual relationships, a diffuse sexual tension with its attendant anxiety and edginess must have wafted through this nineteenth-century city. In these circumstances prostitution not only provided a diversion but a social institution which may have preserved the sanity and tranquillity of urban society as much as the schools or the police, upholding the ideal of the virtuous and earnest young man who deposited his pay in the savings bank as he prepared year after year for marriage. In reality, he probably withheld some of that pay at least occasionally to spend at the brothel around the corner from the bank.

A common pattern, it appears, existed in the experience of young men: when they were about sixteen or seventeen they found employment and left their parents' home to live as boarders in other households until they married, often for as long as ten years. The period of time during which they lived in another household I call the stage of semi-autonomy. It is possible, however, to view semi-autonomy as an artifact of immigration. Most teen-age sons whose parents lived within the city may have stayed at home, and boarders may have been primarily young immigrants on their own. Although it is impossible to identify the parents of boarders, the number of living teen-age sons that the average family should have had can be estimated roughly, as Table 5.17 shows. The ages for which it is important to make an estimate of this sort, against which the actual situation can be compared, are those between seventeen and twenty-five, when boarding was most widespread. Household heads less than forty years old would be very unlikely to have sons in that age bracket, since the average age of marriage was twenty-seven. On the other hand, it is likely that the average married man of forty or more had one living son in this age category, though it is unlikely that the average would be as high as two. On estimate, then, the most likely figure was between one and two. Therefore, should the ratio of young men aged 17–25 to household heads aged 41 and over be between one and two, they all *could* have been the offspring of men living in the city. This does not mean that they necessarily were, but it does mean that if they were not, then the sons of men within the city would have had to emigrate in order to create the number of

TABLE 5.17 Ratios of 17–25-year-old persons to household heads aged 41 and over, 1851 and 1861

Age groups and ratios	1851	1861
(1) Number of 17–25-year-old males	1325	1433
(2) Number of 17–25-year-old females	1615	2091
(3) Number of 17–25-year-old males living with their parents	365	661
(4) Number of 17–25-year-old females living with their parents	409	678
(5) Number of household heads aged 41 or over	966	1573
(6) Ratio of $\dfrac{\text{17–25-year-old males}}{\text{household heads 41 or over}}$	1.4	0.9
(7) Ratio of $\dfrac{\text{17–25-year-old females}}{\text{household heads 41 or over}}$	1.7	1.3
(8) Ratio of $\dfrac{\text{17–25-year-old males living with parents}}{\text{household heads 41 or over}}$	.38	.42
(9) Ratio of $\dfrac{\text{17–25-year-old females living with parents}}{\text{household heads 41 or over}}$	.42	.43

positions filled by the young immigrants. Either case would support the hypothesis that adolescent sons customarily left home to live in another household prior to marriage. Another way of making an estimate that should lead to the same sort of conclusion is to determine the ratio of boys aged 17–25 living with their parents to the number of household heads aged 41 and over. If that ratio should be less than one, it is reasonably certain that a large number of sons were not living at home.

The comparison of the actual situation with these estimates supports the supposition that most young men had left home. Within the city there were 1.4 young men aged 17–25 for every household head aged 41 or over, a figure quite consonant with the preceding demographic assumptions. At the same time, however, only thirty-eight out of every hundred household heads more than forty years old had a son aged 17–25 living at home. If the average man had even one living son, then most of those sons were living somewhere else. They were, in fact, most likely to be living as boarders in the stage I have called semi-autonomy. Laurence Glasco's recent study of Buffalo confirms this point: although at each age, more recently arrived young men boarded than did long-settled young men, a substantial proportion of men who had been in the city for relatively long periods of time boarded as well.[45]

The concept of semi-autonomy as I offer it here connotes more than a place of residence. It implies that young men had more autonomy when they lived as boarders than when they dwelled with their parents, even though as boarders they remained under some scrutiny by an adult household head. Evidence with which to demonstrate the emotional contrast between parents and sons on the one hand and boarders and household heads on the other hand is extraordinarily difficult to unearth. However, by combining what other historians have written about boarding and by drawing a few reasonable inferences from the information about the situation in Hamilton, it is plausible to suppose that boarders lived in a state of semi-autonomy, more plausible, I would argue, than any other inference. I have assumed in the following argument that the relationship between parents and their children is almost always more complex and intense than the relationships between young people and other adults, even adults with whom they dwell and who exercise supervision over their activities.

The two historical works which deal systematically with boarding both argue that it represented something of an emancipation from the family. "The desire for independence from family ties," write Modell and Hareven, "was no doubt a major factor in the decision of boarders to pay rent rather than live with their kin in extended household arrangements. Young men and women in their twenties, employed in semi-skilled or skilled jobs, preferred boarding with a strange family, over their own, because the exchange of rent and services was defined in strict economic terms. Boarding offered the advantages of a family setting, without the affecting and lasting obligations that are woven into family relationships." In mid-nineteenth-century Preston, Michael Anderson argues, the desire for independence motivated young people to consider leaving their family at an early age. "Some children," he writes, "did desert their families and I have presented some evidence which suggested that even where they did not do so many children were conscious of the existence of this possibility and the alternatives it offered, and used it as a way of bargaining a highly independent relationship with their families."[46] Nonetheless, boarders should not be considered completely autonomous, for they lived not on their own but in households which became their "surrogate families."

Young men who lived as boarders were semi-autonomous, less dependent than those who remained at home, though not yet masters of their own households. Evidence for this conclusion rests not only on psychological inference but on a comparison of how children and boarders of the same age actually lived. Consider, for example, the experience of the 138 17-year-old men in Hamilton in 1851. Most of them, seventy-three, did not live with their parents, and most of the seventy-three were boarders, virtually all employed. Given the estimates in Chapter One, it could be expected that five or six of these boarders worked for the head of the household in which they dwelled; the rest worked for somebody else. Their situation contrasts sharply with that of the sixty-five young men who lived with their parents. Of these, nine attended school and thirty-five worked. Probably about fourteen of the thirty-five (using estimates developed in Chapter Three) worked for their fathers, and the other twenty-one worked for other employers. That leaves twenty-one more who were neither at work nor in school. Apparently all of these young men, with the exception of the twenty-one working outside the family, remained economically dependent upon their parents, with whom they lived. And if Hamilton resembled other places, those twenty-one very likely contributed a large share of their earnings to the family income. Thus there is every reason to believe that young men who lived at home remained economically dependent upon their parents more often than those who moved out of the household. Indeed, even if boarders sent money home to their parents, they could not supply as much as if they had remained at home because they had to pay their landlord for room and board. Economic ties between family members, it appears reasonable to suppose, weakened when sons left home. If my psychological assumption is correct, emotional bonds loosened as well.

Young men who dwelled as boarders should have been financially and emotionally closer to independence than men of the same age who remained at home. If this argument is correct, they should have married sooner. And this is precisely what happened. Young men who had been boarders, as Table 5.18 shows, were more likely to have married and established their own households a decade later than men of comparable age who had stayed at home: 7 percent of the young men aged 10–14 in 1851 who had lived with their parents were household heads a decade later compared to 34 percent of those who had lived as boarders. Among the young men aged 15–19 in 1851, 29 percent of those who had been living with their parents headed their own households in 1861 compared to 33 percent of the boarders. For those men aged 20–24 in 1851, the proportions heading their own households a decade later were 60 percent for those who had lived with their parents and 74 percent for those who had been boarders. Leaving home to enter another household appears to have been a transitional step between the status of a child and that of an independent adult. The experience of partial autonomy eased the transition; those men who left home were readier than those who remained to cross the boundary between child and adult.

Experience, however, did not take the form of neat, sequential,

TABLE 5.18 Household and marital status by age[a]

A. Percentage of males who were household heads in 1861

Household	Age in 1851		
status 1851	10–14	15–19	20–24
Child at home	7.2	28.7	60.0
Boarder	34.3	33.3	74.0

B. Percentage of females who were household heads or wives in 1861

Household	Age in 1851		
status 1851	10–14	15–19	20–24
Child at home	1.1	5.8	17.9
Boarder	27.3	28.6	57.2

[a] All people linked 1851 to 1861.

irreversible patterns. Although boarding remained a common phenomenon and roughly the same proportion of households continued to contain kin, individual young people did not remain especially long in any one place. Very few of them, in fact, retained in 1861 the same household status they had had a decade earlier. Many of the boarders, in all 43 percent, had become household heads; 15 percent, on the other hand, had moved back to their parents' home; and only 18 percent remained boarders. To be more exact, 19 percent of the 10–14-year-old boarders and 24 percent of the 15–19-year-olds in 1851 had returned to their families by the end of the decade. Clearly, this indicates that boarding was a transitory form of experience. The same may be said of living as a member of a kinsman's household. Only 30 percent of the men who had lived with kin continued to do so a decade later. By that time 30 percent had returned to their parents and 24 percent had married. Dwelling in another home as a boarder or relative was obviously a transitional phase in the lives of young men. Those who had lived as relatives returned more often than the boarders to the home of their parents; boarders more frequently married and established their own households.

This conclusion returns to both the central theme of this book and to Kett's argument about the random nature of experience. A fluidity in the residential experience of individual young people matched the fluidity in the structure of individual households. Both formed a counterpoint to the overall stability in the distribution of household types throughout a turbulent decade. Although part of both the transiency in the experience of individuals and households related systematically to their life cycle, much of it must remain unaccountable, the product of accident and circumstance in a less predictable and less regulated age.

Young women left home at about the same age as young men in 1851, although Figure 5.2 indicates that in Hamilton even more of the 16–20-year-olds lived away from their parents. Those young women not at home were primarily servants, not boarders, however. By the age of thirteen, three out of every ten girls lived as resident servants in the household of someone to whom they were not related. That proportion remained relatively stable until the age of seventeen; an astonishing 40 percent of the 17-year-old girls were resident domestic servants, a level sustained through the age of twenty when, with the onset of marriage, a steep drop in the proportion of young women living as servants began. Relatively few young women of any age, it should be noted, lived as boarders or as relatives: about 10 percent of the 16–25-year-olds were boarders and 6 or 7 percent were relatives. Most of the young women living away from their parents *could* have been the daughters of families resident within the city, as the same sort of demographic estimate used with young men shows. There were 1.7 young women aged 17–25 in the city for every household head over the age of forty; and only forty-two of every hundred household heads of that age had a daughter aged 17–25 living at home. Again, if it is likely that most men had at least one daughter of that age, then most of the daughters were living elsewhere, either in somebody else's household within the city or in some other town.

Most of the young women who worked, of course, were servants: 363 of the 456 16–20-year-olds who were employed, and 191 of the 263 21–25-year-olds who were employed. Most of the rest were seamstresses or milliners. They began to work after they had left home; at the age of seventeen, when nearly half had left home,

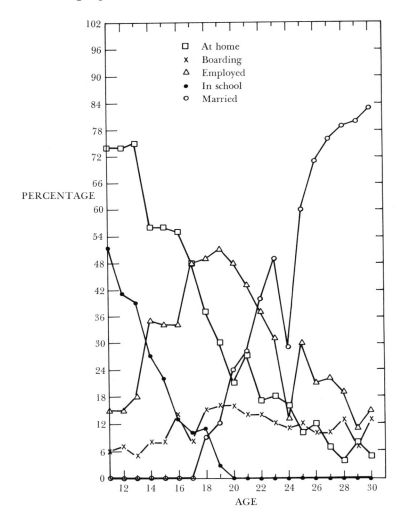

FIGURE 5.2 Young females at home, boarding, employed, in school, and
married, 1851

nearly half were servants. Unlike the young men, young women
began to leave the work force after the age of nineteen, when the
highest proportion of them, 51 percent, worked. As more and
more married during their early twenties, fewer were employed:

37 percent of the 22-year-olds and 15 percent of the 30-year-olds, for instance.

As with young men, the school attendance of young women dropped as the proportion of those employed increased, although the decrease among the young women was rather swifter. Only 26 percent of the 11–15-year-old young women attended school compared to 36 percent of the young men of the same age; and a tiny 3 percent of the 16–20-year-olds had gone to school during the year, a figure half the size of the also very small 6 percent among the men. Young women suffered even more than young men from a period of life in which they neither went to school nor had a job. For more than half of the 11–15-year-old and 34 percent of the 16–20-year-old young women neither attended school nor worked, proportions notably higher than those among young men of the same age. The young women may have had a more traditional and concrete role in these years as apprentice housewives, helping their mothers and preparing in their own way for marriage. Nonetheless, the high proportion neither employed nor in school underlines the restricted situation of women. Limited to employment in domestic service or sewing, most young women had little to do for the long period between the time they left school and the time they married. These years of idleness and dependence probably aggravated the tensions between mothers and daughters, providing young women with a powerful incentive to marry as early as possible and to establish their own households, free at last of the domination of their mothers.

This is perhaps one reason why marriage among women took place so much earlier than among men. The proportion of women who married increased between the ages of twenty-one and twenty-two: 28 percent of the 21-year-olds compared to 40 percent of the 22-year-olds had married. Before the age of twenty, however, marriage was still uncommon; only 12 percent of the 19-year-olds, for instance, were married. By the age of twenty-five, 60 percent of women had married, a proportion not reached among men until the age of twenty-eight, and by the age of thirty, 83 percent of the women, a proportion still substantially higher (17 percent) than for men, had married. Overall, it appears that women married about four years earlier than men.

After they married, most women stopped working at a job: for each age group there was a perfectly inverse relationship between the percentage of women married and the percentage employed. Indeed, almost no married woman with a husband at home listed an occupation. For example, at the age of thirty, 15 percent of women were employed and 83 percent married. Together they account for 98 percent of the 30-year-old women within the city. The absence of married women from the work force signifies as much as anything that Hamilton had yet to reach the industrial age. For one of the hallmarks of the early nineteenth-century factory was its use of female labor; in the industrial city of Preston, for instance, Michael Anderson found that 28 percent of married women with a husband at home were employed, as were nearly a quarter (23 percent) of those with children.[47] Here, then, is a change I expect to discover in Hamilton in later decades. However, the sequence in the relation among opportunity, poverty, and industrialization as they apply to female employment remains far from clear. Did women in commercial Hamilton not take jobs because work was not available, because their husbands earned enough for the entire family, or because they simply did not want to work outside their home? Did the later industrialization lower the wages of men and make it necessary for married women to seek employment in larger numbers, or— equally plausible—did women eagerly undertake factory work, welcoming the growth of employment opportunities which they had lacked and needed to supplement the always meager earnings of their husbands? There exist at present no definitive answers to those very important questions.

Between 1851 and 1861 the relations among home, school, work, and marriage changed. In these years the period of semi-autonomy shortened as the process of growing up assumed a distinctly more modern look. The proportion of young people remaining at home increased at every age, a trend maintained throughout the 1860s as well, though in much less dramatic fashion. All of this happened within a city that was struck hard by the depression of the late 1850s. Although the population had begun to climb after its fall during the nadir of economic difficulties, Hamilton remained in the process of recovery in 1861, and many of the young men had left the city. Whereas in 1851 there had been 1.7 young men aged 17–25 in the city for every household head over the age of forty, in 1861 that figure was almost halved; there was, in fact, only 0.9. Aside from skewing the sex ratios and creating hard times for young women who wished to marry, this exodus of young men reduced the available supply of boarders, and the proportion of households with boarders dropped steeply. The proportion of households employing a servant likewise decreased, as did average household size.

In 1861 the pattern which I have called semi-autonomy still existed. But the proportion of young men living in a semi-autonomous state had diminished sharply. As Figure 5.3 shows, the majority of young men now lived at home five years longer than they had in 1851, until, that is, the age of twenty-one. Whereas less than a quarter of the 20-year-old men lived with their parents in 1851, a decade later more than half, 54 percent, were still at home. Those young men not at home still primarily boarded in another household, but their proportion of each age group, of course, dropped steeply from 34 to 7 percent among 16-year-olds and from 62 to 37 percent among 20-year-olds. Overall, in the age group with the greatest proportion of boarders, the 21–25-year-olds, the proportion shrank from just under half to slightly more than a third.

It might be argued that these data could be an artifact of cross-sectional analysis: they do not indicate a change in habit but simply result from the absence of a large, floating class of young men who had been boarders in 1851 and who left when hard times hit the city. This argument, though plausible in terms of the out-migration already observed, can be counteracted in two ways. One is through the demographic projections made earlier; all the young men in the city in 1851 could have been the sons of its householders, and during the decade the proportion of men over the age of forty with a 17–25-year-old son living at home rose from 38 to 42 percent. More than that, the experience of young men traced across the decade provides confirmation of lengthened dependency. Table 5.19 considers only the young men who were present in both 1851 and 1861 in order to avoid contamination of the results by the presence of transients. Of the men aged 20–24 only 31 percent of those who had been born between 1827 and 1831 were living at home compared to 68 percent of the 20–24-year-olds born a decade later, between 1837 and 1841. Those

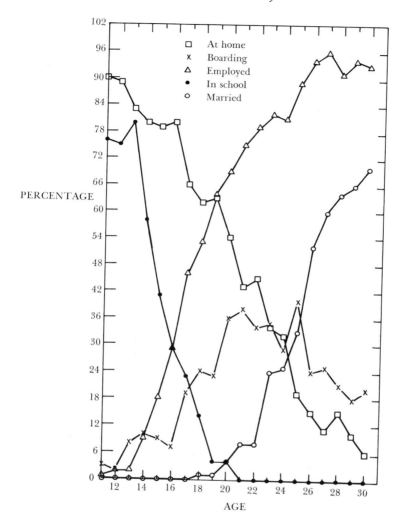

FIGURE 5.3 Young males at home, boarding, employed, in school, and married, 1861

young men who reached their early twenties in the early 1850s, that is, lived at home much less frequently than did those who reached that age a decade later. The same is true of men five years older: 12 percent of those aged 25–29 in 1851 lived with their par-

TABLE 5.19 Men married, living at home, and boarding:
comparison of age cohorts, 1851 and 1861[a]

Age cohort	Birth date	Percent married	Percent living at home	Percent boarding
20–24	1827–1831	19.3	31.3	41.5
	1837–1841	10.7	67.8	15.6
25–29	1822–1826	63.2	11.9	16.9
	1832–1836	36.2	41.3	16.2
40–49	1802–1810	90.3	—	—
	1812–1820	90.0	—	—

a Males linked 1851 to 1861.

ents compared to 41 percent (a massive increase) who reached that age a decade later.

If this increase took place only between 1851 and 1861, it would be less significant than if it were a long-term trend. For it might have been the temporary result of the depression: young men unable to find work naturally would have remained at home longer. But this possibility is countered by the continued increase in the proportion of young men at home in 1871. Although the analysis of the 1871 data is not complete and the proportions given in Figure 5.4 rest on about half the population on the census, that is a large enough sample to yield results representative of the entire population. Unlike the proportions shown in the last paragraph and in Table 5.19, these are based not on people traced from one decade to another but on the entire age group at each point in time. Young men of all ages remained at home longer: for instance, among the 16–20-year-olds the proportion at home rose from 40 percent in 1851 to 66 percent in 1861 and 71 percent in 1871. Clearly, the propensity of young men to remain longer at home, a trend which accelerated during the 1850s, continued to increase during the next decade, though at a slower pace. (Subsequent preliminary inspection of the entire 1871 census confirms the general accuracy of the results given here on the basis of a sample.)

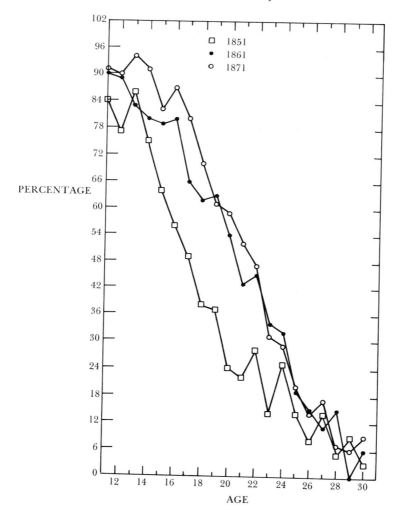

FIGURE 5.4 Young males at home in 1851, 1861, and 1871

It might be thought that young men in the 1850s simply reacted in a traditional way to the problems of the depression. Unable to find employment elsewhere, they stayed at home with their families and worked with their fathers. However, as Chapter

Three has pointed out, young men followed their fathers' occupations considerably less frequently in 1861 than they had a decade earlier. At the same time, they went to school for a longer period. Thus it would seem that the additional years which young men spent living at home with their parents represented a shifting pattern of behavior rather than simply a response to hard times.

As might be expected, young men started work later in 1861 than in 1851; the age at which the majority were employed increased by two years during the decade. A majority of boys were at work at the age of eighteen, but a majority had not left home until the age of twenty-one. If these cross-sectional figures can be translated into a dynamic portrait of the life cycle, young men now were staying at home for about three years after they had begun to work. By the time they reached the age of twenty-five, however, virtually no differences remained between the young men of 1861 and 1851.

Elsewhere I have written in detail about the remarkable increase in school attendance during the decade 1851–1861.[48] The increase in school attendance was sharpest among the 11–15-year-olds, where it increased from 36 to 76 percent. Even among the 16–20-year-olds, school attendance rose notably from 6 to 13 percent. Despite this increase, many young men still neither worked nor attended school. This problem, however, had become most serious among older youths; it had almost disappeared among the younger ones, those who had most often been idle a decade earlier. In 1851, 46 percent of the 11–15-year-olds neither worked nor attended school compared to but 17 percent ten years later, whereas among the 16–20-year-olds the proportion rose notably from 25 to 36 percent. If the increase in school attendance can be taken as a measure of achievement, then the expansion of educational facilities in the 1850s, which undoubtedly had been influenced by the existence of idle youth, was a reasonable success.

It is less easy to specify trends in marriage than in school attendance. For there was a discrepancy between the behavior of all young men, a group composed mainly of immigrants to the city, and of those young men who remained within the city for at least a decade. Among the newcomers, the proportion married fell slightly for men aged 21–25 and rose a bit for men aged 26–30. Overall, the stability of marriage age was striking. By contrast, the pattern among men who remained within the city for at least a decade changed sharply: they began to marry much later than they had a decade earlier. In 1851, 19 percent of 20–24-year-old men married compared to but 11 percent a decade later. Similarly, at the earlier time 63 percent of the 25–29-year-olds married compared to 36 percent in 1861. Young men who remained within the city, quite clearly, were marrying later than men of the same ages ten years before. Very likely, the depression had made it more difficult to acquire the work stability and economic stake necessary to undertake marriage. The discrepancy between the behavior of the newcomers and persisters, however, is not easy to explain. It could be that the young men who remained were more cautious and less adventurous. Confronted with a serious depression and diminished opportunities, the more ambitious and courageous young men simply left in search of opportunity; others stayed behind, refusing even to marry in the unsettled circumstances of the time. The immigrants, on the other hand, may have been more like the young men who had left, adventurous, ambitious, and less daunted by the difficulties of the moment. The opportunity for earlier marriage, in fact, may have formed one important motive for emigrating to North America, for the Irish in Canada married much younger than their counterparts who remained at home.[49] Indeed, this raises the possibility that in general migrants married rather earlier than the more rooted portion of populations. It should not be forgotten, however, that the pattern among migrants included a marriage age that was late by contemporary standards.

Delayed marriage and imbalanced sex ratios confronted young women with bleak prospects if they wished to marry. Indeed, by 1871 the problem had become acute: the proportion of 26-year-old women who were married had dropped from 71 percent in 1851 and 72 percent in 1861 to 52 percent in 1871. Among the 28-year-olds, the decrease was from 79 percent in both 1851 and 1861 to 61 percent in 1871, while among 30-year-olds the drop went from 83 to 80 to 66 percent by 1871. Spinsterhood had become a very real problem.

When these cross-sectional data are transformed into a dynamic pattern, it is evident that the length of the phase of semi-autonomy had begun to shrink. The length of time between the age at which a majority of men were employed and a majority married narrowed from eleven years in 1851 to eight years a decade later. Simultaneously, the length of time between their leaving home and marrying shortened from ten years in 1851 to five years a decade later. It is dangerous to state these conclusions too firmly, for inferences such as these cannot be fully confirmed by cross-sectional data. But they are consistent with the experiences of young men traced across the decade, and hence they form a plausible hypothesis about the changing shape of experience. Young men still lived usually in another household between the time when they left home and when they married, but the length of that time shortened, *not* through any reduction in the age of marriage but, to the contrary, through prolonged residence at home. Finally, despite the difficulties of the depression, marriage still did mean independence, for, as in 1851, almost all married couples immediately established their own households.

Although the behavior of young women changed less than that of young men, they also remained with their parents longer in 1861 than they had a decade earlier (Figure 5.5). The proportion of 16–20-year-olds living at home rose from 30 to 40 percent and of 21-to-25-year-olds from 17 to 23 percent. However, the change was sharpest among the youngest women: the proportion of 14-year-olds at home, for instance, rose from 56 to 71 percent. Nonetheless, the age at which most young women apparently left home did not increase very much, only from 17 to 18 percent, which meant that on the average they moved away from their parents three years sooner than did men, a result, probably, of the availability of employment as domestics. For most young women not at home lived still as servants, though the proportion in domestic work declined notably in accordance with the overall decrease in the proportion of households employing resident servants. The proportion of 11–15-year-old women who were servants dropped from 20 to 9 percent and that of 16–20-year-olds from 41 to 35 percent. However, the proportion of women over the age of twenty-one who lived as servants remained much more steady. As a consequence of the decrease in the proportion of women employed as servants, there was, in 1861, no age at which a majority of women listed themselves as employed. The ages at which the most women were employed, moreover, shifted from

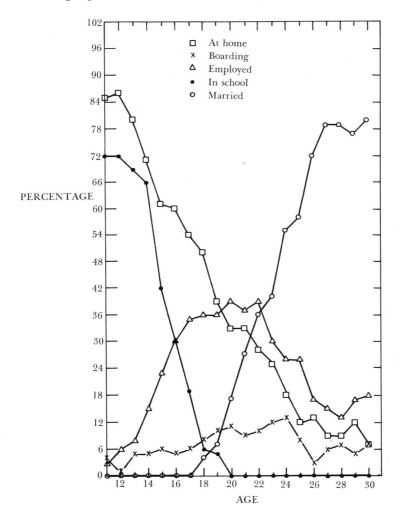

FIGURE 5.5 Young females at home, boarding, employed, in school, and married, 1861

nineteen in 1851 to twenty and twenty-two a decade later, when 39 percent of the women listed an occupation.

School attendance among young women rose in a fashion similar to that among young men: the percentage of 11–15-year-olds attending school more than doubled, from 26 to 57 percent, and the proportion of 16–20-year-olds rose sharply too, from 3 to 9 percent. Nonetheless, at each age fewer young women than men went to school. As in 1851, relations between school attendance and employment were perfectly inverse: 11 percent of the 11–15-year-old young women were employed and 57 percent were in school; for the 16–20-year-olds, the proportions were nearly reversed, 42 percent employed and 9 percent in school. Still, as was the case a decade earlier and as remained the case with young men, many women were neither employed, in school, nor married. Among the younger group, the 11–15-year-olds, the proportion neither employed nor at school dropped by 20 percent, a decrease comparable to that among men and accounted for by increased school attendance, but, again in a manner similar to young men, the proportion of 16–20-year-olds rose to 41 percent, and among the 21–25-year-olds it climbed as well, from 19 to 25 percent, undoubtedly a result of the outmigration and postponement of marriage by some young men. Thus, the proportion of 26–30-year-old young women at home with no visible occupation increased from 4 to 7 percent, a level substantially greater than that among men.

As might be expected, there was by 1861 a slight decrease in the percentage of women in each age category who had married, though the sharp decline brought about by male emigration had just begun to make itself felt. The decline in the proportion who were married among the 16–20-year-olds was from 12 to 8 percent; among the 21–25-year-olds, the proportion dropped from 47 to 44 percent; and among the 26–30-year-olds, who had been married before the economic troubles began, it remained almost steady, slipping only from 78 to 77 percent. The number of years between the time a young woman left home and the time she married may have been decreasing as well, though the evidence is not conclusive: in 1851, the difference between the age at which a majority of women no longer were at home (seventeen) and that at which the majority had married (twenty-five) was eight years; a decade later, it was six years, as a majority of women had left home by the age of eighteen and had married at twenty-four. Figure 5.6 shows that this trend toward prolonged residence at home lasted into the 1870s for women as well as for men. All in

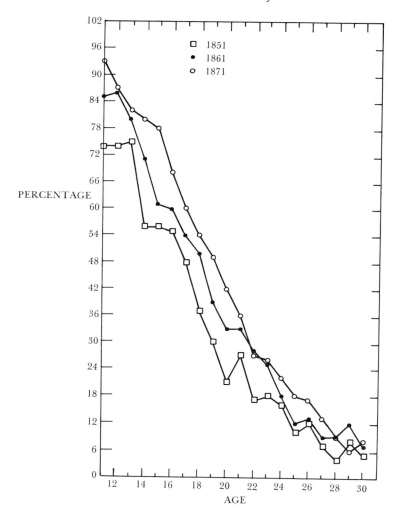

FIGURE 5.6 Young females at home in 1851, 1861, and 1871

all, young people of both sexes remained longer in their parents' home in 1861 than they had a decade earlier.

Did the prolongation of dependency which cut across the experience of the sexes cut across the experience of social classes and ethnic groups as well? It is possible, of course, that there was more than one way of coming of age in nineteenth-century urban Ontario. Marriage provides one clue. Among the small group of marriages referred to before, one pattern stands out: none of the daughters of the entrepreneurial class reported an occupation at the time of their marriage. By contrast, nearly a third, ten out of thirty-six, of the brides in Catholic marriages listed themselves as employed, nine as servants and one as a seamstress. All the Catholic marriages occurred within a year or two of the census, however, while the marriages in the entrepreneurial class spanned a much longer period. Thus, some of the affluent brides may have been working around the time of their marriage but not when they were located on the census. Nonetheless, even if it is not conclusive, this evidence suggests that the daughters of the poor frequently moved from life as a servant directly into marriage, whereas the daughters of the wealthy more often dwelled with their parents before marriage.

Aside from this fragmentary evidence, social class differences in the process of growing up cannot be observed directly, for the parents of most of the young people who lived as boarders, servants, or kin simply cannot be identified. But the religion and birthplace of the young people are known, and, in a rough sort of way, ethnicity can be used as a surrogate for class. Irish Catholics, for example, remained overwhelmingly poor while Canadian-born Protestants formed the most prosperous group within the city.

In a general sort of way, the experiences of young people from all ethnic groups assumed a similar pattern. The differences that did exist set off the experience of the poor from that of other groups, though they were differences of degree rather than of kind. Nonetheless, those variations began to narrow during the decade, and by 1861 the experience of young people from all backgrounds had become much more uniform than it had been a decade earlier. More Irish Catholic young men left home in 1851 than did those of any other ethnic background. Similarly, in Buffalo, New York, in 1855, Irish-born young men left home about a year earlier than those born in the United States.[50] In 1851 the range of variation between the proportion of Irish Catholic young men remaining at home, 18 percent, and the ethnic group with the most sons living with their parents, 35 percent, was much wider than in 1861, when it shrank to between 44 and 53 percent, a distinct increase for all groups and a marked reduction in the gap between them.

Most young men who did not live at home were boarders, a pattern common to all ethnic groups, as Table 5.20 shows. Although the proportion of Catholic young men who boarded was greater than that of any other ethnic group, it dropped dramatically during the decade. To introduce additional figures not

TABLE 5.20 School attendance, employment, and household status by ethnicity and age: selected comparisons for males, 1851 and 1861

Age groups	Percent		Total number	
	1851	1861	1851	1861
Attending school, age 11–14				
Irish Catholic	12.7	42.7	142	75
English Anglican	46.2	50.9	26	53
Scottish Presbyterian	58.3	70.2	24	47
Canadian Catholic	39.5	66.3	43	95
Canadian Protestant	58.6	77.6	198	361
Neither employed nor in school, age 11–14				
Irish Catholic	70.4	52.0	100	39
English Anglican	46.2	47.2	12	25
Scottish Presbyterian	25.0	27.7	6	13
Canadian Catholic	51.2	31.6	22	30
Canadian Protestant	30.3	19.7	60	71
Employed, age 15–17				
Irish Catholic	60.6	45.7	94	70
English Anglican	26.7	24.0	15	50
Scottish Presbyterian	50.0	40.0	14	45
Canadian Catholic	51.7	25.0	29	40
Canadian Protestant	40.3	24.7	144	219
Boarders, age 23–25				
Irish Catholic	41.0	27.5	100	69
English Anglican	26.3	47.2	38	53
Scottish Presbyterian	58.3	41.1	48	73
Canadian Catholic	60.0	35.3	5	17
Canadian Protestant	45.5	30.5	44	105

shown in the table, the proportion dropped from 39 to 9 percent
of the 15–17-year-olds and from 62 to 21 percent of the 18–19-year-
olds. At each end of the decade, moreover, a sizable proportion
of young men from the most well-to-do parents, the Canadian
Protestants, boarded: in 1851 the proportions were 24 percent of
the 15–17-year-olds, 49 percent of the 18–19-year-olds, and 55
percent of the 20–22-year-olds. Similarly, in Buffalo, New York,
in 1855, 36 percent of native-born and 42 percent of Irish-born
21-year-old men lived as boarders.[51] Thus, boarding was widespread among young men of all social origins. In Hamilton,
however, the differences that did exist between the practices of
the affluent and the poor in 1851 had diminished by the end of
the decade.

Likewise, the proportion of young men employed at different
ages revealed surprisingly little ethnic or class variation. For
example, in 1851, more Irish Catholic than other young men were
employed, 17 percent of the 11–14-year-olds and 61 percent of
the 15–17-year-olds; but the proportion of Canadian Protestants
working at the same ages, 11 and 40 percent, did not differ so
much as might have been anticipated. Of special interest, however,
is the ethnic discrimination hinted at by employment patterns a
decade later. By 1861, as Chapter Two explained, competition
from Scottish and English craftsmen, which had intensified during
the depression, had pushed Irish Catholic men out of some trades
in which they had gained a toehold. The experience of young
men reflected this process. Although young Irish Catholic men,
those aged 11–17, worked more often than others, fewer of them
than of men from any other ethnic background were employed
at ages eighteen and nineteen or between the ages of twenty and
twenty-two. After the age of seventeen, young men from other
ethnic groups entered the labor force in sharply increased numbers, displacing the Irish Catholics who had already been working
for a few years. In this way, ethnic prejudice and tough competition for jobs combined to worsen the situation of Irish Catholic
young men in Hamilton; it is no wonder that they left the city
more often than anybody else.[52]

At the same time, men of all ethnic backgrounds sent their
sons to school for increasingly long periods of time. Although
the rise among the Irish Catholics—from 13 to 43 percent of 11–

14-year-olds—was largest, they still ranked lowest in school attendance; but, as with other measures, the distance between them and the other groups decreased. Canadian Protestants and Scottish Presbyterians sent the most 11–14-year-old boys to school, and only they and the English Anglicans sent more than a token proportion—about 12 percent—of 18–19-year-old boys to school. More Irish Catholic young men than those of any other ethnic group, 70 percent of 11–14-year-olds, neither worked nor attended school, a fact which forms a dramatic demographic backdrop to the mounting concern with juvenile delinquency and the creation of reform schools in these years.[53] By 1861, however, the Irish Catholic proportion, 52 percent, still highest, had moved closer to that of other groups; next came the English Anglican young men, nearly half of whom (47 percent) had nothing much to do. The employment problems of Irish Catholics appeared once more among 18–19-year-olds, for 58 percent of them apparently lived in what must have been involuntary idleness. How these young men who neither worked nor attended school actually spent their time remains one of the great unsolved puzzles about everyday life in the nineteenth-century city.

Ethnic variations in marriage patterns point more to the influence of culture than of class. Irish Catholic men married somewhat earlier than others, and very much earlier than men who remained in Ireland. The possibility of early marriage, in fact, could have been one of the most powerful incentives to emigration. Scottish Presbyterians, on the other hand, delayed marriage in both 1851 and 1861 until their late twenties. Canadian-born men, both Protestant and Catholic, began to change their habits, however; by 1861 they were postponing marriage until after the age of 30. Regardless of religion, men born in Canada apparently reacted to economic uncertainty with a similar response. Though many of them must have been sons of Irish immigrants, Catholic men born in Canada behaved like other native sons. Their assimilation had begun.

Like young men, most young women of all ethnic backgrounds began to stay at home longer, and differences between ethnic groups diminished during the decade, as Table 5.21 reveals. Not surprisingly, Irish Catholic young women left home notably earlier in 1851 than did young women of other backgrounds; 52

TABLE 5.21 School attendance, employment, and household
status by ethnicity and age: selected comparisons
for females, 1851 and 1861

Age groups	Percent		Total number	
	1851	1861	1851	1861
Attending school, age 11–14				
Irish Catholic	13.8	43.5	94	46
English Anglican	18.8	62.0	32	50
Scottish Presbyterian	30.0	57.6	10	33
Canadian Catholic	40.6	68.6	32	70
Canadian Protestant	47.7	66.8	155	259
Servants, age 14–16				
Irish Catholic	46.9	31.3	147	96
English Anglican	16.2	31.3	37	48
Scottish Presbyterian	58.3	7.9	12	38
Canadian Catholic	14.3	27.3	28	55
Canadian Protestant	16.2	12.7	148	221
Living with parents, age 14–16				
Irish Catholic	36.7	58.3	147	96
English Anglican	73.0	60.4	37	48
Scottish Presbyterian	33.3	76.3	12	38
Canadian Catholic	57.1	60.0	28	55
Canadian Protestant	70.3	73.3	148	221
Servants, age 17–19				
Irish Catholic	61.2	57.9	178	140
English Anglican	12.0	27.5	25	40
Scottish Presbyterian	34.5	32.7	29	49
Canadian Catholic	21.1	24.4	19	45
Canadian Protestant	21.8	18.3	142	240
Employed, age 20–22				
Irish Catholic	57.8	51.0	161	149
English Anglican	21.1	18.3	38	60
Scottish Presbyterian	51.5	44.3	33	61
Canadian Catholic	28.6	42.9	14	35
Canadian Protestant	26.9	25.9	78	189

percent of 11–13-year-old Irish Catholic young women (not shown
in Table 5.21) remained at home compared to 70 percent of those
from the ethnic group with the next lowest proportion. (In
Buffalo, the differences between Irish and native-born women,
though varying in the same direction, were much greater.)[54] By

1861 this difference had largely disappeared. Interestingly, and inexplicably, English Anglican young women, contrary to the trend among other ethnic groups, began to leave home markedly earlier in 1861 than they had a decade before.

Although at every age Irish Catholic young women were usually more often servants, a sizable share of young women from each ethnic group lived as resident domestics. As might be expected, Canadian Protestants sent fewer young women out as servants, in 1851 no more than 16 percent of 14–16-year-olds, contrasted to 47 percent of Irish Catholic young women of the same age. The highest proportion for any group at any age was 61 percent among 17–19-year-old Irish Catholics. Given the likelihood that most young women did not remain very long in any one household but drifted back and forth between home and work, this strikingly high proportion implies that almost every Irish Catholic young woman who came to Canada spent part of her life as a resident domestic servant, a conclusion which Laurence Glasco also reached about Irish Catholic young women in Buffalo, New York. Nonetheless, it must be emphasized that working as a resident servant did not carry with it the stigma of membership in the lower class. One guide for young and obviously middle-class women emigrating to Canada, for instance, stressed the advantages of years spent as a domestic, which the author viewed as a kind of apprenticeship in housewifery in a new land.[55] And young women from prosperous groups also became servants; for instance, in 1851, 58 percent of 14–16-year-old and 35 percent of 17–19-year-old Scottish Presbyterian young women, daughters of a predominantly middle-class group, lived as resident domestics.

It is not surprising, then, that Irish Catholic young women attended school less often than women from other ethnic backgrounds. Although the proportion attending jumped, doubling from 5 to 11 percent of the 14–16-year-olds during the decade (not shown in table), Irish Catholics still remained well behind women of other origins. Interestingly, the young women who went to school most often at this age as well as at age 11–14 were the native Canadians, both Catholic and Protestant, once again an index of the process of assimilation at work.

Given the trends in employment and schooling, it follows that fewer Irish Catholic young women were idle, that is, fewer

neither attended school nor worked, in their early and late
adolescence (those aged 11–14 and 17–19). In early adolescence
they worked as servants more often than other young women.
In the middle years (15–16) the higher rate of school attendance
among English, Scottish, and Canadian young women boosted
the proportion of those who were occupied above that of the
Irish Catholics. But after the age of seventeen few of them, even,
remained in school, and once again the propensity of Irish
Catholic young women to work as servants kept them more often
occupied. Young women from more prosperous families who did
not live as servants did not marry any sooner than Irish Catholics.
Thus, young women of genteel background spent several years
in what only can be described as a state of semi-idleness, a
circumstance which may have contributed to the incidence of
neurasthenia, hysteria, and other nervous diseases described by
early psychiatrists as common afflictions among more affluent
young women in the latter nineteenth century.[56]

With a couple of exceptions, the ethnic differences in the relationship between the age of leaving school and home, or undertaking work and marriage, appear to have resulted from class
distinctions. It was the ethnic group most clearly associated with
lower-class standing, the Irish Catholics, that differed most
sharply from the others. And those differences by and large had
been shaped by class: lower rates of school attendance, higher
rates of adolescent employment, and consequently earlier ages of
leaving home. Similarly, at times the affluence of Canadians
appears to have placed them at the other end of the rank order
from the Irish Catholics. Nonetheless, this remains the most striking feature of the comparisons among ethnic groups: despite
differences in magnitude, relations among home, work, school,
and marriage for young people of each ethnic background generally varied systematically in the same fashion, changed in the same
direction, and lessened over time.

The major trends in the process of coming of age in nineteenth-
century Hamilton may be summarized as follows:

(1) Most young people spent some time living in a semi-
autonomous state in a household other than their parents'. This
period intervened between leaving school and getting married;
young men lived as boarders, young women as servants.

(2) Between 1851 and 1861 the length of this stage of semi-autonomy shrank as both young men and young women remained at home considerably longer. Although the pace of this change slowed, the same trend continued into at least the early 1870s.

(3) At the same time, the proportion of employed adolescents began to decrease sharply.

(4) In 1851 young men left home at roughly the same time they found a job; in 1861 they lived at home during their first few working years.

(5) The rate and length of school attendance increased sharply during the decade. School attendance and employment varied inversely. Generally speaking, more young men than women attended school.

(6) In both 1851 and 1861 many adolescents, both male and female, neither attended school nor worked. During the 1850s this problem lessened among young adolescents but increased among older ones.

(7) The length of time between leaving home and marrying decreased quite sharply between 1851 and 1861, largely as a function of the prolonged residence of young people at home.

(8) In both 1851 and 1861, nearly all young people who married immediately established households of their own.

The cause of these trends remains more elusive than their identity. In the short run the depression undoubtedly played a major role. For young people apparently altered their behavior to fit a situation in which work had become increasingly difficult to find. According to this explanation, the shortage of jobs caused young people to live at home longer; it was idleness that drove larger numbers of them to attend school.

Though this explanation undoubtedly is an important aspect of the story, it begs two questions. One concerns the pattern of semi-autonomy that existed in mid-nineteenth-century North America. Was that pattern a continuation of the centuries' old practice of sending young people away to live for a time in another household? If that was the case, it raises a second question. What forces sustained this pattern in a new environment and, importantly, what other forces were at work to alter it? For the prolongation of dependence that occurred between 1851 and 1871 forced the process of growing up in the direction of modernity, bending relations in the shape they have since assumed. It is difficult, however, to accept the view that the modern family is merely the result of a number of depressions. It is more likely that forces inherent in the process of social development itself were acting on existing patterns of relations among home, work, school, and marriage. Any adequate explanation of this developmental process must combine the interaction of long-term processes, such as modernization, with short-term crises, like depressions, which may accelerate or retard their pace. Only a theory which accomodates both the general and particular can encompass adequately the kind of data presented here. And those data are, after all, the record of what happened.

The problem of formulating an adequate and comprehensive explanation for the prolongation of dependency leads directly into the last major topic of this chapter: the relation between the family and social change.

The Family and Social Change

Most early-nineteenth-century urban immigrants moved from the countryside to the commercial city. Thus it was upon the family in commercial cities like Hamilton, rather than upon the rural or peasant family, that industrialization first made its impact. Nonetheless, most explorations of the relationships between the family and social change neglect this historical process. For they contrast the rural, peasant family with domestic arrangements in the industrial city. Little work has been done, on the other hand, to help explain the family in cities prior to industrialization. The actual history of the urban family remains obscure.

One recent example should make clear this deficiency in the usual outline of family history: the recent very good and partially historical study entitled *The Symmetrical Family,* written by two distinguished sociologists, Michael Young and Peter Willmott. Young and Willmott argue that the family has passed through three stages. Stage One was the classic rural peasant family in which the household formed the unit of production. There everyone contributed, "men, women and children" working "together in home and field." After a bitter struggle, the Stage Two family, characteristic of early industrialization, supplanted these customary arrangements. In Stage Two the members of the family were "caught up in the new economy as individual wage earners. The collective was undermined," a situation which persisted into the twentieth century, when the Stage Three family gradually emerged. "In the third stage, the unity of the family has been restored around its functions as the unit not of production but of consumption." According to Young and Willmott, the Stage Three family differs from its predecessor in three important ways. It has become increasingly private as the life of its members has centered more and more around their home. Second, the extended family, "consisting of relatives of different degrees to some extent sharing a common life," has declined in importance while the significance of the nuclear family has increased. Third, and most meaningful to them, "inside the family of marriage the roles of the sexes have become less segregated"; and consequently life within the new family merits the label "symmetrical."[57]

Aside from the question of whether or not the characteristics which Young and Willmott attribute to each stage in the history of the family furnish an accurate description, it is obvious that their sequence omits something significant. For nowhere within it can be found families of the sort which existed in Hamilton and, I suppose, in many other commercial cities as well. There the family did not form so cohesive and pervasive an economic or productive unit as it did in the countryside. Although, as in the case of Wilson Benson, husbands and wives frequently worked together or shared in a family enterprise, the customary routine of work in the fields did not characterize life in an urban setting. Many men had jobs in which their wives could give little assistance. Many men, certainly, but by no means a majority, worked at home, thus making some households the scene of both residence and production. In Hamilton, about a quarter of the men at most worked at home, and a maximum of about 40 percent of households served as a location for both residence and work. Relations between the family and the economy, therefore, differed from rural areas, if most writers on the peasant family can be believed. At the same time most of their members did not yet participate in the work force as independent wage earners. For the economic pressures and technological innovations which Young and Willmott assume drove the family apart had not yet appeared. Almost no married women worked outside their homes, and industries which employed children had not yet been established. Of course, Young and Willmott may exaggerate the disruptive effects of industrialization upon the family. Joan Scott and Louise Tilly, for example, have shown that the participation of married women in the labor force was far lower in nineteenth-century and early-twentieth-century England than might be imagined on the basis of Young and Willmott's account alone, and Michael Anderson offers persuasive evidence which counters the commonly held notion of the disintegrating impact of industrialization upon the family.[58] Nevertheless, neither Scott and Tilly nor Anderson provides very much specific assistance with the problem of understanding the urban family prior to industrialization, for despite the greater subtlety and detail of their excellent work they offer essentially the same contrast as Young and Willmott: the peasant family versus the industrial family.

It is especially rewarding, therefore, to turn to Bernard Farber's stimulating book, *Guardians of Virtue: Salem Families in 1800*. For it is the one modern monograph that explores the family in a commercial city whose social structure, family life, and economic activity formed patterns which in important ways made Salem similar to Hamilton. Farber claims that the years between 1775 and 1825 composed a distinct period in the history of Salem, marking "a commercial era which represented neither the Puritan (farming or fishing) village nor industrial New England."[59] Although commercial Salem resembled mid-nineteenth-century Hamilton in important ways, two significant differences between them should be noted: Salem was ethnically homogeneous, and apprenticeship remained common in its crafts at the start of the nineteenth century. These differences make the comparison between the two places especially worthwhile. They point to traditional features of the commercial city whose absence in Hamilton and erosion in other places created the basis for some of the most serious social problems within the nineteenth-century city.

Farber contends that each of the three major classes which formed Salem's social structure—merchants, artisans, and laborers—revealed a pattern of family organization and behavior distinctive in solidarity, stability, marriage, inheritance and socialization practices, and kin relations. In its own way, each family pattern fostered the development of capitalism and economic modernization, either by encouraging capital accumulation and ambitions for upward mobility or by providing a pool of unbound labor. The influence of the family on economic modernization was not entirely unmixed, however; for elements within the family organization of each social class retarded the very process that other, and in the end more powerful, aspects of family life encouraged. The artisans' retention of apprenticeship and strong kinship ties in business diluted the purity of their commitment to profit making and economic progress; merchant-family squabbling over inherited wealth created instability within commercial partnerships, weakened extended family relations, and contributed to the identification of families with political cliques which introduced a divisive acerbity into local politics; and the poverty, deviant behavior, and relative instability of exploited laboring families whose men died distressingly young—younger than those in any other class—created serious social problems.

Artisan kinship solidarity, argues Farber, derived from the special nature of the inheritance which craftsmen provided their sons, namely, a set of skills. Whereas the money bequeathed by merchants became a source of friction, the skills passed on by artisan fathers cemented family relations, binding together the kin network across generations through a solidarity among male relatives like that among "the patriarchal Judaic tribes, the mechanism by which a strong web of kinship was maintained." Their traditional, familial artisan class, rather than the inherently unstable activity of merchants, gave to commercial cities their special character and social stability through time: "The artisan class played an important role in maintaining the stability of the Salem community structure. Here people still had a long life expectancy, fairly large families, a cheap labor supply in apprentices, and an interest in maintaining the old social and economic order implied by their traditional crafts." Industrialization first eroded this traditional pattern, contends Farber, not by eliminating "experienced artisans from the labor market" but by "downgrading . . . the particular skills as valuable family property." Once this process began, sons for the first time had to move away "from the family occupation into competitive, but more lucrative work opportunities."[60]

Farber's thesis might lead to the conclusion that industrialization weakened the relation between kin by sundering the economic bonds that held families together. Very likely, he is right with respect to the experience of individual family enterprises. But his thesis cannot be extended automatically to all kinds of relations between kin, if Michael Anderson's work on industrial Lancashire can be taken as a reasonable portrait of family patterns in mid-nineteenth-century industrial England. Anderson began his research with a paradox. A remarkable amount of literature asserts that industrialization weakened the traditional working-class family, especially by sundering the close relationships that existed among kin. Yet students of modern working-class families in Britain have discovered that kin ties are extraordinarily strong in the areas they have observed, and they have argued that this represents a residue of traditional family patterns in the modern city. Anderson wonders how this paradox can be explained. Is its historical premise in fact true?[61]

He approached the problem by intensively studying an area that was highly industrialized in the mid-nineteenth century, choosing Lancashire because "all through the industrial revolution" it "typified or led industrializing Britain." Within the county he focused on Preston because "the town was in most relevant ways typical of the larger towns of the area." Within Preston, Anderson took a 1-in-10 sample of all occupied residences from the manuscript census returns of 1841, 1851, and 1861. He also selected one enumerator's district for intensive study, listing all the families residing there in each census year and attempting to trace the histories of the ones that remained from decade to decade. In order to compare urban and rural family structure Anderson selected a carefully weighted sample of households from those Lancashire villages which sent a high proportion of migrants to Preston.[62]

Anderson did not rely solely on quantitative evidence for his conclusions. To the contrary, he read deeply in contemporary literature about the family as well as in twentieth-century social theory. Thus he is able to provide traditional documentary evidence to illustrate and support most of the major patterns suggested by his numerical data.

Throughout his book Anderson examines his data from two

perspectives. He looks first at what he terms the "phenomenal" element, the person's own perception of his family and kinship relations. Second, he considers them from a "structural" point of view, assessing the impact which concrete conditions imposed upon relationships. His self-conscious attempt to look at his data alternately through these two lenses adds richness and sophistication to his analysis, although his attempt to synthesize his perspectives into an integrated theory is not wholly convincing.

There remains, however, one perspective from which Anderson did not examine his data, at least in the text. That is the perspective of time, for his analysis generally lumps together findings from different census years or generalizes about all three years from findings based only in one. It is possible that family and household composition changed even within a decade or two, as was the case in Hamilton. Surely, these were not static or uneventful years in the development of Preston, and it seems important to ask about the effects of the town's history on family patterns. Perhaps there were none of any significance, but it would have been useful to know this.

In the most general terms Anderson's careful study shows that industrialization did not destroy the relationship of nuclear family members to one another or the relationships among kin. Despite the fact that most families were nuclear, relatives deliberately maintained close relationships with one another, and kin networks that had existed in the countryside survived migration to the city. More specifically, Anderson provides a great deal of data about the composition, life cycle, residence patterns, and internal relations of the family. Also, on a number of these dimensions he is able to contrast urban and rural family patterns.

Anderson is one of the first writers to emphasize the importance of lodging in studies of the nineteenth-century household. He examines the practice from two perspectives: from that of the household in which the lodger lived and from the viewpoint of the lodger. The lodger's view is especially important because most lodgers were young men or women, usually men. Many were migrants to cities; others grew up in the city but left home when they found employment. Thus lodging, as Anderson recognizes, provided an alternative to remaining at home with parents. Anderson found intriguing differences between country and town.

The figures I have given for Hamilton, a commercial city in mid-nineteenth-century Canada, are much closer to his rural figures than to his urban ones. If in fact there were systematic variations between the proportion of boarders, servants, and relatives living in households in different contexts, this would be a finding of major significance. Living in lodgings, however, was only one relatively common phase of the life cycle with marked implications for household structure. Another was the fact that, in marked contrast to Hamilton, perhaps half the young married couples in Preston lived temporarily with a relative; and it appears that most old, widowed people did so as well. At some point in their life, most people probably lived in a setting other than the nuclear family.

Residential patterns provide strong evidence of the persistence of kinship networks within cities. As Anderson realized, without vital registration data it is impossible to plot accurately and fully the relation between the residence of parents and their married children. Nonetheless, through ingenious methods he was able to arrive at a reasonable estimate of the minimum number of sons who settled near their parents and to compare these figures with the results that would be expected if settlement were random. In fact, it was far from random; sons chose to live near their parents to a remarkable extent. In a similar way people from the same villages in the country clustered together, and, where possible, people migrating from the country often chose to live with relatives when they first arrived in the city.

Relationships among working-class family members, Anderson argues, were not disorganized in the way many writers have implied. Criticism of working-class families as neglectful, exploitative, and abusive has been vastly exaggerated, he maintains. To the contrary, there is a substantial amount of evidence which points to the maintenance of strong and affectionate relations within families, especially between mothers and their children.

In the country, family and economy intertwined as life focused on the family farm. This lack of differentiation, Anderson contends, was one of the sharpest contrasts between rural and urban life. He points out, however, that even in the city the contrast was not complete, for a semi-differentiated relation between family and economy often existed: children assisted their artisan parents, relatives helped one another to find work, and factories employed family work groups. However, the separation and consequently the chance for independence was much greater in the town, and Anderson has found evidence that this sometimes put new strains on the relations between parents and children and made possible the adoption of alternative life styles for those who found the traditional family constricting. Anderson's argument on this point is complicated by the fact that more adolescent boys actually lived away from their parents in the country than in the city, a fact which seems to contradict his interpretation. He dismisses this problem, however, by arguing that people more frequently lived at their place of work in the country than in the city. It is possible, nonetheless, that Anderson has underestimated the significance of this difference between the two types of areas. Indeed, on the basis of his data a quite different explanation is equally plausible, as I shall shortly argue.

Everyone working with manuscript census data about the family faces the problem of placing the mass of available descriptive information within some sort of interpretive or theoretical framework. The task is complicated by the inappropriateness to nineteenth-century data of most of the conceptual constructs developed by scholars working with current data. In terms of family history, the problem might be phrased as one of finding a theory which relates structure to behavior and attitude. We are able to describe with some precision the structural components of households, but what, in fact, do they mean? What consequences for socialization, marital relations, or ego development did various forms of household structure entail? Some correlations can be made by focusing on indexes of behavior—such as the age at which children leave home, the age of marriage, the spacing of children, school attendance, or choice of residence—and relating them systematically to aspects of family and household structure. But that still leaves the problem of constructing or finding an adequate explanation for the correlations that emerge, and this leads once again to the problem of theory, especially as it relates to motivation. Why did children choose to live near their parents? Why, in Anderson's terms, did people in cities choose to maintain close relations with kin rather than with, say, neighbors or workmates?

Anderson is acutely aware of this problem. Indeed, as a sociol-

ogist he appears most interested in the long run in the general
theoretical propositions that can be developed about family behavior. Consequently, he sets his analysis within a fully articulated and complex theoretical structure. The theory itself is
difficult to summarize, and the cumbersome language in which it
is presented makes the task even more problematical. My attempt
at a simplified summary, therefore, runs an especially grave risk
of distortion. Basically, Anderson's theory is one of exchange, a
variant of an outlook current in the social sciences. It is not unlike
the classical economic theory which postulates an economic man
rationally seeking to maximize profit. Anderson depicts people as
entering into social relationships which enhance the attainment
of their personal goals. The extent to which relations form
profitable bargains is the measure of their attractiveness. On this
premise it is possible to locate a number of features which make
relations more or less desirable: the trustworthiness of the other
party, the expected duration of the relation, the degree to which
benefit will come about in the short or the long term. With this
information one may construct a typology which will indicate
the potential appeal of certain kinds of relationships to people in
varying circumstances. By combining this typology with a calculation of the resources available to individuals, Anderson feels that
it is possible to predict the kind of family structures that will be
found within a given society: for instance, kin networks, relations
between parents and children, and the main features of household
composition. He feels that his theory adequately explains the data
he has gathered, particularly the contrast between rural and urban
areas, but here his argument appears the least convincing.

Anderson argues that normative considerations governed relationships in the country more than in the town. By this he means
that in the country the forces of tradition, especially those exerted
by religion and ideology, enforced strong family ties. In the city
these normative orientations broke down, but the family remained a strong unit because it continued to receive support from
calculative considerations, to use Anderson's phrase. That is,
people saw that they had much to gain from maintaining ties
with parents, children, and kin. It is true, of course, that kin ties
in rural areas provided equally important benefits. There, structure and norms, or practice and tradition, nicely reinforced each

other, thus making the rural family stronger than the urban one. Moreover, the presence of alternative life styles provided competition for the urban family and thus further diluted its influence.

Anderson must demonstrate at least three points in order to make the foregoing interpretation convincing: (1) the existence of calculative family behavior in both country and city; (2) a shift in emphasis from a normative to a calculative orientation between rural and urban places; (3) stronger family ties in the country. His evidence satisfies only the first of these conditions.

Using nineteenth-century literary evidence, Anderson effectively argues that people consciously looked at kinship relations in terms of a bargain or an exchange of benefits. Children stayed with parents who were likely to provide them with an inheritance or some material benefit; parents looked on children as sources of support in old age; relatives who could not contribute to the family in some way were not welcome within it. These impressions certainly are supported by the statistical evidence: for example, the children of well-to-do parents stayed longest at home; at those points in the life cycle when people needed help they lived most frequently with relatives; and the presence of grandmothers often made it possible for married women to work.

However, Anderson produces no convincing evidence that the relationships in the city were more calculative than those in the country. The normative system in the country might have been stronger, but every relation he found there had a solid calculative benefit. For his argument to be compelling, Anderson would have to show that people in the country entered into kinship relations that were not materially useful to both parties, that they maintained inconvenient relations because of religious, ideological, or communal tradition. He produces no evidence to that effect.

Likewise, it seems difficult to accept Anderson's statement that "the high commitment to family relationships which was so typical of the rural areas, was not generally to be found in the towns."[63] He has shown that more late-adolescent boys left home in rural than in urban areas. He has demonstrated as well that the diversity of life styles available in the city did not prevent the vast majority of people from making deliberate efforts to maintain strong family bonds and active kin networks. In short, on the basis of

Anderson's own evidence, the degree of commitment to the family evident in Preston does not appear to have been any weaker than it was in the country.

I think it is possible, especially in light of the situation in Hamilton, to draw quite the opposite conclusion from Anderson's book: namely, that family ties and commitments gained strength within the city.

My alternative interpretation of the data rests on a theoretical orientation different from Anderson's: it stresses the performance of certain psychological functions by the family, and these fit very uneasily into the context of an exchange theory. The exchange theory assumes a highly rationalistic approach to life on the part of ordinary people. It postulates that people engage in a kind of mental bookkeeping before they enter into relations, and that they perform a periodic audit of the relationships they have. This conception hardly accounts for the way in which irrational and subconscious factors shape important relations. Thus it takes a narrow view of human motivation, making room for the enhancement of material well-being as a motivating factor, but having no place for guilt. It is hard to see how the kind of theory advanced by Anderson could account for the family relations of Alexander Portnoy. In short, in a general sort of way the premises on which Anderson erects his theory are true; people do generally try to act in their own self-interest. But that is only a marginally useful starting point, and the theory he constructs from his assumptions has three faults: (1) it constricts the range of human motivation; (2) it assumes a greater degree of rationality than probably underlies ordinary behavior; (3) it is not supported by the data in his book.

The nature of my observations about family, household, and life cycle in Hamilton and elsewhere makes possible the abstraction of a process of change which forms a tentative, though plausible, alternative to the one offered by Anderson. Whether the experience of Hamilton during the years of rapid industrialization, let alone the possibly divergent histories of other places, actually conformed to this process remains a very open question. But formulating a possible process even at this stage of research is a useful exercise; for it provides a framework within which to organize my variegated observations about family matters, and it sets out clearly, perhaps too starkly even, a series of questions which deserve the close attention of historians. And, as I have said before in this book, at this stage in historical social research it remains more important to formulate the right questions than to offer correct answers.

If all the world were Hamilton, to borrow Sam Bass Warner's phrase, these, then, are the terms in which the relationship between modernization and the family might be described.[64] Although mostly simple in structure, consisting of married couples with or without children, households had flexible boundaries which frequently expanded to include a relative or boarder—usually a young, single person temporarily seeking a surrogate family in which to pass some of the years between leaving home and marrying, or, in some cases, a young orphan or an elderly widow needing care or support. A large proportion of young men who lived with their parents took up their fathers' occupations; others, who had left school, had no regular employment and lived in a state of partial idleness. When they found work, youths often left home to dwell in another household, where, as quasi-members of the family, they lived a still supervised but more autonomous life than they had before. Upon marriage they established their own households. In this way households shared the task of socialization, blurring the loosely defined boundaries between family and community.

With modernization this situation began to change. Only among the wealthy had complex or extended households—those containing boarders, kin, or servants—been common, and this began to alter as differences in household structure between social classes diminished. The standardization of household structure across social classes paralleled the increasing standardization of the life cycle among young people of different origins. Reduced employment opportunities for young people, the decreasing attractiveness of parental trades, and the heightened perceived advantages of formal education all interacted to keep men at school and at home longer, contracting the period of semi-autonomy. As technology replaced traditional crafts, as railroads fostered the development of industry, and as educational promoters succeeded in establishing the first modern public school systems, traditional relationships and practices shifted. Although the causal nexus remains somewhat obscure, the conjunction of changes within the same span of time is unmistakable. In this period the family gained an increasingly specialized role in socialization and, at the same time, shed some of its responsibilities for formal education and job preparation. Thus, the boundaries between the family and community became more sharply defined as the role of the family became more specific. The family, though reshaped during modernization, remained no less important or cohesive than it had been before. It was, rather, simply different. Marion Levy has put this point especialy well:

> It is frequently noted that activities in terms of the family have been radically reduced in relatively modernized contexts. This does *not* mean that the family units are less important than formerly, unless family importance is defined by the restriction of such activities. It is not at all true, however, that under these conditions the activities still performed in terms of the family are not crucial for the existence of the society. It is not correct to infer that, once the reduction of activities has reached a certain point, family units become negligible or that one can continue to restrict the functions performed on a family basis indefinitely. It is also misleading to imply that this type of family is less critical for this type of society than other types of family are for other societies.[65]

The process of change within the family, however, was probably not unidirectional or simply evolutionary. The initial impact of factories utilizing child labor probably bifurcated the experience of young people from different social classes as the more affluent continued to prolong their schooling and the poor seized the new employment opportunities for young people. With the decrease in child labor the trend toward an increasingly standardized life cycle for young people of different social classes probably resumed. Indeed, as schooling has begun to occupy a growing portion of most lives in the twentieth century a new stage in the life cycle has emerged once again. Kenneth Keniston has called it youth, and it is tempting to consider it a revival of semi-autonomy because young people live away from home at school.[66] But there are two important differences which distinguish the experience of young people at universities today from their counterparts who lived as boarders and servants a century and more ago. First, contemporary young people remain, by and large, economically dependent upon their families. Second, their life cycle increasingly has been regulated by the requirements of institutions integrated in a complex fashion with the labor market. The life cycle of the young, therefore, has been defined by institutional requirements, and this is a fundamentally new development in modern history.

"Whatever the previous ideal of family structure was," writes Marion Levy, "during the transition toward relative modernization, the ideals always change toward . . . a *multilineal conjugal family* unless they already took that form," or, in the terms used here, toward a simple family household. This is what happened in Upper Canada. In early Upper Canada, Alison Prentice points out, people did not yet define the family "as exclusively composed of biologically related people." Rather, they mixed the more inclusive concept of household with the term family, including "people unrelated to the biological family" who lived frequently in households able to support them. In this situation, she writes, "the traditional ideal family . . . was enlarged by the inclusion of friends or dependents over and above those members who were biologically related. It had formal educational obligations beyond the early nurture of its own children. Finally, it was governed by a male parental figure." In the middle of the nineteenth century, more or less coincidentally with the period covered by this book, the ideal of the traditional household began to fade. Increasingly, people came to view the family "more and more as a private retreat from the world and one that for large portions of the week was almost entirely governed by women." This ideal was consciously fostered by the new educational bureaucrats of the 1860s and 1870s, whose statements suggested "a growing commitment to the ideal of the small, self-contained biological family, unencumbered by boarders or related dependents on the one hand, or guardians on the other." About the same time, report John Modell and Tamara Hareven, social reformers in the United States vigorously began to attack the presence of lodgers in families, insisting on the importance of domestic privacy and pointing to the sexual threat that unmarried young men posed to the chastity of women in the family. The lodger evil, as it was called, became a shrill and distorted rallying cry for the battery of reformers who, fearing the weakening of the family, promoted the ideal of the small, private, and sharply defined domestic unit.[67]

The Victorian cult of domesticity endowed Home, Woman, and Mother with transcendent moral force.[68] The elevation of an intense, private model of domesticity as the pillar of civilization and society represented more than an attempt to buttress what many believed to be the crumbling family; it symbolized, as well, the emergence of a distinct and somewhat new idea of what the family should be: two sober, industrious parents dwelling alone with their children, to whom they offered loving care, moral instruction, and close supervision from infancy to adulthood. The strident preoccupation of people with the family revealed an underlying anxiety that all was not well within domestic circles, that ideal and reality matched less often than the future of society required. And one focus of that anxiety became the question of dependency during adolescence. Whether adolescents should remain at home with their parents while at school or whether they should live away became a controversial issue. In New England, for instance, advocates of academies and high schools clashed over the best setting for young people, arguing about the long-term effects on adult character of immersion in the rough and tumble world of the American public school as compared to the seclusion from immorality promised by residential private institutions. The importance that people came to attach to remaining within the family helped decide the issue in favor of the public school. No better educator or guarantor of future morality existed, argued high school supporters, than the domestic circle. The combination of example, supervision, and education within the family could harden the young person to the fleshy and immoral temptations of the rude children in the real world. As long as a virtuous family provided nightly shelter and instruction, a character tempered during youth by exposure to the world as it was would furnish the strongest resistance to the influences that someday would surround the adult.[69]

Demographic evidence shows that theorists who ascribed the emergence of the nuclear family to industrialization clearly erred. But they may have touched, nonetheless, an emotional truth, which concentration on the presence of kin in the household has obscured. What was important was not so much who lived together, for this has not altered very much, but the tenor of the relationships among them, the role of the family within its social world, the relative flexibility of its boundaries, and the length of time it nurtured its children. These, indeed, have changed.

One other point, more specific to the nineteenth century, should be emphasized: the evident crisis of youth in the nine-teenth-century city. For centuries, apparently, it was common for young people of all social classes to spend a prolonged period some-time after puberty and before marriage as a member of a household other than their parents'. For the most part young women worked as servants and young men as either servants or apprentices. Ap-prenticeship probably remained prevalent until early in the nine-teenth century. The erosion of apprenticeship during the first half of the nineteenth century took place prior to the creation of an institutional framework to contain young adolescents. A long period between puberty and marriage still existed for most women and, even more, for most men, but there was in fact less than ever for them to do. Thus the mounting complaints of juvenile vagrancy and idleness made by nineteenth-century social commentators were not merely the distorted perceptions of middle-class moralizers. They were responses, albeit in less than sympathetic and understanding tones, to a demographic prob-lem.[70] There was, in short, a crisis of youth in the nineteenth-century city. "To some citizens" in mid-nineteenth-century Toronto, writes Susan Houston, "the increasingly familiar figure of the street urchin—ill clad, undisciplined, and, most impor-tantly, unschooled—assumed sinister significance . . . 'The idle-ness and dissipation of a large number of children, who now loiter about the public streets or frequent the haunts of vice' were, in the opinion of one prominent Catholic philanthropist, 'creating the most painful emotions in every well regulated mind; and in some degree involving the imputation, that the social condition of the body corporate of which they form a part, cannot be of the highest order.' " Similarly, in New York the problem of idle and vagrant children, writes Carl Kaestle, was "sizeable enough and ominous enough to play a prominent part in school and police reports from the 1820s to mid-century and beyond . . . A school report of 1856 complained that there were 'between 20,000 and 60,000 children now being educated in our streets in habits of idleness, and a knowledge of vice, where they will graduate, enemies to themselves and curses to the community, and enter upon careers of debauchery and crime.' " Idle youth, undoubtedly, formed a supply of willing, cheap labor for the factories that developed in the latter part of the century. Indeed, there may have been a connection between the creation of a labor supply and the timing of industrialization, just as there had been, though for different reasons, in England. In a similar way, the demographic crisis of youth created one of the most powerful forces behind the introduction of public secondary schools in this period and of reform schools, which developed at the same time as high schools for the poor, to use Susan Houston's phrase.[71]

As young people stayed longer in school, they remained longer at home. A prolonged, increasingly regulated and institutionalized dependency created what today we term adolescence, a demographic and social revolution finally recognized by psychologists such as G. Stanley Hall in the late nineteenth and early twentieth centuries, whose theories, thus, did not signal the belated recognition of a perennial biological state but, rather, the codification of a new and socially determined phase in the life cycle.[72]

Conclusion

AT THE DAWN of the twenty-first century when the narrator in *Looking Backward* attempted to convey to readers a vivid sense of nineteenth-century society, he created a metaphor. Society, he claimed, had been "a prodigious coach which the masses of humanity were harnessed to and dragged toilsomely along a very hilly and sandy road." His description of society as a coach captured some of the most important characteristics which, I have argued in this book, marked an earlier urban world.

> Despite the difficulty of drawing the coach at all along so hard a road, the top was covered with passengers who never got down, even at the steepest ascents. These seats on top were very breezy and comfortable. Well up out of the dust, their occupants could enjoy the scenery at their leisure, or critically discuss the merits of the straining team. Naturally, such places were in great demand and the competition for them was keen, every one seeking as the first end in life to secure a seat on the coach for himself and to leave it to his child after him. By rule of the coach a man could leave his seat to whom he wished, but on the other hand, there were many accidents by which it might at any time be wholly lost. For all that they were so easy, the seats were very insecure, and at every sudden jolt of the coach persons were slipping out of them and falling to the ground, where they were instantly compelled to take hold of the rope and help to drag the coach on which they had before ridden so pleasantly. It was naturally regarded as a terrible misfortune to them or their friends to lose one's seat, and the apprehension that this might happen to them or their friends was a constant cloud upon the happiness of those who rode.[1]

Edward Bellamy's metaphor conveyed the rigid structure of inequality that divided the society about which he wrote. From one perspective, the organization of society into relatively permanent constellations of wealth, standing, and power appeared to be its most characteristic feature. Nonetheless, though social classes

retained their essential nature and their relative size, their membership did not remain stable. It was rare, of course, for one of the
multitude that pulled the coach to climb to its roof, but it was
not at all uncommon for someone on the roof to fall. The anxiety
with which those at the top clung to their seats had a basis in
objective fact, for the incidence of falling was frequent, its consequences dreadful. Life among the nineteenth-century poor was
neither romantic nor pleasant; it was a dull and miserable
existence which any sensible person would try to avoid.

The coach metaphor captures, too, the sense of motion which,
along with class, dominated life at the time. For everyone was on
the move. The tremendous population flow into and out of cities,
towns, and villages counterbalanced the rigidity of the social
order. Structures of inequality retained their shape while the
identity of the individual people who lived within them changed
with astonishing speed. Nineteenth-century people, of course,
considered themselves in motion in another way. Motion meant
Progress, the movement of society up the hill away from ignorant
traditionalism to enlightened, scientific modernity. If their notion
now appears naive, at least men of the time thought that the
masses pulling the coach might rest and relax at the top of the hill,
when much of their effort, perhaps, would be superseded by a
locomotive.

But on the way up there were only marginal improvements
that could be made in the fate of those who pulled the coach,
unless the men at the top willingly would assist, which they were
not about to do. They threw much of their weight, in fact, in
just the opposite direction, seeking new means to assure that
their children would continue to inherit their seats. As this became somewhat more difficult to achieve when times began to
change, they tightened their families and created schools, with-
drawing into an ever more private world protected by new
institutions to assure the transmission of status as usual.

Bellamy's metaphor of the coach, nonetheless, breaks down at
three points as an adequate description of social reality. First, it
does not include women, though it is not hard to imagine them
riding in a second coach pulled by the first, linked to the fate of
their husbands and fathers, whose relative position they shared.
Second, the coach metaphor does not allow for any movement

upward out of the multitude. Granted, dramatic upward movement was rare, but some was necessary, and it formed a regulated,
consistent counterpoint to the tumbling of the men from the top
of the coach. Third, a division of society into only two classes does
not quite match the complexity of nineteenth-century stratification. If one group pulled the coach and another directed their
movement from on top, one must still ask who had built the coach
and who rode inside. Those questions point to a third class, one, in
fact, which in many ways gave a distinctive cast to the older urban
order. That would, of course, have been the artisan class. One
could stretch the metaphor to say that the artisan class constructed the coach and then rode within it. Although from inside
the view was not quite so good or the ride quite so exhilarating as
at the top, the dangers were considerably less. Artisans depended
for their position upon their skill, which they often transmitted
to their sons, and this kept them anchored more firmly in their
seats than the uncertainties of credit, markets, and customers,
which kept the hold of the people on top precarious.

Despite the use of metaphor, it is hard to capture the sense in
which life in the past, especially in cities, differed from living
today. One has only to go to any one of the reconstructions of
early pioneer villages to gain at least some sense of a different and
lost way of life among people in the countryside and village. But
it is more difficult with cities. For the recognizable components of
past urban life lull one into imagining a continuity greater than
that which exists. In fundamental ways the patterns and texture
of urban existence have changed. Some of the dimensions of that
change are made clear by Table C.1, which offers a very rough
comparison of some aspects of family and society in Hamilton in
1861 and 1961.

Change appears dramatically not only in Hamilton's immense
growth from a city of nineteen thousand people to one of over 270
thousand, but also in the way in which people ordered their
families. The number of people living within the average household dropped from 5.3 to 3.6, partly a consequence of the reduction in the average number of children living at home from 2.4
to 1.5. The rest of the decrease in average household size came
from the decreasing frequency with which people other than
husbands, wives, and children lived together. In 1861, about a

TABLE C.1 Selected demographic characteristics of
Hamilton, Ontario, 1861 and 1961

Demographic characteristics	1861	1961[a]
Population	19,096	273,991
Household size		
Mean size	5.3	3.6
One member	1.9%	9.1%
Eight or more members	22.3%	3.8%
Simple households[b]	67.8%	79.0%
Children living at home		
Mean number	2.4	1.5
Five or more	16.5%	4.0%
None	20.5%	33.5%
Occupations of household heads[c]		
Professional or public service	6.0%	9.4%
Managerial, clerical, or sales	24.5%	27.4%
Nonprofessional services or recreation	0.8%	7.3%
Transport or communication	3.1%	6.7%
Agriculture and other extractive work	1.3%	3.2%
Craftsmen or production workers	41.0%	41.2%
Labor	23.0%	4.8%
Simple households by economic rank[b]		
0–39th percentile	77.4%	77.9%
40–79th percentile	62.4%	93.0%
80–89th percentile	56.2%	93.9%
90–100th percentile	59.9%	95.3%

[a] Figures drawn from Dominion Bureau of Statistics, *1961 Census of Canada*, Series 2.1, "Households and Families."

[b] Households with only parents and children at home, without co-residing kin or lodgers.

[c] For 1861, based on assessed males; for 1961, household heads.

third of the households contained either a relative or a boarder; a century later that share had decreased to about a fifth, a drop, to be sure, but not one of immense proportions. A sharp contrast undoubtedly would stand out, if contemporary figures were available, between the number of households that employed a resident domestic servant in 1861 and 1961: then over a fifth of the households; in contemporary times, very likely an insignificant fraction.

As might be expected, the number of very large households

dropped considerably, from 22 percent with eight or more members in 1861 to 4 percent a century later; and the number of families with five or more children decreased during the same period from 17 to 4 percent. Of special interest, signifying an important shift in social behavior, was the increase in the proportion of people who lived alone in Hamilton, from just under 2 percent in 1861 to 9 percent a hundred years later. That shift points to the increasing erosion of a fundamental social rule which held that everyone should live within a family setting. In the nineteenth century young people away from home most often lived as kin or boarders in a household, not in separate apartments, and elderly widows whose children had all left home moved in with relatives or neighbors. In these circumstances, households acted not only as sources of lodging and welfare but as agencies of moral instruction and social order.

As the social rule that placed everyone within a family has eroded, the family itself has become increasingly private. No longer does high social rank require the maintenance of an expanded household composed of children, kin, and friends. A new family ideal calls for ever more distinct boundaries between the immediate family—spouses and children—and the rest of the world. Nowhere has this been more clearly evident than in the reversal of the relation between household structure and economic rank. In 1861 the proportion of households containing either a relative of the family or a boarder increased in linear fashion with wealth from about 22 percent of the poorest two fifths of households to 40 percent of the wealthiest tenth. A century later that relation had been exactly reversed. A similar proportion of the poorest fifth—about 22 percent—still had either a boarder or a relative, but by then 95 percent of the wealthiest tenth had none.

Shifts in the world of work have accompanied diminished household size, the gradual acceptance of living apart from a family, and the increasingly private quality of domestic life that have occurred in the last century. Although the figures in the table are crude because the categories are not exactly comparable, they are close enough to indicate some general trends. Striking, first, is the continuity in the proportion of household heads engaged, on the one hand, in commercial and supervisory activity ("Managerial, clerical, or sales"), 25 percent in 1861 and 27 percent in 1961, and in the production of goods, on the other hand, 41 percent in the two years a century apart. Of course, most of those participating in production in 1961 would have worked in factories, a very different setting from the mid-nineteenth-century artisan shop. But the persistence in the proportion of the work force required to manufacture goods remains nonetheless remarkable. The major shift, it is evident, has been at the bottom—the sharp decline in the proportion of household heads in unskilled laboring jobs, a drop from 23 to 5 percent during the last century. This shift reflects primarily a redistribution of effort in particular directions: an increase in the proportion of professionals and of service, transport, and communication workers.

It remains an open, and important, question whether this redistribution of the work force away from unskilled labor reflected also a significant redistribution of wealth or an improvement in the standard of living. The extent and nature of the contrast between past and present on this issue is only one of the many major questions left dangling at the end of this book. In a sense every conclusion that has been reported should be rephrased as a comparative question. The distribution of wealth and power, the experience of ethnic groups, the social ecology of the city, the age at which children left home: all these questions demand comparative study. Was mid-nineteenth-century Hamilton unique, or was it one of a particular type of city, or was it representative of widespread structures and patterns? To what extent did each characteristic alter with time, and exactly when, why, and in what sequence did those alterations take place?

These questions are especially intricate because they require not simply descriptive answers but an explication of the causal mechanisms that underlie social change. They call for a theoretical perspective that integrates family, economy, social structure, geographic patterns, institutions, and demographic behavior into one vision of social development. Any satisfactory theory must permit the assessment of relationships among structure, behavior, and attitudes. It must enable one, for instance, to draw inferences about attitudes toward class from various sorts of evidence about objective patterns of stratification, or to gauge the consequences of life within variously structured households upon their members. At the same time, the development of theory requires greater precision than now exists in the delineation of concepts and their relations to one another. The differentiation and interconnection between class and culture as social forces, for instance, remains an unusually complex and important undertaking, especially for students of ethnically diverse societies. In the last analysis we should not be content to know simply what happened but why it happened, how it all fits together, and what sense it makes. It is this larger vision which must be the goal of historical social analysis.

This larger vision lies many years away, however. If this book has clarified anything, it should be that the past is different from what most people have imagined. Its character cannot simply be assumed. An immense amount of precise social description must remedy our ignorance about the details of the past before we can expect a grand synthesis any more satisfying than the ones which exist already. This is not a call for the mindless accumulation of data but a plea, first, for a systematic assault upon the problem of social description and analysis. At the same time, it is a warning against the continued generation of social theories on the basis of what the past is imagined to have been like.

This book has tried to formulate some of the more important questions and lines of inquiry that systematic historical social research should follow. By no means has it offered a comprehensive list of the major hypotheses about the topics it discusses. For, despite its detail, this book represents a first sweep through immensely rich and complex data, and each topic in it deserves far more extensive analysis than it has received. The greatest omission in the book, as most readers will be aware, is the absence of any information about the destination and fate of the thousands of people who left or passed through the city. They were, indeed, as in most other nineteenth-century places that historians have studied, the vast majority of the people who lived there at any one point in time. The centrality of transiency to nineteenth-century society, and our ignorance about its dimensions, directions, and consequences, give it high priority as a subject for research. The other serious omission in this book concerns the texture of domestic life. I have argued for the existence of a stage in the life cycle that since has virtually disappeared. But that argument rests almost solely on inferences drawn from statistical data. Little direct evidence is available about the way in which people at the time viewed life as a child, as a boarder, or as a servant in different sorts of households. Information is lacking, too, about day-to-day existence. How, for example, did young people neither employed nor at school actually spend their time? This, it seems to me, is the critical area for scholars who undertake systematic but nonquantitative social history.

The task for social history is to seek a level of explanation that mediates between the particularistic specificity of traditional history and the generalizations of social theory. Historical writing which attempts no more than description or simple narrative often remains trivial and of narrow interest. And that is the case whether the data are quantified or not, for quantification itself could become a new antiquarianism if not pressed into the service of more general goals. At the other extreme, social theories which put forward propositions allegedly true for societies in general often appear to be either superficial or little more than codifications of common sense. For it is difficult to write anything that is not commonplace if it is to apply to many different settings. By contrast, social history should fit somewhere between these extremes by demonstrating the interaction of general processes, such as modernization, with particular circumstances or settings, such as a depression in an ambitious nineteenth-century city. For only through analyzing the expression of the general through the particular can we construct subtle and satisfactory explanations of social development.

This book has sought for a middle ground by attempting to refract the general forces at work in the nineteenth-century commercial city through the experience of the people in one particular place. That refraction showed an urban order fundamentally different from that of today, neither fully traditional nor modern, but poised in a moment of transition. At no time did the elements of tradition and modernity fuse more perfectly than on the Queen's Birthday, May 24, 1860. On that occasion, appropriately, the mechanics of the Great Western Railway, builders of the nineteenth century's engine of Progress, led the inevitable procession, one of the most ancient of urban rituals. Marching as urban artisans always had, they carried aloft a newly made banner that reflected at once their traditional deference, their commitment to the future, and the aspirations of their fellow citizens. For their banner read: "God Save the Queen and Success to the Great Western Railway."[2]

APPENDICES

NOTES

INDEX

The Social Geography of a Commercial City, ca. 1853

by Ian Davey and Michael Doucet

[I am] perfectly satisfied that the local trade of the Great Western would present results of the most astonishing and gratifying nature, and that before long the trade of Hamilton would be immensely increased by becoming the port of shipment for the magnificent district of country lying to the west of it. In addition to this the American through travel which would pass along this line would be immense.[1]

In these few words C. J. Brydges, vice-president of the Great Western Railroad Company, expressed the optimism and buoyancy that prevailed in Hamilton as its first railroad neared completion. The Great Western was the first significant railroad in Canada West and stretched from Windsor (opposite Detroit) through London and Hamilton to Niagara, where it connected with routes serving upstate New York. By it Hamilton hoped to establish her hegemony over the rich agricultural hinterland of southwestern Ontario and to challenge Toronto's preeminence in the province. Toward these ends, Hamilton's entrepreneurs, led by Sir Allan Napier MacNab, had committed their own and the city's money to the project. For the city's businessmen, Hamilton's future prosperity depended on the expansion of trade which the railroad would facilitate because, like most North American cities of its time, Hamilton was a commercial center. As such, its functional and spatial differentiation reflected the city's trading base, a base that differed quite markedly from that associated with the modern industrial city. In this appendix we explore the internal spatial structure of a nineteenth-century commercial city through an analysis of Hamilton's commercial, industrial, and residential fabric. Our intention is to show that the commercial city was an urban form distinct from both its predecessor, the feudal city, and its successor, the industrial metropolis.

Introduction

The analysis of the spatial structure and growth patterns of past cities in North America has been particularly influenced by the ecological constructs developed by the Chicago school of sociologists. The most influential of these has been the concentric zone model which was formulated by Robert Park and Ernest Burgess in the 1920s. In essence, the model depicts a series of nested zones with the Central Business District (CBD) at the center, surrounded by four outlying bands of activity—a zone in transition, a zone of workingmen's homes, a residential zone, and a commuters' zone. Although Park and Burgess developed this model to describe the spatial structure of modern North American cities, it has been, perhaps unwisely, applied elsewhere by others. Shortcomings in the concentric zone model soon became apparent when it was tested against the real world. Consequently, it was modified by Homer Hoyt, whose sector model was based on class and real estate values, and by E. L. Ullman and C. D. Harris, whose analysis of cities indicated that the concept of multiple nuclei of activity was often necessary to fully describe and explain structure in modern cities. More recently, quantitative techniques such as factor and regression analysis have led geographers to stress the integration of all three models, and they now view the form of the modern city as a combination of concentric zones reflecting family structure, sectors indicating social status, and ethnic nuclei.[2]

Students of the spatial structure and organization of historical cities also have tested and modified the Park and Burgess model. The most influential of these historical reformulations has been that of Gideon Sjoberg for so-called preindustrial cities. Through observations of medieval feudal places and present-day cities in underdeveloped nations he has delineated the essential features of preindustrial urban spatial structure with a model that contradicts Park and Burgess, though it retains their idea of concentric zones.

In Sjoberg's ideal type the commercial center remains subsidiary to political and religious structures in terms of importance. Moreover, the preindustrial city inverted Park and Burgess' residential zones; the wealthy lived close to the center and the poor on the periphery, reflecting, according to Sjoberg, the premium on access to the center that arises where transportation technology remains undeveloped. Furthermore, the complex residential patterns in the preindustrial city do not fit the model of broad zones, for quarters and streets were often monopolized by particular ethnic, occupational, and family groups. Finally, the preindustrial city was marked by a "low incidence of functional differentiation of land-use patterns," which arose from the absence of marked specialization in the labor force and the lack of separation between home and work place.[3]

Most students of premodern urban places have analyzed spatial structure within a traditional preindustrial-industrial dichotomy. Their aim has been to determine the degree to which a particular city conforms to one or the other of the polarized formulations of Sjoberg, Park and Burgess, or their modifiers. Models derived from either modern industrialized cities or from feudal places, however, are not particularly useful for the study of early North American urban areas. Prior to industrialization these cities thrived as commercial centers. They were never truly feudal cities, such as Sjoberg describes, which are more aptly called precommercial than preindustrial.[4] "Firm evidence of Sjoberg's generalization holding for western cities before they were industrialized," notes A. M. Warnes, "has not been produced. Yet it has frequently been applied to early nineteenth-century European and North American cities, even if only implicitly." Nor can the commercial city be viewed simply as an early version of the modern metropolis, for industrialization has drastically altered the form and function of urban places.[5] The commercial city must be studied as a distinct type rather than as a merely transitional form on the road to the industrial metropolis.

Fortunately, a number of scholars recently have begun to point out the major features of the North American commercial or, as it is sometimes called, mercantile city.[6] Thus far they have paid more attention to the location of economic activities than to the residential distribution of the people. Martyn Bowden, for one, has located the origins of the commercial city in seventeenth-century mercantilist London; from there it spread to Europe and those parts of the world affected by European expansion and exploration. The predominance of wholesaling in central areas, reflecting the leadership of merchants in the development of commercial cities, has been clearly illustrated by both Bowden and David Ward. Similarly, Allan Pred's discussion of the American mercantile city has shown the dominance of retail and wholesale trading activities in both ports and inland service centers, while manufacturing remained small in scale, frequently related to the trade of the city, and often carried on in the home.[7] Nevertheless, although a number of specialized activities could be found in the center of commercial cities, Ward suggests that the retail trades remained relatively undeveloped prior to 1870, and his discussion of the residential pattern in Boston indicates that neither Park and Burgess, Hoyt, nor Sjoberg provided an adequate model of the commercial city. For the immigrant poor lived both close to its center and on its periphery.[8]

It is quite apparent that the North American commercial city did not resemble a feudal place, though it also differed from the modern city in a number of significant ways.[9] Aside from the obvious difference in its economic base, it was smaller, reflecting market limitations, and, as a pedestrian city, necessarily more compact. Its relatively small size may have led scholars to oversimplify the complexity of the commercial city, especially the degree of spatial differentiation of activities. Here, through a fine-grained analysis, we attempt to show the complex economic and residential patterns within one mid-nineteenth-century urban place. If Hamilton was at all like other places, we must conclude that existing models do not capture the complex spatial order within the commercial city.

The Setting

For any time period it is important to place the social geography of a city within the context of both its sphere of influence and the physiographic limitations of its site. Originally laid out in 1813, Hamilton's location at the head of Lake Ontario brought many advantages. Although it was designated the administrative center for the newly created District of Gore in 1816,[10] Hamilton's subsequent growth owed more to its situation than to its place in the administrative hierarchy. For, as L. J. Chapman and D. F. Putnam point out, there are "many reasons why a lakehead location is likely to result in the building of a city. It is likely to be a port—a point at which transfer is made between water carriage and land carriage of persons and goods, a place of trade with a large hinterland, a place of processing of goods brought thither by both land and water, and a place for the establishment of secondary manufacturing." Nonetheless, Hamilton's site imposed certain physiographic limitations on its growth and development. It might have been expected, for instance, that the center of town would be located near the harbor, but, one commentator noted in 1846, "on account of the swamp in the vicinity of the bay, the principal part of the town has been placed about a mile back from the bay, on a gently rising ground."[11] To the south, the presence of the 300-foot-high Niagara Escarpment, the Mountain, further constrained the city's expansion. Though neither of these barriers was insurmountable, they affected Hamilton's configuration throughout the early years of its development.

The town grew within these physiographic limitations. It attained city status in 1846 and had a population of some fourteen thousand in 1851, making it the next largest urban place in Canada West after Toronto. Although by that date the boundaries of the city encompassed about 3.4 square miles, actual urban development had taken place only on about 1.03 square miles, or 30 percent of the total area. As Figure A.1 illustrates, the built-up area focused on the intersection of King and James streets and radiated out along those roads that served the surrounding communities. Broadly, three zones of development can be recognized. The first, an intensively built-up area covering approximately 314 acres, centered on the nodal point of King and James. The second, occupying about 346 acres, surrounded the core to the north, west, and south and was either partially developed or taken up by large estates. (Large estates were found especially in the south end of the city near the Mountain.) The third zone, a very large area of over 1,517 acres, remained undeveloped. Some

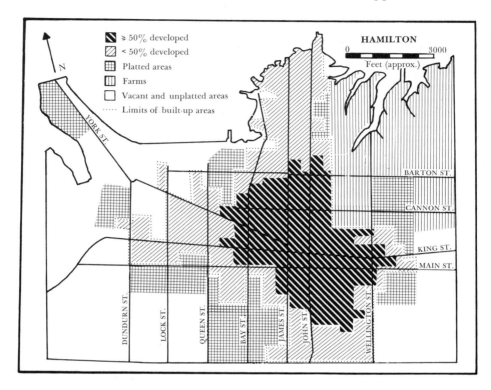

FIGURE A.1 Land development, ca. 1852

sections of this zone, especially to the east of Mary Street, remained in agricultural use, while others already had been platted in anticipation of future growth.[12]

Midway through the nineteenth century, some forty years after its establishment, Hamilton was growing rapidly. It was a city which had not yet experienced the full impact of the industrial transformation to factory production. In fact, for the majority of its workers, small-scale, home-centered activities were the norm and large-scale work settings were only found in construction firms, foundries, and coach and carriage factories. This is clearly indicated by the *Census of Canada* statistics for 1851. Of the 282 industrial establishments in Hamilton, 52 percent listed no employees aside from the owner, and fully 93 percent employed fewer than ten persons. Furthermore, there were only nine establishments employing more than twenty people, none of which employed more than a hundred.

The source of the city's booming character lay in its commercial activities. As a port it rivaled Toronto. Moreover, it had a well articulated commercial center comprising a number of wholesale firms and numerous retail outlets which were supported by financial institutions and a variety of professional services. Although overshadowed by Toronto forty miles to the east, Hamilton was clearly the focal point and service center for an expanding hinterland of farms and small towns in south central Ontario, a fact that did not go unnoticed at the time. As the *Spectator* noted during the staging of the Provincial Exhibition in Hamilton in 1853, the city "possesses, from its location, peculiar advantages for drawing a crowd . . . At the head of Lake Ontario, it is easy of access by water, and on the other hand, it is an outlet for a tract of country exceeding in extent, productiveness, wealth and enterprise, any other section of this favoured province."[13]

This burgeoning commercial place was dominated by immigrants. Only 9 percent of the household heads had been born in Upper Canada, whereas 32 percent had come from Ireland, 29 percent from England and Wales, 18 percent from Scotland, and 7 percent from the United States. The fruits of the commercial boom, however, were unequally divided among Hamilton's immigrant inhabitants. Already the city was markedly stratified in terms of wealth and power, with a clearly discernible elite effectively controlling the livelihood and potential well-being of the rest of the population. The class divisions were drawn particularly along ethnic lines: Irish Catholics were overrepresented among the 40 percent of the household heads who earned only 1 percent of the income for the city and could be considered poor.[14]

Thus, even in its commercial phase of development, Hamilton was a city of contrasts. It was easy for those who participated in the city's prosperity to eulogize its progress. But at the same time, it was difficult to ignore the plight of those who became its victims. For example, in a period of less than a month at the end of 1852, the *Spectator* carried two articles which contrasted the fortunes of Hamilton's inhabitants. On the city's growth, it declared that "strangers, visiting the place, after one or two years absence, are actually astonished at the evidences of solid prosperity and enterprise which have sprung up, as if by magic. On every street new, and in many cases elegant, buildings have been erected . . . Hamilton has, during the present season, made more rapid strides in improvement than any of the sister cities; and yet we are but on the dawn of that progress and prosperity to which we look forward." Three weeks later, fearing an outbreak of cholera after reports of a number of "sudden deaths," the *Spectator* noted that "there are several dwelling houses in this city which are in a far filthier state than the dirtiest alley or yard that can be found, and . . . these dens of disease and infamy are not confined to the backstreets and the suburbs." The article chastised the wealthy owners of a large house on James Street, immediately alongside the imposing Bank of Upper Canada: "This house has long been the resort of the lowest and most abandoned creatures of both sexes; the victims of poverty and of vice have both taken advantage of the cheap rents and squalid tenements . . . The inmates have long been the terror of the neighbourhood—and yet this house is situated near the centre of the city, and is . . . the property of men who are rich, and who could afford to allow their barrack to remain idle unless respectable tenants offered themselves."[15] Although minor by twentieth-century standards, these statements suggest that mid-nineteenth-century Hamilton was a very complex place. Certainly, its spatial structure did not conform to the pre-industrial ideal type. It was a city about to undergo the transformation from a commercial to an industrial place. At the same time, it was experiencing rapid population growth and turnover and residential differentiation along class and ethnic lines.[16] These processes in consort shaped the city's social geography in 1853.

Economic Activity

Given the compact nature of mid-nineteenth-century Hamilton, it is not surprising that most economic activity took place in and about its core. This was true not only for small-scale artisan activities and shops, such as grocery stores, that catered to the everyday needs of the populace, but also for most of the city's larger establishments, as Figure A.2, which plots the addresses for a number of different categories of manufacturing concerns, shows. Of the six industrial types displayed there, only one, con-

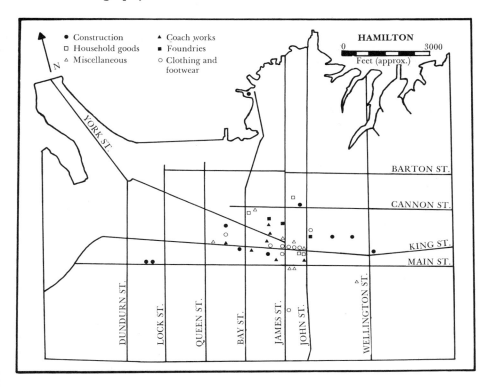

FIGURE A.2 Industries employing more than five workers

struction, occupied a consistently peripheral location, undoubtedly either to be close to raw material supplies, as in the case of brick yards and stone quarries, or, for construction firms, to be near those parts of the city undergoing development. By way of contrast, near the center of the city, the intersection of King and James, clustered the other types of industry, especially the heavier ones, foundries and coach works (the largest manufactories in Hamilton), and consumer industries such as clothes, footwear, and household goods. Obviously, the factors which have led to the exclusion of industry from the core of the modern city were not operative in commercial Hamilton.[17]

The distribution of retail grocery stores also shows the importance of a central location and underscores the contrast between a commercial city of the mid-nineteenth century and a modern industrial one. For the location of grocery shops, which, after all, catered to the everyday needs of the community, might have been expected to reflect population density in a pedestrian city. This, however, was not the case in Hamilton, where, as a comparison of Figures A.1 and A.3 will show, the clustering of stores related more to the existence of market places within a strong and viable central area than to the distribution of the population. The location of grocery shops also reflected the major access routes to the agricultural hinterland, as their concentration along King, John, and York streets reveals. Obviously, the advantages of a central location outweighed the convenience of people who lived beyond the core of the city and who, lacking the benefits of modern refrigeration, had to walk a considerable distance to buy everyday necessities.

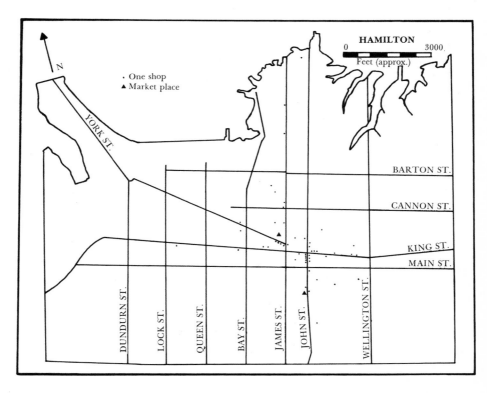

FIGURE A.3 Retail grocery shops

The Central Area

The concentration of economic activities in central locations is one way in which the commercial city was distinctive, and that concentration makes a detailed examination of the central area especially important. In contrast to Sjoberg's preindustrial city, commercial rather than religious and governmental activities dominated the center. The range and type of activities, however, were not those commonly associated with the modern Central Business District (CBD).[18] Manufacturing, for example, was a much more important component of the commercial city's core, while large offices only developed later. It is not sufficient simply to trace the present-day central business activities back to their origins in the nineteenth-century city, because the functions of central areas have changed through time. For this reason we have chosen to use the broader term "central area" rather than Central Business District, which implies a greater specificity of function than we intend.

The exact boundaries of the central area of any city remain problematical. Geographers have defined them in a number of ways, although fundamental to the idea of a central area is the concept of a "central place" serving the *entire* city and its hinterland.[19]

Martyn Bowden, in the most important empirical attempt so far to delimit a central area historically, has developed indices of height and intensity and a standard of contiguity. He calculated the height index on the basis of the number of floors devoted to CBD-forming uses and the intensity index on the amount of floor space devoted to these uses. He considered an establishment contiguous, and therefore part of the CBD, if it connected with the core area on at least one of its four fronts. The distinctions that Bowden made among different kinds of activity, however, imply a greater degree of specialization than existed in the commercial city, and his indices of height and intensity do not work well in a setting in which people lived above their shops and artisans combined work and residence in the same structure. Bowden recognized these problems himself, for he wrote that in the San Francisco of 1850 "specialization was not marked at this embryonic stage in the development of the central district and it was often difficult to decide whether an establishment could be considered CBD-forming or not. Distinctions among retailing, wholesaling and manufacturing were not always clear and place of work and residence were frequently one and the same."[20]

We have adopted a simpler standard than Bowden's. Our measure of contiguity is the same as his: all *work places* contiguous to the core on at least one side form part of the central area. But instead of using his measures of height and intensity, we have adopted two economic processes put forward by James Vance, exclusion and segregation.[21] For even though there was a lack of functional specificity, economic processes were actively shaping the form and content of the central area. According to Vance, exclusion operates through the mechanism of the rent gradient, under which "a lot at the very heart of the city has the highest value and all lots grading out towards the edge have successively less value." As similar activities have similar rent-paying abilities, the central area becomes more exclusive in content. Within this framework, the process of segregation operates. Although exclusion drives some activities, such as residences, from the center of the city because of their inability to pay high rents, groups of similar and interconnected activities concentrate together, resulting in internal differentiation of functions based upon rent-paying ability.

Other scholars have assumed that the concentration of activity made the center of the commercial city a jumble of undifferentiated enterprises. This observation only holds at a distance, however, for our more detailed reconstruction shows that even at an early stage in its history the central area of a commercial city could reveal a surprising degree of specialization. Peter Goheen's description of Toronto in 1860 provides one example of the more conventional view: "By comparison with the end of the century, the city was a jumble of confusion in 1860. Commerce, industry and high class residential properties were tightly intermixed. The central commercial district was also the focus for the larger industrial plants of the city. Intermixed with these were the main institutions of the city and many of the estates of the wealthiest and most prominent citizens." David Ward's model of Central

Business District growth makes the same point. He argues that the central business districts of North American cities experienced two distinct periods of growth in the nineteenth century. In the first, from 1840 to 1870, there was "minimal internal differentiation of activities," although wholesaling and its related financial and warehouse activities dominated commercial life. "Before 1870 most general retailing was unspecialized and widely dispersed throughout the city. General stores provided essential staples." In the second period, 1870–1900, the retailing and administrative areas, which had been of minor importance in the early period, expanded rapidly.[22]

Although our findings modify Ward's conclusions about the lack of internal differentiation, they support his argument about the process of growth. Reflecting Vance's argument about the mechanism of the rent gradient, Ward contends that "because locations on the major arteries of a city are more accessible to local markets than sites in intervening areas at the same distance from the city centre, the outward expansion from the original cluster of centrally located activities tended to be spoke-like."[23] Similarly, in Hamilton, as Figure A.4 indicates, development moved outward from the intersection of King and James streets in five ribbons: King Street West leading to the town of Dundas and King Street East toward the village of Stoney Creek; York Street, the main road to Toronto; James Street, leading north to the port; and Upper John Street, the major road over the Mountain to the south. It is especially significant that the central area did not extend along James Street South, or Upper James Street, for this road did not continue past the city limits in 1852. Hamilton's central area occupied all or part of forty-one blocks, or about 17 percent of the blocks that had been partially developed by 1852.

We have reconstructed the central area itself from the city directory of 1853 (the first in the city) and relied on the designations there to distinguish among seven major categories of central functions: retailing, wholesaling, manufactories and crafts, professional services, financial institutions, administrative establishments, and hotels and boarding houses.[24] Distinctions between retail and wholesale activities in the commercial city cannot be made with precision. Some wholesalers did sell directly to the public, and artisans often sold their own products in their shops, to cite two examples which complicate matters. Consequently, our distinctions among activities sometimes are arbitrary.

Nonetheless, even our imperfect distinctions show a considerable differentiation of activity within the central area. Of the 450 establishments there, 34 percent were retail, 33 percent manufacturing or artisan, nearly 11 percent professional, almost 8 percent wholesale, about 9 percent hotels and boarding houses, and the remaining 5 percent financial and administrative. As Figure A.4 shows, an inner and an outer central area could already be distinguished. Trading and financial establishments dominated

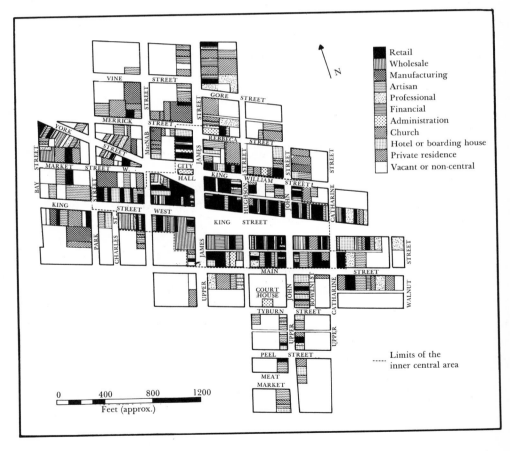

FIGURE A.4 Ground floor land use, central area of Hamilton, 1853

the inner area, which focused on the junction of King and James streets. Retail trading dominated the northern side of King Street; stores marked the two blocks on either side of the junction with James, extending particularly to the east. Virtually all the wholesale establishments, on the other hand, were located along the south side of King Street in the same area. In the small financial section, banks concentrated close to the wholesalers and almost at the central junction.[25] Lawyers also worked within the inner central area, congregating on Main Street close to the Court House. Thus, the processes of exclusion and segregation had been at work in Hamilton before 1853: artisan activities virtually had been removed from the inner central area, and the trading, financial, and professional activities that existed there had grouped themselves into small, specialized sub-areas.

Artisan shops and manufacturing establishments dominated the outer central area, while hotels and boarding houses intervened between that area and the city center. The most prominent feature of the outer portion was the relative concentration of the city's largest enterprises—the foundries and coach works—in its northern and western segments. Otherwise, much of the outer central area looked residential: many artisans combined their place of work with their residence, and completely separate residences were also common. By contrast, everyone who dwelled within the inner central zone lived above a business; there were no separate houses, and businesses were not located on the upper levels of buildings, except for a few professional offices near the junction of King and James streets.

From one perspective, the central area of Hamilton reflected the characteristics geographers have attributed to commercial cities. For virtually all activities were located within it: manufactories, artisan shops, banks, stores, wholesale houses, even homes, all clustered close to the center of the city. However, a more precise examination reveals that Hamilton's core district differed in two very significant ways from prevailing concepts regarding the commercial city's central area. In contrast to the "minimal internal differentiation" claimed by Ward, Hamilton's central area displayed a reasonably clear spatial segregation of activities. The central area of the commercial city only appears a "jumble" when the number of activities within it is compared to the modern CBD and analyzed at a highly aggregated level, rather than lot by lot as we have done here. Again in contrast to Ward, in 1853 Hamilton had a well-defined retail district.[26] In fact, the retail business had already become fairly specialized: only one retailer described himself in the directory as simply a "merchant"; all the others specified the nature of their trade. Thus, if Hamilton was at all like other commercial cities, our analysis of the spatial distribution of its economic activities suggests that geographers have underemphasized both the internal spatial differentiation of central areas and the importance of the retail sector. Perhaps it was not the jumble of activities in its central area but the concentration of a wide variety of enterprises into specialized segments of a compact center that gave a commercial city its distinctive spatial pattern.

Who Lived Where?

The spatial distribution of its homes as well as of its work places created a distinctive pattern in the commercial city. Neither the geographic models of the industrial metropolis nor those of the preindustrial city match the reality of residential patterns in mid-nineteenth-century Hamilton. This section will examine those patterns through an analysis of the residential locations of three major groups defined by occupation, ethnic origin, and economic position. Although residence partially reflected the social class divisions within the city, it did not conform completely to social structure. Rather, residential patterns blurred the otherwise sharp divisions among social groups; for the boundaries that separated the homes of different social classes remained, for such a stratified society, surprisingly ambiguous.

To facilitate the analysis of residential patterns we have divided the city into eleven sub-areas, as Figure A.5 shows. Some of these areas were easy to define. The Core could be defined through an analysis of land uses. The Port could be circumscribed with reference to such physical features as the shore line and the railway, while Cork Town has long been recognized as a distinctive part of Hamilton.[27] The South West, North East, and South East, the largely unsettled areas, could be fairly easily differentiated from the built-up environment of the city. The other five districts—

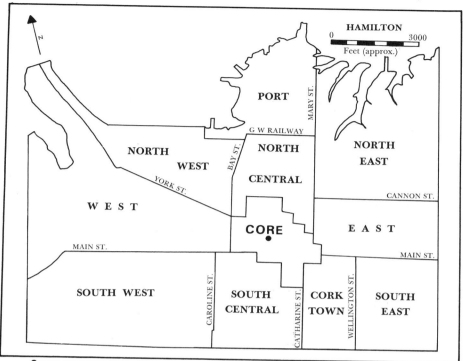

FIGURE A.5 Hamilton sub-areas

North West, West, North Central, East, and South Central—were convenient subdivisions of the remainder of the built-up area.

Six selected occupational groups—the carpenters, shoemakers, merchants, laborers, clerks, and lawyers—accounted for 38 percent of Hamilton's total assessed population in 1852.[28] Table A.1 reveals that the residences of members of each of these selected occupations were not equally distributed throughout the city.

Carpenters were overrepresented in districts that contained or were very close to employment opportunities, either in developing new subdivisions (North West, West, and East) or in wood-processing industries, such as lumber yards and shipping in the Port and coach building and furniture making near the North Central district. Their underrepresentation in the Core reflects, no doubt, the high cost of family accommodation there.

In terms of residential location, shoemakers were remarkably

TABLE A.1 Distribution of selected groups by sub-area, 1852[a]

		Sub-areas										
Group name	Number of men	North West	West	South West	Port	North Central	Core	South Central	North East	East	Cork Town	South East
Occupation												
Carpenters	195	3.6%	15.4%	—	11.3%	30.8%	17.9%	1.5%	—	9.7%	9.7%	—
Shoemakers	128	1.6	10.2	—	4.7	16.4	38.3	5.5	—	10.2	13.3	—
Merchants	149	1.3	3.4	—	2.0	9.4	59.1	12.1	—	8.7	4.0	—
Laborers	375	2.4	10.7	—	9.6	25.6	16.8	2.4	—	9.1	23.5	—
Clerks	142	0.7	5.6	—	3.5	14.2	57.7	6.3	—	4.2	7.7	—
Lawyers	17	—	23.5	—	—	11.8	23.5	17.6	—	23.5	—	—
Ethnicity												
English Anglican	255	3.1	15.7	0.8%	5.9	18.0	30.6	8.2	—	7.5	9.8	0.4%
Irish Catholic	269	0.7	5.6	—	10.4	23.0	26.4	6.7	0.4%	5.6	21.2	—
Irish Protestant	333	3.3	8.1	0.3	9.6	18.3	29.1	5.7	—	11.4	13.8	0.3
Canadian Protestant	168	2.4	6.5	—	6.5	16.7	42.9	6.0	0.6	8.9	8.9	0.6
Scottish Presbyterian	235	3.4	11.1	0.8	2.6	19.1	35.3	7.7	0.4	11.1	8.1	0.4
English Methodist	119	2.5	8.4	—	1.7	21.8	37.8	5.0	0.8	13.4	7.6	0.8
Wealth												
Statute laborers	130	—	5.4	—	—	6.9	63.8	7.7	—	4.6	11.5	—
Wealthiest 5%	131	4.6	4.6	—	0.8	6.1	60.3	15.2	2.3	4.6	0.8	0.8
Entire city	2636	2.1	9.4	0.2	7.1	19.8	36.0	5.6	0.2	8.8	10.4	0.3

[a] Sub-area as delineated in Figure A.5.

in step with the overall distribution of Hamilton's population. Their dispersal throughout the city was probably due to at least two factors. First, as with most artisan groups, shoemakers varied greatly in terms of wealth and status, ranging from large-scale shoe manufacturers down to employees in such firms, with independent craftsmen occupying a position somewhere between. The 38 percent who resided within the Core were, in all probability, engaged in Hamilton's retail and wholesale shoe business. Second, the ubiquity of the shoemakers was related to their major function in society. Everyone needed shoes and everyone had to have shoes repaired. Shoemakers, then, often catered to the needs of quite local populations.[29] Unlike the artisans of Sjoberg's preindustrial cities, Hamilton's shoemakers did not dominate any of the streets or quarters of the city. In fact, their distribution gives a reasonable indicator of population density in Hamilton in 1852.

Those who called themselves merchants constituted one of the wealthiest groups in mid-nineteenth-century Hamilton.[30] Their residential distribution reveals a concentration in two parts of the city and an underrepresentation in all the other sub-areas. Almost 60 percent of the merchants lived in the Core, as might be expected in a commercial city. Of the remaining 40 percent, many had been drawn to the more spacious outlying parts of the city, especially the South Central district near the base of the Mountain, where they had built large homes. These individuals retained their access to the central area by locating on or near the major thoroughfares of the city. The modern suburban trade-off between increased travel time to work and more spacious residential lots and dwellings had its antecedent in the residential choices of some of the merchants of Hamilton and probably of other commercial cities like it.

The most numerous occupation recorded in the mid-nineteenth-century Hamilton assessment rolls was that of laborer. In 1852, 14 percent of all the assessed individuals fell into this category. Laborers were generally a poor group: only about one in five owned a home.[31] Moreover, they tended to reside on the periphery of the city. Almost a quarter of them lived in Cork Town, Hamilton's Irish district. They were also overrepresented in the Port, West, and North Central regions. The largest portion, almost 26 percent, resided in the last area. On the other hand, 17 percent of them lived within the Core, presumably to be near the heavy industries located there. Thus the complexity of the residential patterns in Hamilton becomes obvious: laborers were overrepresented in the poorest section of the city, but they were also highly visible in the center of town. The residences of the poor in commercial Hamilton corresponded to neither the pre-industrial peripheral pattern nor to the modern central one. Despite the social distance between merchants and laborers, they were sometimes neighbors in the commercial city.

The residential locations of Hamilton's clerks were closely tied, naturally, to the commercial district. Almost three fifths of them resided in the area we have called the Core. Indeed, almost half of that number resided on four blocks of King Street in the vicinity of James. The clerks' overall residential pattern corresponded quite closely to that found by Bowden for the clerks of San Francisco at roughly the same time. However, the separation between home and work place was to increase markedly for clerical workers during the second half of the nineteenth century, as Goheen has illustrated.[32] As members of the middle class, they would then be able to take advantage of advances in urban transportation, such as the streetcar; but at mid-century the restrictions of the pedestrian city kept them near the core.

Like laborers and carpenters, Hamilton's lawyers tended to dwell on the periphery of the city. Even though all of them had offices within the central area, most of which were near the Court House at the corner of Main and John streets, fewer than one quarter of them resided within the Core. The remainder, however, lived on or very near the main streets of the city. Like some of the merchants, particularly the wholesalers, the lawyers had consciously opted for lower-density living and a longer journey to work. The economic circumstances of these wealthy groups very likely enabled them to ride to work in a private carriage. Their tendency to reside on major thoroughfares insured that their journey would be direct and would carry them through the most handsome streets of the city.[33] The consistently peripheral location of the lawyers' residences contrasted notably with what would be expected in a preindustrial city.

A combination of three principles determined the residential location of people in different occupations. The desire to be close to their place of work affected the least wealthy, indeed all of those who could not afford carriages: laborers lived near the principal enterprises that employed unskilled workers, clerks concentrated near offices and shops, and carpenters resided near construction sites and wood-utilizing industries. Some of the well-to-do, on the other hand, exchanged the convenience of proximity to work for an especially pleasant location. Finally, some tradesmen, such as shoemakers, defied the pull of the central area in which, perhaps, they could not afford a shop, and scattered themselves near their customers. The effect of these three principles was to moderate the tendency toward class segregation that otherwise might have occurred in such a highly stratified society.

For the most part, residential patterns moderated ethnic distinctions as well as social divisions. Despite its ethnic diversity, mid-nineteenth-century Hamilton contained no real ghetto. Table A.1 summarizes the residential distributions of the six ethnic groups that comprised over 70 percent of the city's population— the English Anglican, Irish Catholic, Irish Protestant, Canadian Protestant, Scottish Presbyterian, and English Methodist.[34]

As with the occupational groups, the figures for the residential concentration of the selected ethnic groups do not point to an even distribution throughout the population. Specific areas attracted certain groups and repelled others: Irish Catholics were overrepresented in Cork Town and the Port and underrepresented in the Core; Scottish Presbyterians were overrepresented in the West and North West and underrepresented in Cork Town; and Canadian Protestants were overrepresented in the Core and underrepresented in the West and Cork Town. What is most remarkable about the residential patterns for the various ethnic groups, however, is not the partial clustering of some people with similar ethnic origins, but rather the tremendous intermixing of the various groups within small areas of the city. To be sure, Cork Town was predominantly Irish, but it was not an exclusive ghetto, and, furthermore, the majority of Hamilton's Irish-born residents did not reside within its boundaries in 1852. In a rapidly growing city like Hamilton, perhaps the available housing and the house building technology of the time placed great constraints on residential location.[35] According to the assessment of 1852, fifty-seven of the city's slightly less than two thousand dwellings were vacant. This yields a vacancy rate of only 2.95 percent, an almost miniscule figure and one that indicates a housing shortage in a rapidly growing city. Perhaps proximity to work and the availability of housing were the strongest factors in determining where Hamiltonians lived.

Any final notions that the commercial city consisted simply of a well-to-do core and a poor periphery can be dispelled by examining the residential patterns for the poorest and wealthiest groups in the city. The former consists of the statute laborers, individuals who possessed neither real property nor taxable income. Over half, 55 percent, of the statute laborers actually called themselves unemployed at the time the assessment was taken; yet, in terms of residential location, they were surprisingly similar to those who constituted the wealthiest 5 percent of Hamilton's residents. As Table A.1 reveals, both groups were highly clustered in the Core. The statute laborers, however, were prominent on the edge of the Core, while the well-to-do congregated close to the nodal intersection of King and James streets. Almost 40 percent of the statute laborers lived in three cheap hotels and one boarding house located along John Street, south of King.[36] This pattern of the urban poor residing in cheap hotels near the heart of the city is much more typical of the modern industrial city than of the feudal town. Nevertheless, the degree of juxtaposition of the two groups, representing as they did the extreme rungs on mid-nineteenth-century Hamilton's economic ladder, could not have been predicted from the structural models of either preindustrial or modern cities.

The relationship between the patterns of residential location and occupation, ethnicity, and wealth in commercial Hamilton underscores some of the very real differences between its spatial structure and that of both preindustrial and modern cities. The commercial city tended toward both other types; yet, because of its complexity, it emerged as a distinct urban form. Therefore models designed to account for the preindustrial or the modern city cannot do justice to the commercial city.

Conclusion

Hamilton did not conform either to the sort of preindustrial city described by Sjoberg nor to the ideal types of modern industrial places. Rather, it was a North American commercial city, not yet influenced by the full impact of industrialization and never really a feudal place. The commercial city must be studied on its own terms.

The spatial structure of commercial Hamilton in the mid-nineteenth century was both small and compact, like that of preindustrial cities. Internally, however, its functional differentiation was closer to that of a modern industrial city, for a viable and highly visible commercial core dominated the city. Within the core, economic activities were grouped into small, specialized retail, wholesale, and financial sections from which purely residential structures had been excluded. Though still within the central area, manufacturing firms and artisans' shops marked an outer zone separated in some places from the core by hotels and boarding houses. Expansion outward from the center followed the major arteries to the hinterland in a spoke-like pattern. Interstices between the spokes generally awaited later development, especially near the periphery of the built-up area. This pattern approximates Ward's model for urban expansion in the streetcar era; yet Hamilton was still a pedestrian city. Perhaps major arteries exerted an influence on residential development that was quite independent of the technology of transportation.

The complex residential structure of commercial Hamilton defied simple core-periphery contrasts between the homes of the rich and the poor. Both rich and poor lived in and about the city's core. In fact, some of the very poorest men in the city, the statute laborers, clustered in the hotels of the central area. Moreover, a significant number of the elite had traded convenience for a scenic location and had built fine homes at the base of the Mountain, well south of the core. As in both preindustrial and modern cities, some areas of Hamilton had a distinctly ethnic character. Yet there was no exclusive area and no ghetto. The implications of this residential pattern are intriguing. For Hamilton had a rigidly stratified society in which wealth, power, and sometimes ethnicity coalesced into clear, identifiable social groupings, which its residential structure did not reflect in any very straightforward way. Did the social mixture of the city's neighborhoods moderate class tensions, or did the nearby presence of the merchant's fine home continually aggravate the laborer's resentment? At this point we can do little more than ask the question. But that is worth doing, for this puzzle about the consequences of an imperfect fit between the arrangement of people in geographical and social space could be our most significant finding.

Occupational Classification

THE VERTICAL OCCUPATIONAL classification used in Chapters Two and Three is an adaptation of the five-cities scheme explained there. The 113 occupations classified in that scheme account for well over three quarters of all employed males. I have added all the other occupations, putting them into the categories that seemed most appropriate. Although this scheme is probably quite useful for studying a nineteenth-century city prior to industrialization, I would not, without much further study, recommend its use in a period after industrialization. I have discussed the problem of occupational classification in "Occupational Classification in History," *Journal of Interdisciplinary History,* III, 1 (Summer 1972), 63–88.

The occupations are divided into five socioeconomic ranks, with rank I at the top. A sixth rank has been added for occupations that could not be classified according to the five-cities scheme.

I (High)	City councillor	Hardware merchant
Alderman	Clergyman	High Bailiff
Ale merchant	Clothier	High Constable
Archbishop, Catholic	Coal merchant	Importer
Archdeacon	Coffee merchant	Insurance agency owner
Attorney	Commission merchant	Insurance manager
Banker	Company manager	Jobber
Bank manager	Corn merchant	Judge
Barrister	Councillor	Judge of Vice Admi-
Bishop	Crockery merchant	ralty Court
Bishop, Catholic	Dry goods merchant	Ladies goods merchant
Chancellor	Feed merchant	Leather merchant
Chief Engineer of the	Financial director	Liquor merchant
railroad	Flour merchant	Marble dealer
Chief Justice	Forwarder	Mayor
Chief of Police	Gentleman	Member of Supreme
China dealer	Glass dealer	Court

Merchant
Merchant Tailor
Minister of religion
Patent rights dealer
Physician
Police Magistrate
Porter merchant
Priest
Private means
Professor
Prothonotaries
Provision merchant
Publisher
Seed merchant
Solicitor
Spice merchant
Surgeon
Tea dealer
University officer
Vicars
Vice Chancellor
Wharfinger
Wholesale druggist
Wholesale merchant
Wine merchant
Wooden ware merchant
Wool merchant

II

Accountant
Actor
Actress
Agent, General
Agent, Insurance
Apothecary
Appraiser
Architect
Art exhibitor
Artist
Assessor
Auctioneer
Auditor
Author
Baggage master
Bandmaster
Bank teller

Billiard room keeper
Boarding house keeper
Boarding school keeper
Bookkeeper
Bookseller
Bookbindery owner
Booking agent
Bowling alley keeper
Brewer
Bridge inspector
Broker
Broom merchant
Builder
Cab owner
Canal inspector
Cartage agent
Cashier
Caterer
Cattle yard keeper
Cemetery agent
Checker
Chemist
Chief Constable
Cigar maker
City or county clerk
City or county inspec-
   tor
City or county registrar
City or county surveyor
City or county treasurer
Civil engineer
Clerk
Clerk of the Crown
Clerk of the Peace
Cloth manufacturer
Club president
Coal oil dealer
Collector
Commercial traveler
Commissary
Commission agent
Contractor
Cooperative storekeeper
Coroner
Custom House broker
Custom House keeper

Customs clerk
Customs collector
Customs officer
Dairyman
Dancing master
Dentist
Deputy City Clerk
Deputy Commissary
Deputy Reeve
Deputy Sheriff
Detective
Druggist
Dry goods clerk
Editor
Emigrant Agent
Fancy storekeeper
Farmer
Fire inspector
Fish dealer
Founder
Freight agent
Fruiterer
Furrier
Gaoler
Geologist
Grain dealer
Grocer
Harbor master
Hide dealer
Homeopathist
Hotel keeper
House agent
Ice dealer
Immigrant Agent
Indian Interpreter
Innkeeper
Inspector
Inspector of Locomo-
   tives
Insurance man
Insurance agent
Ironmonger
Jeweler
Journalist
Junk dealer
Justice of the Peace

Land agent
Land surveyor
Landlord
Librarian
License inspector
Lighthouse keeper
Livery stable keeper
Lock keeper
Lumber inspector
Lunatic asylum keeper
Mail conductor
Manager
Manufacturer
Market stable keeper
Medicine dealer
Mercantile agent
Merchant's clerk
Milkman
Miller
Mill owner
Mineral water agent
Money broker
Music teacher
Musician
Music seller
News agent
Notary
Oil agent
Oil dealer
Optician
Organist
Overseer
Pawnbroker
Phrenologist
Photographer
Piano dealer
Piano seller
Picture dealer
Poet
Pork dealer
Postmaster
Post office inspector
Postal clerk
Pound keeper
Principal
Produce dealer

Private school owner
Race agent
Rag dealer
Rag sorter
Railroad agent
Railroad clerk
Real estate agent
Recorder
Renovator
Reporter
Restaurant keeper
Road contractor
Road inspector
Salesman
Sawmill owner
Scribe
Sculptor
Secretary
Secretary for School
    Board
Section boss
Sexton
Shipper
Shipping agent
Shoe dealer
Shopkeeper
Showman
Small ware shopkeeper
Speculator
Stage agent
Stage proprietor
Stationmaster
Stationer
Steamboat proprietor
Stenographer
Stone and slate dealer
Storekeeper
Store manager
Stove dealer
Street inspector
Sub-agent
Superintendent
Superintendent of
    Canals
Superintendent of
    Fishing

Superintendent, Hos-
    pital
Superintendent, Rail-
    road
Surveyor
Tobacconist
Tavern keeper
Tax collector
Teacher (male)
Telegraph operator
Temperance House
    keeper
Ticket agent
Timekeeper for rail-
    road
Trader
Travel agent
Traveling agent
Trustee
Turkish bath operator
Undertaker
Veterinary surgeon
Victualler
Warehouse keeper
Weigh master
Yeoman

III

Ax maker
Bailiff
Baker
Bandbox maker
Basket maker
Bellows maker
Billiard maker
Blacking maker
Blacksmith
Block maker
Boat maker
Boiler maker
Bookbinder
Bracket maker
Brakesman
Brass founder
Bricklayer
Brick maker

Bridge builder
Broom maker
Brush maker
Butcher
Cabinetmaker
Carpenter
Carpet maker
Carriage maker
Carriage trimmer
Carver
Caulker
Chain maker
Chain and bedstead
     manufacturer
Chair maker
Chandler
Cheese maker
Cloth cleaner
Cloth cutter
Coffee roaster
Comb maker
Compositor
Conductor
Confectioner
Constable
Cook
Cooper
Coppersmith
Cordwainer
Cork manufacturer
Cotton manufacturer
Cutler
Daguerreotypist
Dealer
Distiller
Draughtsman
Draper
Driller
Dyer
Edge tool maker
Engine driver
Engine fitter
Engineer
Engraver
Fanning mill manu-
     facturer

Farrier
File maker
Finisher
Fireman
Fireman for railroad
Fireworks maker
Fire engine manu-
     facturer
Fishing tackle maker
Fitter
Florist
Fringe maker
Fuller
Furnace maker
Furniture manufacturer
Gas fitter
Gas worker
Ginger beer maker
Glass maker
Glazier
Glover
Glue maker
Goldsmith
Grate maker
Guilder
Gunsmith
Hatter
Hoop maker
Hop grower
Horse trainer
Horticulturist
House mover
Implement maker
Iron fitter
Japaner
Jewelry manufacturer
Joiner
Knitter
Lace maker
Ladder maker
Last maker
Lathe maker
Letter carrier
Lithographer
Locksmith
Looking glass maker

Lumber merchant
Machinist
Marble cutter
Marble manufacturer
Mason
Match maker
Mattress maker
Mechanic
Melodeon maker
Millwright
Molder
Nail maker
Net maker
Nurseryman
Oar maker
Oculist
Oil cloth manufacturer
Oil manufacturer
Operator
Organ builder
Pail maker
Painter
Paper hanger
Paper maker
Patent medicine maker
Pattern maker
Patent leather dresser
Pianoforte manu-
     facturer
Pilot
Plane maker
Plasterer
Plate worker
Plough maker
Plumber
Policeman
Polisher
Potash manufacturer
Potter
Powder maker
Printer
Pump maker
Railroad car builder
Railroad policeman
Rake maker
Reed maker

Rifle maker
Rigger
Rope maker
Sabot maker
Sack maker
Saddler (harness maker)
Safe maker
Sail maker
Salaratus (baking soda) maker
Sash maker
Sausage maker
Sawyer
Scale maker
Scythe maker
Seedman
Sheriff's officer
Shingle maker
Shipbuilder
Ship chandler
Shipwright
Shirt maker
Shoemaker
Shoe manufacturer
Sign painter
Silk manufacturer
Silk printer
Silver platerer
Silversmith
Slater
Soap maker
Soda water manufacturer
Spade maker
Spinner
Spirit gas maker
Spoon maker
Spring maker
Starch maker
Stave maker
Stay maker
Steamboat steward
Steward
Stove fitter
Stove maker
Streetcar driver

Stucco maker
Sugar maker
Switchman for railroad
Tailor
Tallow chandler
Tanner
Taxidermist
Trashing mill maker
Tile cutter
Tinker
Tin plate worker
Tinsmith
Tobacco manufacturer
Toll bar keeper
Tray maker
Trimmer
Trunk maker
Turner
Twiner
Type founder
Typesetter
Umbrella maker
Upholsterer
Varnisher
Vinegar maker
Wagon maker
Watchmaker
Weighing machine maker
Well digger
Wheelwright
Whip maker
Wine manufacturer
Wire drawer
Wire worker
Woodworker
Wood seller
Woolen manufacturer
Yardsman

IV

Barber
Barkeeper
Bell hanger
Bill poster
Boatman

Bus driver
Cab driver
Caretaker
Carrier
Carter
Chimney sweep
Coachman
Colporteur
Courier
Drover
Errand boy
Factory operator
Ferryman
Fisherman
Gardener
Gas lighter
Grave digger
Groom
Hairdresser
Hewer
Hospital worker
Hunter
Huxter
Landing waiter
Lime burner
Lumberman
Mariner
Market clerk
Messenger
Miner
Omnibus driver
Packer
Peddler
Porter
Quarryman
Railroad worker
Restaurant worker
Sailor
Soldier
Stableman
Stage driver
Steamboat mate
Stevedore
Stoker
Stone cutter
Teamster

Turnkey
Waiter
Watchman
Weaver
Whitewasher
Wool sorter

V (Low)

Laborer
Rail layer for railroad
Unemployed

VI (Unclassifiable Occupations)

Apprentice
Assignee for estate
Bank clerk
Chamberlain

Charwoman
Clogger
Colored man
Deceased
Dressmaker
Embroiderer
Foreigner
Governess
Handicapped
Indian
Journeyman
Keeper of house of ill-
  fame
Lady
Law student
Lunatic
Matron of hospital or
  asylum
Midwife

Milliner
Mother Superior
Nun
Nurse
Pensioner
Prisoner
Prostitute
Seamstress
Seminarian
Servant (female)
Servant (male)
Spinster
Student
Tailoress
Teacher (female)
Unknown or not given
Washerwoman
Widow
Wife

Record Linkage

THREE DIFFERENT SORTS of record linkage have been used in assembling the data for this book. At the start of our work, we linked the 1851 census to the 1852 assessment by hand. Ian Winchester then developed the first automated record-linkage system to replicate that linkage. To join the 1861 census and assessment John Tiller and I devised a semi-automated record-linkage system which we described in "Record-Linkage for Everyman: A Semi-Automated Process," *Historical Methods Newsletter,* V, 4 (September 1972). To join the 1851 census to the 1861 census we used an automated system. The weights for this system, however, were derived from a hand-linked sample which we managed to replicate. We did not have sufficient data at the time to use a probability weighting system, which would have been superior. Hence, ours is an additive scheme. We do not contend that these weights are the most appropriate ones for all studies, but by using them other scholars could at least provide results comparable to ours. The weighting system we used is described below. The record-linkage process begins with the compression of names into a SOUNDEX code (also described below) which has been developed by Ian Winchester especially to account for Irish and Scottish names and to compensate for some of the problems posed by nineteenth-century penmanship. Each SOUNDEX code consists of one alphabetic character and three numeric characters.

Rules for Converting Surnames into SOUNDEX Code

1. The first letter of the surname is not coded but written down as is and serves as the prefix letter:
   WHEELER = W
2. Internal W and H are ignored entirely.
3. A, E, I, O, U, Y are also not coded.

4. B, P, F, V   coded 1
   C, G, J, K, Q, S, X, Z   coded 2
   D, T   coded 3
   L   coded 4
   M, N   coded 5
   R   coded 6

If the three digits are used up before the end of the name, the remaining letters are ignored:

MacDONALD = M235

No SOUNDEX code can have a double number (except 0). If two adjacent consonants have the same code, write the number only once:

STEDLER = S346, *not* S334

If the surname is short or has many vowels and has only one or two consonants that can be coded, fill up the remaining space(s) with 0's, so that there are three digits:

WHEELER = W460
BERRY = B600

Weighting System for Linking 1851 and 1861 Censuses

This weighting system is based, first of all, on the requirement that in all linked pairs the SOUNDEX and the sex must be identical; second, the disagreement in age must be twelve years or less; third, the religion must be either Catholic or a Protestant denomination on both sources.

There are eight identifying items to be considered besides SOUNDEX and sex: birthplace, religion, age (in different categories), race, surname, first initial, initial of spouse or parent, and marital status. Of these at least three must be identical, and at least two of the three must be birthplace, surname, or age plus or minus 3.

I. Not a Match
    (a) If sex not identical on both files, then not a match.
    (b) If religion on one file is Catholic and on second file is non-Catholic, then not a match.
    (c) If age plus 9, minus 1861 age, is greater than 12, then not a match.

    Do not treat missing initials as disagreement unless specified.

II. Conditions for a Match (match = +4)

| Variable | Special Conditions | | Score for | | |
			Agree	Dis-agree	Miss-ing
Birthplace	Call the following identical:		+3	−3	0
	Group 1	Germany and Holland Russia, Poland, and Prussia			
	Group 2	Native of Canada (French origin) Native of Canada (not French origin) Nova Scotia and Prince Edward Island New Brunswick Newfoundland Indians			
	Group 3	Egypt South Africa Africa			
	Group 4	England and Wales Guernsey Jersey and other British Isles and Gibraltar			
Religion	Call the following identical:		+2	−1	0
	Group 1	Church of Scotland Free Church Presby-terian Other Presbyterian			
	Group 2	Wesleyan Methodist Episcopal Methodist New Connection Methodist Other Methodist			
	Group 3	No creed given Free Thinker			

	Group 4 Anglican		
	Established Church		
Age	(a) If 1851 + 9 = 1851 ± 3	+3	
	(b) If 1851 + 9 = 1861 ± 4–6	+2	
	(c) If 1851 + 9 = 1861 ± 7–9	+1	
	(d) If 1851 + 9 = 1861 ± 10–12		−1

Initial	+3	−4	−2
Name	+2	−1	0
Surname (after compression)	+3	−3	0
Father's first initial	+3	−4	0
Mother's first initial	+3	−4	0
Spouse's first initial	+3	−4	0

Marital status of females
          Call the following identical:

Group 1 Married	0	−4	0
Widowed			

Notes

Introduction

1. *Hamilton Spectator and Journal of Commerce,* Sept. 29, 1847, 3, Jan. 1, 1861, 2. Cited hereafter as *Spectator.*

2. Canada Life Assurance Company, *Hamilton, the Birmingham of Canada* (Hamilton, Ont., 1892).

3. See, e.g., *Spectator,* Sept. 27, 1860, 3; on the Buchanan move to Hamilton see P. Douglas W. McCalla, "The Buchanan Business, 1834–1872: A Study in the Organization and Development of Canadian Trade," unpub. diss., Oxford University, 1972, 86–91, 108–116.

4. *Spectator,* June 14, 1848, 2, April 5, 1848, 3, Jan. 15, 1848, 3, Jan. 19, 1848, 2, August 7, 1847, 2.

5. *Spectator,* Jan. 30, 1861, 2, May 15, 1850, 2, May 23, 1860, 3, Oct. 20, 1860, 2.

6. See, e.g., *Spectator,* Oct. 9, 1847, 2, May 25, 1860, 2.

7. *Spectator,* June 20, 1849, 2, Dec. 26, 1849, 3.

8. *Spectator,* Dec. 23, 1848, 3, May 25, 1860, 2.

9. *Spectator,* Oct. 20, 1860, 2, July 24, 1847, 3, Sept. 27, 1848, 3, Feb. 16, 1848, 2, Nov. 6, 1859, 2.

10. *Spectator,* Dec. 23, 1848, 2, Dec. 12, 1860, 3.

11. *Spectator,* May 11, 1860, 2, May 16, 1860, 2, Nov. 5, 1860, 3, April 11, 1861, 3.

12. *Spectator,* Jan. 22, 1851, 4, June 21, 1860, 3, Aug. 18, 1849, 3; Ian E. Davey, "Social Reform and School Attendance: The Hamilton Central School, 1853–1861," unpub. M.A. thesis, University of Toronto, 1972.

13. *Spectator,* Aug. 3, 1860, 2, Aug. 7, 1860, 3, Aug. 15, 1860, 2, Aug. 23, 1860, 3, Jan. 28, 1861, 2, Feb. 6, 1861, 3, Feb. 23, 1861, 2, May 17, 1861, 3, Dec. 19, 1861, 3; McCalla, "Buchanan Business," 363–365. On the economic history of the region see R. W. Roberts, "The Changing Patterns in Distribution and Composition of Manufacturing Activity in Hamilton between 1861 and 1921," unpub. M.A. thesis, McMaster University, 1964; and James Muckle Gilmour, "Structural and Spatial Change in Manufacturing Industry: South Ontario, 1850–1890," unpub. diss., University of Toronto, 1970.

14. E. A. Wrigley, "The Process of Modernization and the Industrial Revolution in England," *Journal of Interdisciplinary History,* III, 2 (Autumn 1972), 225–260.

15. Philip Abrams, "The Sense of the Past and the Origins of Sociology," *Past and Present,* 55 (May 1972), 18–32.

16. For example: Stephen Thernstrom, *Poverty and Progress: Social Mobility in a Nineteenth Century City* (Cambridge, Mass., 1964), shows what can be done working essentially by hand.

17. Abrams, "Sense of the Past," 29; Peter Laslett, *Household and Family in Past Time* (Cambridge, Eng., 1972); Michael B. Katz, "Occupational Classification in History," *Journal of Interdisciplinary History,* III, 1 (Summer 1972), 63–88.

18. See my comments on Lee Benson's book, *Toward the Scientific Study of History,* in *Historical Methods Newsletter,* VI, 2 (March 1973).

19. Hayden V. White, "The Burden of History," *History and Theory,* 5 (1966), 111–134.

Chapter One. The People of a Canadian City, 1851–52

1. For more detailed quantitative information than is given in the rest of this book, see the first four interim reports of the project, available on microfilm from the Department of History and Philosophy of Education of the Ontario Institute for Studies in Education. See also my essay, "Social Structure in Hamilton, Ontario," in Stephan Thernstrom and Richard Sennett, eds., *Nineteenth-Century Cities: Essays in the New Urban History* (New Haven and London, 1969), 209–244. I have rounded all percentages in this chapter and in most sections of the book to whole numbers. Considering the inexactness of historical data, this seems quite appropriate, especially when it increases ease of reading. In a few cases, however, where it seemed important, proportions have been rounded to one decimal in the text.

2. Record linkage is one of the central technical problems of this type of study. For a discussion of the problem and of our approach to it, see Ian Winchester, "The Linkage of Historical Records by Man and Computer: Techniques and Problems," *Journal of Interdisciplinary History,* I, 1 (1970), 107–224. The hand-linkage of the 1851 census, 1852 assessment, and 1853 directory was done by Mr. John Tiller, who also has done most of the coding of the 1861 census and assessment. I should like to acknowledge Mr. Tiller's invaluable participation in this project. On the problem of record linkage in general and the variety of possible approaches, see E. A. Wrigley, ed., *Identifying People in the Past* (London, 1973). The record-linkage techniques used here are explained in Appendix Three.

3. The *Spectator* and the *Gazette.*

4. Stephan Thernstrom and Peter Knights, "Men in Motion: Some Data and Speculations about Urban Population Mobility in Nineteenth Century America," in Tamara K. Hareven, ed., *Anonymous Americans: Explorations in Nineteenth-Century Social History* (Englewood Cliffs, N.J., 1971), 17–47; Peter R. Knights, "Population Turnover, Persistence, and Residential Mobility in Boston, 1830–1860," in Thernstrom and Sennett, *Nineteenth-Century Cities,* 258–274; E. J. Hobsbawm, "The Tramping Artisan," in his *Laboring Men: Studies in the History of Labor* (London, 1964), 34–63; Howard P. Chudacoff, *Mobile Americans: Residential and Social Mobility in Omaha 1880–1920* (New York, 1972); Anders Norberg and Sune Åkerman, "Migration and the Building of Families: Studies on the Rise of the Lumber Industry in Sweden," in Kurt Ågren, David Gaunt, Ingrid Eriksson, John Rogers, Anders

Norberg, Sune Åkerman, *Aristocrats, Farmers, Proletarians: Essays in Swedish Demographic History*, Studia Historica Upasliensia XLVII (Uppsala, 1973), 88–119; David Gagan, unpublished material from Peel County History Project, Department of History, McMaster University.

5. Unpublished papers by Mrs. Judy Cooke and Mr. Dan Brock, Ontario Institute for Studies in Education (OISE).

6. The mean assessed wealth of all the people engaged in commerce was £96, of the transients in commerce, £63; of resident professionals, £71, of transient ones, £21; of resident artisans, £25, of migrants, £13; of resident laborers, £9, of migrant ones, £7.

7. The existence of a similar phenomenon—a division of success within trades—is clearly revealed by Henry Mayhew's description of the organization of various trades in London in the middle of the nineteenth century. An example is the distinction between the "honorable" and "dishonorable" parts of the tailoring trade. See E. P. Thompson and Eileen Yeo, *The Unknown Mayhew* (London, 1971), 181–277, on tailors.

8. Robert Dreeben, *On What is Learned in Schools* (Reading, Mass., 1968), 95, provides an example of this point. See also Talcott Parsons and Robert F. Bales, *Family, Socialization and Interaction Processes* (Glencoe, Ill., 1955).

9. Not all employed men necessarily worked away from their homes. As Mayhew points out, it was common for manufacturers of various sorts to give out work to craftsmen to perform in their own homes.

10. See, for example, Proceedings of the Council of the City of Hamilton, 22 January 1851, 398–399, 19 January 1850, 128–129, available on microfilm in the Ontario Archives.

11. For studies of residential patterns in nineteenth-century cities, see two recent monographs: David Ward, *Cities and Immigrants: A Geography of Change in Nineteenth Century America* (New York, 1971); and Peter Goheen, *Victorian Toronto* (Chicago, 1970).

12. I have discussed the construction of these scales in the project's Working Paper No. 21, "The Measurement of Economic Inequality."

13. Fifty-one percent of the working population born in England and Wales were in the middle (fortieth to eightieth) economic ranks, as were 46 percent of the Anglicans. On the argument for drawing the poverty line at the fortieth percentile see my "Social Structure in Hamilton, Ontario." Of the Free Church Presbyterians 26 percent were poor, compared to 16 percent of the Wesleyan Methodists. At the same time 31 percent of the Free Church Presbyterians were well-to-do (eightieth to one hundredth economic ranks), as were 29 percent of the Wesleyan Methodists. Concerning the other major ethnic and religious groups: the Scottish-born were predominantly middle-income, much like the English; the adherents of the Church of Scotland, and those who called themselves simply Presbyterians, were likewise middling in terms of wealth, except that the former had few wealthy adherents; the figures for Methodists were much like those for Presbyterians, and those for Baptists were much like those for members of the Church of Scotland.

14. For the actions of the City Council with respect to immigrants, see, e.g., Proceedings of the Council, 20 August 1849, 31, and 10 September 1849, 149–150. On the institutionalization of poverty in the United States see the recent provocative book by David Rothman, *The Discovery of the Asylum* (Boston, 1971); for the same subject in Canada see Susan E. Houston's superb work,

"The Impetus to Reform: Urban Crime, Poverty, and Ignorance in Ontario, 1850–1875," unpub. diss., University of Toronto, 1974, which treats poverty especially on pp. 185–322. See also Haley P. Bamman, "The Ladies Benevolent Society of Hamilton, Ontario: Form and function in Mid-Nineteenth Century Urban Philanthropy," in Michael Katz, _The Canadian Social History Project Interim Report No. 4_ (Toronto, 1972), 161–217. The records of the Ladies Benevolent Society are available in manuscript at the Hamilton Public Library.

15. E. J. Hobsbawm, _Industry and Empire_ (London, 1969), 157.

16. Mrs. Anne-Marie Hodes coded the 1851 and 1852 newspapers for the project.

17. Only the top three quarters of the assessed population were eligible to serve on the jury. I suspect that those actually chosen did not represent a cross section of that group.

18. For the idea of constructing a scale of visibility based on mentions in a newspaper, I am indebted to the work of Professor Walter Glazer of the University of Pittsburgh.

19. Robert E. Gallman, "Trends in the Size Distribution of Wealth in the Nineteenth Century: Some Speculations," in Lee Soltow, ed., _Six Papers on the Size Distribution of Wealth and Income_ (New York, 1969), 2, 6; Lee Soltow, _Patterns of Wealthholding in Wisconsin since 1850_ (Madison, 1971), 29; Edward Pessen, _Riches, Class, and Power before the Civil War_ (Lexington, Mass., 1973), 39, 41.

20. The marriage registers were coded by Mrs. Margaret Zieman.

21. The figures are supported by those found for European countries. See, e.g., Peter Laslett, "Size and Structure of the Household in England over Three Centuries," _Population Studies_, XXIII, 2 (July 1969), 199–223, and his recent book, _Household and Family in Past Time_ (Cambridge, Eng., 1972). Only 20 percent of Scottish grooms were less than twenty-five years old compared to 39 percent of all grooms, while 30 percent of Scottish grooms were in their thirties compared to 18 percent of all grooms. Among people born in Canada West, 51 percent of the grooms, compared to 39 percent of all grooms, had been married before the age of twenty-five; of the brides 82 percent, compared to 75 percent of all brides, had been married before they were twenty-seven years old.

22. For an overview of Canadian population history that makes this point, see _Census of Canada,_ 1931, chapters ii and iii of the excellent monograph on the family.

23. Of the poor, 18 percent had a large family; so did 20 percent of the middle-income group and 21 percent of the well-to-do. Similarly, 38 percent of the poor had a small number of children, as did 35 percent of the middle rank and 38 percent of the well-to-do.

24. The means are as follows: U.S.-born, 2.40; Canadian, 3.18; English, 3.35; Irish, 3.52; Scottish, 4.01. The Scottish rank third in mean number of children among 20–29-year-olds, fifth among 30–39-year-olds, and first among the 40–49-year-old group. The mean for members of the Church of Scotland is 4.39 and for Free Church Presbyterians, 4.62. The Baptist score is 2.17. I should point out, in fairness to traditional ideas, that a preliminary inspection of the 1861 results indicates that the family size for Catholics and Irish was slightly larger than average. At this point the change is inexplicable.

25. For comparative figures on class and birth control, see E. A. Wrigley's excellent book, *Population and History* (New York, 1969), 186–187. On the method of studying birth control in past societies, see E. A. Wrigley, "Family Limitation in Pre-Industrial England," *Economic History Review*, 2d ser., XIX, 1 (1966), 82–109. For more on the relation between status and birth control in the nineteenth century, see J. A. Banks, *Prosperity and Parenthood: A Study of Family Planning among the Victorian Middle Classes* (London, 1954); and D. E. C. Eversley, *Social Theories of Fertility and the Malthusian Debate* (Oxford, 1959).

26. On general patterns of household size in England over four hundred years, see Laslett, "Size and Structure of the Household."

27. There has been amazingly little written on the history of school attendance. The only monograph in English that I know to be specifically devoted to the topic is David Rubenstein, *School Attendance in London, 1870–1904: A Social History* (Hull, 1969). My own article is "Who Went to School?" *History of Education Quarterly*, XII, 3 (Fall 1972), 432–454. See also Selwyn Troen, "Popular Education in Nineteenth Century St. Louis," *History of Education Quarterly*, XIII, 1 (Spring 1973), 23–40; Carl F. Kaestle, *The Evolution of an Urban School System: New York City, 1750–1850* (Cambridge, Mass., 1973), esp. 89; and Ian E. Davey, "School Reform and School Attendance: The Hamilton Central School, 1853–1861," unpub. M.A. thesis, University of Toronto, 1972.

28. Tables comparing these cities are in the project's Working Paper No. 23, Third Interim Report.

29. Historians who are interested but hesitant about venturing into quantitative social history can gain some knowledge of how to proceed from four recent books: Edward Shorter, *The Historian and the Computer: A Practical Guide* (Englewood Cliffs, N.J., 1971); Charles M. Dollar and Richard J. Jensen, *Historian's Guide to Statistics, Quantitative Analysis and Historical Research* (New York, 1971); E. A. Wrigley, ed., *Nineteenth-Century Society: Essays in the Use of Quantitative Methods for the Study of Social Data* (Cambridge, Eng., 1972); and Roderick Floud, *An Introduction to Quantitative Methods for Historians* (Princeton, 1973).

Chapter Two. The Structure of Inequality, 1851 and 1861

1. Peter Laslett, *The World We Have Lost* (London, 1965), 148.

2. I base this statement on an impressionistic look at the industrial census for 1871, which will be subjected to systematic study in the near future, and on the data in James Muckle Gilmour, "Structural and Spatial Change in Manufacturing Industry: South Ontario, 1850–1890," unpub. diss., University of Toronto, 1970, 69 and 309–310.

3. On this topic see Robert Nisbet, *Social Change and History: Aspects of the Western Theory of Development* (New York, 1969).

4. Clifford Geertz, *The Social History of an Indonesian Town* (Cambridge, Mass., 1965), 142, 145.

5. Donald J. Treiman, "Industrialization and Social Stratification," in Edward O. Laumann, ed., *Social Stratification: Research and Theory for the 1970's* (Indianapolis and New York, 1970), 207–234.

6. Ibid., 228.

7. Talcott Parsons, "Equality and Inequality in Modern Society, or Social Stratification Revisited," in Laumann, *Social Stratification,* 13–72.

8. See, e.g., Peter Laslett, ed., *Family and Household in Past Time* (Cambridge, Eng., 1972).

9. Parsons, "Equality and Inequality," 15.

10. There is not much more than fragmentary evidence that this may be the case, but see A. H. Turritten and Louis J. Mulligan, "Who Moves Up; Who Moves Down? Problems of Data Analysis in the Historical Study of Social Mobility in Hamilton, Ontario, 1901–1940," paper presented at the Annual Meeting of the Canadian Sociology and Anthropology Association, Queens University, Kingston, Ontario, May 27–31, 1973.

11. Stuart Blumin, Laurence Glasco, Clyde Griffen, Theodore Hershberg, and Michael Katz, "Occupation and Ethnicity in Five Nineteenth Century Cities," paper presented at the annual meeting of the Organization of American Historians, Chicago, April 1973.

12. Michael Katz, "The Measurement of Economic Inequality," in Michael Katz, *The Canadian Social History Project, Interim Report No. 3* (Toronto, 1971), 36–46.

13. Barbara Welter, "The Cult of True Womanhood: 1820–1860," *American Quarterly,* XVIII, 2, pt. 1 (Summer 1966), 151–174. See also Carroll Smith-Rosenberg and Charles Rosenberg, "The Female Animal: Medical and Biological Views of Woman and her Role in Nineteenth-Century America," *Journal of American History,* LX, 2 (September 1973), 332–356; Kathryn Kish Sklar, *Catherine Beecher: A Study in American Domesticity* (New Haven, 1973).

14. *Daily Spectator and Journal of Commerce,* Dec. 15, 1860, 2.

15. Ibid.

16. *Hamilton Spectator and Journal of Commerce,* Feb. 19, 1851, 2.

17. E. P. Thompson and Eileen Yeo, *The Unknown Mayhew* (London, 1971), 24, 147.

18. For detailed tables documenting the social and demographic characteristics of women, see my working paper, "On the Condition of Women, 1851–1861," in Michael Katz, ed., *Canadian Social History Project, Interim Report No. 4* (Toronto, 1972), 16–25.

19. On the provision of welfare for women see Haley P. Bamman, "The Ladies Benevolent Society of Hamilton, Ontario: Form and Function in Mid-Nineteenth Century Urban Philanthropy," in Katz, *Canadian Social History Project, Interim Report No. 4* (Toronto, 1972), 161–217.

20. Stanley Lieberson, "Stratification and Ethnic Groups," in Laumann, *Social Stratification,* 172.

21. Ibid., 176, 180.

22. The percentages given here are for those individuals linked between census and assessment at each end of the decade. They are thus biased toward the upper economic ranks, though not sufficiently to invalidate my conclusions.

23. See, e.g., *Hamilton Spectator and Journal of Commerce,* June 14, 1848, 2, January 15, 1848, 3, and January 5, 1848, 2.

24. In his *Blacks in Canada, A History* (New Haven, 1971), 484–489, Robin Winks points to the underenumeration of Blacks in the mid-nineteenth-century censuses. The low number of Blacks on the census for Hamilton may

be due to the fact that many Blacks lived in an area just outside the city limits. For a statement praising the Black community and comparing its prosperity, not altogether inaccurately, to the situation in the United States, see *Hamilton Spectaor and Journal of Commerce,* May 15, 1850, 2.

25. As a beginning of the sort of work that should be done, see the superb recent book by Charlotte Erickson, *Invisible Immigrants: The Adaptation of English and Scottish Immigrants in 19th Century America* (Coral Gables, Florida, 1972), and her essay, "Who Were the English and Scots Immigrants to the United States in the Late Nineteenth Century?" in D. V. Glass and Roger Revelle, eds., *Population and Social Change* (London, 1972), 347–381.

26. Blumin et al., "Occupation and Ethnicity."

27. One of the difficulties with the manual-nonmanual distinction is the placing of clerks, whose status varied widely. The occupation of clerk, which suffered quite early from an oversupply of labor, was precarious and certainly below that of master craftsmen in stable trades. See, e.g., *Hamilton Spectator and Journal of Commerce,* January 17, 1849, 2.

28. "Social Structure in Hamilton, Ontario," in Stephan Thernstrom and Richard Sennett, eds., *Nineteenth Century Cities: Essays in the New Urban History* (New Haven, 1969), 209–244.

29. The nature, distribution, and significance of household structure is examined more fully in Chapter Five.

30. Blumin et al., "Occupation and Ethnicity." Philadelphia was a clear exception, having less than half the proportion of home owners in comparison to the other cities. The size of a city may have been a critical variable in the proportion of home ownership, with the percentage declining along with size beyond a certain point.

31. Parsons, "Equality and Inequality," 23; Robert Hunter, *Poverty* (New York, 1965), 46 (first published 1904).

32. The propensity of Irish-born men to buy property has been noted by Stephan Thernstrom in *Poverty and Progress: Social Mobility in a Nineteenth Century City* (Cambridge, Mass., 1964), 156–157.

33. The choice of these dimensions is not accidental. It reflects the distinctions that recur and are especially useful in analyzing the spatial distribution of various social features. See, e.g., R. J. Johnston, *Urban Residential Patterns* (New York, 1973), 19–63.

34. The characteristics of the various districts of the city are discussed fully in the appendix and also in Michael J. Doucet, "Spatial Differentiation in a Commercial City: Hamilton, 1851–2," in *Canadian Social History Project, Interim Report No. 4,* 307–351.

35. *Hamilton Spectator and Journal of Commerce,* May 24, 1848, 2, and December 12, 1849, 3.

36. For a similar conclusion about the nature of a mid-nineteenth-century city, see Peter R. Knights, *The Plain People of Boston 1830–1860: A Study in City Growth* (New York, 1971), 91.

Chapter Three. Transiency and Social Mobility

1. *Life and Adventures of Wilson Benson, Written by Himself* (Toronto, 1876), 5. Benson's autobiography was privately published and has not been republished. I found it in the University of Toronto library.

2. Ibid., 7.

3. Ibid., 9.
4. Ibid., 14.
5. Ibid., 17. In Ireland as a whole the percentage of unmarried 25–34-year-old men in 1851 was 61 percent, of women, 39 percent. In 1861 the percentage of unmarried 20–24-year-olds was 92 percent for men and 76 percent for women. Robert E. Kennedy, Jr., *The Irish Emigration, Marriage and Fertility* (Berkeley, Los Angeles, London, 1973), Statistical Appendix, Table 5, 215.
6. *Life of Benson,* 17–18.
7. Ibid., 24.
8. Ibid., 24–25.
9. Ibid., 26, 27.
10. Ibid., 30–31.
11. Ibid., 31.
12. Ibid., 32.
13. Ibid., 34.
14. Ibid., 37.
15. Ibid., 39.
16. Ibid., 40.
17. Ibid., 48.
18. Ibid., 53–54.
19. In a small but suggestive study, Peter Knights, tracing native-born men who had lived in Boston in 1840 and left during the following decade, found that in 1850, 66.3 percent lived within ten miles of the center of the city and only 12.5 percent lived fifty or more miles away. Peter R. Knights, *The Plain People of Boston, 1830–1860: A Study in City Growth* (New York, 1971), Table VI-7, 113.
20. On the use of the term "friends" during this period see Alison Prentice, "Education and the Metaphor of the Family: The Upper Canadian Example," *History of Education Quarterly,* XII, 3 (Fall 1972), 283–284.
21. *Life of Benson,* 6. On the irregularity of work see, for instance, Stephan Thernstrom, *Poverty and Progress: Social Mobility in a Nineteenth Century City* (Cambridge, Mass., 1964), 20.
22. Thernstrom, *Poverty and Progress,* supports this contention.
23. Benson, 47, 5.
24. Joan W. Scott, "The Glassworkers of Carmaux, 1850–1900," in Stephan Thernstrom and Richard Sennett, eds., *Nineteenth-Century Cities: Essays in the New Urban History* (New Haven, 1969), 3–38. Stephan Thernstrom and Peter R. Knights, "Men in Motion: Some Data and Speculations about Urban Population Mobility in Nineteenth-Century America," in Tamara K. Hareven, *Anonymous Americans: Explorations in Nineteenth Century Social History* (Englewood Cliffs, 1971), 39.
25. Clyde Griffen, "Workers Divided: The Effect of Craft and Ethnic Differences in Poughkeepsie, New York, 1850–1880," in Thernstrom and Sennett, *Nineteenth-Century Cities,* 49–97 (quotation on 92–93). Thernstrom, *Poverty and Progress,* 181–182.
26. T-H Hollingsworth, "Historical Studies of Migration," *Annals de Demographie Historique 1970* (Paris and The Hague, 1970), 87–96, and James W. Simmons, "Changing Residence in the City: A Review of Intraurban Mobility," *The Geographical Review,* LVIII, 4 (1968), 622–651 are two useful re-

views of the literature which include a consideration of the relation between mobility and the life cycle.

27. Hollingsworth, "Historical Studies"; Sidney Goldstein, *Patterns of Mobility, 1910–1950: The Norristown Study, A Method for Measuring Migration and Occupational Mobility in the Community* (Philadelphia, 1958), 50; Kennedy, *The Irish*, 68–73.

28. Simmons, "Changing Residence"; Peter H. Rossi, *Why Families Move: A Study in the Social Psychology of Urban Residential Mobility* (Glencoe, Ill., 1955).

29. Goldstein, *Patterns of Mobility*, 52; Simmons, "Changing Residence," 626; Stephan Thernstrom, *The Other Bostonians: Poverty and Progress in the American Metropolis, 1880–1970* (Cambridge, Mass., 1973), 228.

30. Gareth Stedman Jones, *Outcast London* (Oxford, 1971), 81–83.

31. Thernstrom, *The Other Bostonians*, 232.

32. Hollingsworth, "Historical Studies"; Goldstein, *Patterns of Mobility*; Julian Wolpert, "Behavioral Aspects of the Decision to Migrate," *The Regional Science Association Papers*, 15 (1965), 159–169; Barbara A. Anderson, "Internal Migration in a Modernizing Society: The Case of Nineteenth Century European Russia," unpub. diss., Princeton University, 1973. For an excellent example of the complex relation of the type of migrant to a variety of conditions and of migration of less qualified men, see C. J. Erickson, "Who Were the English and Scots Emigrants to the United States in the Late Nineteenth Century?" in D. V. Glass and Roger Revelle, eds., *Population and Social Change* (London, 1972), 347–373, esp. 368.

33. Wolpert, "Behavioral Aspects of the Decision to Migrate." Charlotte Erickson, *Invisible Immigrants: The Adaptation of English and Scottish Immigrants in 19th Century America* (Coral Gables, 1972), 22, 24, 27, 29, 233, 238, 395.

34. Goldstein, *Patterns of Mobility*, 216.

35. Hollingsworth, "Historical Studies," 88.

36. Thernstrom, *The Other Bostonians*, Table 9.1, p. 222; Goldstein, *Patterns of Mobility*, 129. See also, A. H. Turritten and Louis J. Mulligan, "Who Moves Up; Who Moves Down? Problems of Data Analysis in the Historical Study of Social Mobility in Hamilton, Ontario, 1901–1940," paper presented at the Annual Meeting of the Canadian Sociology and Anthropology Association, Queens University, Kingston, Ontario, May 27–31, 1973, which analyzes shifting rates of persistence in Hamilton.

37. This has been true of our work and of Theodore Hershberg's Philadelphia Social History Project as well.

38. R-S Schofield, "Age Specific Mobility in an Eighteenth Century Rural English Parish," *Annals de Demographie Historique 1970* (Paris and The Hague, 1971), 261–274. Ingrid Eriksson and John Rogers, "Mobility in an Agrarian Community: Practical and Methodological Considerations," in Kurt Ågren, David Gaunt, Ingrid Eriksson, John Rogers, Anders Norberg, and Sune Åkerman, *Aristocrats, Farmers, Proletarians: Essays in Swedish Demographic History* (Uppsala, 1973), 60. Gagan's study, conducted at McMaster University in Hamilton, is called the Peel County History Project. Thernstrom, *The Other Bostonians*, Table 9.1, p. 222.

39. See E. A. Wrigley, *Identifying People in the Past* (London, 1973); Ian

Winchester, "The Linkage of Historical Records by Man and Computer," *The Journal of Interdisciplinary History* I, 1 (1970), 107–24.

40. Knights, *Plain People,* 144–147. Thernstrom and Knights, "Men in Motion."

41. It could be tested by the straightforward but laborious procedure of coding assessment rolls year by year.

42. Seymour M. Lipset and Reinhard Bendix, *Social Mobility in Industrial Society* (Berkeley, 1960); Peter M. Blau and Otis Dudley Duncan, *The American Occupational Structure* (New York, London, Sydney, 1967), 435–436.

43. Thernstrom and Knights, "Men in Motion," 39.

44. Blau and Duncan, *American Occupational Structure,* 2–3. For a critique of mobility research which makes some of these points plus others, see Anselm L. Strauss, *The Contexts of Social Mobility: Ideology and Theory* (Chicago, 1971), 1–14.

45. This is the most obvious weakness in the admirable work of Peter Laslett and his associates in the Cambridge Group in England. See, for example, his "Introduction: The History of the Family," in Peter Laslett, ed., *Household and Family in Past Time* (Cambridge, Eng., 1972), 1–89.

46. Knights, *Plain People,* 118; Blau and Duncan, *American Occupational Structure,* 243–275.

47. Clyde Griffen has achieved such precision in his work on Poughkeepsie. For a contemporary discussion of the complexity of the concept of mobility, see Charles F. Westoff, Marvin Bressler, Philip C. Sagi, "The Concept of Social Mobility: An Empirical Inquiry," *Behavioral Science,* IX (1964), 207–218.

48. Thernstrom, *Poverty and Progress,* 132.

49. Clyde Criffen in a personal communication to the author.

50. See Chapters One and Two.

51. This classification is discussed in Chapter Two.

52. Michael B. Katz, "Occupational Classification in History," *Journal of Interdisciplinary History,* III, 1 (Summer 1972), 63–88.

53. Thernstrom, *Poverty and Progress,* 97; Blau and Duncan, *American Occupational Structure,* 420.

54. Blau and Duncan, *American Occupational Structure,* 422.

55. Thernstrom, *The Other Bostonians,* 232–241, discusses the surprising consistency in mobility rates that have turned up in American studies. On the fear of downward mobility at the time—and on perceptions of occupational status more generally—see Alison Prentice, "The School Promoters: Education and Social Class in Mid-Nineteenth Century Upper Canada" (unpublished Ph.D. thesis, University of Toronto, 1974), pp. 148–182.

56. Joseph L. Fleiss, *Statistical Methods for Rates and Proportions* (New York, London, Sydney, Toronto, 1973), 41–43. Also helpful on chi square is Roderick Floud, *An Introduction to Quantitative Methods for Historians* (Princeton, 1973), 129–132.

57. In the five-cities project we found a decrease in property owning by age among artisans in each city. On the relation between aging and economic decline see Jones, *Outcast London.*

58. Clyde Griffen in a personal communication to the author.

59. Blau and Duncan, *American Occupational Structure,* 402–403. The impact of education on life chances in the nineteenth century remains very much a matter for speculation. See, for instance, the discussion in Harvey J. Graff,

"Towards a Meaning of Literacy: Literacy and Social Structure in Hamilton, Ontario, 1861," unpub. M.A. thesis, University of Toronto, 1971. On the Central School see Ian E. Davey, "School Reform and School Attendance: The Hamilton Central School, 1853–1861, unpub. M.A. thesis, University of Toronto, 1972. Michael Olneck has made some helpful comments about the relation between fathers' and sons' occupation, which indicate that I shall need additional evidence to document fully the decline in occupational inheritance which I believe occurred.

60. Blau and Duncan, *American Occupational Structure*, 435–436; David Crew, "Definitions of Modernity: Social Mobility in a German Town, 1880–1901," *Journal of Social History*, VII, 1 (Fall 1973), 51–74.

Chapter Four. The Entrepreneurial Class

1. *Hamilton Spectator and Journal of Commerce*, Feb. 5, 1851, 2, Feb. 15, 1851, 3.

2. For a partial description of these sources see Chapter One.

3. These are the manuscript records of the R. G. Dun and Company (which in 1933 became Dun and Bradstreet) for Wentworth County, Canada West. Dun and Bradstreet Collection, Baker Library, Harvard Business School. I should like to thank Mr. Robert W. Lovett of the Baker Library for making these records available to me. They are cited hereafter as RGD. Entries in the ledgers usually contained abbreviations, which I have generally expanded in the quotations for ease of reading. The records are cited with the permission of Dun and Bradstreet, at whose request I have omitted the last names of a number of individuals whose heirs might have legal grounds for objection.

4. Buchanan Papers, Public Archives of Canada, vol. 93, pp. 65130–65143.

5. They represent, that is, 161 of the roughly 500 men in the top 20 economic percentiles, which is where I draw the boundary of the class.

6. Based on information throughout RGD. Unfortunately, not enough information is available to show in detail the differences in behavior between businessmen and professionals. There were, in any case, too few professionals to form a distinct class, though in larger cities they may have been a more viable and distinct social grouping.

7. See Chapter Three.

8. Ian E. Davey, "School Reform and School Attendance: The Hamilton Central School, 1853–1861," unpub. M.A. thesis, University of Toronto, 1972.

9. Haley Bamman, "The Ladies Benevolent Society of Hamilton, Ontario: Form and Function in Mid-Nineteenth Century Urban Philanthropy," in Michael B. Katz, ed., *The Canadian Social History Project, Interim Report No. 4* (Toronto, 1972), 161–217. See also Susan E. Houston, "The Impetus to Reform: Urban Crime, Poverty, and Ignorance in Ontario, 1850–1875," unpublished diss., University of Toronto, 1974, esp. chaps. vi and vii.

10. *Hamilton Spectator and Journal of Commerce*, Aug. 18, 1849, 2–3.

11. Eric Ricker, "Consensus and Conflict: City Politics at Mid-Century," unpub. essay, Toronto, 1973.

12. Walter S. Glazer, "Participation and Power: Voluntary Associations and the Functional Organization of Cincinnati in 1840," *Historical Methods Newsletter*, V, 4 (September 1972), 165.

13. In general, the argument I offered about class in a much earlier essay, "Social Structure in Hamilton, Ontario," in Stephan Thernstrom and Richard

Sennett, eds., *Nineteenth-Century Cities: Essays in the New Urban History* (New Haven, 1969), 209–244, still seems reasonable, though some of the specifics, especially that concerning the sharp line between manual and nonmanual work, require substantial modification. A recent and very provocative argument for basing definitions of class firmly on a conflict model is in R. S. Neale, *Class and Ideology in the Nineteenth Century* (London, 1972).

14. For more on these marriages see Chapter Five.

15. See the last section of this chapter.

16. RGD, 117, 144, 208H, 228A.

17. On the nature of credit in nineteenth-century Hamilton, see the excellent recent study by P. Douglas W. McCalla, "The Buchanan Businesses, 1834–1872: A Study in the Organization and Development of Canadian Trade," unpub. diss., Oxford University, 1972. My sample of fifty-one entrepreneurs is biased toward the more well-to-do, who more often sought credit in New York. This makes the incidence of failure among the group especially striking. On the origins of credit rating see James H. Madison, "The Evolution of Commercial Credit Reporting Agencies in Nineteenth-Century America," *Business History Review*, XLVIII, 2 (Summer 1974), 143–186.

18. Recently Edward Pessen, in *Riches, Class, and Power before the Civil War* (Lexington, Mass., 1973), ch. vii, has argued a position that seems contrary to the one taken here, namely, that the wealthy retained their fortunes with remarkable success. The contradiction between our findings is apparent rather than real. Pessen dealt with only the very rich, whereas I deal in this chapter with a much wider group. Nonetheless, it remains an open question whether the pervasive impression that fortunes often fell was based on the experience of the richest few, as Pessen would contend, or upon the experience of a broader group, such as the entrepreneurial class, as I would argue. If I am right, then Pessen has not really disproved the assertion which he set out to attack.

19. Anselm L. Strauss, *The Contexts of Social Mobility: Ideology and Theory* (Chicago, 1971), esp. pp. 1–14; Michael B. Katz, *The Irony of Early School Reform: Educational Innovation in Mid-Nineteenth Century Massachusetts* (Cambridge, Mass., 1968), and *Class, Bureaucracy and Schools: The Illusion of Educational Change in America* (New York, 1971); E. A. Wrigley, *Population and History* (New York, 1969).

20. McCalla, "Buchanan Businesses."

21. Bernard Farber, *Guardians of Virtue: Salem Families in 1800* (New York, 1972), esp. 199–211. McCalla, "Buchanan Businesses."

22. RGD, 132, 240, 112, 95, 164, 100, 101. The nineteenth-century land market deserves a great deal of study. Fortunately the sources—land records, personal papers, and newspapers—are at hand.

23. *Hamilton Spectator and Journal of Commerce*, April 5, 1848, 2; *Life and Adventures of Wilson Benson, Written by Himself* (Toronto, 1876), 38.

24. J. K. Johnson, "The Businessman as Hero: The Case of William Warren Street," *Ontario History*, LXV, 3 (September 1973), 128.

25. McCalla, "Buchanan Businesses," 277.

26. The continuities, including deference, between nineteenth-century and contemporary Canadian political culture, as described recently by Robert Presthus, are striking. Robert Presthus, *Elite Accommodation in Canadian Politics* (Cambridge, Eng., 1973), 20–63.

27. RGD, 117, 144, 208H, 228A; McCalla, "Buchanan Businesses," esp. 391–397, 454–466.

28. RGD, 107, 101, 122.

29. RGD, 97.

30. RGD, 107.

31. RGD, 96.

32. RGD, 94, 127.

33. RGD, 103.

34. RGD, 165.

35. RGD, 149, 214, 231; McCalla, "Buchanan Businesses," 267.

36. RGD, 116.

37. RGD, 94.

38. RGD, 105.

39. RGD, 100.

40. RGD, 98.

41. RGD, 160D, 228, 208H. The information about Daniel D.'s family situation is from the manuscript census.

42. Katz, "Social Structure in Hamilton, Ontario."

43. Farber, *Guardians of Virtue.* My conclusions about class structure are quite similar to Farber's.

Chapter 5. Growing Up in the Nineteenth Century: Family, Household, and Youth

1. Peter Laslett, ed., *Household and Family in Past Time* (Cambridge, Eng., 1972), ix.

2. For an excellent and important recent discussion of changes in child-rearing during the late eighteenth and nineteenth centuries, see Daniel Calhoun, *The Intelligence of a People* (Princeton, 1973), 134–205.

3. Published in London, 1965.

4. Laslett, *Household and Family,* 1–90, 125–158.

5. Ibid., 23–28.

6. Ibid., 28–32.

7. Ibid., 72.

8. Ibid., 66, 152–153.

9. Lutz K. Berkner, "The Stem Family and the Developmental Cycle of the Peasant Household: An Eighteenth Century Austrian Example," *American Historical Review,* 77, 2 (April 1972), 408; Michael Anderson, *Family Structure in Nineteenth Century Lancashire* (Cambridge, Eng., 1971), 123; Bernard Farber, *Guardians of Virtue: Salem Families in 1800* (New York, 1972), 48.

10. Berkner, "Stem Family," 406–7; Anderson, *Lancashire,* 48.

11. Laslett, *Household and Family,* 20–21; R. S. Schofield, "Age-Specific Mobility in an Eighteenth Century Rural English Parish," *Annals de Démographie Historique 1970* (Paris and The Hague, 1971), 261–274.

12. Laslett, *Household and Family,* 66; Marion J. Levy, Jr., "Aspects of the Analysis of Family Structure," in Ansley J. Coale et al., *Aspects of the Analysis of Family Structure* (Princeton, 1965), 1–63.

13. Laslett, *Household and Family,* 73.

14. Laslett, *Household and Family,* 81, 85; Michael Anderson, "Household Structure and the Industrial Revolution: Mid-nineteenth Century Preston in

Comparative Perspective," in Laslett, *Household and Family,* 220, 222; Laurence Admiral Glasco, "Ethnicity and Social Structure: Irish, Germans and Native Born of Buffalo, New York, 1850–1860," unpub. diss., SUNY, Buffalo, 1973, 149.

15. Laslett, *Household and Family,* 151.

16. Anderson, "Household Structure," 220–232; Susan E. Bloomberg et al., "A Census Probe into Nineteenth Century Family History: Southern Michigan, 1850–1880," *Journal of Social History,* 5, 1 (Fall 1971), 26–45; John Modell and Tamara K. Hareven, "Urbanization and the Malleable Household: An Examination of Boarding and Lodging in American Families," *Journal of Marriage and the Family,* August 1973, 467–478.

17. Anderson, "Household Structure," 235; Bloomberg et al., "Census Probe."

18. For instance, middle-ranking people seemed to decline especially in the employment of servants.

19. Richard Sennett, *Families against the City: Middle Class Homes of Industrial Chicago, 1872–1890* (Cambridge, Mass., 1970). The argument about the expansion and contraction of family structure is also made persuasively in Philip J. Greven, *Four Generations: Population, Land, and Family in Colonial Andover, Massachusetts* (Ithaca, 1970), 288.

20. On occupational classification see Michael Katz, "Occupational Classification in History," *Journal of Interdisciplinary History,* V, 3 (Summer 1972), 63–88. The quotation is from Richard Wall, "Mean Household Size in England from Printed Sources," in Laslett, *Household and Family,* 160; see also Glasco, "Ethnicity," 141.

21. Modell and Hareven, "Urbanization," 470, 478 (sources of quotations), 475; Anderson, *Lancashire,* 135.

22. Orvar Löfgren, "Family and Household among Scandinavian Peasants: An Exploratory Essay," *Ethnologia Scandinavia* (1974), 23.

23. Glasco, "Ethnicity," 167.

24. Modell and Hareven, "Urbanization," 475.

25. Laslett, *Household and Family,* 154; Anderson, *Lancashire,* 123; Farber, *Guardians of Virtue,* 48; Berkner, "Stem Family," 408; W. A. Armstrong, "A Note on the Household Structure of Mid-Nineteenth Century York in Comparative Perspective," in Laslett, *Household and Family,* 207.

26. Alison Prentice, "Education and the Metaphor of the Family: The Upper Canadian Example," *History of Education Quarterly,* XII, 3 (Fall 1972), 281–303.

27. Laslett, *Household and Family,* 73.

28. Levy, "Aspects of Family Structure."

29. Howard H. Irving, *The Family Myth* (Toronto, 1972).

30. Michael Young and Peter Willmott, *The Symmetrical Family* (New York, 1973), 35.

31. Philip J. Greven, Jr., *Four Generations;* see my review in *Canadian Historical Review,* LII, 2 (June 1971), 198–202. Anderson, *Lancashire,* 56–62; Michael J. Doucet, *Nineteenth Century Residential Mobility: Some Preliminary Comments,* York University Department of Geography, Discussion Paper No. 4 (Toronto, 1972). Michael Young and Peter Willmott, *Family and Kinship in East London* (London, 1960); Irving, *Family Myth.*

32. On marriage and class in the nineteenth century see John Foster,

"Nineteenth Century Towns—A Class Dimension," in H. J. Dyos, ed., *The Study of Urban History* (London, 1968), 281–300.

33. Anderson, *Lancashire*, 202.

34. Berkner, "Stem Family," 405–406.

35. Anderson, *Lancashire*, 48, 56.

36. Laslett, *Household and Family*, 20–21.

37. Young and Willmott, *Symmetrical Family*, 361.

38. Robert V. Wells, "Demographic Change and the Life Cycle in American Families," in Theodore K. Rabb and Robert I. Rotberg, eds., *The Family in History: Interdisciplinary Essays* (New York, Evanston, San Francisco, London, 1973), 85–94.

39. Joseph F. Kett, "Growing Up in Rural New England, 1800–1840," in Tamara K. Hareven, ed., *Anonymous Americans: Explorations in Nineteenth Century Social History* (Englewood Cliffs, 1971), 1, 13.

40. Steven R. Smith, "The London Apprentices as Seventeenth Century Adolescents," *Past and Present*, 61 (November 1973), 149–161. For an assertion that a stage of "semi-dependence," defined much as I define semi-autonomy, characterized the experience of European youth prior to industrialization, see a book which appeared after the discussion here was written: John R. Gillis, *Youth and History: Tradition and Change in European Age Relations, 1770–Present* (New York, 1974), 7–9; for a similar argument about the Scandinavian experience see Löfgren, "Family and Household," 25.

41. Alan Macfarlane, *The Family Life of Ralph Josselin, A Seventeenth Century Clergyman: An Essay in Historical Anthropology* (Cambridge, England, 1970), 205–210; Edmund Morgan, *The Puritan Family: Religion and Domestic Relations in Seventeenth Century New England*, rev. ed. (New York, 1966).

42. Schofield, "Age-Specific Mobility."

43. Anderson, "Household Structure," 234.

44. Glasco, "Ethnicity," 181–201.

45. Ibid., 212–216.

46. Modell and Hareven, "Urbanization," 472; Anderson, *Lancashire*, 135.

47. Anderson, *Lancashire*, 71.

48. "Who Went to School?" *History of Education Quarterly*, XII, 3 (Fall 1972), 432–454.

49. Robert E. Kennedy, Jr., *The Irish Emigration: Marriage and Fertility* (Berkeley, Los Angeles, London, 1973), 215.

50. Glasco, "Ethnicity," 181–201.

51. Ibid.

52. This is especially evident in the skewed sex-ratios. Among the Irish-born 21–25-year-olds the percentage of men dropped from 74 to 46 percent during the decade.

53. Susan E. Houston, "Victorian Origins of Juvenile Delinquency: A Canadian Experience," *History of Education Quarterly*, XII, 3 (Fall 1972), 254–280.

54. Glasco, "Ethnicity," 201–211.

55. Ibid., 205; Catherine Parr Traill, *The Canadian Settler's Guide* (Toronto, 1855; New Canadian Library ed., Toronto, 1969), 5–7.

56. Carroll Smith-Rosenberg, "The Hysterical Woman: A Case Study in Sex Roles and Social Stress in 19th Century America," *Social Research*, 39 (Win-

ter 1972), 652–678; Carroll Smith-Rosenberg and Charles Rosenberg, "The Female Animal: Medical and Biological Views of Woman and Her Role in Nineteenth Century America," *Journal of American History*, LX, 2 (September 1973), 332–356; Nathan Hale, *Freud and the Americans: The Beginnings of Psychoanalysis in the United States* (New York, 1971), 57–64.

57. Young and Willmott, *Symmetrical Family*, 28–30.

58. Joan W. Scott and Louise Tilly, "Women's Work and the Family in Nineteenth Century Europe," unpub. essay, October 1973.

59. Farber, *Guardians of Virtue*, 2.

60. Ibid., 64–65, 105–108.

61. Anderson, *Lancashire*, 1.

62. Ibid., 18, 19.

63. Ibid., 91.

64. Sam Bass Warner, Jr., "If All the World Were Philadelphia: A Scaffolding for Urban History, 1774–1930," *American Historical Review*, LXXIV, 1 (October 1968), 26–43.

65. Marion J. Levy, Jr., *Modernization and the Structure of Societies* (Princeton, 1966), 75.

66. Kenneth Keniston, "Youth as a 'New' Stage of Life," *American Scholar*, 39 (1970), 631–654.

67. Levy, *Modernization*, 74; Prentice, "Education," 281–303; Modell and Hareven, "Urbanization," 467–469.

68. Barbara Welter, "The Cult of True Womanhood: 1820–1860," *American Quarterly*, XVIII, 2, pt. 1 (Summer 1966), 151–174.

69. I have written about this issue in *The Irony of Early School Reform: Educational Innovation in Mid-Nineteenth Century Massachusetts* (Cambridge, Mass., 1968; paperback, Beacon Press, 1971), pt. I.

70. Katz, *Irony*, pt. III.

71. Houston, "Juvenile Delinquency," 255–257; Carl F. Kaestle, *The Evolution of an Urban School System: New York City, 1750–1850* (Cambridge, Mass., 1973), 113–115; Houston, "Juvenile Delinquency," 274. See also Alison Prentice, "The School Promoters: Education and Social Class in Mid-Nineteenth-Century Upper Canada," unpub. diss., University of Toronto, 1974, 66.

72. On the background of the concept of adolescence, see Dorothy Ross, *G. Stanley Hall: The Psychologist as Prophet* (Chicago and London, 1972), 333–337. See also John and Virginia Demas, "Adolescence in Historical Perspective," *Journal of Marriage and the Family*, XXXI (1969), 632–638.

Conclusion

1. Edward Bellamy, *Looking Backward: 2000–1887* (Chicago, 1888), 5.

2. *Hamilton Spectator and Journal of Commerce*, May 25, 1860, 2.

Appendix One

1. The authors wish to thank James T. Lemon and Michael B. Katz for their very helpful criticism of earlier drafts of this paper. The quotation is from *Hamilton Spectator and Journal of Commerce*, Sept. 7, 1853, 3 (cited hereafter as *Spectator*).

2. Robert E. Park et al., *The City* (Chicago, 1967), 50–58 (originally published in 1925). Homer Hoyt, *The Structure and Growth of Residential Neigh-*

borhoods in American Cities (Washington, 1939). C. D. Harris and E. L. Ullman, "The Nature of Cities," *Annals of the American Academy of Political and Social Science*, 242 (November 1945), 7–17. Robert A. Murdie, *Factorial Ecology of Metropolitan Toronto, 1951–1961*, University of Chicago, Department of Geography Research Paper No. 116 (Chicago, 1969), 167–172. For a description and evaluation of these models, see R. J. Johnston, *Urban Residential Patterns* (London, 1971), 64–98; and James T. Lemon, "Approaches to the Study of the Urban Past: Geography," paper presented to the annual meeting of the Canadian Historical Association, Kingston, Ontario, 1973, which has recently been published in Canadian Historical Association, *Historical Papers* (Ottawa, 1973), 179–190.

3. Gideon Sjoberg, *The Preindustrial City* (New York, 1960). For a discussion of the importance of Sjoberg and of Park and Burgess, see Harold Carter, *The Study of Urban Geography* (London, 1972), 166–170.

4. Martyn J. Bowden, "The Internal Structure of the Colonial Replica City: San Francisco and Others," paper presented to the annual meeting of the Association of American Geographers, Kansas City, April 1972. We are indebted to Professor Bowden for permission to cite this paper.

5. A. M. Warnes, "Residential Patterns in an Emerging Industrial Town," in B. D. Clark and M. B. Gleave, eds., *Social Patterns in Cities,* Institute of British Geographers (I.B.G.) Special Publication No. 5 (London, 1973), 171. For a discussion of some of the morphological changes incident with industrialization, see Peter G. Goheen, *Victorian Toronto 1850 to 1900,* University of Chicago, Department of Geography Research Paper No. 127 (Chicago, 1970).

6. See particularly: Allan R. Pred, *The Spatial Dynamics of U.S. Urban Industrial Growth, 1800–1914* (Cambridge, Mass., 1966); James E. Vance, *The Merchant's World: The Geography of Wholesaling* (Englewood Cliffs, N.J., 1972); Martyn J. Bowden, "Internal Structure," and "The Dynamics of City Growth: An Historical Geography of the San Francisco Central District," unpub. diss., University of California, Berkeley, 1967; and David Ward, "Nineteenth Century Boston: A Study in the Role of Antecedent and Adjacent Conditions in the Spatial Aspects of Urban Growth," unpub. diss., University of Wisconsin, Madison, 1963, and his book *Cities and Immigrants* (New York, 1971).

7. Bowden, "The Internal Structure" (see also Vance, *Merchant's World*); Ward, *Cities and Immigrants,* 89–101; Pred, *Spatial Dynamics,* 143–195.

8. Ward, *Cities and Immigrants,* 94, and "Nineteenth Century Boston," 64.

9. See, for example, Sam. B. Warner, Jr., *Streetcar Suburbs: The Process of Growth in Boston, 1870–1900* (Cambridge, Mass., 1962); Ward, *Cities and Immigrants;* and Goheen, *Victorian Toronto.*

10. Lois Evans, *Hamilton. The Story of a City* (Toronto, 1970), 78–83. Other local histories of the city include Mabel Burkholder, *The Story of Hamilton* (Hamilton, 1938); Marjorie Campbell, *A Mountain and a City* (Toronto, 1966); and C. M. Johnston, *The Head of the Lake: A History of Wentworth Country* (Hamilton, 1966).

11. L. J. Chapman and D. F. Putnam, *The Physiography of Southern Ontario* (Toronto, 1966), 325–326. W. H. Smith, *Canadian Gazetteer* (Toronto, 1846), 75.

12. Much of the city had already been subdivided into lots. This is illustrated by Marcus Smith's *Map of Hamilton, 1850–1* (New York, 1851), which forms the basis for Figure A.1.

13. *Spectator*, Oct. 13, 1853, 2.

14. For a discussion of the definition of wealth employed here, see Michael B. Katz, "The People of a Canadian City, 1851–2," *Canadian Historical Review*, 53 (December 1972), 401–426.

15. *Spectator*, Oct. 28, 1852, 3, "Progress of Hamilton," and Nov. 18, 1852, 2, "Sanitary State of the City."

16. Evidence of this rapid population turnover can be seen in the fact that only about three quarters of those listed on the Assessment Rolls of 1852 could be linked back to the census, taken just three months earlier. For a discussion of nineteenth-century residential mobility see Peter R. Knights, *The Plain People of Boston, 1830–1860* (New York, 1971), and Stephan Thernstrom, *The Other Bostonians* (Cambridge, Mass., 1973), 220–261. For a discussion of some of the problems involved in record linkage see E. A. Wrigley, ed., *Identifying People in the Past* (London, 1973).

17. According to advertisements placed on page 101 of the *Canada Directory* (Montreal, 1851), some of the heavy industries employed upwards of seventy workers. For a discussion of some of the factors which led to the suburbanization of industry during the first third of the twentieth century see Charles C. Colby, "Centrifugal and Centripetal Forces in Urban Geography," *Annals of the Association of American Geographers*, 23 (March 1933), 1–20.

18. See, for example, John Rannells, *The Core of the City* (New York, 1956); M. J. Doucet and L. S. Bourne, *Core Area Structure and Development Trends: Toronto*, Special Report No. 2, University of Toronto Centre for Urban and Community Studies (Toronto, 1970); and Raymond E. Murphy, *The Central Business District* (London, 1971).

19. Absolutely fundamental to the notion of the central area is the concept of a central place composed of those functions that serve the central area itself, the whole city, and its hinterland. For a discussion of the central areas as a central place see Martyn J. Bowden, "Downtown Through Time: Delimitation, Expansion and Internal Growth," *Economic Geography*, 41 (April 1971), 121–135. Here Bowden introduces the concept of absolute centrality, which refers to the amount of central or service functions necessary to serve both the hinterland and the central place (as distinct from the immediate neighborhood of the central area). In Bowden's terms CBD-forming uses are "those central functions that contribute to the absolute centrality of the CBD." In other words, the CBD is the ultimate service center within an urban region because it is the only such center that serves the entire area.

20. Bowden, "Downtown Through Time," 127.

21. James E. Vance, "Focus on Downtown," in L. S. Bourne, ed., *The Internal Structure of the City* (Toronto, 1971), 112–120.

22. Goheen, *Victorian Toronto*, 84; for a further illustration of this idea see Sam B. Warner, Jr., *The Private City* (Philadelphia, 1968), 50. Ward, *Cities and Immigrants*, 85–103 (quotations from 94).

23. Ward, *Cities and Immigrants*, 86.

24. W. C. Cooke, *City of Hamilton Directory* (Hamilton, 1853).

25. This arrangement agrees with Ward's characterization of the early CBD; see *Cities and Immigrants*, 88.

26. For a description of the decline of wholesaling in the period see Douglas McCalla, "The Decline of Hamilton as a Wholesale Centre," *Ontario History*, 65 (December 1973), 247–254. Bowden has also argued that retailing attained considerable significance much earlier than Ward has suggested. See Martyn J. Bowden, "Review of *Cities and Immigrants*," *Annals of the Association of American Geographers*, 62 (December 1972), 713–715.

27. For a discussion of the history of Cork Town see J. G. O'Neil, "Chronicles of Corktown," *Wentworth Bygones*, 5 (1964), 28–39.

28. The data on these groups have been derived from the City of Hamilton Assessment Rolls for 1852. The occupations were selected to reflect the major occupational groupings in the mid-nineteenth-century city: business, unskilled, clerical, skilled or artisanal, and professional. The members of each occupation were mapped by the block upon which each resided, and the maps have been summarized in Table A.1. The same methodology was employed for the ethnic and wealth groups discussed below.

29. Pred, *Spatial Dynamics*, 205–207, discusses the pattern for a similarly localized market-oriented group, the bakers of New York City in 1840. He notes that their scattered distribution was simultaneously a reflection of the stage of transportation, the state of technology, and the dynamic applications of central-place theory. The same forces were acting to shape the locations of Hamilton's shoemakers a decade later.

30. According to Katz, merchants had the highest mean wealth of all occupational groups in the city by 1861. See "The Structure of Inequality: Occupation, Wealth and Ethnicity, 1851 and 1861," in Michael B. Katz (ed.), *The Canadian Social History Project, Interim Report No. 4* (Toronto, 1972), 156.

31. At this time 35.6 percent of assessed Hamiltonians owned at least one house, but property ownership was concentrated in the hands of a relatively small group of individuals: 7.2 percent of the population owned 49.4 percent of the city's 1,922 houses. These figures were calculated from the Assessment Rolls.

32. Bowden, "Dynamics of City Growth," 97; Goheen, *Victorian Toronto*, 201–205.

33. For a discussion of the differences in the residential locations of wholesalers and retailers see Ian Davey, "The Central Area of Hamilton in 1853," in Katz, *Canadian Social History Project, Interim Report No. 4*, 238–241 and Map 3. Engels' observation concerning the "plutocrats" of industrial Manchester in 1844 was almost equally applicable to commercial Hamilton in 1853: "the plutocrats can travel from their houses to their places of business in the centre of the town by the shortest routes . . . without even realizing they are close to the misery and filth which lie on both sides of the road . . . because the main streets . . . are occupied almost uninterruptedly on both sides by shops." Friedrich Engels, *The Condition of the Working Class in England in 1844*, quoted in W. O. Henderson, ed., *Engels: Selected Writings* (Harmondsworth, Eng., 1967), 28.

34. Although information concerning ethnic origin and religious affiliation is contained in the census, our data base for this analysis has been the 1955 people who could be found on both the census and assessment records for the period 1851–52. This was necessary because the census did not give precise address information. In Chapter Two Michael Katz elaborates on the conception of ethnicity in this study and its relation to social structure.

35. In the interval between 1846 and 1851, the population of the city climbed from 6,832 to 14,112, an increase of 106.6 percent.

36. According to a provincial statute of 1850 (13 & 14 Vic., Cap. 67, Sec. 22), statute laborers were defined as males aged 21–60 who had neither taxable income nor property. Such individuals, most of whom were single, were compelled to either pay a tax or work a specified number of days for the city. In identifying the wealthiest 5 percent in the city, wealth was determined by the total amount of property and taxable income held by individuals according to calculations based upon the Assessment Rolls of 1852. The percentages given for laborers were derived from the maps we constructed to depict the precise residential location of each statute laborer and each member of the city's wealthiest 5 percent.

Index

Abrams, Philip, 1, 7–8, 9, 354n
Adolescence, 212, 256–292; and ethnicity, 284–287; standardization of, 304–305, 306, 307–308; crisis of youth, 306, 307–308
Age distribution: and number of children, 34; of boarders, 36; and marriage, 40; and occupation, 73, 75; and wealth, 75; and property ownership, 83, 162–163; and transiency, 114, 123–124, 132; and social mobility, 138, 160–163, 173; and household structure, 244–249, 249–253, 255. *See also* Life cycle
Ågren, Kurt, 354n, 361n
Agriculture, 2, 319, 325; and occupations, 51–52
Åkerman, Sune, 19, 354n, 355n, 361n
American Occupational Structure, The (Blau and Duncan), 135
Anderson, Barbara A., 361n
Anderson, Michael: Preston study, 217, 218, 235, 239, 242, 243–244, 251, 259–260, 267, 273, 294, 296–299, 365n, 366n, 367n, 368n; exchange theory, 300–302
Andover, Massachusetts, 239
Anglicans, 26, 37, 127. *See also* English immigrants
Architecture, 326; public edifices, 4, 5; homes of wealthy, 28, 41, 43
Armstrong, W. A., 366n
Artisans: as social class, 4, 27, 311; tramping, 19; shops of, 23, 333; economic rank, 25, 71; political power, 27, 28; school attendance, 39; outmigration of, 62; as immigrants, 117; occupational inheritance, 138; social mobility, 145, 146, 173; occupational mobility, 170, 171–172; in entrepreneurial class, 179, 187, 194, 207; kinship solidarity, 295; residence patterns, 337; property ownership, 362n

Assessment rolls, 18, 19, 20
Associations, voluntary, 6, 29, 30, 183; and entrepreneurial class, 186, 191, 197, 198
Austrian village: household structure, 217–218, 235; life cycle, 243, 244

Bales, Robert F., 355n
Bamman, Haley, 183, 356n, 358n, 363n
Banking, 65, 69, 188. *See also* Credit system
Banks, J. A., 357n
Baptists, 32, 34–35
Bellamy, Edward, 309, 310, 368n
Bendix, Reinhard, 134–135, 174, 362n
Benson, Lee, 354n, 360n
Benson, Wilson, 94–111, 113, 117, 175, 192–193, 293, 359n
Berkner, Lutz, 217–218, 235, 243, 244, 249, 251, 365n, 366n, 367n
Best, T. N., 179, 198–199, 201, 205
Bickle, T., 179, 196, 205
Birmingham, Alabama, 19
Birth control, 35
Birth rate, 33–35, 40; decline in, 214; and ethnicity, 233–234
Black Abolitionist Society, 3
Blacks: as immigrants, 2, 3, 61; economic rank, 62–63; occupations, 65, 68; property ownership, 68
Blau, Peter, 135, 136, 139, 144, 147, 174, 362n, 363n
Bloomberg, Susan E., 366n
Blumin, Stuart, 358n, 359n
Board of Trade, 182
Boarders, 60, 77, 297, 305; and wealthy, 35, 36, 40, 41; and household structure, 36–38, 215, 217, 222, 225, 226–227, 229, 233, 234, 235, 236, 244, 248, 249, 312, 313; as transients, 124, 125; of widows, 254; adolescents as, 262, 264–269, 274; young men as, 285–286, 290

HARVARD STUDIES IN URBAN HISTORY